ISBN 978-0-260-86877-0
PIBN 11193585

1 MONTH OF
FREE
READING

at
www.ForgottenBooks.com

By purchasing this book you are eligible for one month membership to ForgottenBooks.com, giving you unlimited access to our entire collection of over 1,000,000 titles via our web site and mobile apps.

To claim your free month visit:
www.forgottenbooks.com/free1193585

English
Français
Deutsche
Italiano
Español
Português

www.forgottenbooks.com

Mythology Photography **Fiction**
Fishing Christianity **Art** Cooking
Essays Buddhism Freemasonry
Medicine **Biology** Music **Ancient
Egypt** Evolution Carpentry Physics
Dance Geology **Mathematics** Fitness
Shakespeare **Folklore** Yoga Marketing
Confidence Immortality Biographies
Poetry **Psychology** Witchcraft
Electronics Chemistry History **Law**
Accounting **Philosophy** Anthropology
Alchemy Drama Quantum Mechanics
Atheism Sexual Health **Ancient History**
Entrepreneurship Languages Sport
Paleontology Needlework Islam
Metaphysics Investment Archaeology
Parenting Statistics Criminology
Motivational

For COUNTY RECORDER

DAN FLANNERY

REPUBLICAN NOMINEE

Election November 6, 1906

For CONGRESS   Fifth Congressional District

E. A. HAYES

(Incumbent)

Election November 6, 1906

For JUSTICE OF THE PEACE

CHAS. A. THOMPSON

Regular Democratic and Union Labor Party Nominee

Santa Clara Township, Comprising the Precincts of Agnew, Campbell, Hamilton, Jefferson, Moreland, Santa Clara and University.

Election Tuesday, November 6, 1906

For SHERIFF

LANGFORD

Regular Nominee

UNITED LABOR PARTY========and========DEMOCRATIC PARTY

Election Tuesday, November 6, 1906

Vote for————————————————

JAMES H. CAMPBELL

For DISTRICT ATTORNEY
(Present Incumbent)

————————————————Election Tuesday, November 6, 1906

MR. CAMPBELL was elected by the people to enforce all the laws all the time. He has enforced them including them against vice, immorality and gambling. He has run the District Attorney's office for the people, and has not allowed the bosses to run it for themselves. That is why the political czars, their newspaper monopoly and their allies, the gamblers are fighting him. Are you with them?

FOR JUSTICE OF THE PEACE

I. HERRINGTON
(Present Incumbent)

REGULAR REPUBLICAN NOMINEE

SANTA CLARA TOWNSHIP

————————————————Election Tuesday, November 6, 1906

For County Superintendent of Schools

D. T. BATEMAN
(Incumbent)

Regular Nominee

Democratic Party.   Union Labor Party

Election November 6, 1906

For————————————————

COUNTY TREASURER

Ernest W. Conant

For SENATOR 27TH DISTRICT

FRANK N. SMITH

REGULAR UNITED LABOR AND DEMOCRATIC NOMINEE

Election, Tuesday, November 6, 1906

For COUNTY SURVEYOR

J. G. McMILLAN
(Incumbent)

Regular Republican Nominee

Election November 6, 1906

B. E. KELL
—FOR—

Coroner and Public Administrator
(Present Incumbent)

Regular United Labor and Democratic Nominee

JAS. E. GLENDENNING
(Present Incumbent)

Regular Republican Nominee for.....

JUSTICE OF THE PEACE

Sana Clara Township: Comprising the Precincts of Agnew, Campbell, Hamilton, Jefferson, Moreland, Santa Clara and University.

Election, Tuesday, November 6, 1906

Contents.

Nace Printing Co.   Santa Clara, Cal.

The Redwood

Entered Dec 18, 1902, at Santa Clara, Calif. as second-class matter, under Act of Congress of March 3, '879.

VOL. VI. ·SANTA CLARA, CAL., OCTOBER, 1906. No. 1.

AMBITION

Far from the enchanted kingdom held in fee
    By Fancy, clustered round with fairies bright,
Across the shadowland of Revery
Faint echoing music fills me with delight.

I hear it by the lone, surf-beaten shore,
In many a dreamy vale and cloud-girt hill,
Amid the city's tumult and the roar
Of crowded marts I feel its mystic thrill.

Ah, who may read the meaning? Yet to me
Whose darkling steps it oft hath nerved to rise
Above the baleful depths of Lethargy
It seems an angel-song from Paradise.

Sophomore

THE DIVINA COMEDIA

The "Divine Comedy" is not a comedy in the sense in which we now understand the word. This was a term the ancients used to classify productions whereof the denouement was a happy one, and in which the style was neither the studiously elegant nor the common, but couched rather in a middle tone. Hence the fitness of this unique title; for its final scene was one of happiness, and its story was told in the poet's native tongue, the Tuscan, which was considered neither as refined nor as elegant as the Latin. It was not, however, called "Divine" by Dante, but was so styled subsequently by transcribers owing to the sacredness of the theme and the seeming inspiration of the author.

The poem presents an unequalled unity of construction. It consists of a hundred cantos each containing from 130 to 140 verses, the whole scheme divided into three sections of thirty-three cantos each. The first canto is a kind of an introduction to the three sections devoted respectively to Hell, Purgatory and Paradise. The *measure* of the poem is the *terza rima*, consisting of a triple recurrence of the same rhyme alternated by another series of three. The verses, thus interlinked, are composed of eleven syllables, divided into five iambics, the last being an overbeat; so that all through the lines have an undertone of vibrant sonorousness.

All immortal poetry is the chant of the mystery that everywhere surrounds us, an investigation of the primal questions—What are we? Whither do we tend? Are we sailing into the sunset, to vanish, when night has come, in the sea of oblivion, or is the bark of life straining towards the dawn? This is the question that comes to us all, that is solved only in the light of faith, that presents an enigma to the haughty, resulting in atheism. Dante, proud and strong-willed, his heart scalded by the injustice of his countrymen, gazed into the west with its sinking sun; but the light afterwards rose again for him unto another day.

Drawn to Rome by the jubilee instituted by Boniface VIII, he was thrilled by the intensity of the faith that brought the whole of Christendom on a pilgrimage to the Vatican, and thus impressed with the sincerity of the faithful, in the splendor and pomp exhibited he saw something of the splendors of heaven. Chastened as he had been by pain and sorrow, he was now inspired to take up his visionary pilgrimage into the life that lies beyond the visible, with its three kingdoms of punishment, purification and happiness.

Having in vision entered the path of death, Dante begins his descent into the infernal regions. These according to him are situated directly beneath Jerusalem, consisting of gradually narrowing circles terminating in the centre of the globe. On the antipodes of this the mountain of Purgatory rises in terraced plains to a Terrestrial Paradise on the summit, whence the entrance to Heaven.

The poet is first beset by three wild beasts, and retreats in terror, when he is intercepted by the spirit of Virgil, who promises to guide him through the regions of woe. Thus reassured he follows the Roman to the portal of Hell, over which stands the inscription,

"Through me is the road to the dolorous city,

Through me is the road to everlasting sorrows,

Through me is the road to the lost people,

Justice was the motive of my exalted ruler!"

They enter the sightless gulf, containing the souls of neither the good or bad. Collecting the multitude on the banks of a stream into his boat, the fiery-eyed Charon

'Beats with his oar whoever lags behind:

As in the autumn time the leaves fall off,

First one and then another, till the branch

Unto the earth surrenders all its spoils;

In similar wise the evil seed of Adam Throw themselves from that margin one by one.'

The limbo of the unbaptised opens, impenetrable through sooty clouds and mist, and noticing even Virgil pale, Dante asks, "Master, if thou art afraid what is to become of me!" "Pity, not fear," replies his guide, "causes me to blanch." Thence they come to a second gulf narrower than the first, at the entrance of which Minos sits as judge. Here driven before an unceasing wind appear the multitudes brought thither by unrestrained passion, and Francesca di Rimini with her silent companion at her side, tells that touching tale of love and woe, which Dante concludes,

"While thus one spoke, the other spirit mourned,

With wail so woeful that at his remorse I felt as though I should have died. I turned

Stone-still; and to the ground fell like a corpse."

Virgil conducts him by Plutus, guardian of the avaricious and sullen; Phlegyas, ferryman over the stagnant water of Arragonce; the city of Dis with its iron towers and battlements, glowing dull-red through the gloom; the cemetery of the heretics, laid with red hot tombs to be sealed on the day of Judgment; Alexander, Attila and other wielders of the sword in a river of blood; the sombre forest of the suicides—each tree, black-boughed, leafless, charred, enclosing a self-murderer; the desert of burning sand on which

'Were raining down dilated flakes of fire

As of snow on Alps without a wind.'

In a hole of ice Count Ugolino, betrayer of the Pisans, is discovered devouring Ruggieri. He tells the horrible tale of his imprisonment along with his children in the Tower of Famine where one by one they famished through lack of food.

"I saw my three wee children, one by
   one,
Between the fifth day and the sixth, all
   die:
I became blind; and in my misery
Went groping for them, as I knelt and
   crawled
About the room; and for three days I
   called
Upon their names, as tho' they could
   speak too,
Till famine did what grief had failed to
   do."

The final scene that Hell presents is
the Titan. Lucifer immersed in a lake
of ice in the centre of the earth devouring the great betrayers, among them being Judas. Here at the centre of
gravity of the globe they become in-
verted and pass through the earth,
emerging on the other side at the foot
of the mount of Purgatory.

Carried in sleep to its threshold by
Lucia, or Divine Grace, Dante beholds
the kingdom of purification where the
same sins punished forever in Hell, are
pardoned after true repentance. The
envious dressed in vile sack-cloth have
their eyes sewed in by wire; the angry
are wrapped in black mists; the gluttons
tormented with visions of sweets they
are powerless to obtain. Confronted by
a path of fire he dare not proceed further until, encouraged by Virgil with
word of Beatrice's presence on the
other side, he surmounts the horrors of
the flames and emerges in the terrestrial Paradise. Here Virgil takes his
leave and Dante wanders forth alone
into the fragrance of the celestial forest,

ringing with the music of warbling birds
and the soft winds swelling through the
trees. At the bank of a crystal rivulet
a beautiful lady appears culling flowers.
She explains to him the name and
nature of the stream: it is Lethe, the
river of forgetfulness. She wanders
along its bank until of a sudden she
stops and cries, "Behold and listen!"
and a light of exceeding lustre comes
streaming through the woods. On
closer inspection Dante sees that it is a
chariot, brighter than the sun, surrounded by angels, and seated within
it, garbed in white and crowned with
olive, is Beatrice. She speaks to him,
but filled with shame for his frailties he
turns his gaze to the ground. Commanded to lift up his eyes he is so overcome by her beauty that he falls sense-
less to the earth. After this meeting he
is carried through the Lethe and having been immersed in the waters of the
Eunoe is regenerated and prepared for
Paradise.

Dante's idea of the structure of the
universe is taken from Ptolemy of
Pelusium, the celebrated astronomer,
who supposed the earth to be the centre
of the universe and the planets to revolve around it. The seven planets
constitute Dante's first seven heavens;
the eighth heaven is the region of the
fixed stars where the host of Christ
triumphant march; the ninth is the
crystalline heaven from which all the
former receive their motion. Through
each of these increasing splendors Dante
has been carried upward by Beatrice's
look, and now he is in the Empyrean,

the heaven of heavens, in the region of light—the light of transcendent love. A river of light 'effulgent with flashing splendors' sparkles before him. Beatrice bids him dip his eyes into the light, and no sooner do his eyelashes touch it, than the stream becomes a vast circle, of greater circumference and brightness than the sun, wherein the combined courts of heaven are revealed. Myriads of blessed souls, white-mantled and golden-winged, are seated in rising tiers, in the form of a great white rose. He sees Beatrice now shining among them; he beholds the Blessed Virgin resplendent with light; surrounded by thousands of angels; he hears the angelic choirs thundering forth the Ave Maria; and lifting his eyes towards the greater vision, he beholds what he neither has power to describe nor the memory to endure.

Carlyle declares this poem an 'architectural harmony,' 'a supernatural world cathedral.' He says, 'It is, at bottom, the *sincerest* of all Poems. It came deep out of the author's heart of hearts; and it goes deep through long generations, into ours.' In its idea it is the grandest of all poems; embracing all that is seen by the mind and eye,— to speak with the poet, "A sacred poem built with earth and heaven." It is the song of a soul that believes, of a soul that raises itself out of the finite, and which, having crossed the confines of space and time, goes into the eternal splendors of the Deity. He dwelt not on objects, that fall under the perception only of senses, weaving fantastic romances, or lauding the grandeur of the mountain, or the glory of the field. He was too intense to be a mere pastoral poet, too ethereal to indulge in hero-worship. Being no less a philosopher and theologian than poet, he opened to his imagination new fields extending over the broad and deep areas of reason and faith, and caused beautiful flowers of poetry never before seen to blossom along his path.

"Mine eyes did look
On beauty such, as I believe in sooth,
Not merely to exceed our human; but,
That save its maker, none can to the full
Enjoy."

Dante is a sovereign painter, presenting whatever he wishes us to see, as real and lifelike, by catching the most luminous point in the scene and bringing it out with a few bold strokes. We might say, of his pictures, such is their magnitude and strength, that his canvas is infinite space; his background, the universe; and his strokes, flashes of lightning? Yet so graphic and exact are his descriptions, so particular is he about truth, so conscious of detail as opposed to the deliberately practised obscurity of Milton; that the very measurements of Hell are given, the height of its mountains, and dikes, and the time that elapsed during his pilgrimage; and modern Dantists have computed the measurements of, surveyed, and even charted, his visionary universe.

Energy and life constitute the singular charm of his style. As he accompanies his images with concise, robust,

and figured speech, they remain indelibly pictured in our mind. What sublime pictures are those of the city of Dis, the entrance to Purgatory, with
The beauteous star which lets no love despair,
Making the Orient laugh with loveliness,
the summit of the mountain of Purgatory, and the Cross and Rose in Heaven? What marvelous pieces of sculpture are the Charon, Phlegyas, the Furies, Ugolino, Lucifer, the Angels and Cacciaguida.

The richness and splendor of Dante's similitudes are known to all. The poet is such a master of the matter which he has in hand, that while he is thinking of one thing, he has time and leisure to fix his eyes on the rest of creation, and to match those objects that bear some relation to his own, placing them face to face. Hence we have that superabundance of comparisons taken from all orders of things, be they sensible or rational, subjective or objective.

Allow me here to make a brief distinction on the excellence of Dante's similes. When they are compared to those of other classics, one would think that those of our poet are superior, but we must recall that in the criticism similes are regarded from two points of view,—the form, and the matter. The form of the figure is beautiful when the thing is said with elegance and style; the matter, when it not only appropriately fits the other term of the comparison, but also when the resemblance is not an ordinary one, but needs for its discovery the eye of a genius; for it is by this the poet offers you new knowledge, and therefore a new delight. It is certainly a proof of great merit to see a point of resemblance between two things which to others appear most unlike and furtherest removed from each other. To apply this to our poet, we may grant that other classics in some particular cases exhibit the better form; but if we take into account the matter, we must acknowledge him to excel all in power of invention, profundity, and genius.

But his inventive merit lies not so much in creation as organization. There was many beautiful visions recounted before his time, such as those of Bede, St. Patrick, St. Farcy, and Albeir of Monte Cassino, but through the fault of the narraters these were confused and eccentric, awaiting a ray of heat and light to give them order and beauty, and this ray was the subtile intellect of Dante. Like the prophet of the Testament he beheld a plain covered with the scattered bones of an army which under his scrutiny became revivified, and rose once more a living army. Without sign of strain or evidence of effort he produces a continuous series of new ideas, bright fancies, and stern truths, using all the while, in his account of Hell and Purgatory, himself, Virgil, the tormented, and the torment: yet his variety is inexhaustible. In his description of heaven the scenes hinge on two elements, song and light, but with these two he paints scenes so sweet, so novel, so wondrous and entrancing that it is indeed a Paradise.

But that which is particularly characteristic of the poet is his uniting intellect with the imagination, visions with scientific speculation; in three kingdoms he has combined the encyclopedic knowledge of his times, in theology, philosophy, mythology, and science, with intellect and erudition so as to make one whole. It can as well be called a work of the reason as of the imagination: its uniqueness among all visions is its scientificness. He who reads it finds no less food for the intellect than for the fancy, and he moves in a sea whither the rivers of all the sciences bring their tribute. To have known how to produce this wonderful harmony of mind and imagination, to have been able to assimilate as materials of craftmanship the total knowledge of one's age; to have thrown a halo of religion over it all is surely the test of the supreme artist; and Pallen justly calls it 'the supremest literary production of the greatest intellectual epoch in History.' I could go more into detail regarding Dante's style and invention; I might dwell at length on his sublimity, his immensity, his accuracy, his systematization, his fine moral and religious tone, by infringing upon your patience; but I must content myself with this humble endeavor, hoping that I have enkindled within you some sort of an appreciation that may prompt you to read him. Our lives are bounded by mysteries, our entrance and our departure clouded to our mental sight; faith like an impalpable magnetism draws us onward over the right path, but imagination illuminates the gloom, making the hitherto darksome avenues shining vistas towards the eternal splendors. If you would increase this light, this iridescence of the mind, take up in your leisure hours this pilgrimage with Dante as your guide. At first you will perhaps find the way strange and laborious, encountering the vale of night, but again the beams of morning will descend, rewarding your perseverance; and, finally, dipping your eyes into the light as did the poet, you may become enraptured with the angelic symphony and behold the Vision of which Dante, even Dante, could not speak.

JOHN H. RIORDAN, A. M. '06.

THE OLD ADOBE

[The old adobe building used for many years by Santa Clara students for their debates, was so badly shattered by the earthquake that, in spite of its romantic associations, it had to be razed to the ground. Erected in 1818, it served as the residence of the Majordomo of the Mission Indians; then it was seized and used as a wayside inn, until it was purchased by Fr. Nobili in 1854. Right near it was an old Indian burying-ground.]

Let others hail the walls that rise
　　Upon thy hallowed site,
They wear scant beauty in my eyes,
　　Nor give delight.

Thy walls to me were ivy-grown
　　With memory's magic leaf,
Adown a century was sown
　　Mid joy, mid grief.

Mid joy, mid grief, in truce and feud,—
　　For thou had'st braved them all!
And varied empires had'st thou viewed
　　Arise and fall!

The mind and heart of Serra's days
　　Stood bodied in thy frame;
The simple and the kindly ways,
　　The exalted aim.

Lo! comes the Mexican dread blight,—
　　The Mission ruined lies,
As when, a cold October night,
　　The floweret dies.

Then saw'st the Indian in thy shade
Sink wearily to rest
Where he his gray-haired sires had laid
In days more blest.

Hark! loud resounds the drunken broil!
And rusts thine ivy now;—
The focus erst of Christian toil
A tavern thou!

The changes ring! Commingled rays—
Faith, science—on thee fall
And green the ivy fresh arrays
Th' adobe wall.

Before me files a shining band
Of eager youth sublime,
Strong-armed by thee for high command
Of mellowed time.

And tones I hear ring light and gay,
Destined the world to thrill:
Tones, even were they hushed for aye,
Thou'dst echo still.

Echo still, Adobe?—Fancy kind,
That vanishes anon!—
I ope my pensive eyes and find
Thou too art gone!

R. S., '07.

THE HERITAGE OF NELSON

The very first inkling I had of the whole affair came that night when I dropped in on Nelson unexpectedly. The room was dark, but over on the divan under the window I could make out the dim outline of his form. I turned on the light.

He was lying flat on his stomach but with his head turned so that his face was towards me and his right ear pillowed on that old sea shell of his. His eyes were closed, so I started to leave the room. And then I noticed that his lip was curled up, baring the strong white teeth. That was Nelson's way of showing excitement, as he had often told me. So I stopped.

"Asleep, Nels ?"

He opened his eyes at once, not blinkingly or stupidly, like a man regaining consciousness, but alertly and—as I thought—a little impatient.

"Oh hello, Mac,"—he sat up—"glad to see you. Sit down, won't you ? Just taking a little snooze, you see."

He laughed carelessly, but his eyes burned. There was something wrong, I knew. I never stood on ceremony with Nelson.

"What's the matter?" I asked.

He looked me in the eye for a full minute, without answering. I noticed that his hair curled a little in front from the moisture on his forehead. The room was cool. Then he took the sea shell, laid it on the table, and picked up a cigar.

"No, thanks," said I, anticipating the offer.

"Mac,"—he struck a match and lighted the weed—"I'm going to resign my position tomorrow."

I thought he was joking and laughed. He snapped his finger nervously.

"I mean it."

I gazed at him through the smoke mist.

"Sick or crazy?"

He did not answer at once. He was puffing furiously, and the tip of his cigar was brighter than his eyes.

"I don't know," he answered gloomily —at length, "A little of both may be, Mac."

I saw he was serious so I turned out the light. Whenever Nelson wanted to talk seriously he always liked the dark. He was a great fellow for talking about primordial instincts and all that.

"Mac," he began, "did you ever hear much about my parents?"

I hadn't, and told him so.

"Neither have I. I know that I was born on shipboard coming to America from Sweden. My mother died on the boat and I was raised in a foundling's home in New York. I afterwards heard that when my mother had been buried at sea, my father in despair had plunged in after her. It was night and they couldn't help him."

He puffed on his cigar and his strong square face glowed a curious copper in the darkness. I sat silent and somewhat awed. Nelson, I knew, had never told as much to any other man. I watched his face and saw his teeth bared under the curling lip. What a strongly individual characteristic that was. And yet, I thought, everything about him was strongly individual. The man was a power.

He broke the silence.

"Do you believe in hereditary instinct?"

"I don't know exactly what you mean," I answered, "Why?"

"Oh, never mind. Anyway of late years I have learned that I am from a strong Swedish family, the men of which for the last six generations have been sailors and have died at sea. Indeed there is an old legend in the family that we are decended from Eric, the Norseman."

He stopped. I waited for him to proceed but he sat on and on, unspeaking. When he puffed his cigar I could see that he was gazing dreamily into space. A clock on the table ticked steadily. Presently I spoke gently.

"But why are you going to give up your position, Nels?"

He drew up his chair closer to mine.

"Mac," he said, quietly, "I am going to tell you something I never told anybody before—the secret of my life."

For the first time in our six years of friendship he fell into a Swedish accent.

"I'm going to quit my job for one in San Francisco because there is something like a mighty hand drawing me to the ocean. I am like a child seeking its mother, or like the compass needle seeking irresistibly the north. I can't resist, I can't fight against it. It is in my blood, a part of me. I belong to the ocean, and the longing, the craving to reach it, to touch it, to wade in it so that the waves break in my face and the salt sting my eyes is awful. 'Tis burning me up."

He ceased abruptly. We sat silent for a long time. Then he pulled himself together and struck a match to light the student lamp. I could only stare. Nelson dubbed the Silent, the Stoic, with his eyes blazing like that, and his hand shaking so that the lighted match threw wavering, fantastic shadows on the wall!

———

That was in September. A year later I met Nelson in San Francisco. Jack Stillman was with me. After I made them acquainted, Nelson said:

"Say, I want both you fellows to come out to the ocean with me, will you? Going to take a little dip, you know."

"A little cold isn't it?" Jack asked.

Nelson looked at him steadily.

"I go in every day, rain or shine, Mr. Stillman," said he.

On the car I heard Nelson saying to Jack, "Do you know I think I'm absolutely indefatigable in the water. Before I took my present position with the S. P., I was employed in St. Paul by the Great Northern. I always thought that if it wasn't for the matter of food that I could easily swim Lake Superior."

Jack looked at me questioningly. I

knew that he was beginning to think Nels a little queer.

We got off at the Cliff House. Nelson did not stop here, however, but walked rapidly on down the beach. He had become very silent. I noticed that a nerve in his cheek twitched relentlessly and that his eyes were bright with a peculiar reddish light in them. It recalled vividly that night in the dark.

The tide was out and the breakers were storming sullenly under the leaden sky. Nelson turned to me, his eyes ablaze,

"It's a beautiful sound, don't you think, Mac?"

His tone was low and conventional, but I could see he was holding himself strongly in check.

We walked steadily for two hours and a half, and then Nelson stopped and began to undress.

I looked about. There was no sign of the works or the presence of a human hand within a radius of two miles. Ten miles down the beach the Cliff House was discernible, at that distance merely an inelegant squarely symmetrical pile of windows.

"Aren't you coming in?" Nelson asked us, presently.

We both were afraid of the cold and said so. He looked at us wonderingly but offered no comment.

A little later he caught me glancing about.

"No sign of civilization, eh Mac? Only the old ocean just as God and nature left it. You won't find any boats about

here." He laughed loudly and unmusically.

Then he waded in, not hastily or boisterously as I had half expected, but steadily with his two arms stretched out in the form of a cross, almost in ecstacy. Once a big wave broke roughly in his face and I heard him suck in his breath in delight.

We watched him curiously for a while and then sat down and fell to talking. Jack and I had been chums at college and had much in common.

For half an hour my mind was diverted from ths man in the water. And then Jack's eyes wandered casually towards the ocean and I saw them leap into sick, livid horror. Then I looked.

The sun had sunken sulkily, swathed in gray clouds, and the sky was beginning to clear. Nelson, his yellow head silhouetted sharply a mile away in the dull afterglow of the sunset, was swimming with strong joyous strokes straight out to sea.

I looked at Jack. In his throat I could see the great pulse pumping wildly. I tried to shout, but my voice broke ludicrously. Jack burst out into a laugh, harshly hysterical.

I cleared my throat and cupped my hands about my mouth.

"Nels," I shouted, "Oh, Nels, come back!"

Night was descending and sea and sky were starlessly purple. Above the boom of the breakers the man, a mile and a half out, heard, for he turned his head for an instant.

We stood there stupidly and watched the man swim on and on. The bobbing head was growing so faint in the darkness that only at times could I make it out on the black water.

Once I thought he turned and waved his hand, but perhaps it was only a dash of foam.

I watched, fascinated, until my sight was blurred with the monotonous, desolate perspective.

Then I shut my eyes tightly to clear the vision. The waves boomed drearily but I could hear Jack's thick breathing.

When finally I opened my eyes the sea and sky were one, and the head had disappeared.

JAMES FRANCIS TWOHY, '07.

AUTUMN

The golden season now is born,
    Autumn is here,
And the drooping leaves all mourn
    The dying year.
And we realize the strife
    Never ceases,
That the space twixt Death vnd Life
    E'er decreases.
But though death brooks no delay,
    We'll not fear her,
For the passing of each day
    Brings us nearer:
Nearer to eternity
    O'er paths untrod,
Nearer the shoreless sea,
    Nearer to God.

Robert E. Twohy, '08.

BACK TO ROME

———

(AN INCIDENT OF AVIGNON.)

———

Christ's Vicàr halts; amazement thrills his limbs,—
Then pain,—then fearful hesitation,—while
He eyes and eyes the prostrate form outstretched
To bar the path of his departing.

                               Rome,
Art thou again defrauded of a meed divine,
Ere it return unto the eager clasp?
Long hast thou waited for this gladsome day,
When Avignon, now three score years and ten
Thine all unequal rival, should repent
Her folly and deliver thee the spouse
That's thine, the Papacy not circumscribed
To any country's narrowness but broad
As are the mighty world and thou! So grand
Erstwhile, reduced to dire, dire wretchedness,—
Sombre th' historic lanes and desolate,—
The owlet nestles in thy temples rare
And hoots the night to morn,—thy glory gone!
For he is far from thee and lingereth still,
Thy Pontiff-King, thy soul, thy joy,—despite
His heaven-recorded vow.

                              Ah, well he may
Since there athwart his steps a parent lies,
Beseeching by the hoar frost of his locks
For pity from that son.

                         Fierce struggles heave
The breast one moment, till his duty bids
The Church release from bonds nor yield to ought
"Upon the asp shalt walk, the basilisk,
Upon the dragon and the lion tread."
                              He speaks
And sunders nature's fondest tie forthwith.

Th' Eternal City sheds her weeds of woe
Hailing a Gregory with loud acclaim.
                              SPECIAL.

RICARDO

When in that year of madness and unrest, the dire summons came for the Padres to leave their home, Carmel, around whose cloisters their hearts clung closer than the aged ivy reaching up its walls, little six year old Ricardo was weeping and sobbing with a vehemence quite unusual for his gay little heart.

He cared not for the others; (for was not Padre Edmunde cross to him) but he was to lose his loved Padre Francisco, who told him stories, taught him his prayers and filled his pockets with good things.

"And we shall never see him again? Then I want to stay and die near him."

And Padre Francisco was loathe to leave; for how could he go far away, nay, place an ocean between himself and his children?

And the sea! How could he live away from its roar so musical to him, voicing from out the restless blue depths the might and strength of God? As he fancied himself thus removed from this loved home, and for a moment allowed himself to dream, every spot, every sound, every movement seemed to beckon to him to return. And as he came to himself he was surprised to find his cheeks wet, his hoary head bent still more, and his feeble step rendered still more uncertain.

The night when the stars came out to keep their vigil, he dropped on his knees before his skull and Crucifix, and prayed that if he must go, it would be to the one place dearer to him, Heaven. Long and earnestly he wrested in prayer, and when they came into his cell the next morning to serve the writ, they found him there on his knees, his white hair flowing caressingly over his shoulders, dead.

Out beneath the willows they carried him, and while the birds he had loved so much and fed so often with his own hands chirruped the requiem, they laid him to rest in the valley of his love.

Long after the others had gone away, a little "Mexican" stole softly up to the newly made grave, and having breathed a little prayer planted there his only treasure, a red rose-bush, and quickly stole away.

II.

Just at dusk when the summer sun had bidden farewell to the little town of Monterey, and had thrown a shower of gold on the restless waves which lapped its shores, a handsome, manly young Mexican rode proudly into the town. The prancing of his blooded horse, who seemed as he tossed his head and champed his bit, to be consciously proud of his master, awoke for a moment the slumbering streets from their drowsy lethargy; and as he passed through the Spanish portion of the little hamlet, many were the greetings from the vine covered verandas, and many a "Mamma" wished within her heart, that he were one of the family.

But as he gained the English speaking district, these expressions of welcome were no longer heard, but in their stead, remarks of contempt or of spiteful envy. For no white man could ride as he, no one could brand the struggling heifer as well as or as quickly as he, and consequently no one was hated among them so much as he. He seemed, however, not to heed these ill-boding glances, and as he flung himself from his horse before the door of the principal hotel of that place, a smile played around his dark handsome features. Apparently unconscious of the malignant looks shot at him from the lowering eyer of the rough bearded men lounging there, he threw himself in a chair near the door and began to converse quietly with another Mexican. Now and then he could hear muttered epithets not calculated to pass muster as compliments, but he ground his teeth and said nothing. At last one of the men, intoxicated enough to be vicious, and no doubt urged on by his companions, reeled toward him and in a voice choked with rage, growled, "You Mexican dog, if you don't pull up your stakes and light out of this here camp in ten minutes, there will be one Greaser less to account for in this town of Monterey."

"Why?"

"Why?" the other retorted, "you beast, don't you know that you ain't got no business here among white men. Git!"

But as he reaches for his revolver, a shot rang through the air,—a dull thud —and the self constituted Vigilante was bargaining with Charon for a passage across the Styx.

When the smoke and the confusion cleared away, a trail of blood through the doorway, and the maddened gallop of the fleetest horse in the county spoke sufficiently for themselves.

Within the little town all was ablaze with excitement. A Mexican had shot and killed a respected white man. What mattered it that he shot in self defense? What mattered it that he was wounded perhaps mortally in return? Such an outrage must not go unpunished. The coyote must be tracked, captured and brought back to heal the wounds of suffering justice. If it were a white man, he,——well, justice is blind.

"Jesu, Madre Mia-you knew it was my life or his! I did not mean to kill him! Oh, this pain; this torture!—shall I end all? Shall—but no! no!—they must not catch me! Fly, my sweet Caramillo!"

Onward through the companionless night his faithful steed bore him; onward mile after mile, never seeming to grow weary. Now and then some night bird flew across the path, and started the air with its hideous screech, and now and again a coyote yelped and whined sulkily, as if resenting the intrusion. But the rider heeded not; crazed by the pain, he felt nothing but the torture of the jagged bullet holes; nothing but the thought of his life fast ebbing away with every heart throb, nothing but the thought of going to his God. "Now—oh, any time but now! Jesu! Maria! But I shot in protection! Madre mia ! He would have shot me!"

And then a quiet peace settled over him, (as often happens to a dying man) through all the scenes of his life he rambles; back to the rancho, where his young wife was waiting for him, back further to the day when his mother went to the Angels, back further still— what a loving memory,—to the pleasant hours of his childhood at the Mission, the kindly old face of Padre Francisco— the vineclad porch, the stories—the sad parting.

But he is swaying to and fro! Will he fall? With one hand grasping the pommel of his saddle, making desper- ate struggles at every lurch, he still clings on. He is making a desperate attempt to cling on, but slowly and surely, as his life's blood oozes from the ragged wounds, he is losing his last hold, when all at once his horse, thor- oughly exhausted and wayworn, stumbles over an obstruction of bushes, throws him to one side—and his misery is over forever.

And there lying prostrate, with a shower of of red rose leaves scattered around his head, the posse found him in the early morning, and as the others muttering turn their horses' heads homewards, the sheriff noted in his memorandum: "Ricardo found dead on a grave at Carmel. Headstone: In Memoriam—Padre Francisco."

A. C. F. 2nd Acad.

MY THOUGHTS

My thoughts, they come, they go,
In a continual flow,
They never leave me to my peace,
And never cease,
Importunate!
Even when I rest, e'en when I eat,—
Breakfast, and sup and dine,—
Yet—they are mine.

T. J. S. '12.

BRYAN J. CLINCH

By the death of the learned author of "California and Its Missions," Santa Clara College has lost one of its best and most distinguished friends. Whenever Mr. Clinch could do us a good turn, whether as an architect or as a writer, he always did it in his own quiet, unostentatious way. He was the reconstructor of the old Mission Church, badly battered by an earthquake some thirty years ago, and its blending of modern requirements with the old-world devotional atmosphere of the Spanish Mission days is a striking monument to his skill and taste. He also designed the Boys' Chapel which withstood the shock of April 18th better than almost any other brick building of equal dimensions in the country. Beyond these material favors, however, were the researches which he made into the history of Santa Clara Mission and College and the essays published from time to time in book and magazine, wherein he drew with a master hand the successes and failures, the joys and the sorrows of our bygone years.

Mr. Clinch was a native of Dublin, and was related to the Kenrick family that gave to the United States two of its greatest Archbishops. He studied at the Catholic University of Dublin, probably under its famous rector, Dr. afterwards Cardinal, Newman. There he had for class-mates some ardent Irish spirits, such as the late Edmund O'Donovan, all full of eagerness and enthusi-asm for the liberation of their country from the tyranny of England. To the end of his life Mr. Clinch was filled with this passionate love for Ireland, and he followed with the zeal of a patriot and the keen insight of a philosopher all the plans for her betterment. He took up the cause of the Gaelic Revival with his characteristic energy and a most erudite article on this subject in the Messenger was almost the last of his literary labors.

He was a man of the most varied and wonderful erudition. He seemed to have read everything and to have retained all he read. I heard a story, a really bona fide story, told of him that would have done credit to the omniscient Gladstone. A certain clergyman who had lived for some years in India, and had made a special study of Indian manners and history, was very fond of making his experiences and studies in that country the topic of his conversation. He was a master of his subject and was always listened to with the greatest interest. On one occasion, however, he had Mr. Clinch for an auditor. What was the narrater's surprise when the modest listener now suggested a name, now supplied a date, now filled out a half forgotten anecdote and, in a word, showed an acquaintance not merely with the obscure and confused history of India, but such a vivid knowledge of its topograpny, such an intimate familiarity with its peculiar manners and traditions as to give a stranger the impression that he had spent half his life in that country. When our reverend traveler was informed that Mr. Clinch had never even seen India, he exclaimed: "Well, his powers are more than human."

Though he was by profession an architect, and one of exceptional ability at that, as many churches in California bear witness, yet it is as a literary man that we think of him. He was known throughout the country as a writer on historical, ethical, political and sociological subjects, and the leading Catholic magazines of the United States are indebted to him for many a valuable contribution. His greatest achievement in this line was undoubtedly the "California and Its Missions," a large work in two volumes, highly prized on account of its painstaking character and the interest of its style. It won for its author the highest encomiums from within and without the church, and it was on account of it principally that Santa Clara College honored itself by conferring upon him last year the degree of doctor of philosophy.

For some time previous to the epoch-making April 18th, he had been engaged on a "History of Santa Clara Mission and College," but the precious manuscript perished, along with the rest of his books and papers, in the fire.

This great loss, as well as the horrors of the earthquake and the ensuing conflagration, seemed to have proved too much for a constitution never the most robust. For some hours, he was, in company with several others, hemmed in by encircling walls of flame with no prospect of escape. This was a situation to unnerve the strongest. The earthquake itself, however, did not much disturb him; while it lasted, he calmly prayed, after the example of one of the early Mission Fathers, to the Lord of the earthquake, and when it was over, he continued his repose.

His death, which occurred on May 17th, was quite unexpected, notwithstanding that he had had one or two heart-spells a short time previously. But he was well prepared; his life had ever been moulded on the highest christian principles. He was a Catholic in thought and word and deed. With this we take leave of him, trusting that the memory of his worth will ever remain green and fruitful among us. In him California has lost one of its most able architects; the historical world, one of its most painstaking and energetic workers; and all of us an exemplar of vast learning joined with equal modesty and virtue.

J. D. '07.

AN AUTUMN LAY

One autumn I essayed some verse
In diction simple, pure and terse:
I sang of how the lovely trees
Were rudely shaken by the breeze;
And how the ripply purling stream
Made love-lorn gentry sit and dream,
While kine came lowing through the rye
And birds sat on a fence near by;
Observed that now the sun's bright rays
Were cooler than on summer days;
Then drew the moral: "All things change
'Tis sad, but not so very strange."
"Immortal Bard!" I proudly said,
"This shall remain when thou art dead
And mingle with thy kindred clay!"
—Up to the Sanctum, no delay,
My lines were sent, but lack-a-day
I sore misjudged the kind of stay
Awaited my sweet roundelay
For there it lay!
              and lay!

                                    Sophomore.

A COLLEGE FRIENDSHIP—ITS BEGINNING AND END

Who would ever have prophesied that Clair Stephens and Frank Leat were to become such affectionate friends? Why, they seemed to have scarcely anything in common. The old proverb says that friendship finds people alike, or makes them alike. Well, it certainly did not find our two heroes alike, and as to making—but that we'll see later on. They differed in mostly everything. Clair was dark-haired; Frank's curly locks were of a beautiful pale gold, though, truth to tell, they won him the nickname of Towhead. Clair's eyes were deep dark brown, very beautiful, but so hard and cross! Frank's face, on the contrary, was lit up with soft pleading blue orbs that seemed equally akin to smiles and tears. Clair was rather reserved, self-sufficient, very matter-of-fact, of but average intellect, and full of common sense, while Frank was open-hearted, extremely clever and a trifle imaginative. Above all Clair was nearly fifteen and was an old student of two years' standing, while the other was more than a year his junior, and a new boy at that, and therefore deserving of mild contempt *ex officio*.

Yet the fact is that Frank had not completed his first decade of days at Clarantas when he and Clair Stephens filled a very large part in each other's lives. But nature did not tamely yield to such a violation of one of her proverbial laws. The friendship was to be founded in enmity. It happened in this way.

It was just a week after the opening of College. Dinner was over and the boys were filing out of the refectory. Right in front of Frank walked a boy with a Panama hat in his hand. The hat was so new and natty; the owner did handle it so carefully! Our mischief-loving Frank was in temptation: he fell. No sooner was the door reached and the precious hat deposited upon the owner's head than off he snatched it and was away like the wind.

The bereaved Panamaian was dumb with astonishment. To be treated with such undue familiarity by a boy smaller than himself and a newcomer at that was an entirely new sensation. At last, however, astonishment gave way to anger.

"Say, Johnnie, just bring that back."

The words were not so uncivil; the tone and the dark look meant unutterable things.

"Yes, I will—nit," laughed the other, with unruffled coolness—but carefully keeping at a safe distance. "What a cheap old Panama this is!" And he twisted it and tortured it and eyed it contemptuously.

"Look here, you mamma's pet," cried the other in a voice that said a vast deal to those who knew him—"just hand over that hat or I'll make you the sorest kid in the yard."

Frank grinned and enjoyed the situation immensely. "Why, you don't mean to call this a hat, do you? I thought it was a dish-rag." And smiling benignly on his fuming victim, he knocked the disputed headdress inside out.

No reserve or dignity could stand this and Clair gave chase. But Leat was unusually quick, and what with dodging and doubling, and turning and twisting he had his pursuer baffled most ignominiously. Now he would feign exhaustion, and when the enemy was right upon him, off he would dart to one side with a bound and a shout; now he would offer to return the hat, and then at the last moment, withdraw it from the tantalized owner's hand. Finally, he was willing to come to terms.

"Now," said he, "You promise to call it square, and I'll return the hat."

"All right, hand it back, and I'll make it square," was the ambiguous reply. "What are you afraid of? Won't you take my word?"

Reassured by this, Frank surrendered the hat. At the same moment he received a stinging blow in the face that bore him to the earth. But he recovered instantly and giving Stephens a look in which surprise and sorrow mingled with reproach, he walked away in dignified silence.

Clair was humiliated; more than that, he was touched. Rather "tough" as he was and careless of others, that look of mute, angerless reproach had wakened a latent chord into life. Leat had evidently had a good opinion of him; perhaps he had even liked him. Possibly he had but wanted to "make friends" and had taken that way to break the ice. Poor Clair was miserable. Vindictive as he was, and prone to anger, a sullen anger that smouldered long, even when no flame showed, his was a genuinely tender heart. Rough and selfish home treatment had frozen the springs of kindness, but a new influence was to thaw them out, and to sweeten his character forever.

The only thing for him to do was to go to Leat and "make it up." But when he came face to face with the clear eye and the well-bred self-possession of his former victim, his courage strangely forsook him, he blushed and trembled and at last turned away in confusion. However, when a moment later he again faced Frank who to improve the occasion, had kindly come after him, he had regained his usual self-control,

"Let us be friends," said Frank.

"Yes, let us," replied the other, earnestly, "and if I don't make up for that cowardly blow, you—

"You've made up already," interrupted Frank, "besides I deserved it, is I guess we both mean the same thing if we call it square this time."

And in the smile which ensued their friendship was cemented.

* * * *

The stream of friendship so stormy in its beginning, had flowed on for more than a year in its joyous music hardly marred by the slightest breaker. Day after day found it growing broader and deeper, and it appeared as if Clair and Frank were destined to be borne all their lives upon its sparkling, sun-re-flecting tide. They had done each other a great deal of good. Clair was fast losing his chilling reticence, while main-taining the reserve of a thoughtful self-reliant character. A certain dark sus-piciousness and a general conviction of the selfishness of human nature, which a motherless home training had taught him, gave rapid way before the ever re-curring evidences of his friend's sunny nature and unstinted generosity.

Even his studies felt the impulse. He was in the same class with Leat and he deemed it humiliating to lag be-hind one a year his junior. Frank, however, was so clever that to keep up with him was no easy task, and Clair had to work hard to stay abreast. Per-haps there was a bit of jealousy in all this. In the study-hall, for instance, when Clair, tired with the rules of pros-ody or the subtleties of Euclid, would fain rub his eyes, stretch out his arms and have a good yawn, if at this mo-ment his glance chanced to fall, as often it did, upon his friend and rival at his desk, the tired feeling was at once for-gotten and he was buried in his books again.

Frank was no less a gainer. Clever, lively, generous as he was, there were yet some slightly weak points in him, that contact with Clair tended to re-move. He was too confiding, and dan-gerous companionship would find in him a prey. Not that he was not one of the most pure-hearted boys on earth, but angels have fallen, and if he had not had the advice, ay! and the scold-ings of Clair to guide him, he might have come under injurious influences. Clair's scoldings, by the way, were en-tirely characteristic. Did he see his protegé, for instance, associating too freely with undesirable companions, he bluntly expressed his disapproval, and until the fault was corrected, refused even to speak to the sinner, or, as Leat put it, he kept within his shell.

It was shortly after Christmas of Frank's second year in school. The baseball 'season' was on and all was ex-citement. Many and eager were the surmises in the Junior Division about the issue of the great 'try-out' for the Junior Team, and keen and energetic was the competition. Clair had been second pitcher in last year's nine, and this year he was to be the first. Frank was not so sure of a place; he was rather new to the game, but he had had the advantage of almost daily practice with his coach, Stephens, besides being the fastest runner in his Division, so that the scales turned at last in his favor, and Frank Leat was the Center-fielder of the Junior Nine. Clair ex-pressed his congratulations in his char-acteristic way: "Well, I guess you are not as glad as I am."

But alas! too zealous in practicing, Frank had, on the very day of his pro-motion, overheated himself and caught a severe cold, in consequence of which he was confined to the infirmary for a few days. In the meantime, the team held its meeting for the election of officers. Two aspired for the post of captain, the pitcher and the first baseman; they were both nominated; the voting took place, but resulted in a tie. The Faculty director of athletics had now the deciding vote, but for reasons of prudence he preferred not to avail himself of his privilege. It was then suggested that a committee call upon the ninth voter in the infirmary and let his vote decide the matter. This was acted upon, although it was a foregone conclusion that Clair would get the vote. The delegates found the "balance of power," as they called him, engaged in conversation with Mr. Healy, his teacher, who retired, however, "before superior force." Frank's answer was given without hesitation, and the committee returned with the announcement that Harley was captain of the team.

Upon hearing this, Clair turned for an instant, deathly pale. He had not been very desirous of getting the captaincy; in fact he "ran" for it only to please some of the team, and he felt that, on the whole, it would be a good thing not to get it: "It'll do me good in one way, I guess," he said to himself, "it'll teach me how to manage people so that later on I can be President, but, on the other hand, what about my studies? Frank will get ahead of me, and what honor can make up for that?"

But he was not elected. Frank had prevented that! His best friend had voted against him! He whom he had ever stuck by, through thick and thin, had gone back on him at the very first chance. And to think that he had day after day trained him and practiced with him just to get him into the First Nine! And now that he was in, his first step was to "throw down" his faithful friend before the whole school. "I'll never forgive him! No, never," was the passionate cry of his heart,—"I won't say a word about it, but after this he is dead to me." Poor Clair, you prophesy better than you know.

All these thoughts passed through his mind in a twinkling, unguessed of by his companions. They, in their thoughtlessness, teased him about his friend's backsliding, and he rallied sufficiently to take it all in good part, and to congratulate the new captain very cordially. But as soon as appearances allowed, he stole away to a corner of the yard and there, alone and in silence, brooded over the injury he had received. A tense, hard look overspread his face, a dark, ominous cloud settled upon his forehead, and a deep, enthralling anger burned in his eyes with the hidden subdued light of a nature strong, reserved and implacable. "I wonder what bribe Leo gave him," he muttered sardonically—"we'll see if he'll prove as true a friend as I have been."

The director of athletics had noticed the sudden paleness of Clair and had guessed the cause. Happening to pass by him now, he thought of turning the incident to the boys' spiritual profit, and said to him as he walked by: "Cheer

up, my boy, cheer up; after all, if our
dear Lord is with us, what matters it
who is against us?" Alas! the last
phrase alone fixed itself in Clair's mind.
"Joe against me—even the prefects say
that!" And, in spite of all his efforts, a
tear coursed down his cheek.

But pride and anger at once regained
their mastery, and Clair was steeled the
harder on account of his momentary
weakness, for

" To be wroth with one we love
Doth work like madness in the brain."

Springing to his feet, he determined
to be up and doing, to play and laugh
and look and feel as if nothing had
happened, as if his false friend had
never darkened his path. But the
laugh was hollow and the smile was
forced, and when night-study was on,
and his eye fell upon the vacant desk of
Joe, a terrible pain clutched at his heart
and almost unmanned him. He found
that nothing whatever could

"Wholly do away, I ween
The marks of that which once had been."

Next day, Frank was back in the
yard again, having prevailed upon the
infirmarian, almost against the latter's
better judgment, that he was sufficiently
restored.

Of course, his first move was to seek
his friend. He found him, chatting with
unusual gaiety—Clair had seen him
coming—among some companions. All
circled around the newcomer, who was
a universal favorite, but Clair, taking
advantage of the melee, walked carelessly away.

The stab was not thrown away on

Frank. He saw Clair was angry in
good earnest and divined the cause. He
bode his time however, until some hours
later when he saw his angry friend sitting in the shade of a tree, absorbed in
a book. Stealing up cautiously behind
him, he had his arms around his neck
before resistance could be made.

"Say, Clair, aren't we friends any
longer?" Clair freed himself fiercely.
"No," he cried, choking with bitterness,
"we are not friends, and never shall be.
Wr're quits,—remember that." And
he arose and left.

Frank had in the past encountered
his anger more than once, in fact, Clair
was inclined to be a trifle unreasonable
and exacting at times, but never had he
seen his eye lit up with such a baleful
light as now, or his face so unyieldingly
stern. He was overwhelmed with sorrow and lonesomeness.

"And it was for this, I left the infirmary," he muttered. "Why did I not
obey the infirmarian?"

He had no one to go to in his distress.
Hitherto Clair was the confidant of all
his school-boy woes, but now—to whom
could he go? Oh yes! he would go to
Clair in spite of him; he would write
him a letter and explain everything.
He would have to listen then.

That evening in study hall a folded
piece of paper was thrown cautiously
upon Clair's desk. Looking around to
see the author of it, his eyes fell upon
the eager face of his former friend,
turned towards him pleadingly, How
strangely the face was flushed! "No

wonder he feels guilty," thought Clair to himself.

Inspecting the paper, he read: "To Clair Stephens, from Frank Leat—Please read immediately." For a moment the old kindness tugged at his heartstrings, and his face softened, but in an instant it was clouded more darkly than ever, as a wave of anger broke over his soul. He held up the letter and in full view of Leat tore it deliberately into small pieces, which he swept together finally into his little waste-box on the corner of his desk.

Early next morning when the infirmarian answered a violent ringing of his bell, he found Frank Leat, haggard and flushed, before him. "Well, Brother," said he, "I guess I flew from the nest a little too early. I haven't slept a wink all night, and I feel, oh; so—"

But the infirmarian had no need to hear more. He saw that the boy was in a very high fever, and sent him to bed immediately. His lips were cracked, his tongue was brown-coated, and though he was suffering violently, his forehead and face were burning hot. The doctor came and declared it pneumonia in its most violent form. He advised the infirmarian to prepare him for the worst.

Shortly after the patient became delirious and the boys in the yard were notified of his danger. It fell upon Clair like a thunderbolt, but, incredible to say, it did not break the barrier of pride. Yet such is the inconsistency of human nature that he spent nearly all his free time in the office praying for the patient. "What does he care for me he bitterly reflected—"he did not even send for me." None the less, he sat up in bed that night, rosary in hand, until exhausted nature could no more and he fell asleep.

On awaking in the morning he heard the softly whispered news that Frank was dead. Clair uttered no cry; did not even shed a tear, but the mortal agony that gleamed in his white face showed that the blow had gone to the heart.

The chaplain called him after Mass, "Clair," said he, "almost the last words of poor Leat were about you. Shortly before dying he recovered perfect consciousness, and he begged me, oh so earnestly! to tell you he had always done what he thought best towards you. He tried to explain to me something about some note or other but his strength gave way, and I bade him leave all these things in the hand of God. Now, do not cry, my boy, you'll be a long time together in Heaven."

A thought struck Clair. He went to study hall, gathered from his waste box the little bits of Frank's last note, and with incredible labour, put them together in their original places. And this is what he read—read through a mist of tears, for every tear in the letter seemed to him a wound in his dead friend's heart:—

My dear Clair: So I am not fit to talk to now. You think I have gone back on you. Have I ever before shown myself such a mean character that you may judge of me now without even knowing the facts? Mr. Healy told me he hoped you wouldn't be captain because it would interfere with your studies in which you were doing unusually well this year. Besides he said that you yourself at bottom really disliked the idea, and wanted Harley for Captain. I ought to be in the infirmary now, but I left it just to get a chance to have a long talk with you and explain all. Come along now, dear old Clair, let's be friends again. Honestly, I feel awfully lonesome.   Yours as ever,

                                        Frank.

"Awfully lonesome," echoed poor sobbing Clair,--oh, my God! Yes, awfully lonesome—all my life."

                              WM. HIRST, '10.

THE AGNOSTIC

I used to strive, with straining eyes,
  To penetrate the gloom;
To grasp the mystery that lies
  Beyond the silent tomb.
To slake my burning soul I tried
  Each day, some new, vain hope,
That left me helpless on the tide,
  Left me to blindly grope.
I floated on, year after year,
  On thru the silent night,
And waited for the clouds to clear
  And show my soul the light.
And now at last my strength is spent,
  And still no light, no rift;
My heart is dead, and I'm content
  Merely to drift, to drift.

                    James H. Twohy, '07.

The Redwood.

PUBLISHED MONTHLY BY THE STUDENTS OF THE SANTA CLARA COLLEGE

The object of the Redwood is to record our College Doings, to give proof of College Industry and to knit closer together the hearts of the Boys of the Present and of the Past.

DIRECTOR
RODERICK CHISHOLM, S. J.

EDITORIAL STAFF

EXECUTIVE BOARD
JAMES F. TWOHY, '07
President

J. DANIEL McKAY, '07   HARRY A. McKENZIE, '08

ASSOCIATE EDITORS

COLLEGE NOTES - - - - -	IVO G. BOGAN, '08
IN THE LIBRARY - - -	ROBERT J. O'CONNOR, '08
EXCHANGES - - -	ANTHONY B. DIEPENBROCK, '08
ALUMNI - - - - -	MERVYN S. SHAFER, '09
ATHLETICS - - - -	HARRY A. McKENZIE, '08

BUSINESS MANAGER
J. DANIEL McKAY, '07

ASSISTANTS

FRANCIS M. HEFFERNAN, '08   REIS J. RYLAND, '09

M. T. DOOLING, 09

Address all communications to THE REDWOOD, Santa Clara College, California

Terms of subscription, $1.50 a year; single copies, 15 cents

EDITORIAL COMMENT

Old Father Time, as is his inexorable wont, has swept another school year into the mists of the past, and with it has gone a host of cherished friends and associations. Life, after all, is merely a revolving cycle, more or less intermittent of greetings and farewells. All our terrestial pleasures must be transitory, for that is one sorrowful heritage from the great ancestral fall. Time is a mysterious entity, an ever flowing point which is the Nunc or the Now; and so swiftly does the present dwindle to the past and the future swell into the present that our joys almost always find us smiling through our tears.

The REDWOOD this year misses many old familiar faces from the staff: Martin V. Merle, John W. Byrnes and Michael R. O'Reilly, the executive board of last year have all departed by the degree route—which does not mean by degrees. In fact their departure has been all too sudden for the good of the RED-WOOD. For three years they have toiled earnestly and conscientiously on the magazine for the greater glory of their Alma Mater.

In Mr. Merle we are losing one of the most conscientious workers that ever graced our sanctum. As for Messrs O'Reilly and Byrnes their departure is especially to be lamented; for besides being a loss in efficiency, their departure marks the passing of the last pioneer REDWOOD men. Here are three more added to the many, many answers of College men to the Call of the World, and of these three we are proud indeed.

Robert E. Fitzgerald, '06, Leo J. Atteridge. '06, and Robert H. Shepherd ex-07 are three associate editors of last year whose names will not appear this year on the staff. The first two named have returned to college to direct their efforts towards an attainment of an A. M. degree. Owing to press of work, they are not on the staff, but they are still with us and we shall profit by their

estimable advice. In fact, Mr. Fitzgerald has kindly consented to chronicle College notes this month, during the illness of the editor of that department. Robert Shepherd has elected a life above and beyond even the echo of the clattering press. We shall miss him; but as we have his interest at heart we resign him willingly. Then there is Floyd E. Allen a member of last year's staff who this year goes to the University of California. He is a prince of good fellows, and no student in the yard last year was more respected or more loved. We hate to see him go but if good will and best luck wishes have any potency, his lines are ever going to fall in pleasant places.

And the new staff? Well, not eagerly or presumptuously, but with extreme diffidence do we assume the duties of our departed predecessors. We recognize their superiority, but we realize that we have one thing in our favor which they had not. That is their own distinguished example, which will always be for us a kindly light.

Away out here in the west of the Western Hemisphere San Francisco is unconsciously raising a great cry against the wail of the pessimist and the muck rake spirit of the day. Beaten down by one of the greatest, if not the very greatest calamity of modern times, these people have risen and are striving undaunted against an overwhelming force of circumstances. In that respect, it seems to us, there is very little difference between men and horses: it is the class that counts, and the strength of class lies in the pedigree.

It is a terrible thing to see a care free, pleasure pursuing, convention-bound people, plunged, in a trice into the throes of a lawless, unformed, primordial chaos. In such a case the worth of the individual is the only thing that can preserve the number. And therein lay the crisis. In those first moments of that great retrogression the unselfishness of the individual San Franciscan was weighed in the balance and was not found wanting.

Convention fathered the doctrine of self aggrandizement. The law of Class and Mass has ever been an implacable enemy to true benevolence. And in those first moments of the common disaster the people shook off the shackles of convention and the degrading law and instinctively turned to the docrine of the helping hand. Out of the ashes of dead convention, there sprang the phoenix of true charity. Everybody's sympathies and assistance were turned to his neighbor. Patrician and plebeian rubbed elbows in the mutual evincement of real altruism. And that was the class portraying itself. The courage of hundreds and hundreds of ancestral heroes reproduced and demonstrated in the third and fourth generation. Ah, it is the pedigree that counts after all.

And now that San Francisco is feeling the logical effects of such an upheaval in strikes and panics, there are those who prophesy dire things, They do not realize that these disturbances follow such a disaster as inevitably as thunder follows lightning, and go to make up the obstacles which future ages will eulogize these people for overcoming. The pessimists are busy crying that the city is gone and forever. Such words are but the natural offspring of a weak mind fearful of a battle against odds, and should be ignored. Every great enterprise that was ever floated has been assailed by such cries. But San Francisco will rebuild. It will not be weeks or months but many years, for it must be borne in mind that the old town is standing in the shadow of one of the world's greatest disasters, and its recovery must be slow. But it will come; already the crash of falling beams and rending timber has found an echo hopeful, in the blows of the hammer, And the blows will not cease. For back of the shoulder is the indomitable spirit of the ancestors who pressed on doggedly in the stormy days of '49. Truly opportunity is a great alchemist, and his favorite crucible is affliction. At present we speak of two San Franciscos; one will live in the future and the other has lived in the past. They are called San Francisco the Strong and San Francisco the Stricken. And to them with a heart full of hope and sorrow the world is saying, "San Francisco. city of tomorrow and yesterday, ave atque vale."

The REDWOOD avails itself of this opportunity to extend to the old boys a hearty welcome, and to the new a sincere hand of good fellowship.

JAMES F. TWOHY, '07.

Back Again

It is now a month since the close of vacation, "that sweet joyful period of rest and recreation" as one divinely inspired muse has it, and the lengthened faces of the mournful newcomers are gradually but surely regaining their proper expression. Cheer up, fellows, the worst is yet to come. But to return, verily we are back. Athletics are again booming under the management of one of the ablest staff of officers seen here in many a day. The new social hall is soon to be opened, the gym will shortly be ready for us again and amid the universal excitement and enthusiasm which will soon prevail the newcomer will speedily forget his mournful recollections and reminiscences of "down home," and enter into the spirit of the occasion.

You are ere now deep in your studies, or you should be, if you are not. But one word of advice. If you who are engaged with Xenophon or Demosthenes, Cicero, Plautus or Livy, if you must use a "pony" to go galloping through your translations, why do so; keep a whole stable of them, but be careful lest they escape. You who are deep in the works of Euclid and his equally puzzling followers, you who are absorbing the bacilli of lockjaw at every class in the mysteries of the Pterodactyl, the Plesiosaurus dolichodeirus, or the annals of the frisky Rhamphorhyncoi and stately Diplocynodons which in the Mesozoic ages romped around this mundane sphere, if you will cut your recitations for the more pleasant sunny parlors of the Infirmary, remember your exam's and beware. Finally, my dear fellow students, if you can't be good, be careful, oh be careful.

The Faculty

We were glad to find that the College faculty remains nearly as it was last year. Father Ford, however, our Prefect of Studies for the past two years is very conspicuous by his absence, having gone to fill the same office at St. Ignatius. Truth to tell, though he did spur us on when we tried to lag behind, and did assign us an exorbitant amount of work for each year, we nevertheless miss him very much. His place is admirably filled by Father J. Lydon, whose learning and painstaking interest in his work won him golden opinions from the Junior class two years ago, This class he has taken up again this year, in addition to his other duties. Father Giacobbi succeeds Father Culligan as Chaplain of the boys. Father Ricard teaches the post graduate course. Mr. Wall, S. J. and Mr. Boesch, S. J. have gone to St. Louis to complete their theological studies, in which we wish them every success.

The Staff

With this number the new staff steps into the full glare of the footlights and makes its bow to the public, meanwhile awaiting its verdict. In great part it has been changed, most of last year's members are no longer at college but to those few remaining have been added the names of some of the contributors who helped to make last year's volume the success it was. Martin Merle, editor for the past two years, has left us, but the example he set us of earnest and conscientious work still remains to stimulate us. We miss also three of our literary editors, Leo Atteridge and Robert Fitzgerald, who have graduated, and Robert Shepherd who has entered the novitiate at Los Gatos. Their loss will be felt but we hope it will not be irretrievable. The Business Depart-

ment is also stricken; Michael O'Reilly who has joined the Alumni is now engaged in business in Los Angeles, and Floyd Allen, one of his very capable assistants, has entered the State University. John Byrnes, Secretary of the Executive Board, and the pioneer manager af the REDWOOD, is also numbered among the missing.

Mr. Merle has been succeeded as editor by James Twohy, '07, who will be remembered by his many contributions during the past year. The REDWOOD is to be congratulated in having secured a writer of such ability to fill the editor's chair. J. Dan McKay, one of Michael O'Reilly's busy and capable assistants, succeeds his chief in office. His past experience as assistant manager coupled with his natural ability and strenuousness will make the REDWOOD, at least as far as its business and financial side is considered, a complete success. He has been fortunate in securing as his assistants Francis Heffernan, '08' Maurice Dooling, '09' and Reis Ryland, '09' The clipping shears and paste will be under the resourceful care of Anthony Diepenbrock, '08, whose fertile pen will direct the Exchange Department. His name is not a new one to the REDWOOD. One of the most successful departments in last year's volume was Athletics, and this year it promises to be even better under the same capable editing of Harry McKenzie '08' Ivo Bogan, '08' succeeds Robert E. Fitzgerald in the chronicling of College Notes. Mervyn Shafer, '09' will follow up the "doings" of the old boys in the alumni column, and it is safe to say that it will be to his department that the old grads will turn first. His is an important position and he is the man for the work. The books of the day will be thoroughly reviewed by Robert O'Connor, '08, in the Library Department.

Senate

The upper branch of the Literary Congress, or rather what is left of them, —for graduation made their Roll Call look like the list of directors at an insurance investigation, conspicuous mostly by their absence,—held an impromptu meeting in impromptu quarters on the evening of September 17 for the purpose of electing officers for the coming session and also to fill out their ranks from the eligible candidates in their Recruiting Agency, the House. They were obliged to meet in a vacant class room since the new building which is to replace the old historic structure in which the Senate had held their sessions for nearly half a century, has not as yet been fitted up for their reception.

The old building, a relic of pioneer mission days, was one that had withstood the onslaught of time for nearly a century and it took the shock of the greatest 'quake in the history of California to disturb its old adobe walls. But it is perhaps as well that it is gone, precious as were its historical associations and reminiscences of bygone days. For dear as it was as the birthplace and

shelter of the Literary Congress through all her many years, much as we valued our historic surroundings, and greatly as they did inspire the future orator preparing to startle the world with his eloquence, yet how could we return to it again and be reminded on every side, by the library which was the Senate's pride, by their pictures on the walls, by their vacant seats, by their names carved in inspired moments in their desks, by all the individuating traces which great men leave behind them, of the loss which the commencement of 1906 has brought upon us? How could we, I ask, go back to that hall which so often rang with the mellifluous silver tones of those budding orators and not have been reminded of our loss. Senator Merle of San Francisco no longer occupies the chair of Recording Secretary which he held so long and well; the position of Corresponding Secretary, filled so faithfully by the Senator from New York, Mr. O'Reilly, was vacant; Senator Belz of Visalia who during the past year had the painful duty of separating various Senators from their hard earned cash no longer answers to the roll. A visit from him would make a wad of bills that formerly might have choked up the New York Subway shrink so small that it would rattle as it passed through a pipe stem, —and yet he is gone.

Senator Carter of Irvington is also numbered among the vast majority, the alumni. 'Tis well our boisterous visitor of April 18th destroyed our Library for what would it have been without our

Librarian,—and he is gone. Gone too is Senator Lejeal of San Francisco, his weighty words are heard no more. So it is through all the roll, gone—gone is Senator Riordan of Santa Clara, Senator Plank of Mexico, Senators C. and J. Byrnes of San Rafael. Senator Allen of Berkeley no longer answers to the call to arms, and Senators Leonard of Leonards, and Shepherd from Oakland are also silent; and of all that year's assemblage of toga-clad students, but six are left, Senators Atteridge, Budde and Fitzgerald who have returned to the fold under the guise of post graduates, and Senators Aguirre, Donlon and Schmitz of the class of 1907.

It was, then, with heavy hearts we proceeded to elect our officers, but even in our grief, taking care to give our absent members the ablest successors.

After the air had cleared, the chairs and desks, such of them as had survived the contest, had been readjusted and the rest thrown out, the results were announced.

The winning tickets were as follows: Recording Secretary, August Aguirre, '07; Corresponding Secretary, Tom Donlon, '07; Treasurer, Leo Atteridge, '06; Sergeant-at-Arms, J. W. Schmitz, '07; Librarian, Robert Fitzgerald, '06; Chairman Committee on Invitation, Hermann Budde, '06·

We took a rest and then began again until the Sergeant-at- Arms discovered that there was not enough furniture left to go round and the meeting was forced to adjourn after having put Representatives Twohy, Brown, Casey and

McKay of the class of 1907 through the three degrees entitling them to wear the toga of Senatorial dignity.

House of Philhistorians

After a most unexpected adjournment of five months, caused by the eventful catastrophe of April 18th last, the House of Philhistorians was once again called to order on September 17th by the memorable Kearsage gavel in the hands of Mr. Fox, S. J., the Speaker of last session.

Although in temporary quarters most unsuggestive of a Literary Congress the meeting was carried on with all the interest and business-like manner that has been characteristic of the past.

The magnificent new quarters which will occupy the ground hallowed by the old adobe Congress, are being hastened to completion through the zealous efforts of the Faculty. When thrown open for occupancy they will furnish us with a debating hall as commodious and elegant as the most fastidious could desire.

It is the earnest intention of the members of the House of Philhistorians to furnish their quarters in a befitting manner. It was principally on this account that the members convened on Monday evening.

But sad to relate the House is to lose some of its most distinguished debaters. The Senate has already bereft it of Messrs. Twohy, Brown, Casey, McKay and Fisher. Others are likely to follow.

This by no means, has disheartened the remaining members, who are fully determined to train themselves into orators 'whose words all ears take captive.'

The election of officers together with some excellent suggestions in regard to the new quarters of the Literary Congress of Santa Clara College took up the greater portion of the evening.

The following is the result of the ballot:

Clerk, F. Heffernan; Librarian, J. Lappin; Treasurer, C. Kilburn; Sergeant-at-Arms, H. Broderick; Corresponding Secretary, R. O'Connor; Assistant Librarian, R. Browne; Assistant Treasurer, H. McKenzie; Assistant Sergeant-at-Arms, H. Cunningham.

Committees:

Ways and Means—M. Schafer, H. McKenzie, R. Ryland.

On Debate—Mr. G. G. Fox, S. J. ex-officio, R. Birmingham.

Entertainment—R. Caverly, C. Mullen, M. Schafer.

Reporter, H. Broderick.

The Student Body

A happy augury of a coming successful athletic season is the capable list of officers chosen to direct Student Body affairs for the present scholastic year. An enthusiastic meeting was held in the Scientific Building on September 19, the popular ticket being elected by acclamation. They have all taken prominent part in athletic affairs before this and have succeeded in earning the con-

fidence of the Student Body. The outgoing or rather outgone officers may rest assured that their official shoes will be well filled and capably navigated. August Aguirre, '07, Captain of the '05 football team and not unknown in baseball circles, succeeds Floyd E. Allen, '07 as athletic manager. Tom Donlon, '07, takes Leo Atteridge's chair as President, "Att" being engaged in the strenuous work of post graduating. Luke Feeney, '06, Com,, who handled the cash for this able body of financiers, has also left us, but his place is well filled by Frank Heffernan, '08, while Harry McKenzie, '08, succeeds Francis Lejeal, '06, as Secretary. The REDWOOD's door will always be open to these frenzied financiers, with a word of caution to the Treasurer. We still remember with a feeling of pain some visits of his predecessors.

With the Players

The Senior Dramatic Club has efficiently reorganized under the direction of Mr. Fox S. J., and have already commenced active work in preparation for a play to be given for Thanksgiving. The name or character of the play has not as yet been made public, but at least the past record of these able entertainers would be a sufficient guarantee of a successful performance. In reorganizing the staff care was taken to preserve in office as many of the past incumbents as possible, and though the absence of Martin Merle will be greatly felt, the staff hopes to repair their loss by hard and conscientious work.

The new line up is as follows:

George Fox, S. J., President and Stage Director; August M. Aguirre, '07, Stage Manager; J. Walter Schmitz, '07, Assistant Stage Manager; J. Dan McKay, '07, Business Manager; Robert E. Fitzgerald, '06, Leo J. Atteridge, '06 Press Agents; Professors G. C. Buehrer, A. W. Kaufmann, Musical Directors; Thos. W. Donlon, '07, Property Master; Lester C. Wolter, '09, Assistant Property Master; Professor John J. Montgomery, Electrician; Cleon P. Kilburn, '08, Assistant Electrician.

Junior Sodality

The election of the officers of the Junior Sodality held on September 16th resulted in the selection of the following:

Director, G. G. Fox, S. J.; Prefect, Wm. C. Gianera; First Assistant, Alex-ander T. Leonard; Second Assistant, Walter I. Sweeney; Secretary, Christopher Degnan; Censor, Martin Leahy; Vestry Prefects, Chas. L. Brazell, Jas. R. Daly; Consultors, Thomas J. Lannon, Louis F. Putman, Ignatius H. McCarty, Wm. I. Barry, Alexander Oyarzo, Robt. J. Flood.

Sanctuary Society

As we go to press news comes to us of yet another gathering to elect officers; this time the Sanctuary Society. On the evening of September 22, amidst much excitement the following officers were installed:

Henry Brainard, S. J., Director; George Fisher, '07, President; Robert E. Fitzgerald, '06, Secretary; August Aguirre, '07, Treasurer; Ernest Watson, Charles Brazell, Arthur Watson, Robert Browne, Censors; Robert O'Connor, William Gianera, Reginald Archibold, Sacristans.

From Los Angeles comes the announcement that Henry Haack ex-o8 has joined the ranks of the Benedicts. The bride was Miss Marie Petit, a prominent member of AngelCity Society. —We offer our sincerest congratulations. "Heinie's" reputation outlives him at Santa Clara. Heinie was one of the best ends that ever displayed his ability on our gridiron. He did not confine himself to foot-ball alone, but was a hustler in every line of college activity. It was on "band concert" nights particularly that Heinie's ginger displayed itself. If the band got demoralized and failed to "discourse sweet music" Heinie would always manage to fill the gap with some brilliantly humorous idea; for instance, by mounting the old water-faucet stand and starting an auction. And what an inexhaustible supply of second hand goods he would have to sell! Anything from Joe Kohlbecker's base-ball franchise to Gasty's bump of vanity and Tom Feeney's hair crimpers. And speaking of Feeney reminds us—

if we need a reminder—that Luke Feeney is with us no longer. He got his Commercial Degree last June and made tracks for Gilroy. Rube seems to have taken some of the life of the yard with him. No more will the stentorian tones of "Captain Feeney" summon the "Colts" to practice; no more will the Literary Club meet for its daily wrangles out of which the Rube always came forth with flying colors. He is now settling down to a staid, corpulent, commercial man in Gilroy where he has charge of his father's business during the latter's absence in Europe. Our advertising manager is seriously thinking of taking a trip Gilroyward in the hopes of securing an ad. Success Luke!

Roscoe Jacobs ex-'o8 and Martin Carter, '06 are to study surgery—Won't they be the real "cut up kids?"

Santa Clara loses four of her brightest students in the persons of Robert Shepherd and Edward McFadden, ex-'07, and Peter Dunne and Eugene Ivancovich, ex-'08, all of whom have chosen "the better part" and exchanged the cares of the world for the peace of the Jesuit Novitiate at Los Gatos. They are very much missed. all of them, and nowhere more than in base ball circles where Rob was official scorer for two years, and the others were among the star performers of the Junior team. They have the best wishes of all their companions.

Mr. Joseph Ryland, '84 (B. S.) met with a very serious accident several weeks ago. While inspecting the new pumping station of the San Jose Water Works he fell into the pit forty feet below. Mr. Ryland's right leg was badly fractured and he sustained numerous minor injuries. We glad to hear that he is rapidly recovering.

Harry Wolter, ex-'09, Captain of our last year's base ball team and now a member of the Fresno Club of the Pacific Coast League, has been drafted by the Cincinnati National League Club. Congratulations, and all kinds of success next year, Harry!

One of Santa Clara's bright and manly sons of "ye days of old," is Mr. Charles D. South—at present of San Jose, and on the Mercury staff of that city. Mr. South was a student at Santa Clara in 1876, and he is still endearingly remembered by the older members of the Faculty as a "good boy" and an earnest student. He has followed journalism as a profession for many years past and has obtained honorable prominence in his chosen field of labor. He wields a clear and ready pen, which ever and anon positively scintillates. He has moreover to answer to the soft impeachment of being a poet, an impeachment which we would justify by a few quotations from his poems, did not space forbid. To our great sorrow, we have to turn aside from his poetry just now to say that he has lately met with a very severe accident from a collision of electric cars in San Jose, wherein he sustained a compound fracture of the left leg, besides minor injuries, owing mainly to the fact that he heroically yielded his chance of escape to women and children. But with a happy temperament he is now rapidly recovering, and we hope soon to see him up and around once more.

Among the political announcements found in our present issue is that of Hon. James H. Campbell, A. M. '71, who has already distinguished himself as District Attorney. He is now seeking re-election to that same office, which he fills so creditably.

So too, Dan Flannery is in the field. "Genial" Dan enjoys the popularity in politics which ever characterized him not only in the class-room, but likewise, and especially, on the diamond where he was the favorite with the Fans as first baseman of yore.

MERVYN S. SHAFER, '09.

Well to begin. For that is what a beginner always has to do. We must first remark that *The Dial* for May contains better poetry than any other Exchange on this month's file. Both "Caesar" and "The First Bud" are very excellent. But the best we came across is "The Stricken City" which the great catastrophe that ruined the best part of our dear old San Francisco, inspired. In our humble opinion it is poetical from any point of view; poetical in its conception, in its development and in its language. The rhythm is of a quality not found in most College verse and the rhyme is noteworthily unstilted. Listen to this, tyro, if you wish to learn:

Oh, how vain are man's boastful achieve-
　　ments!
Where now is the work of his hand?
Go, ask the wild winds of the ocean,
Ask the breakers that beat on the strand.
A prayer for the souls that were sum-
　　moned
From earth at the Maker's decree;
A tear for the stricken city
That once stood so proud by the sea.
　　　　　　　　　—The Dial.

After running over a number of Exchanges, all more or less meritorious, we come across the *Bowdoin Quill*. Somehow or other the sight of this diminutive, unpretentious-looking little bundle of wisdom strikes a tired ex-man like a breath of fresh air on a hot day. It is up to its usual standard in everything and a little above it in "Julian's Apostasy" which is the best story that we have reviewed this month. The plot is very original and is a pleasing change from the usual weak attempt ending in a live-happy-ever-afterwards style. A story like "Julian's Apostasy" now and then would show that Bowdoin is living up to her precious inspirations in Hawthorne and Longfellow.

"College Education," in the *Red and Blue* of the University of Pennsylvania, surpasses any other essay to be found in the late ex's lying upon our desk. It is full of good solid sense and sound reasoning. The author here has something to say and says it, or rather he has a proposition to prove and he proves it to the satisfaction of anyone who will take the trouble to read it. The proposition to be proved comes to this, that a man who does not profit by a College education will regret it greatly in after-life because he will be excluded from all intellectual, artistic, and social circles. Again he will regret his loss in after-life because, if he gets sense enough to see his fatal mistake, and becomes ambitious enough to mend it, the trials and difficulties which he will have to strive against will be much greater, since he must depend upon his talent alone, and will have to struggle with a memory that is rusted by long years of inactivity. The writer graciously remarks in concluding, that any poor erratic, who has become enlightened enough to know that he should place before himself a higher ideal, can depend upon the help of U. of P. men Christian charity is a healthy spirit to foster, *Red and Blue!*

Another little note-worthy fact about the *Red and Blue*. There is a little burlesque entitled "Pearson" between its covers, which we took favorably to. A burlesque is a rarity in College magazines, especially as good a one as "Pearson" is. To us it pictures very well the character of many College and University men, who enter their College or University more with the intention of having a good time than for serious study. Pearson is made to say: "Gentlemen, do not let your studies interfere with your College education." A good paradox, isn't it? And it expresses the truth of the situation better than any jumble of words we can think of.

The Viatorian for June-July is a neat little paper, nicely covered, artistically designed, and tastily colored and ——? we were going to enumerate more of its good qualities, that are worthy of mention, but we will break off and substitute after our little conjunction, this little · question— what is inside? Unless at the time we reviewed it we suffered from a severe attack of optical illusion there is no fiction in any manner, shape, or form and merely one little attempt at verse. What has happened, *Viatorian?* We hope your editor has done nothing rash. If so profit by your mistake, Mr. Viatorian Editor.

Well, we see the Georgetown *Journal* has associated with bad companions and followed the example of the wicked *Viatorian* in not giving us one smack of fiction, not even the kind we gulp down hard! Or did the editor reject any good stories that might have been handed in to make space for prize essays and that sort of thing. "The Founding of the Colony of Virginia" is a dry combination of events. That's about all we will say about it except to theorize on how it happened. Did not the writer pressed by time condense his article much more than he would have done, were he working at his leisure? More than this we cannot hold against you, *Journal*, because you usually are one of the best papers on our desk.

A. DIEPENBROCK, '08.

·IN THE LIBRARY·

THE NORTH STAR

MRS. M. E. HENRY-RUFFIN, LITTLE, BROWN & CO.

Mrs. M. E. Henry-Ruffin's novel of Norway, "The North Star" which was favorably reviewed by the REDWOOD some years ago has met with such a cordial reception since its appearance two years ago, that publishers Little, Brown & Co., will issue a large new edition this fall. It is an interesting co-incidence that the hero of Mrs. Ruffin's novel, Olaf, the first king of a united Norway was crowned at Trondhejm, the same city that witnessed the recent cor-onation of King Haakon VII. The arrival and coronation of King Olaf at "Nidaros" as it was called in his day is a very fine picture in this stirring tale of the vikings. King Haakon lately sent an autograph letter of congratula-tion to the gifted authoress, who, by the way,—and let us say it in all modesty—takes a special interest in the REDOOOD.

TOM LOSELY: BOY

FR. COPUS, S. J.—BENZIGER BROS. 85 CTS

This is one of the most charming and at the same time most instructive and beneficial books we have come across for many a long day. It is a story of a real American Catholic boy, full of life and fun and mischief, and, at the same time, endowed with a delicate sense of honor, and a tender, if unobtrusive piety. He never gets too good for human nature's daily food, he never is made to pose before us an angel—his assiduous diplomacy in securing cream-puffs and tarts from Jane effectually check any over-idealizing on our part— but in spite of all that, or perhaps on account of all that, we love Tommy all the more, and his little theft of the fig from the fruit stand, with his consequent heroic penance, endears him much more to us than if the "happy fault" had never been committed. Every page in the book teems with fun and yet each manage to convey its own serious and impressive lesson. We should like to see it in the hands of every young Catholic in the country.

"JACK"

BENZIGER BROS, 45 cts.

This is quite an interesting little book of the juvenile class. While the plot is not very elaborate, the language is simple and easily intelligible to young readers. The principal character brought out is "Jack." whose high ideals concerning restitution in the Sacrament of Penance are remarkable. On the whole the story is well calculated to interest and instruct the young people for whom it is meant.

Instead of awaking to greater activity after the shake, our athletic spirit merely rolled over like the proverbial log and slept for three months. But with a vivacious spring it has bounded out of these somnolent quilts and now fresh as a new born daisy it rubs its eyes and looks around for something to do. It has not been decided up to the present writing what game will replace the abolished collegiate football. Rugby has been suggested and probably will at least be given a fair trial. It will be difficult for the erstwhile collegiate stars to accustom themselves to this innovation; however, fellows, if this be the inevitable, we must go after it with all our oars in the water. And if Rugby fails to materialize, or to hold its own among us,—well! there is no use in moping for all that. We can be up and doing in other sports. There is classical track to give lung power and speed; there is handball to give agility and dislocations; there is tennis to give you grace and grit; and basket-ball to give you the strength of an Atlas with the eye of an eagle. Last but not least, there is baseball—the American Game. Out of dear old football—may I so call it?—we get pleasure, hard knocks and an abundance of glory, but there are other sports by which we may secure beneficial exercise. It is wonderful how exercise supports the spirits and keeps the mind in vigor. There is no better preventive of mental exhaustion than regular muscular exercise. So, fellow students, especially the bench-warming fraternity, get off the bench and be at least a molecule in the athletic activity. It will strengthen your average in the class room, it will make your brain act quicker, it will develop your body toward its proper proportions. Like the every-day street fakir, I merely ask the bashful and backward to try. It is a safe investment in which to put some of the time and energies which have been so liberally given you.

It is hardly proper to be forecasting the baseball outlook just now, but a word in this connection, however, is hardly ever out of season. A. Shafer, after a year furlough, has returned to his Alma Mater. During his absence, "Art" attended St. Vincent's College, Los Angeles, where he made an enviable record on the track and diamond. Then we have the following from the Gibraltars of 1905: J. Collins, C. Kilburn, J. Brown, J. Twohy, M. Shafer, C. Freine, H. Broderick and J. Lappin.

Harry Wolter, last year's captain, is now the premier outfielder and leading sticker of the coast league. Harry is sought after by the eastern league magnates and will no doubt nestle in an eastern tree next season. He has a host of admirers in college, who will watch his progress with much interest. Congratulations, Harry!

Cleon Kilburn, '08, was unanimously elected to the captaincy left vacant by Harry Wolter. Cleon has been a star performer on the varsity team for the past three years and has all the requisites of a proficient captain. We look forward to a very successful season with Kilburn at the head of the nine.

Tennis

The students who wear the rubber and duck on the bituminous court, have at last taken some beneficial elixir. The man with the hoe annihilated in one day the filthy weeds that have kept the court in obscurity for three months. The treasurer turned tainted money into pure chalk and marked the court according to Spalding. The club members are practicing zealously for the coming tourney which will give Santa Clara a criterion to go by. The motto of the club, so Pres. McClatchy said, will be "Racket." During the vacation the old net was confiscated and used by the chef-de-cuisine to secure our annual supply of fish. Treas. McLane reports progress financially——"but," quoth he, "we can crowd a few more in." One dollar initiation and twenty-five cents a month gives one the right to belong to the chosen few. Here is the roll call and the results of the last campaign. President, C. McClatchy; Treasurer, H. McLane; Secretary, E. Wood; Members, J. Maltman, A. Shafer, H. Yoacham, A. Donovan, R. McClatchy and G. Duffey.

Basket Ball

The personnel of last year's team has not been changed and as a result the collegians should more than outdo their splendid efforts of '05. A manager will be elected shortly who will arrange games with Stanford, Berkeley, University of Pacific, and others. Any student who has played the game before is urgently requested to don a uniform, for new material is always welcome. Twohy R., Schmitz, Aguirre, Murphy, Bogan and McKenzie are now in training.

Athletic Rally

An enthusiastic athletic rally took place on Sept. 19th, at which, besides the transaction of other business, the officers for the year were elected. August Aguirre was chosen Manager of athletics. A wiser choice could not have been made. "Augi" has been tried and true in many an office, and we all can look forward with confidence to a very successful athletic year under his management. Cleon Kilburn is Captain of baseball. Anyone who knows the whole-souled earnestness with which Cleon confronts all his duties, in class or in campus, knows full well that the Captain's mantle could not have fallen upon more worthy shoulders.

Second Division

(By WILLIAM BARRY, '10.)

So many of the good players of Second Division have attained their "majority" and passed over to the First Division, that the baseball outlook for us was just a bit cloudy at first. However, after some figuring, two pretty good leagues of three teams each have been put together. In the "Big League" several of last year's veterans are still to be found,—such as R. Foster, our sole survivor of the Junior Team '06; H. Gallagher; L. Putman; J. Sheehan; E. Moraghan; and H. Lyng. Moreover, other good players, such as Gianera and Cuda, who last year were content to warm the bleachers during the games, are now trans-

formed into enthusiastic players. So, although there has not yet been any too much interest shown in their work by the big leaguers, we expect things to brighten up rapidly, and this season to turn out fully as successful as the last.

But the "Little League"—they are small, but oh my! The fur begins to fly from the first instant the umpire calls the game, or rather it begins its flight during breakfast on holiday mornings and ends it somewhere in the tired evening. In our next number we shall give a more detailed account of their doings.

A new game has been started in Second Division — Indoor Baseball, played, however, outside. It excites a great deal of interest. As most of the players are rather "green" to the work, the rules are yet very pliable, and errors, for obvious reasons, do not count —all of which puts a vast deal of fun into the contest, as its uproariousness testifies.

The Gymnasium officers for the term are as follows: R. Foster, Pres.; Wm. Barry, Treas.; C. Smith, Sec'y; Censors: A. Leonard, F. Cuda, D. Di Fiore, H. Hogan, C. Deignan.

Those of the Junior Tennis Club are: W. Hirst, Pres.; H. Hogan, Treas.; E. O'Rourke, Sec'y; J. Sheehan, M. Lohse, Censors.

H. A. J. McKENZIE, '08·

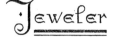

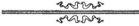

THE REDWOOD

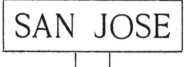

SAN JOSE

Brick Company

MANUFACTURERS OF

Common and . . .
Ornamental Brick

Yards at Dougherty Station

SAN JOSE OFFICE

17 North First Street   San Jose, California

Telephone Main 594

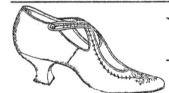

Labor Party

Democratic Ticket

Sheriff—Arthur B. Langford

County Assessor—L. A. Spitzer

County Recorder—Thomas Treanor

District Attorney—James H. Campbell

Tax Collector—W. A. January

County Clerk—H. A. Pfister

County Treasurer—Thomas Monahan

County Auditor—Bert Schwartz

Superintendent of Schools—D. T. Bateman

County Surveyor—Henry Fisher

Coroner—B. E. Kell

Supervisor, 4th District—John Roll

State Senator—F. M. Smith

Assemblyman—John Stanley

Justices of the Peace—Santa Clara Township
Chas. A. Thompson and D. R. Oliver
Constables, Santa Clara Township
J. J. Toomey and Mat Hite

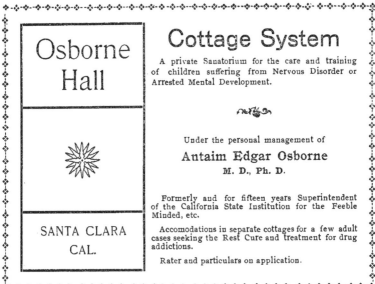
PAINLESS EXTRACTION   CHARGES REASONABLE

DR. H. O. F. MENTON
DENTIST

Res. Phone Clay 13
Office Phone Grant 373
Office Hours—9 a. m. to 5 p m
Most Modern Appliances

Rooms 3, 4, 5, 6, 7, 8 Bank Building, over Postoffice
Santa Clara, Cal

For COUNTY RECORDER

DAN FLANNERY

REPUBLICAN NOMINEE

Election November 6, 1906

For CONGRESS   Fifth Congressional District

E. A. HAYES

(Incumbent)

═══════════════════Election November 6, 1906

For JUSTICE OF THE PEACE

CHAS. A. THOMPSON

Regular Democratic and Union Labor Party Nominee

Santa Clara Township, Comprising the Precincts of Agnew, Campbell, Hamilton, Jefferson, Moreland, Santa Clara and University.

Election Tuesday, November 6, 1906

For SHERIFF

LANGFORD

Regular Nominee

UNITED LABOR PARTY═══════and═══════DEMOCRATIC PARTY

Election Tuesday, November 6, 1906

Vote for——————————

JAMES H. CAMPBELL

For DISTRICT ATTORNEY
(Present Incumbent)

————————————Election Tuesday, November 6, 1906

MR. CAMPBELL was elected by the people to enforce **all** the laws **all** the time. He has enforced them, including them against vice, **immorality** and **gambling.** He has run the District Attorney's office for the people,' and has not allowed the bosses to run it for themselves. **That** is why the political czars, their newspaper monopoly and their allies, the gamblers are fighting him. **Are you with them?**

FOR JUSTICE OF THE PEACE

I. HERRINGTON
(Present Incumbent)

REGULAR REPUBLICAN NOMINEE

SANTA CLARA TOWNSHIP

————————————Election Tuesday, November 6, 1906

For County Superintendent of Schools

D. T. BATEMAN
(Incumbent)

Regular Nominee

Democratic Party.   Union Labor Party

Election November 6, 1906

For——————————————G

COUNTY TREASURER

Ernest W. Conant

For SENATOR 27TH DISTRICT

FRANK N. SMITH

REGULAR UNITED LABOR AND DEMOCRATIC NOMINEE

Election, Tuesday, November 6, 1906

For COUNTY SURVEYOR

J. G. McMILLAN
(Incumbent)

Regular Republican Nominee

Election November 6, 1906

B. E. KELL
—FOR—

Coroner and Public Administrator
(Present Incumbent)

Regular United Labor and Democratic Nominee

JAS. E. GLENDENNING
(Present Incumbent)

Regular Republican Nominee for.....

JUSTICE OF THE PEACE

Sana Clara Township : Comprising the Precincts of Agnew, Campbell, Hamilton, Jefferson, Moreland, Santa Clara and University.

Election, Tuesday, November 6, 1906

Contents.

Nace Printing Co. Santa Clara, Cal.

Photo by Bushnell

OFFICERS OF THE STUDENT BODY

FRANCIS M. HEFFERNAN, Treasurer; THOMAS W. DONLON, Vice-President, HARRY A McKENZIE. Secretary

The Redwood

Entered Dec. 18, 1902, at Santa Clara, Calif. as second-class matter, under Act of Congress of March 3, 1879.

VOL. VI.   SANTA CLARA, CAL., NOVEMBER, 1906·   No. 2.

NEW AND GREATER SAN FRANCISCO

(A Vision)

I draw aside the veil of future days,
And peer into the ages yet to be
A new-born city by the Western sea
Meets my enraptured vision. Halo rays
Of glory deck her brow. Bright sunshine plays
About her form ethereal. Cheeringly
The Western wave creeps on in majesty
About her. How wondrous are God's mighty ways!
She who but yesterday had sat in woe,
Amid the ruins of her desolation,
To-day, stands forth, in fullest noontide glow
Of fame, prosperity and exultation!
How meet, O City of St. Francis' love,
Eternal thanks to render to the God above!

B. A. '10

A MEMORY OF AN ADOBE FORUM

I. THE LANDMARK

The old adobe home of the Literary Congress of Santa Clara College has been razed to the ground.

The passing of this venerable landmark is like the death of a friend. We view the remains, recall familiar virtues of the departed, breathe a few words of eulogy, and tearfully surrender the lifeless clay to memory and the grave. Here, in my humble way, would I perform a last office for the old adobe.

It was a decree of fate, and not a vandal-stroke, that laid the building low; and the hand of Progress obeyed necessity in finishing the work that the earthquake had too well begun.

The structure was erected by the Indians, under the supervision of the Franciscan padres, about thirty years before James Marshall found the glittering treasure that maddened half the world. It was solidly built with standard adobe bricks, each earthen cube being two feet long, one foot wide, and three inches thick; while the thickness of the walls was from three to four feet.

. When this fabric was reared, in 1818, the Mission had already seen its halcyon days. Four years later witnessed the Mexican occupation, and then followed a period of political greed and avarice culminating in the secularization of the Missions and the seizure of the Mission lands and flocks and herds.

From the downfall of the religious system, under the Mexican rule of plunder and confiscation, to the declaration of American sovereignty, lawlessness reigned and violence usurped the place of right. It was under these deplorable conditions that the adobe, which had been the dwelling place of the Majordomo, or superintendent of the Mission Indians, was boldly seized, by sheer physical force, and converted into a wayside inn.

In the latter '40's, the adobe was styled the "California Hotel." No register nor record of any kind remains to enlighten us as to the identity of any of the guests, and even the name of the host is lost forever. It is probable that many of the pioneers of the golden era were harbored there—that the Gwins and Fremonts, the Sutters and Kearneys, the Larkins and Rileys and Danas made it a halting place in their journeys up and down the "King's Highway."

We know, however, for an absolute fact, that the beloved Father John Nobili, founder and first president of Santa Clara College, in order to avoid friction with the claimants of the hotel, paid their price for it in the year 1854. From the time the school was established in 1851, the boarders had been lodged in the various small rooms of the Mission, and the old Mission pump was the scene of their morning ablutions. The acquirement of the California

Hotel, which faced the campus from the east, signalized a change.

The old adobe, like all the original Mission buildings, was only one story in height; but no sooner had Father Nobili secured possession than he added a second floor; the new story being built of a peculiar light-colored brick, fire-baked and durable. The upper floor was used as a dormitory; the lower floor for classrooms; but the name of "California Hotel" clung to the building for decades.

In that old dormitory, Thomas I. Bergin, Bernard D. Murphy, D. M. Delmas, Clay Greene, James V. Coleman, Charles J. Martin and William Brown, among others, had their beds and lockers.

Bergin, one of California's ablest counsellors, was the law partner of the late Hall McAllister, the acknowledged leader of the San Francisco bar; Murphy, the great-souled, big-hearted "Barney," whose friends are as numerous as the sands of the sea, was six times Mayor of San Jose and has been frequently mentioned as a prospective candidate for gubernatorial honors. Delmas, brilliant lawyer and scholar of the classics, today bears the palm of eloquence and has no rival in finished oratory on the Western shore. Clay Greene, of New York, eminent author and playwright, has delighted millions of Americans with the productions of his clever and versatile pen. Smiling "Bill" Brown was chief of the old volunteer fire department in the Garden

City, and afterward chief of police. Charley Martin followed a mercantile life, and has been Mayor of the city of his home. And "Jim" Coleman is the San Francisco millionaire, known for his large benevolence, his scholarly gifts and his influence in the sphere of politics.

In 1871 Father Aloysius Varsi constructed the imposing Exhibition Hall at the extreme northeast corner of the college grounds, and the dormitory for the elder students was removed from the California Hotel to the first floor of the new building. The lower story of the adobe continued to be used for classes, while the upper floor was converted into apartments for the secular employees of the college. This disposition lasted until 1876, when the two college debating societies were organized into a Literary Congress, under the presidency of Rev. Aloysius Brunengo, and at the inspiration of Father Edmund Young. Then the partitions were removed and the upper floor was divided into two roomy halls, the one on the south side being the Senate Chamber, the one on the north the House of Representatives. That was the arrangement until the epochal April morning when the foundations of the valley were rendered more secure by the correction of a serious fault in the coast range of mountains.

Thus far have I dealt with little more than the bare history of the adobe hostelry. Now, let me draw, if I can, another and a fairer picture.

II. The Senate

Musing, I tread the ashes of a memoried hall. I close my eyes. The past rises before me. Once more I stand in the spacious Senate Chamber, with its splendid, carved, high-backed chair under the tasseled canopy, fronting the familiar semi-circle of desks.

From the walls look down, out of old-fashioned frames, the strong faces of mighty men who shaped the destinies of the Nation.

On this pedestal stands the marble effigy of Webster, the invincible; and yonder is the Parian counterfeit of Clay, who dazzled crowds and Senates with his witchery of speech.

There, stacked against the rear wall, its shelves bending underneath the weight of thousands of useful volumes, is the old library, rich with the lore of the statesmen of the land.

And now the chandeliers are ablaze—the hall is peopled, and voices break the solemn silence.

Behold! In the massive chair, gavel-in-hand, sits the noble old Jesuit, Edmund Young—broad of brow, benevolent of face and soul; his eyes and heart full of sympathy and love—a man of giant form, but gentle as a lamb. Peerless as a rhetorician, he was both poet and orator. As a boy, he had listened to the thunders of Dartmouth's Titan of the forum; to the fascinating voice and seductive reasoning of the author of the Missouri Compromise; and to the deep tones and deeper thoughts of Calhoun, the metaphysician.

As a scholastic at Georgetown, Edmund Young had found in near-by Washington his intellectual recreation and delight; and he was the first to conceive and put into practical execution the idea of a mimic Senate and House of Representatives, as a substitute for the ordinary debating society.

The first American Literary Congress was instituted at Santa Clara College by Father Young. It was composed of two co-ordinate branches, the Philalethic Senate and the House of Philhistorians. In its form and method of procedure the Congress of the United States was taken as a model; the president of the college filling, ex-officio, the place of the executive. By this organization the members enjoyed not only all the advantages afforded by debating societies, but they acquired, at the same time, a practical knowledge of parliamentary law and the manner in which legislative bodies are conducted.

Father Young was a native of Maine, and he bore for the Pine-Tree State a truly filial love. It was a New Englander, then, who developed in Santa Clara the ideal forum for collegians. Only a decade ago, Yale University placed the seal of its approval on the model congress as exemplified at Santa Clara, and paid the western institution the notable honor of adopting the identical idea at New Haven.

New England has thus been repaid by the west for that which New England gave to the west through Edmund Young, the Jesuit. And the plan of the mimic Congress is destined to find its way into every thoroughly American college and academy.

III. Out of the Past

I linger about the sight of the old hall, while the handmaid of the Night is drawing the "gradual, dusky veil;" and I fancy spirits of the lamented dead assembling, in a shadowy host, where the historic building stands no more. And first among them I distinguish Stephen M. White, statesman without fear and without reproach. In the mimic Senate, as in the real, he displayed that potentiality of character which made California proud to bestow upon him her most coveted and exalted honors. Stephen M. White was a man!

Let me be understood. In the California lexicon, man comprehends all that is best in human nature. Man is a higher, broader, deeper, grander designation than gentleman. Man is the solid gold nugget; gentleman, refined gold alloyed with baser metals. Man is the true diamond; gentleman, a highly polished ornament that may be a diamond, but bears a suspicion of paste. Man "tells truth and shames the devil;" gentleman equivocates by the art of diplomacy. Man is one who fulfills a mission rather than one who acts a part; he is real, not artificial; he is honest, frank, generous, sympathetic; whereas, gentleman, often pictured with gloved hands, has too often a gloved heart and a gloved conscience.

Man is a republican who stands upright; gentleman, a courtier who fawns.

Man is an image of his Maker; gentleman, also an image, but with the character sometimes blurred by the chisels of dissatisfied human amateurs.

Of Santa Clara College let this be said: "She has made men."

Among the shadows gathered on the old site, I mark the form of one who abandoned law for the stage. John T. Malone was admired of Edwin Booth, and was a favorite in the great theaters of the East. His Richelieu and his Richard III, discovered in him a standard quality, and the laurels he strove for were within reach when death rang down the curtain and life's fitful drama closed.

I know but few of the shadows, yet I see in the dimness some stately figures and shapely heads, and I know there is learning and dignity and courtesy in the company that appears at twilight and departs, as if obedient to some vesper call, when God's candles illume the azure temple of the sky.

The living members of that old Senate are many, and it were vain for me even to attempt to recall the names of all those who have shed luster on their Alma Mater by reason of the mental adroitness and mastery of speech attained in the Literary Congress.

There is one, however, who led a band of warriors to the other side of the world, bearing his country's flag to victory in the isles of the Orient seas. But his triumphs did not cease with the war, for he then took up and solved more difficult problems of peace. He framed just laws for the country he pacified, and the President of the Nation gave him high command in the army, then placed upon his shoulders the ermine of a Supreme Justice, and finally elevated him to the enviable rank of Governor General of all America's possessions in the Far East. James F. Smith needs no encomium. He has carved out for himself a lasting fame; but the intellectual weapons he used were sharpened till they glistened in their keenness, there, in the homely old adobe, of which all that is left is a picture and a story.

Charles and Valentine McClatchy, who direct the policy of that paper of sterling character, the Sacramento "Bee," were Senators here; so were Hon. Reginald Del Valle, of Los Angeles; Judge M. T. Dooling, of Hollister; United States Civil Service Commissioner Samuel J. Haskins, of San Francisco; Superior Judge Bradley V. Sargent, of Monterey; former District Attorney Lewis F. Byington, of San Francisco; District Attorney James H. Campbell, and Deputy District Attorney James P. Sex, of Santa Clara county; Peter Martin, the Newport multi-millionaire; Assistant District Attorney John O'Gara, and Attorneys John J. Barrett and William Humphrey, of San Francisco, and Harry Wilcox, Charles M. Lorigan and Charles W. Quilty, of San Jose; and the Rylands—John, Joseph, Frank and Tacitus; and Victor Scheller, president of the San Jose Chamber of Commerce; and those commercial princes of the Bay City—the Welches —Charles, Aloysius and Andrew. The roll of honor, as I might call it, would

stretch out far beyond the space allotted me, and reluctantly I fold the unfinished scroll of names.

IV. Adobe Dust

The old adobe, with its roof of tile, its rude exterior, and its long, low-ceiled halls; with its ten thousand treasured memories and associations, and a history extending far back into an age "before the Gringo came"—the old adobe has gone the way of all structures material. It served many a turn; it answered many a purpose; it furnished the educators of the country with an immeasurably-valuable, original American idea; and, when its time came, it went down all of a sudden, and buried itself in its own congenial mold.

Yet, even there—its dust commingled with its mother dust—the old adobe will be eloquent still; for, when the winds of winter blow, and moisture clouds the air, and the soil of the valley drinks its annual libation to prosperity—then will there be a re-awakening of the life that was imprisoned in the adobe's massy walls, and the scattered remains of the building will be robed in springtime verdure.

Is there not a symbolism here?

The excellent seed planted in young minds at a college wherein commerce is rated secondary to morals, may be neglected in after life and remain long unfruitful, even as the seed locked up in the adobe. But, even so, the argument is with the moral teaching still. The time will come—it may be after dissipated years, when the snows of age are on the brow and the clouds of the winter of life form above the soul; the time will come when the mind will go back in retrospect and things will be seen in the light of what they are worth. Then may the tears of repentance fall, and, quickened by those precious drops—as the adobe with the rain—the old seed latent there will burst its bonds and flower in beauty, and the regenerated spirit will bear testimony of the truth that good seed is never planted in vain.

I am not wont to moralize—but the theme is there!

"What is writ is writ!

Would it were worthier!"

CHAS. D. SOUTH.

IN VAIN

Do not hesitate Muse
    For I need thee to-night !
E'en did I abuse,
    Do not refuse !
For can'st thou not see I must write?
    Come now beside me
And make my dark celly brain light,
    Or alas! what will betide me ?

But naught could I say to her;
    In vain did I pray to her !

            A. D., '08.

MARY QUEEN OF SCOTS' FAREWELL TO FRANCE

(FROM THE FRENCH)

Adieu, oh sunny land of France,
    Dear by so many a tie,
Fond nurse of fairy youth's romance
    Adieu! to leave thee is to die.

The fates to exile lone compel,
My chosen fatherland from thee
Hear Mary's soul-outpoured farewell,
O France, and guard her memory.
Now sighs the breeze, we quit the shore,
And though I prayed the storm to rave,
And, kindly cruel, thy queen restore,
Yet God will not awake the wave!

When in the gaze of Gallia's eyes,
They twined the lilies on their queen,
The people cheered my royal guise
Less than my beauty's vernal sheen.
The sovereign rank in vain, in vain,
Attends me to dark Scotia's strand;
And never had I wish to reign
Save over France's happy land.

Love, glory, genius, all allied,
Have led through flowers my youthful days;
But these cold Scotland bids aside;
Henceforth I wander thorny ways.
Alas! an omen evil-fraught
Would numb mine every faculty;
I saw in troubled sleep, methought,
A scaffold dread loom up for me.

When girt around with courtier fears
The daughter of the Stuart line
As on this day that sees her tears
For thee, O France, will tearless pine.
But God! the swiftly-gliding barque
Moves even now 'neath alien skies
And night, with dewy mantle dark,
Conceals thee from mine aching eyes.

Adieu! O sunny land of France,
    Dear by so many a tie!
Fond nurse of fairy youth's romance,
    Adieu! to leave thee is to die.

A. M. D., 2ND FRENCH.

"THE WAY OF THE WORLD"

Richards closed and locked the door. Then he turned and faced the younger man.

"Billy," he said calmly, "Mr. Redding has just telephoned me from the bank that they have discovered a large shortage in my accounts. How much have you taken?"

The other's face went chalk white.

"Why I—why, what—"

"Now don't tell any lies. I took you into my department to give you a chance on account of—well, you know why. I entrusted you with my books and I know that if there's a shortage that you are responsible. How much is missing?"

The other sat with eyes sullenly averted, and did not answer.

"Come now, Billy, tell me and we'll see what can be done."

The young man's eyes narrowed craftily.

"Oh, no you don't. You don't work me for a confession, Richards. I'm not that green."

Richards threw up his hands.

"Great Heavens, boy, can't you see that I may be able to help you, if you tell me? I'm going to try and get you out of this thing for—for the sake of your sister."

His companion threw off the mask.

"I didn't mean it, Jack, I didn't mean it. I'm sorry. Oh, don't let them put me in jail, don't let them for Margaret's sake. It'll break her heart."

He covered his face with his hands and sobbed. The other man's face was white.

"Come now," he said soothingly, "Pull yourself together, Billy."

The younger man wept uncontrolably, hysterically. Richards crossed the room and seized him by the wrist.

"Stop it," he said sharply, "Don't be a baby." Billy looked up startled, his weak chin quivering.

"Cut that out," Richards went on. "We haven't got much time. The officers have been notified. Mr. Redding trusted me, but the police won't. They'll be here at any moment."

Terror gripped the other.

"At any minute," he repeated hoarsely, "My God."

Then he went to pieces.

"Jack," he whispered, falling on his knees and grasping Richards' hand, "Get me out of this, save me. Can't you think of some way, old man?"

His face was mottled like an artist's pallette.

Richards pulled him to his feet.

"Stand up," he said, "You're contemptible."

Billy wiped his forehead with the back of his hand.

"Jack," said he, pitifully, "You don't know how Margaret will feel. It will kill her, I swear it will. Don't let them take me. Promise you won't."

The older man gulped.

"They'll not take you, Billy," said he

simply, and handed him the key. He walked over to the window and stood motionless, gazing out. His companion watched him out of the corner of his eye.

"You promise?" he asked.

Richards did not answer. Billy slipped on his overcoat and reached for his cane.

"I trust you, Jack, and-er—I thank you." Then he was gone.

The other remained at the window. A thin typically London rain was hanging in the air, and through it as through a gauze curtain gleamed the lights of the city. Directly under the window a gas lamp sputtered, and threw its dingy yellow reflection on the wet pavement. The man at the window saw a figure swing out of the building into the light. It was a young figure, clad in a long overcoat, and jauntily swinging a cane. Richards turned away.

The next day the London Times said: "The police have succeeded in capturing a man who has been systematically robbing the Fifth Exchange National Bank. In fact the criminal was none other than the cashier of that bank, John K. Richards. The young man enjoyed the unlimited confidence of the bank officials, and the news of his dishonesty comes as a great shock to them. It seems that he has been making heavy drafts, as his shortage for a year and a half amounts to four thousand pounds. He was prominent in society circles and was engaged to marry Miss Margaret Sanger. It is rumored that William Sanger, Jr., who is employed in the same bank, made some efforts to save his prospective brother-in-law from disgrace. Mr. Redding, the president of the bank, was a close personal friend of the prisoner's father and regrets the affair very much. The young man's father was Knighted by Queen Victoria for superior literary efforts and he himself is a graduate of Cambridge University. Of course, in accordance with an old custom of that institution, his degree will be taken from him and his name stricken from the list of alumni. We sympathize with the relatives and friends of the prisoner, but it is best for the community to have a man so dead to love, gratitude and family pride, in confinement. The young man, contrary to expectations, has refused counsel. He will undoubtedly receive a severe sentence.''

That was what the paper said.

When London society read it, a whispered 'I told you so' crept around the circle. When the London slums read it, those of the 'Great Unwashed' cried delightedly, "The police have caught another college crook."

When Mr. Redding, president of the Fifth Exchange National Bank, read it at the breakfast table, he laid the paper down with a sigh, and picked up his cup of coffee. When Margaret read it, her lips were firmly compressed, but a tear rolled down her cheek, unchecked.

When Billy read it he smiled bitterly and went on with his game of billiards.

When the Man in the Cell read it, the paper slipped from his nerveless fingers, and he laid his head on the table, wearily.

JAMES F. TWOHY, '07.

A HOARY SINNER

The great yellow disc grew bolder before descending, then gathered in her penetrating rays—the shadows of twilight fell on Albion Cemetery. This was Decoration Day as could easily be seen from the profusion · of beautiful flowers. Hundreds had been there this day to go through the ordeal of true affection and pay tribute to their departed friends and relatives.

But now a deeper feeling of loneliness came over the place. · The throng had disappeared; the silence of death reigned supreme. One remained—a broken down old man. Upon his face some excessive sorrow had left its terrible story; undying love and regret, sadness and dejection were legibly written thereon.

He sat on a flowerless mound beneath whose barren surface lay the dead body of his only son—once the pride and joy of his life. He had buried him ten years before after a protracted illness.

There the old man remained for some time buried in sorrowful thought. At last he arose, surveyed the surrounding graves with their array of luxuriant flowers. His eyes rested on the flowerless grave before him, his aged form shook convulsively, as raising his dimmed eyes to heaven he muttered, "Yes, I must do it!"

He looked cautiously around, then passed nervous and trembling from grave to grave culling flowers. Blushing roses, modest violets, snowy lilies—these he placed tenderly on the barren grave of his son. "There, my boy, I have not neglected you though old and feeble. I did not shirk my duty even though the world has no use for decrepit men. Frank, my boy, won't you look at them, the beautiful flowers? They are yours. Of course you will." Suddenly he buried his face in his hands—a piteous sob unnerved me. "God forgive me," he ejaculated, "I have stolen!"

H. A. J. McKenzie, '08.

AFTER

Merrily drifts my bark to-day
On the breast of life's deep throbbing stream
And the sunny banks with their cities gay
Fade like a fitful dream away
As I float in my fairy bark to-day
                  Down to the silent sea,

But where are the friendly ships that passed
Laden with argosies rich and rare,
Last night, when the clouds came scurrying fast
Borne on the wings of the howling blast ?
Oh! where are the friendly ships that passed
                  Out on the ruthless sea?

                      F. J. H., '09.

A BIT OF BARK

So you want to know why I keep that piece of fir-bark in that glass case, and both of them in the center of the mantelpiece. Well, perhaps I had better tell you its whole history, though it may not interest you so much as it did me when first I heard it.

Some thirty years ago, I indulged in a little silver prospecting tramp through the northern part of what is now the State of Nevada. It was a very wild country then and inhabited by still wilder settlers and squatters. Silver there was through the length and breadth of the country, but, strange to say! I never came across any of it—the only mine it ever yielded me was a mine of memories, some of them sweet, more of them bitter, and some pathetic. Of the latter class is a story that was one day related me by a rough but good-hearted old fellow, who, in a particularly lonesome section of the country, acted as my guide. He had been a miner himself, but having lost an arm in an accident, and having lost faith in the country as well, he took to living on such shifts of Providence, combined with his own native shrewdness, brought in his way. The poor fellow and I became good friends, and though our pathways ran together for two short days only. I have never forgotten him. In fact it would be rather difficult for me to do so, for this homely piece of bark holds its honored place through a pathetic tale which he told me, and which I now relate to you, as far as my decaying memory will serve, in his own words:

"Do you see that white rock pile over there across the canyon? Well, if you want to do any prospecting, I'd advise you to begin there. That's Bill Denver's old shaft. Poor Bill! he thought he had sight of a mighty good claim when he sunk that shaft, but now it has been lying idle and abandoned for over eight years."

"Yes," I asked, getting interested, "why is that?"

"Oh, well, thereby hangs a tale. Let's hit the trail across the canyon, and like the buffalo, we can graze as we go. Bill came here about twelve years ago. It was in the time of what is known around here as the Big Boom. The whole hillside before us was covered with tents, although God knows! it is lonesome and forsaken enough now. Why, about five miles from here they built a big city, so it seemed to us, of nearly a thousand inhabitants. Many of the houses are still standing, it's a fact; perhaps we can go up there some day if you want to. But I am getting off from Bill Denver. Bill came here with the crowd, but when they, one after another, pulled up their stakes, he stayed with it; he evidently had not lost his faith in the country. Anyhow, he was a very determined sort of a fellow, not saying very much, but meaning all he said. and generally a great deal more. He was a handsome, strapping lad, about six feet two or something, and weighed in the neighborhood of two hundred and thirty. He never seemed to have any failings like the rest of us chaps, never played poker or gambled in any fashion, and, what was more wonderful still, he didn't drink or swear. He was as kind as he was strict. He was one of nature's noblemen, so to speak, and had some education to boot, as I had myself in a mild degree, though I do say it. He had a sweetheart back east somewhere, and he used to save up all his money for her sake. He carried her picture in a little gold locket which he wore under his shirt, and he often showed it to me. It was certainly a very pretty face, but it seemed to me there was a mighty little heart in it; in fact I couldn't think of her at all as good enough for such a royal fellow as Bill. At first he would talk and talk about her to me, and I used to like to listen to him, so warmed-up and so ruggedly eloquent he would get about her good qualities. But after a while he stopped talking about her, and once or twice, when I tried to start him on his favorite topic, he avoided the subject. I began to smell a rat. At last, I came upon him immediately one beautiful summer evening, as he sat alone by that fir-tree over yonder. His head was bowed down and his face buried in his hands, but when he heard my footsteps he looked up suddenly. I saw it all. The locket was in his fingers, his eyes were swollen and red, and his breast was heaving as if he had been

sobbing. I guess I felt as bad as he did; I certainly would have given a great deal to comfort the poor fellow, but all I could do was to blurt out: "That's all right, Bill, I've been there myself; I'll keep your secret, but she wasn't half good enough for you anyway." Just as I turned away, I saw, in a mere casual glance, her initials carved on the fir-tree. I suppose Bill had cut them there in happier days. These were A. C. for Anastasia Carlson."

"After the boom died down, Bill prospected around here for a while in a half-hearted, downcast way. He seemed to have nothing to live for, and I believe if death had come in his way he would have welcomed it. He never locked his cabin, and if anyone ever asked for food or money, Bill never hesitated to give more than he ought to. One night an Indian came to his cabin—Firewater Ike we used to call him, on account of his wonderful capacity for that liquid. He carried in his arms a little Indian boy, probably his son, about nine or ten years of age. He offered to sell the little fellow to Bill for the exorbitant sum of ten dollars. "He keep your house," pleaded the wretched Ike, "same good watch dog." Bill gave him one dollar and promptly kicked him out, but he kept the boy, and from that moment there was a great change in Bill. He became another man entirely. It was wonderful how the big white man and the little Piute took to each other. He called the boy Anastasius Carlson.

"Bill taught the boy how to read and

write, in fact, he taught him all he knew himself, and that was no small quantity for these diggings. Anastasius was a very bright pupil, and he picked up his teacher's ways and ideas very fast, for he loved him with his whole little heart, Bill in turn, found all his delight in his little foster son—that's the very title he gave him—and hour after hour would he tell him, as they sat in the evening on the cabin steps, of the big city in the east, where he was going to send Anastasius to college when he had put money enough together. It was not such a bad idea, after all, for the little Indian was brighter than most white boys I've seen, and though tawny, was strikingly good-looking.

"All this time Bill's mine was beginning to yield pretty good, and Bill was putting a little by. One morning about one or two o'clock, a stranger came over to the cabin and began prowling around. Bill saw him first, and that means a good deal out here in the West, especially when you have the distance measured off with your colt. Bill came out of his door, and as he did so, the moonlight gleamed on the barrel of the revolver that he held in his hand. "Sort of late," says he, "to make a call." The stranger, seeing himself covered, got a severe attack of coughing and began bending over. Bill was on to his scheme, and he invited the gent to travel or he would be unable if he lingered much longer. The fellow knew what was healthy and made off accordingly. But that wasn't the end of it. Next morn-

ing, when Bill and Anastasius were at their breakfast, a boulder bounced over his cabin. It was pretty plain that that rock had never started of its own accord. Bill never said anything about it except to me, but he watched—watching especially a certain drummer who was stopping in camp, and whose conduct he didn't relish. This was no place for a drummer; who cared to buy brass-plated watches and gilt jewelry? But Bill kept silent.

"By this time Anastasius had got to love his guardian as a father. He simply adored him, and whatever Bill said was right. One day he was telling a bunch of rough young fellows how Bill loved him and taught him to say his prayers with him every night before they went to bed. "Why," said one of them, with the contempt which is so strong in ignorant people,—"why, you don't believe in that sugar-candy stuff about God and all that kind of talk, do you?" Anastasius answered not a word, but gliding behind one of the fellows, snatched his gun from him, and levelling it at the loud-mouthed infidel, made him retract everything he had said. When I asked him afterwards if he had meant to shoot him in case of non-submission, he replied: "No, that would not be right, but I knew I could scare him, for Bill told me that every man who does not believe in God is a coward."

"But to return to the drummer. One morning Bill was digging for dear life at the bottom of the shaft, thinking perhaps of a fair "dead love" somewhere in the east, or, more probably, of a swarthy little boy at his cabin. All at once he heard a noise above, and looking up, he saw the drummer in the act of throwing a stick of lighted dynamite at him. He tried to seize it as it came down but it fell out of his reach, behind a mass of rock not yet broken. Anastasius had seen the fiend light the dynamite, and with the anxious instinct of love, had run for the spot. He shouted for me and a chum of mine, who happened to be not far away, but that copper-colored angel got there before us. "Jump," he yells to Jim, "jump into the bucket." I saw what he meant. Bill was too dazed to think and blindly obeyed. The other bucket was plumb full of ore, and that with the lad's weight brought it down like a shot. As Bill flew up, something with dark streaming hair flashed past him. He seized the windlass as soon as he reached the top, but all too late! There was a sharp report and a rumbling and all was over,"

"Bill buried Anastasius under this fir tree right ahead of us. Let's go and see it!"

"And what became of Bill?" I asked.

"Well, he sort of lost heart and went clean to the dogs. Sold his mine for a song, and then went off, no one knows where. But two years after I found the skeleton of a man right here under this tree. How he could have died alone half a mile from camp I cannot guess. Perhaps he was caught in a snow storm. I could tell from a gold locket who it was. Buried him with the boy. See those initials?"

"I used to feel bad about it," added my guide musingly, "but that was nine years ago."

*   *   *   *

And now you have the history of my piece of fir bark. Do you see those letters carved in it—yes, of course, they're A. C. I took them with me, with my guide's permission. They read me a story of the faithlessness of a shallow-hearted white girl, and the brave and true love of an Indian boy, who gave his life for his friend. It's worth keeping; don't you think so?

PAUL O. TROPLONG, 2nd Acad.

ST. STANISLAUS

A fair young flow'ret meekly bowed its head,
The sweetest of the garden; through the air
Its fragrance, like Arabia's perfume rare,
No more exhaled—for Stanislaus was dead !
Her crowning feast had come, and Mary said
Unto her angels, "Call a blossom fair
From out my garden, the most fragrant there;
Its color that of love, vermilion red."
As morning's happy blush suffused the sky,
They came, and bore away earth's fairest rose;
Too fair for earth, more meet for Heaven high,
In cloudless Paradise 'twill ever bloom.
Weep not when youthful saints droop to the tomb:
The florist Death but life unending sows.

                                    R. J., '08.

THE KING OF CREATION

I gazed upon the starry night,
    Yon orbs how vast, how far, how fair !
    O lowly me beneath compare !
Clear shone in their ecstatic light.

I walked the beetling cliff alone,
    The sea stretched out to meet the sky;
    Oh what a very atom I !
Long sang the booming solemn tone.

Yet boast ye not, O stars, O sea !
    Ere flashed your rays, ere stretched thy sands,
    God held me graven in His Hands,
And sea and stars, you're made for me.

                                    G. C. W., '09.

KIPLING AS A POET

It is with a more than ordinary amount of diffidence that we essay -to gauge the poetical merits of Rudyard Kipling. He is too near us to measure him with much accuracy. We need perspective for such a task. A foothill at close range shuts out the sight of the snow-covered mountain. On the other hand, it is a proverb that no man is a prophet in his own country, and, let us add, his own time. We are apt to overrate our men of genius; and the history of poetry from the days of Homer down to those of Poe shows that we are apt as well to underrate them. Moreover, so fertile is Kipling as a writer, so unweariedly active has been his pen for the last twenty years, in poetry and in prose, that proximity to him is doubly embarrassing.

That this is not a mere personal experience, a glance at the diverse estimates made of Kipling will establish immediately. He is a giant or a pigmy; an inspired poet or a grinder of jingling verse; a man of vast political conceptions, developing and cementing the bonds of Enland's imperialism, or else a loud-mouthed ranter, disturbing with his tinkling banjo the ear of England's literary conservatism, so long attuned to the lyre of classic poets. It does not require much philosophy to deduce the conclusion that our author's real worth lies somewhere in the mean; this is of course to argue *a priori*, but a study of him will lead, we think, to the same result.

It seems pretty clear that while Rudyard Kipling may live in some of his short stories, he is not destined by the fates to wear the laurel of the deathless poet. The Recessional will live as a classic gem, but one swallow does not make a summer. He is too matter-of-fact to be a great poet; we had almost said he is too sane for that 'fine madness which should rightly possess a poet's brain.' If his eye doth include the earth and heaven in its glance, yet it is a common-place earth that he sees, and an unlovely heaven that but serves to dome the earth, not those unutterable visions of the master-poets where the soul loses itself in shining vistas of marvellous beauty and sublimity. Poetry as we know, is the breath and fine spirit of knowledge. All sensation, thought, and feeling, in a word the sum of man's entire spiritual and intellectual existence can be expressed in it, but it must be expressed in terms of beauty; it must forsake dry facts for the 'breathing, living realm of the imagination.' Now here is where Kipling falls short of the classic poet; he has not the fine spirit of knowledge. His touch does not transmute clay into fine gold. He does not 'unsensualize the senses,' the poet's first office. He views things too materially, and is utterly too realistic. He creates no lofty, grand, or inspiring characters. Their virtues are certainly none too good for human nature's daily food, and their vices are often gross enough, and told without any of that delicate reserve that we had learned to associate with the very name of poet. Many there are, it need hardly be said, who defend such a course; 'This is being true to Nature" say they, 'it's human.' To the devil in the poem who "bubbled below the keel,' "It's human but is it art?" these gentry answer, "Yes."

But Browning would not answer yes. It is the reverse of true art, according to him, for a painter to represent a road by drawing a trail of mud across his canvas. And in presenting the mud of human nature the poet should _be equally delicate.

Kipling sees everything and he tells us all he sees in plain, outspoken bluntness. We look in vain for the modesty of the figure of reticence, for everything is shown us and there is nothing more behind. The mysteries of life appear to be naught in his eyes; his answer to all questions is the Saviour's aye, aye; nay, nay. It is evident how this at once clips the wings of the reader's imagination. His poetry has no unsounded depths where abyss calls upon abyss; no 'dim, religious light' where the soul may brood in solemn silence; no faintly-heard echoes to lure the fancy's rove into dreamy Elysian fields. In the Paradise Regained we have a striking example of the evil in this want of reticence, where Milton dares to bring the reader face to face with Him whom man cannot behold and live.

Kipling has another fault at his door

besides ultra-frankness—he is at times somewhat irreverent in his treatment of God and of scriptural characters. He blesses with a text some of his most nonsensical barrack-room verses. In his poem "Sappers" we read such things as these:

When the Flood came along for an extra monsoon
'Twas Noah constructed the first pontoon,

*   *   *   *   *

But after fatigue in the wet and the sun,
Old Noah got drunk, which he wouldn't have done, etc.

—all of which reminds us of a vulgar series of pictures—now happily dead of old age—in one of our comic Sunday Supplements.

Added to this, there is, as one has already been led to expect, a cheap sort of smartness about his diction that seems to aim at the shocking and the sensational. Poetry borne up on such wings as these will never mount Parnassus. Of course, this is to be found chiefly in his earlier poetry; as he advanced in years he advanced in grace, and it would be gross injustice to judge of England's 'uncrowned laureate' by his Departmental Ditties. Yet this uncouthness of diction, though getting beautifully less, still adheres to his writings like the odor of the first liquor to an earthen jug.

Thus when describing the far-extending sway of England's flag, he says,

"Take 'old of the wings o' the Mornin',
And flop round the earth till you're dead;
But you won't get away from the tune that they play
To the bloomin' old rag over'ead."

Where the thought is assuredly very lofty but the language that of a barrack-room ballad indeed. Take this again,

"We're poor little lambs who've lost our way,
  Baa! Baa! Baa!
We're little black sheep who've gone astray,
  Baa—aa—aa
Gentlemen-rankers out on the spree
  Damned from here to eternity
God ha' mercy on such as we
  Baa! Yah! Baa!"

However, this is looking at our poet at his worst. That he has a better side is evident at first blush from the immense popularity which he has enjoyed so long and so steadily. He is the real laureate of England, crowned with the bays of the Nation's acclaim. Still, while this argues solid worth in him, we must be careful not to take this popularity at its face value. Homer had naught of it; Milton had little of it —he had to be discovered by Dryden. Wordsworth, as he himself foresaw, was destined at once to unpopularity and to immortality. Moreover, there is another motive for the *cultus*, which Kipling enjoys, besides the 'true inwardness' of his poetry—the *'arma virumque'* of which he sings, are just what the people like to hear. The grandeur of British Imperialism!—the life of the British Soldier in the Colonies, and in strange, mysterious India especially! Kipling has, with great skill, felt the pulse of plethoric old King Demos; he has studied, felt with the intuition of genius, how and when he is to be pleased. He gauges the very moment when some sentiment gathering in the people's breast is about to reveal itself, and he anticipates it by an hour. He expresses what the people most want expressed; he gives vent to their wrought-up feelings, and thus figures in their eyes as a 'long-felt want.' He does more; being the mouthpiece of public feeling, he directs the feeling, he diminishes or intensifies it; he identifies himself with it. It becomes, as it were, incarnate in him, and thus the slowly accumulated product of the national mind is accredited in the Book of Fame to him who has made himself its oracle.

So it was with the Imperialistic idea. He took hold of it at the time this idea, in a vague and undefined form, was most swelling out the breasts of Englishmen. He became its exponent, and a most vigorous and exhilarating one at that. The natural consequence followed. To read Kipling became the fashion. It was necessary for an adequate sense of one's birthright as an Englishman. To back him up with hearty applause, to throw your hat in the air and huzza for the new poet was only to be evincing a due amount of patriotism, and a becoming satisfaction that "Fair is our lot, goodly is our heritage." Unction it was to the soul to repeat such strains as

"Under an alien sky
Comfort it is to say,
'Of no mean city am I.' "

And then his imperialism is so practical and full of common sense. It falls in with John Bull's humor exactly. This stout gentleman is not over-fond of abstractions; and theories, unless they have a practical bearing, do not at all upset him. He wants to see and hear and feel. Accordingly Burke's splendidly vivid imperialism impressed him; that of Kipling, less splendid but more vivid,—as it feeds more upon details,—impresses him still more. In ringing the glories of Britain's world-encircling rule the latter thus stands alone and unrivalled. He has brought the East and West into a mutual sym pathy that no code of laws has done; he has bound England to her colonies by a chain more potent than a common tariff.

" . . . There is neither East nor West, Border. nor Breed, nor Birth
When two strong men stand face to face thougn they come from the ends of the earth."

Besides this national good work that he has done, Kipling has another of a directly literary character to his credit. Before his advent, Engiish literature was getting maudlin in sentiment, spineless and nerveless, or, in the words of an English writer, it was 'erotic, neurotic, and Tommyrotic.' This was true of prose more than of poetry, but both were getting more and more psychological, and, like the speeches of Burke, kept on refining and refining until for the reader of ordinàry ability and sanity, the meaning of it had become so etherealized as to have quite evaporated away. All at once the bold, breezy imperialist burst in on the scene, and it is laughable to think of the havoc he wrought with the nerves of English literary conservatism. Of all men be was the very one to give it a good rous-

ing shock that might restore it to a more manly constitution—despising, as he did, books, tradition, conventionality; speaking 'in straight-flung words and few'; riding roughshod over the little laws, and some big ones too, within which English writers had entrenched themselves; 'whistling like a free lance and swaggering like a buccaneer.' No wonder that some of these writers held up their hands in holy horror, and gazed upon the progress of the invader as tbey would upon that of a bull in a china-shop! No wonder that one of them sighed for some far-away land

"Where the Rudyards cease from Kipling, And the weary are at rest."

However, whether the 'weary' have become resigned to their fate or not, there is assuredly no rest for the wicked Kipling, whose pen is never idle and never ceases to write large on the face of modern English literature the influence of the most vigorous and original personality it knows today.

His ditties and ballads, with their wild exotic realism—which is even' more marked in his prose—their free-and-easy lilt, the broken sentence, the local word, the highly-colored phrase have produced an impression that would at first seem beyond them. The style may be jagged and uncouth and careless, but it is evidently a style nevertheless. and though it may set the reader intellectually on pins and needles, it at the same time holds. him by a peculiar fascination. He is a past master of rythm, and his sprightly tripping verses haunt the reader's ears whether he will or no. Read this:

"For the temple-bells are callin' an' it's there
    that I would be—
By the old Moulmein Pagoda, looking lazy at
    the sea;
On the road to Mandalay,
Where the old Flotilla lay,
With our sick beneath the awnings, when we
    went to Mandalay!
On the road to Mandalay,
Where the flyin' fishes play,
An' the dawn comes up like thunder outer
    China 'crost the Bay?''

Throughout most of his writings, Kipling's humor, when it does assert itself, is apt to the cynical and harsh, though in the Barrack-Room Ballads we find some specimens of pure humor entirely free from rancor. Here is an extract from his description of Fuzzy-Wuzzy:

" 'E rushes at the smoke when we let drive,
    An' before we know, 'e's 'acking at our 'ead;
'E's all 'ot sand an' ginger when alive,
    An' 'e's generally shammin' when 'e's dead.
'E's a daisy, 'e's a ducky, 'e's a lamb!
'E's a injia-rubber idiot on a spree,
'E's the only thing that doesn't give a damn
    For a regiment of British Infantry!"

Tenderness is rarely to be met with in the pages of our author. In his prose his most tender creation by far is Ameera, but as a rule he has none of the great poet's delicate sympathy about him. Perhaps, as in the case of Samuel Johnson, an early exposure to the hard trials of life nipped the green leaves of a sensibility, never very promising. But he is good-hearted and always loyally upholds the cause of the oppressed and the suffering. Proud though he be of the Mother-land,

no one is yet more ready than he to score her for her misdoings. His latest poem is a bitter arraignment of England's conduct towards a South African colony. We quote—

"But we—what God shall turn our doom,
    What blessing dare we claim,
Who slay a nation in the womb
    To crown a trickster's game?
Who come before amazed mankind
    Forsworn in party feud
And search the forms of law to bind
    Our blood to servitude?"

Kipling's test of virtue is action: "By their fruits you shall know them" must be a favorite text of his. This is his test of religion also—a true one, no doubt, but needing to be supplemented by a study of the intrinsic value of a religion's principles. His view of God is deep-dyed with the same utilitarian sentiment. He is a God of righteousness, true! but He seems to exist merely to keep the world in order. His *raison d'etre* is that the welfare of man requires Him. Naturally enough, therefore, Kipling's reverence is not of the most edifying—his use of scripture phrases and his invocations upon God's name are rather familiar, to say the least.

"But what about the Recessional?" the reader will say. We answer that it is a noble poem, full of lofty inspiration and very sincere in feeling. Yet it does not impress us as a great hymn. It does not so excite gratitude in the English reader, as a feeling of smug self-satisfaction at the thought that, let him hide it as he may with a veil of modesty, after all he does 'beat all creation.' A story is told of two vet-

erans of the British Navy who were discussing Nelson shortly after his death.
"I wonder," said one, "if he went
straight to Heaven when he died!"
"Well," burst out the other indignantly,
"I'd like to know who'd stop him." We
trust this is a story and nothing more,
but only of the Englishman however
could it be related. A sentiment re-
motely akin to this seems to pervade
the Recessionàl. Let us not forget that
though the world from palm to pine
has been given to our charge, yet it is
only given in trust—to us. In those
days of Jubilee, when we as a nation
are taking a rest from land-grabbing
and loving our neighbor—in his goods
—as we love ourselves, let us remember
that 'the earth is the Lord's and the
fullness thereof,' and that we are
merely his favorite and predestined
stewards. Let us keep a dignified
silence, let us exhibit the modesty
which so well sits on true greatness,

and not indulge in boasts like the Gen-
tiles,

"Or lesser breeds without the Law."

How hard and unspiritual this feels
after reading the Lead, Kindly Light of
Newman! how false rings its note of
humility when heard after the child-like
prayer,—

"Keep thou my feet; I do not ask to see
The distant scene; one step enough for me."

But we must take leave of Rudyard
Kipling. We part from him with feelings, on the whole, of respect and admiration. We are convinced that his
great influence is used for good, that the
world is the better off for the work of
his tireless pen. This pen may have
sputtered and blotched here and there,
but it has been guided by a desire for
the furtherance of his country's interests and the alleviation of human suffering.

J. D., '07.

> *Hush !   he is dying !*
>   *Ah !   how calm he is, my dear !*
> *See !   his soul is trying*
>   *To fly to God, my dear !*
> *Yes !   he then was sighing !*
>   *—To us how sad, my dear !*
> *He smiles—he is defying*
>   *Death's gloomy scowl, my dear !*
> *How still and white he's lying !*
>   *Oh !   let us pray, my dear !*
> *His soul to God is flying.*
>   *A. J. D., '08.*

"A TWO-EDGED SWORD"

Big Jim leaned back against the counter. The store was deserted. The clerk was in the post office in the rear distributing the weekly mail and Jim was all alone. Having nothing better to do he rolled a cigarette and calmly drove another nail into his coffin. Meditatively he spat again and again on the floor and thoughts surged into his lazy brain far too numerous for him to handle. He gave up trying and was about to make up his mind to leave the store, whence all but he had fled, when someone entered.

Lazily he looked up toward the door. Jim did everything lazily. It was a young girl that entered, not beautiful but fair. Deep black rings encircled her eyes, her face was pale and wan. She gazed timidly about as she came in and stood waiting at the counter.

Jim finished his cigarette, dexterously tossed the stub behind a cracker-box and sauntered over to the girl.

"How's your ma to-day?" he asked.

No answer. A moment's silence, and then a sudden and violent trembling of the ill-clad figure.

Jim moved closer. He knew she was crying. How he did long for the right to put his strong arm around her and soothe away her little heart-wrung tears! How he did long for the right to share her troubles, or rather bear them all upon his own strong shoulders! How tempted he was to ask her for the privilege. But he knew that such was not to be, for, qualified as he was in every other way, Jim was of Indian blood.

But Jim moved closer to her and she did not resent. For she loved Jim; he was so big and strong, and as generous as he was strong. He continued--

"Not so well to-day, little girl?"

A nod of the shawl-covered head

"Where's the old man?"

No answer; more sobs.

"Is he drinking again?" Jim had taken her hand in his.

"Yes"—and the tears flowed uncontrolably.

A loud laugh at the door startled her, and also Jim, as much as a man of his lazy temperament could be startled.

He released the hand he held and and stared at the stranger. The girl clung to him frantically.

The newcomer was loud and boisterous. Liquor plainly had the better of him.

"Well, I done it, Jim! I got old Mac drunk again. He won't ever get over this one. I played him cards and won all he had, even his house and home, I run his old woman out and all the kids. The old girl tried to sham sick, but she can't work me. She's out in the street now on an old cot. It was great, Jim, to see them kids bawl and raise a rumpus. I just roared," and the man laughed loudly.

Jim had forgotten the girl in contemplating the scene the man presented or rather he made her sobbing figure the background of the heart-rending picture.

He started forward, "You dog," he began.

A loud report behind him made him jump and a horrible shriek pierced the air.

Jim for a moment was dazed. Gradually he realized.

He grabbed the smoking weapon from the girl's hand, and as she swayed unsteadily he caught her in his arms.

"He killed my mother," she murmured sleepily and fell limp and motionless.

Jim laid her gently down and turned to meet the startled storekeeper just entering. He laid the gun upon the counter.

"Good God, man! what's up?"

"Nothin', just killed a man," said Jim, reaching for his tobacco—"send for the sheriff."

"Keep quiet now, little girl, what's the use of crying? I'll make it all right with you before the law, but see that you make yourself right before God. This hand has taken two lives, little girl—his and mine. But run home to your ma. Have my brother help you move her, and take her to my old home. It's yours now."

He turned to the sheriff and smiled sardonically.

"I won't need it for some years to come, I guess."

He stooped and kissed the tragic hand. "I trust my blood will wash off his," said he, solemnly. "Good bye."

"Come along," said the sheriff.

And Jim went.

IVO G. BOGAN, '08.

The Redwood

PUBLISHED MONTHLY BY THE STUDENTS OF THE SANTA CLARA COLLEGE

The object of the Redwood is to record our College Doings, to give proof of College Industry and to knit closer together the hearts of the Boys of the Present and of the Past.

EDITORIAL STAFF

EXECUTIVE BOARD

JAMES F. TWOHY, '07
President

J. DANIEL MCKAY, '07 HARRY A. MCKENZIE, '08

ASSOCIATE EDITORS

COLLEGE NOTES - - - - - IVO G. BOGAN, '08
IN THE LIBRARY - - - ROBERT J. O'CONNOR, '08
FXCHANGES - - - ANTHONY B. DIEPENBROCK, '08
ALUMNI - - - - - MERVYN S. SHAFER, '09
ATHLETICS - - - - HARRY A. MCKENZIE, '08

BUSINESS MANAGER

J. DANIEL MCKAY, '07

ASSISTANTS

FRANCIS M. HEFFERNAN, '08 REIS J. RYLAND, '09

M. T. DOOLING, 09

Address all communications to THE REDWOOD, Santa Clara College, California

Terms of subscription, $1.50 a year; single copies, 15 cents

EDITORIAL COMMENT

The REDWOOD has ventured a prize story contest, which is open to every embryonic Kipling in the College. We firmly trust that every boy in the yard will avail himrelf of this opportunity to improve his mind, store up a few filthy shekels for a rainy day, and discharge a duty to his college paper. Competition in collegiate journalism is keen, and for us to keep the representative of Santa Ciara in its proper strata we must have the sincere indorsement and assistance of everyone. Besides the time spent in this literary labor will be rewarded, we assure you, a hundred fold. So you see, fellows, that anyone who does not enter this contest is hurting himself and hurting his college journal. So pitch right in, all of you, and with fervent apologies to one Billy Jordon—may the best man win.

Now that higher education has reached its present broad and unprecedented popularity, the thinkers of today are beginning to turn towards our great universities in forecasting the nation's future. Annually a vast throng of the nation's brightest youth is pouring into the higher itstiturions of learning, and it is patent that the university men of today are the leaders, the legislators of tomorrow. The self-made man as a nation's leader is a thing of the past. The type of men of fifty years ago, who, as far as education is concerned, stepped from a country school house into the Capitol or Senate is gone. We will not have other Jacksons and Lincolns and Garfields; not that the strength and spirit of these men is weakened, vitiated in their posterity. The posterity has not altered; rather it is the times and the demands of the times that hrve altered. The charge is objective rather than subjective. There will be Americans who will arrive at a summit of greatness equal to Lincoln's but the road Lincoln followed is closed and another and newer road is opened. The reason is simple. As a nation grows older its life and manners become more complex. The elemental simplicity of new crea-

tion, of the nascent state, disappears as the nation progresses and evolves surely into the marvelously intricate maze of modern civilization. Today more is demanded than yesterday. Our successful man must combine rugged strength with a polish, a veneer, which education alone can give. Hence from this fact the question naturally arises among earnest college men, "What are the most important attributes we should strive for? Is there any quality which is a cornerstone of greatness." Presupposing that the college man in his rudimentary education is firmly grounded morally, we think that the greatest, the most practical, the most fundamental attribute to be aimed at is self-reliance. This, however, we emphatically distinguished from independence. Independence we understand to be exemption from entrinsic support and control, and as such it is impossible. Man has an innate social instinct and cannot succeed without assistance and encouragement from his fellow beings. But this is far from our idea of self-reliance. Self-reliance is not self-assertiveness or conceit, which is often mistaken for it; it is simply a firm, reasonable, trust in one's own ability, a frank knowledge of self-strength and self-power. It teaches a man to lean on himself, to think, to decide, to act for himsslf. And this quality is the keynote of success. It is what draws the line between the dumb, driven cattle and the heroes in the strife. There never was a great man who lacked it nor a weak man who possessed it. It is fuel to the fire of genius, the foundation of the courage that makes us break away from the heard. It is the foundation of the greatness of all great men; and after all the world's history may be told in the lives of a few remarkable men. One man may arise and the long shadow of his might will stretch far into the future and fall on future generations. How many a chapter of United States history may be told in the life and principles of Washington and Lincoln. A whole epoch of Roman history has been called the Scipioness of Rome, and is found in the life of one man. And this is what all college men should strive for, for without it there is no success. We should look at a thing with calm eyes. Study not only the flesh but also the skeleton of everything through the X ray of those talents bestowed on us by the Almighty. And while we must ever show all respect to authority we should never be overawed by insignia, by titular buttons and badges. Underestimation of ourselves is wrong; for it is the belittling of a gift of the munificent God. We should stand fixed and constant and unafraid modestly confident in and unaffectedly conscious of the powers of self.

What is the cause of the present wave of pessimism which is sweeping the newspaper world and causing the wholesale attack on our public men? Is it because our public men have degenerated, and that they deserve all this?

It might prove easy to answer these questions with some small witticism or even to break a clever epigram upon it. But we think that the question is too vital for jest and too vast to compress within the four corners of an epigram. It is developing into an evil, the proportions of which make it impossible to be overlooked. Therefore consideration of it is in order and timely. Every man is more or less of a "laudator temporis acti." Perhaps this is because our vision in the heat of life's battle is destroyed; or because our close proximity to the thing observed robs it of its beauty as proximity to an elegant oil painting would; or maybe the spectacles of retrospection are rose-colored. Whatever the reason the fact remains that there is a glamour, a halo around men of the past which those of the present can never attain. Washington in his time met with much bitter domestic opposition; Lincoln in his day and generation was regarded by many as the destroyer of his country. And yet in the calm, impersonal light of a later day these figures stand on twin pedestals, in the eyes of a grateful country, the greatest Americans that have lived. Somehow men can not get a right perspective of today's greatness. They scan the horizon through a telescope, seeking what often lies right under their noses. And undoubtedly there is something of this spirit underlying the present popular renunciation of our public men.

But more than in this; the trouble lies in the American press itself. Our newspapers which, as the strongest popular factor in the Nation, should be the most zealous watchdog of the popular weal, have almost without individual exception, become political organs.

The paper is run on a system, and the primal, and frequently the only object is the political advancement of the boss. There is no individual, party or organization where absolute freedom from political shackles is so necessary as our press, for it is the most powerful, the most democratic, the most universal organ in the country, and yet it is deeply meshed in the net of boss ownership. Nothing is frank, personal, spontaneous. A man's worth in journalism lies in his ability to help the boss and strengthen the system. Quality has given way to quantity, self is submerged in impersonality; the doctrine of the American press is the doctrine of anonymity.

The independent newspaper, the friend to right and foe to evil has passed and in its place stands this new giant whose strength is sufficient to break the country. Monopoly, the curse of the twentieth century, has attacked the most powerful defender of the land, and is slowly sapping its strength.

A few moneyed philanthropists claim to be seeking new chances for charities. What could be more beneficial than the endowment of independent newspapers? What we need are personal writers— men like Dana and Greeley and Waterson who, Spartan-like, have arrayed quality against bulk. There are still a few in the field fighting manfully for the right of honest criticism. But their strength is fast failing and unless they are strongly re-enforced our much-mooted freedom of the press will perish, for government restraint would be mild as compared to the tyrannous control of political parties. It would be true philanthropy to aid in the support of that pillar of our society, press freedom, which is the staunchest of all barriers between us and tyranny.

JAMES F. TWOHY, '07.

Senate

The upper branch of College States-men, with their roll-call once more at its usual length, have resumed the strenuous life interrupted last April and have been hard pressed to dispose of the amount of work that has accumulated since that memorable month,—so much so indeed, that debates have so far been dispensed with and special business meetings are the order of the day. Senators Fisher of Coyote, Griffin of Boston, Heffernan from San Francisco, Kilburn from Salt Lake, Murphy of San Jose and McKenzie of San Francisco are the new names on the roll-call and they are now dodging the muck rake.

A special meeting was necessitated to elect committees to carry on the regular business of the session. Senators Fitzgerald, McKay and Atteridge attend to the Ways and Means, with Senator Fitzgerald chairman of the committee. The resolutions are in the hands of Senator Casey, while Senator Fisher controls the Senate in the Committee on Rules. The Building Committee has Senator Aguirre as chairman, assisted by Senators Fisher and Heffernan. Senators Atteridge, Twohy, and Schmitz are to provide for the spreads under the guise of Committee on Entertainment, and they are promised the hearty co-operation of the members. But here the muck raker made his entrance and brought the postal service to trial. Several of the junior Senators had not been receiving their sky-blue-pink, violet-scented missives as regularly as usual and cries of "graft" and "investigation" disturbed our peaceful atmosphere. A committee was immediately appointed from among the most interested and Senators Brown, Schmitz and Kilburn pledged themselves to probe the iniquitous proceedings to their deepest depths and spare no one in their grand exposé. At the next meeting they sadly and solemnly, but with deep determination, reported that the excessive heat had caused the "mail man" to fail in his duty. A loud crash was heard and upon examination it was found that Ida M. Tarbell, who had been lurking in a corner of the gallery, had fainted at the awful news and Thomas W. Lawson was weakly endeavoring to restore her to consciousness.

The project of an Inter-Collegiate debate with St.. Mary's College, to take place before Christmas, is now under consideration and in all probability before this issue comes from press the plans will have been consummated.

House

The House of Philhistorians is once again getting into old-time form and its ranks once more begin to assume normal proportions. Although as yet, through unforeseen circumstances, we are not established in our quarters, it is sincerely hoped that the day is not far distant when the members can take their seats before the speakers in the new debating forum.

The evening of the 10th witnessed a very interesting debate. So warmed up to the argument were the participants that the concluding remarks were postponed until next meeting on account of the lack of time. The subject was the ancient but till now unsettled question: Resolved, "That the confinement of Santa Clara College is too strict." Representatives Bogan, Diepenbrock and Caverly upheld the affirmative side, and O'Connor, Ryland and Cunningham opposed them.

By the drafting into the Senate the House loses some of its most eminent members. Representative F. M. Heffer-

nan, clerk; C. P. Kilburn, treasurer; H. A. McKenzie, assistant treasurer and chairman of several committees. These gentlemen were zealous in the execution of their duties and in debates. Leander Murphy also answered the cal. of the Senate and has gone to its fold The House feels the loss of these clever speakers, but is proud of their advance. Representative M. Shafer was chosen to fill the office of clerk, and Representative Lappin that of treasurer. Representative Diepenbrock was chosen to fill the office of librarian, vacated by the promotion of Representative Lappin.

The debate for next meeting is, "Resolved, That trade unions are a menace to the public weal."

The following were initiated into the House at the last meeting: Messrs. R. Archbold, H. Yoacham and T. Farrell.

Band

In the art of Orpheus "Labor omnia vincit" is as true as it is of any other art or undertaking. Thus, it seems, soliloquize the disciples of that ancient god. Sturdily they work under sturdy leaders. Prof. Austin Morris directs them. "Nuff sed." We all know Prof. Morris. The Sodality band stands out a bright luminary in Austin's firmament of success. It was this same unassuming Mr. Morris who started the first band of League of the Cross Cadets which, at the time of the great shake enjoyed the reputation of being the best amateur band in the West. He has good material and hopes are high that we will have good stirring music to make things lively on band concert nights and to blow us on to victory in our athletic undertakings. The earnest support of every boy in the yard is, or should be tendered to Prof. Morris. The following are his officers: Vice President, August Aguirre; music keeper, J. W. Schmitz.

Orchestra

The old students remember well the sterling working qualities of Prof. Buehrer. Not long ago our old friend returned from a tour in Europe, where he has conferred with the very best masters in Italy and France. He is with us once more resolved to devote his best energy to the orchestra and glee club. The orchestra has already begun to flourish.

Behind the Scenes

Slowly but surely the "Blind Prince" begins to see a grand success not far distant. J. Twohy, who will have the title role, needs no introduction to our readers. You all know him by his stories and able work in the REDWOOD. August Aguirre is another old timer who plays the important part of Oberto, the honest, ambitious farmer. Harry McKenzie, the jovial joker, will appear as Molino, the happy-go-lucky good-time seeker, with plenty of noise and little to say. Leander Murphy, the

veteran of many wars, is still in the masks and will receive the hisses and hoots of the gallery, and stain the waters of the river with his villainous blood, in the last act. Fred Sigwart, another idol of days gone by, will once more grace the boards and come before the audience. Ed. Lowe, a new member of the Senior Dramatic Club, will appear for the first time upon the stage in a play. Ivo G. Bogan will play the part of Elvins, son of Oberto. The play will be the finale of a grand vaudeville in which will be seen A. Aguirre and H. McKenzie in a skit. The glee club will be in evidence and P. Troplong, G. Mayerle, F. Lyman and W. Barry will entertain the audience in a side-splitting sketch entitled, "Which Town," written by Paul Troplong.

The Junior Dramatic Society Notes

Though late last month in forwarding the current doings, the J. D. S. was not tardy, however, in throwing open the portals to its first enthusiastic meeting of Sept. 17th. And even if the absence of a few faces are deeply felt, the happiness of a reunion, the prospect of a glowing future and the energy of the present members threw a charm and color over existing circumstances otherwise gloomy and foreboding. For the higher life had beckoned some of our best members to its noble field. We make the sacrifice willingly. Then First Division held out its jealous hand to rob us of our few distinguished members; but right is might. Will First Division crush out the life of the J. D. S.? will it be guilty of the dastard tragedy?

"Is such · resentment in heavenly minds?"

For a few months, "The Venerables" will grace the meetings with their presence until the new members, aided and abetted by the speeches and doings of their forefathers, have become adepts in the eloquent art and conversant with the rules and customs of the society.

Mr. R. Henry Brainard, S. J., will still guide the destinies of the society.

After a few remarks from the President on encouraging the members to hold aloft the standard of the society, and push it to the front rank, thus witnessing the finish crowned with the victorious eagle, it was in order to proceed with the nomination and election of the various officers.

Mr. H. Shields' name was judged fit and placed on scroll of vice-presidents; while Mr. L. Pierce heard with ears tingling either with joy or embarrassment his unanimous election as secretary. Mr. E. Watson was again called upon to count how much the society was in, and the members out. Mr. W. Gianera, Mr. G. Hall and Mr. S. Heney were voted to the office of Censor, Sergeant-at-Arms and Prompter respectively.

The election ended, the officers and members set about re-enforcing their shattered ranks. Messrs. R. McCabe, L. Putman, W. Barry, Robert Flood, A. Watson, A. Oyarzo, J. Sheean were their happy choice. These we know and feel will follow hard in the footsteps of those who have borne aloft bravely and nobly the reputation of the J. D. S.

Return of Rev. John Cunningham, S. J.

The evening train on October 22nd brought to us back from Mexico this very much beloved former professor of Santa Clara College, and the founder and for many years the director of the Young Men's Sodality Club. The Sodality band awaited his arrival at San Jose and escorted him to the sound of lively and joyous music to the College. Next morning after his Mass at 8 o'clock, the Father tried to say a few words to his cherished "boys" of the Sodality, but emotion choked his utterance, and the sermon was left unpreached verbally, it is true but preached nevertheless in a more eloquent way than he had intended. Next week Father Cunningham sails for Manila, to help the Jesuit Fathers there in their educational work. The best wishes of all his friends—and all who ever knew him are his friends—will cross the seas with him.

IVO G. BOGAN, '08.

A number of Commercial Alumni have been heard from, mostly through letters to their former Professors. Follow their example, you who have attended Santa Clara in the past. Let us know where you are and what you are doing. Don't get the idea that when you leave this historic pile, you have severed all connections with your Alma Mater. She is still your affectionate mother and is glad to hear of your success. Nothing pleases an "old boy" more than to glance over the REDWOOD and to see the name of a college companion in the columns. He recalls many an old friendship, perhaps a broken one, which he may be led to renew. This is what holds the alumni together. Don't be backward. We do not speak from a disinterested point of view. The more you write the less hustling we have to do for matter. "Come one, come all."

James A. Chichizola of Amador, Commercial, '03, is managing the Chichizola estate consisting of a large mercantile business and several mines. "Chick" played center on the famous '02 foot

ball team, probably the greatest eleven that ever represented Santa Clara on the gridiron.

William R. Curtin of Madera, California, Commercial Cert. '04, is a candidate in the coming county election. Bill is of the old school and there are few students here now who remember him. He was one of those fellows whose "college spirit" is the stimulus of every action. Bill was always helping somebody or something, and if an enterprise, got tangled up through mismanagement, he was there to straighten things out. Curtin was a prominent member of "The House." He was stage manager the year "The Passion Play" was produced and contributed much towards its success. We wish you the biggest kind of a plurality vote, Bill.

Some more Commercial—Joseph Grifon of Winters, Cal., Com. '04. He was formerly head bookkeeper for the Earl Fruit Company. But Joe has struck out for himself. He has one of the largest orchards in the Oroville region which yielded him handsome returns last year. Joe was an all around athlete and it is hard to decide in which branch he excelled. His great speed in base-ball made him a dangerous man on the bases and his ability on the cinder path is well known. Joe was a monster in statue and looked the very personification of slowness, but many a third baseman, to his sorrow, found him to be the opposite, for Joe had a happy faculty of bunting the ball down the line and beating it to first. May your success be as rapid as your course down the hundred yards, Joe!

Ralph C. Harrison, '05, has received an appointment to West Point Military Academy. Ralph was a member of the staff and defended the House of '04 in the annual debate.

John Byrnes, '06, is in real estate with his father. Jack should make good. He is a business man in every sense of the word, as his numerous successes while at College testify. Jack had the honor and responsibility of being the first manager of the REDWOOD which office he held a year and a half; he was manager of the foot ball team for two seasons, and manager of the '05 base ball team. Besides he held the position of Seargent-at-Arms in "The Senate." Charles Byrnes, ex-'07, has registered at Georgetown University. Charlie was an excellent performer on the diamond, playing 3d base two years ago. and 1st base last year.

We were favored during the past month by a visit from ex-District Attorney L. F. Byington, B. S,, ,84.

John Leibert, ex-'09 is in the employ of the Builder's Exchange in San Francisco. Jack was obliged to leave college on account of ill health but we are glad to hear that he has entirely recovered and is again able to assume his "social duties."

Vincent Durfee, Com. '05, is on the Surveying Staff of the Ocean Shore Railroad.

It gives us much pleasure to announce that Mr. Charles South A. M. '01 (Honorary) is rapidly recovering from his injuries. In another section of this issue of the REDWOOD will be found a delightful account of 'the old adobe' that until lately stood on our grounds to act as a link between the present and the past. The sketch first appeared in the Mercury.

"Commodore" Jack Shea, ex-'09, was badly wounded in a recent engagement with the arch enemy—Cupid. He was quietly married October 20th to Miss Aloha Agnew of San Jose. Coincidentally Jack got a reception at the station. The S. A. A. band was waiting for Father Cunningham (see College Notes) and as the train pulled out gave the couple a parting send-off. Miss Agnew is well known in social circles at San Jose, where her genial temperament and winning ways have made her a host of friends. Ad multos annosi

Cupid again—Herman E. Berg, ex-'00, was married October 9th to Miss Lorrine Goodspeed of San Francisco. The bride is a graduate of Notre Dame Convent, Marysville. The REDWOOD offers its sincerest congratulations.

Andrew Bunsow, ex-'09, is helping his father in his large emporium in Chiuahua, Mexico. Andrew will long be remembered by his classmates here for unassuming modesty joined to talents of no ordinary calibre, When he competed for a prize, all others felt their chances were pretty attenuated. How he feels toward Santa Clara may be seen from the following extract of a letter which he wrote to a friend:

"You can't imagine how sorry I feel sometimes when I think of Santa Clara College. I really love that College. It almost makes me cry sometimes, when I think that I shall never go there again. That is, to study there, sleep there, eat there, play there, and so on. When I was there, I never thought that I would feel sorry after leaving it, but now I can't forget it. However, what can a fellow do? He has to get in and work sometime. When I think of all the school-mates I left, and the good teachers, I feel like flying and going to take at least a little glimpse of the place. Still, I hope I may soon go and visit the old College; the old Santa Clara College which I shall never forget, and the good Fathers to whom I am so grateful for all they did for me, during the four years that I attended their College.

Kindly give my regards to all the Fathers and my schoolmates."

MERVYN S. SHAFER, '09.

At last we come to something good in the fiction line. After reading long and feverishly we find that only three stories that stand aloft above the plain of mediocrity. The difficulty now is in picking out the winner.

In the *Villa Shield* "Waiting of Two Hearts," is cleverly done but the writer seems to be a trifle inexperienced. At least the story is written in a style that strikes us as being decidedly "young'' and on that very account it drops out of the race. This leaves "The Man with the Green Eye" in the *University of Virginia Magazine* and "About College" in the *Georgetown Journal* to finish the run. Now the "Man with the Green Eye," though the style of it would be a credit to anyone, has a ten-cent-magazine-story plot to it. It is original, yes, in spite of the fact that here and there it reminds one just a little of the popular Sherlock Holmes stories. But we do not mean to charge it with unoriginality, Therefore "About College"is first to the string and the crown of laurels falls on its worthy head. About College! Rather an unattractive title, isn't it? But we are not going to judge by titles or that story would have been cautiously

dodged long ago. The thing we note particularly about this is the ease and naturalness of the conversation in the story. Another little attribute not to be overlooked is the clearness with which characters of the 'dramatis pérsonæ' are drawn. As for the plot, there is no need saying it is good and well developed and all that, for if it hadn't all these good qualities we would have ranked "The Man with the Green Eye" first in class.

Now for the poetical contributions.

In our opinion "Finis Vitæ" which is also between the covers of the *University of Virginia Magazine* is better than any other attempt we could find. Here the author imagines himself to be an old man who sees his life departing from him inch by inch. He very beautifully likens his life to a smouldering fire whose "ashes fall in silence one by one till all have heaped the pyre," and continuing in this strain he concludes in the last stanza that he will "like these embers, pass to join the universal mass awaiting birth.'' Now this grows a little obscure. What does he mean by "universal mass awaiting birth?" This is a question that we could not answer.

Probably he means the resurrection, at least we hope so, though to a suspicious ear it might seem to have a pantheistic or materialistic ring to it. But despite this little obscurity we cannot deny that it is a very excellent little poem, and one well worth quoting at the end of our article.

In the *Villa Shield* there is a pretty neatly written article on "Father Marqueltte," the Jesuit explorer. Though it is very much condensed, it is quite interesting. This is no easy thing to do, to write a series of facts in anything but a dry and unreadable manner. For this we must compliment the young lady who signs herself 'Alumna.' But the most we can say for this account of Father Marquette's life is this, that it is undoubtedly first in the essay class this month. However the compliment just paid is not such a very great one after all, for if October's showing in this branch of college literature were indicative of any permanent condition instead of being, as we trust, merely a temporary depression, we should say that our essays are taking a lower standard of merit. Nothing has met our eyes this time that can compare with "College Education," in September *Red and Blue.*

It is too bad, but, though the *Georgetown Journal* is first in fiction and has, in our humble opinion, improved a great deal all around, it has a less meritorious essay than before on its pages. Its title —fashionable enough—is the French "Le Tiers Etat." It is a trifle annoying to find such mediocre work in a magazine that we have learned to look upon as almost ideal.

There is nothing of the remarkable, but it cannot be denied that what is done is well done in the Mills College *White and Gold* for August-September. "A Matter of Numbers" might be noted as being good, especially because of the unexpected and wild improbability of the ending. The verse it contains is also clever.

The *Exponent* from St. Mary's Institute came in the other day from Dayton but there are only three pages in the magazine proper and then we came to the departments. What you have, Exponent, is all right but what you haven't may be better.

FINIS VITÆ.

Here on the embers of my fire
  I gaze and see the ashes fall,
In silence, one by one, till all
  Have heaped the pyre.

Here on the embers of my life
  I gaze and see each feeble power
Fade noiseless with the passing hour
  To rest from strife.

And, yet, no murmer of complaint;
  For, like the embers of this fire,
Some gleam of warmth did I inspire
  Ere I grew faint.

And once more to my mother, earth,
  Shall I, too, like these embers, pass
To join the universal mass
  Awaiting birth.

           "H."
In the University of Virginia Magazine.

    A. B. DIEPENBROCK, '08.

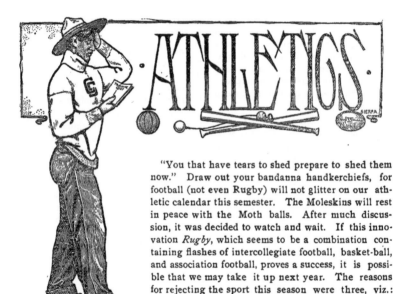

"You that have tears to shed prepare to shed them now." Draw out your bandanna handkerchiefs, for football (not even Rugby) will not glitter on our athletic calendar this semester. The Moleskins will rest in peace with the Moth balls. After much discussion, it was decided to watch and wait. If this innovation *Rugby*, which seems to be a combination containing flashes of intercollegiate football, basket-ball, and association football, proves a success, it is possible that we may take it up next year. The reasons for rejecting the sport this season were three, viz.: Inability to secure a coach, scarcity of outside games and lateness of the season.

The sanguine fraternity declare with vehemence that the deceased game will surely come to life ere the year of '07 is visited by the good St. Nicholas. Of course, this prophecy depends entirely upon Rugby itself. If the students now playing the game receive beneficial exercise and plenty of glory; if the game is a success from the spectators' view point, then the wiseacre will have to join the army of the unemployed instead of gracing the boards as a modern Isaias. However, fellows, we must confine our talents to something else for this winter. Basket-ball will be taken up with a vengeance, while baseball can be served as desert. This latter is the cream of our athletic menu here at Santa Clara, but don't swallow voraciously of this cream; check your appetites a trifle for the present; then eat everything in sight when the bell rings next season.

The death rate should be very high around the keystone sack, with Jim Twohy and Art. Shafer doing the tagging. Chas. Freine, who played the outfield in such masterly style last season, has been studying puzzles during his leisure hours and will endeavor to solve the intricate corner on the first team.

Collins worked as an officer of the law while in San Francisco this summer and will as of yore swing the stick with a vengeance. Pudgy Shafer, our midget short stop, spent the long vacation on a chicken ranch near Petaluma. He solved the chicken business to a nicety and knows the fouls thoroughly. While in the land of nod, the little fellow unconsciously exposed his scheme. Those who lay awake at night heard him voice his sentiments in the following language: Heavy breathing—a nasal number—"Yes sir, you bet—I am going to wear the cage next baseball season, I know a foul when I see one, take the tip from me—I'm from Petaluma," Brown, who will do a little twirling, positively excludes the free list and will issue few passes when on the firing line. Capt. Kilburn is digging in the garden continually; he is storing up a rare assortment of bait with which he will keep opposing stickers at his mercy. Lappin & Broderick, the daisies of the outer garden, have been daily practicing on the numerous windows about the college.

Basket Ball

With the winter baseball men polish the diamond on the inside, the College basket ball tossers have full sway on the outside campus. There is some very promising material among the new candidates. These students will make some of the veterans hustle to hold their places. The quintet has played together for over a year now and should put up some rattling good games for basket ball is a sport in which team work is the most potent factor.

Aquirre at center is passing with accuracy and hits the goal with precision. Schmitz and Murphy are playing with renewed vigor at the guard positions. R. Twohy and Bogan work in a manner very baffling to their opponents, while Fisher, Gray and Casey are taking rapid strides in the game. The Santa Clara High School will organize shortly and the college will clash with them in a friendly game once or twice a week.

Tennis

Play—Thank you—Thirty Love! Breezes from the tennis court. Treas. McLane and Pres. McClatchy are the only rivals of Mr. Duffy of debris fame. These energetic young students have taken a contract to remove the debris from the tennis court. This they have accomplished fairly well and promise the yard that the much advertised tournament will take place surely—before Christmas. Mr. McLane will positively appear in duck trousers. This will be a gala day for the racket wielders. Harold will defend his title against the redoubtable Yoacham.

Swimming

To our eastern brethren it would seem entirely out of season to write on the above, but in this salubrious climate we may dip in the folds of old Neptune without serious results even on Christmas Day.

During the hot weather the boys took frequent dips in the college natatorium. There is some very likely material among the students and these with proper training may develop into championship timber. Swimming is the most beneficial exercise we have if taken moderately. One should not remain in the water more than thirty minutes to derive any physical benefit. The length of time of course depending on the physical condition.

Every student in college should take up this branch of athletics as we get better all around results than all other sports combined. Before the school year is over, the athletic management intends holding a series of races. The events will in all probability be handicap, so that every student will have a fair opportunity of capturing honors.

Second Division

(REPORTER, H. W. LYNG, '09.)

As my worthy predecessor in this corner of the REDWOOD said in the last issue, the school year opened with rather cerulean prospects for the 2nd Division baseball. Two of the best players of last year's invincible Junior Nine, captain and catcher "Gene" Ivancovich, and left-fielder "Pete" Dunne, have left us for the "hill," as the Jesuit Novitiate at Los Gatos is ycleped among us irreverent laymen. Ws miss both of

them extremely, they were not only good baseball players but they diffused around them a spirit of gentlemanliness and good will towards all, that served as oil for all the little wheels of our athletic machinery. They were really "good fellows," with a strong emphasis on 'good,' and another on 'fellows.' Then, again, some of the boys did not show up this year, and the majority of those that did, having tried to look as big and manly-looking as possible during the holidays, and having even cultivated and coaxed incipient mustaches with a deal of microscopic success—having done all these things and more, I say, were allowed to go and mingle with and admire and imitate the "big boys" in the 1st Division.

But now the baseball world of the 2nd Division is marshalling its molecules and its atoms out of the chaotic condition into which they have been and, in a word, is pulling itself together. New and splendid material bobs up every now and then in the most unexpected places, Who would have thought that Putnam, for instance, and Cuda, J. Sheean, Leonard and Robertson would have sprouted up in a twinkling, like the gourd of Jonah, into the crack players we all now see they are? It would have taken a false prophet to foresee such an outcome.

Joseph Sheean and Louis Putman are taking to the game with an ardor that springs not only from an innate love of sport, but from a laudable purpose of reducing their equatorial measurement and their tailor's bills into the bargain.

As their girth is sinking their batting and fielding averages are swelling in exact proportion. Indeed I have heard it said—I think by Francis Lyman, a most reserved and cautious statistician—that in order to get the weights of these athletics in question you have only to apply the "rule of three" to their respective batting averages. That is, all you have to do is to subtract that figure from 1000 and divide the result by three, and the thing is done. Prefects can take a hint from this—they should not allow these gentlemen to go out to the back yard to get weighed, as there is absolutely no need for it. What can be more precise and reliable than mathematics, anyway?

And Francis Cudal—what shall we say of him? Having warmed the benches last year until they were too hot to hold him, he has betaken himself to the diamond from the word go, this term, and he is now the despair and the envy of divers and sundry who are creeping on way behind him. He is a fast outfielder and when he hits the ball, it travels on a mileage ticket.

As these three forenamed students are richer in avoirdupois than we are ourselves, we had to be a trifle careful how we treated them. The following, however, are our inferiors in that valuable article; we think we can emerge from a collision with them in safety if not in honor, and hence we will have more regard for plain facts hereafter.

Alex. Leonard is not yet an adept on the diamond but he is tending in that direction. Alex. gets there by head work. For instance, the glasses that he wears—and he got them for this very purpose—are such powerful reflectors that they cancel all the curves the pitcher can use, and thus every ball that comes to him is a straight ball. No wonder then that his batting is improving!

R. J. Robertson is autochthonous with respect to San Jose. In plain English that means he knows something about baseball. Still he has no "swell-head" about it, but feels that there is a large field for improvement. This field is the Second Division yard in which he practices sedulously every day.

With the above players to help out, we see no reason why the Junior team '07 shohld not be on a par with its predecessor. Yes! we think that this year's team will prove as unconquerable as any that have preceded it.

As a sort of prelude to this team, a select nine has been lately put together. Mr. Galtes, S. J., is president, ex-officio. Wm. Gianera was elected manager, and he is certainly a splendid choice. "Gulie" has had charge of the tamale stand for a year or more, and he proved his capacity in that office beyond all cavil. The financial end of the institution is thus in good hands. The captaiu is Victor Salberg, who knows the game from alpha to omega, and who has besides all the energy and tact of a leader of men. Archbold and Lyng form the battery; Gianera, Foster, Salberg, and Watson occupy the infield, and Sheean, Gallagher, and Jones the outfield.

The only thing that remains for the team to do in order to furnish a brilliant prologue to the coming season is to get a few games. This is a somewhat difficult matter at this time, but we trust that Manager Gianera will not have, like Alexander, to sit down and weep because he has no worlds left to conquer.

We were pledged, weren't we, to record the doings of the new indoor baseball game that made the southern corner of the yard so stentoriously vocal on holidays. But we never hear of it now. Perhaps it has died! Perhaps the business manager speculated away the funds, or perhaps it was a house divided against itself. In any case, we should like to hear more about it. It was a good thing for the Benjamins of the family and should have been pushed along. Who had charge of it, anyhow?

In view of our next number, the REDWOOD reporter will keep his sporting eye on the smaller leagues of the Second Division and record as faithfully as he can whatever and whomsoever he finds worthy of mention.

H. A. J. McKENZIE, '08·

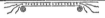

F. T. SOURISSEAU

Manufacturing
and Repairing

Extra Fine Assortment of Sterling Silver and Solid
Gold Jewelry

No Plate Goods—Only 10-14-18 Karat Gold

69½ South First Street, San Jose

Rooms 2-3-4   Phone White 207

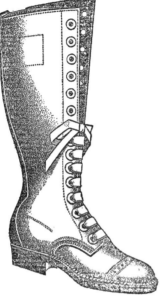

SAN JOSE

Brick Company

MANUFACTURERS OF

Common and . . .
Ornamental Brick

Yards at Dougherty Station

SAN JOSE OFFICE

17 North First Street   San Jose, California

Telephone Main 594

EAST

If going East secure Choice of Routes, of Limited Trains and Tourist Excursions by calling on nearest agent

Southern Pacific

Ask for Particulars

E. SHILLINGSBURG, D. F. and P. A.,

40 E. Santa Clara Street, San Jose, Cal.

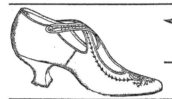

=====THE=====

Senior Dramatic Club

—OF—

Santa Clara College

Will Present

THE BLIND PRINCE

Thanksgiving Eve., Nov. 29, 1906

AT THE

College Theatre

Proceeds for Benefit of Literary Congress

Admission   -   -   -   25 and 5o Cents

Labor Party

Democratic Ticket

Sheriff—Arthur B. Langford

County Assessor—L. A. Spitzer

County Recorder—Thomas Treanor

District Attorney—James H. Campbell

Tax Collector—W. A. January

County Clerk—H. A. Pfister

County Treasurer—Thomas Monahan

County Auditor—Bert Schwartz

Superintendent of Schools—D. T. Bateman

County Surveyor—Henry Fisher

Coroner—B. E. Kell

Supervisor, 4th District—John Roll

State Senator—F. M. Smith

Assemblyman—John Stanley

Justices of the Peace—Santa Clara Township
Chas. A. Thompson and D. R. Oliver
Constables, Santa Clara Township
J. J. Toomey and Mat Hite

)WOOD

ECEMBER, 1906

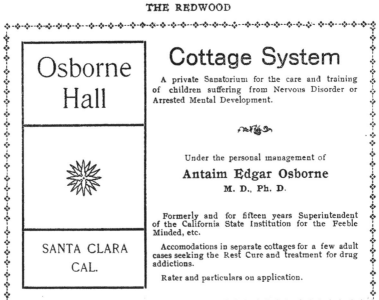

Contents.

Nace Printing Co.   ⬛⬛⬛   Santa C

THE REDWOOD STAFF OF '06

Photo by Bushnell

Reading from left to right, A. B. Diepenbrock, '08, Exchange, I G Bogan, '08 College Notes; H A. McKenzie, '08, Athletics, M. S. Shafer, '09, Alumni, J. F. Twohy, '07, Editor-in-Chief, R J. Chisholm, S. J., J. D. McKay, '07, Business Manager; M T Dooling, '09, Assistant Business Manager, R. H O'Conner, '08, In the Library, F. M Heffernan, '08, Assistant Business Manager, R A Ryland, '09 Assistant Business Manager

The Redwood.

Entered Dec. 18, 1902, at Santa Clara, Calif. as second-class matter, under Act of Congress of March 3, 1879

| VOL. VI. | SANTA CLARA, CAL., DECEMBER, 1906. | No. 3. |

IMMACULATA

Fair Mother-Maid, what subtle, sweet constraint
   Lures me to sing thy wondrous purity !
No more presumptous theme the crystal sea
Of radiance round the Godhead's throne, where Saint
And Seraph bathe eternally, and 'faint
O'erpowered by the glory, for in thee
God willed his brightest throne of grace to be
And kept thee pure of the least shade of taint !

Ah, might a sinful voice, uncensured, praise
The marvel of thy maiden loveliness,
'Twere mine to swell the hymn the heavens raise
In universal rapture, thee to bless !
For little though thy glory thence would gain
One heart must needs be purer for the strain !

F. J. H., '08.

NEWMAN'S "IDEA OF A UNIVERSITY"

Ireland in 1850 was beginning to a-waken from the lethargy induced by many years of British despotism and mis-rule. The penal laws which had made education for Catholics a crime and the educators criminals, which forbade Cath-olic worship and hunted priests and ped-agogues from one place of concealment to another and finally either exiled or imprisoned the greater part of them, had lately been repealed and the Catholics of England and Ireland were beginning to realize their position. Robbed, op-pressed and thrust aside, they had not been for centuries in a condition to at-tempt the education necessary to put them on an equal footing with their more fortunate Protestant brethren as land owners, as statesmen, or as men of the world. It was now time to avail them-selves of the means to acquire "the force, the comprehensiveness, the steadiness, the versatility of intellect, the command over our own powers, the instinctive just estimate of things as they pass be-fore us", which Newman outlines as the marks or characteristics of a true gentle-tleman, "sometimes indeed a natural gift but commonly not gained without much effort and the exercise of years."

It was soon after the beginning of this revival, if it may be so called, that John Henry Newman accepted the Rectorate of the newly organized Catholic Univer-sity of Dublin. But a word as to New-man.

Born in London, February 21st, 1801,

he was the son of Mr. John Newman a banker, while his mother was a member of one of the old Huguenot families, with moderate Calvinistic tendencies. From her Newman no doubt received some of his early prejudices against the Evan-gelical school of Theology. Studious from his youth, he read much and often, and his books were the moulders of his character. After an early education in a private school he went up to Oxford, and he received his degree before he had reached the age of twenty years. In 1822 he was elected to a fellowship in Oriel, where he himself says he pass-ed for some years a lonely life. Here his religious views began to change and he gradually left his evangelical beliefs in favor of the Higher Anglican doc-trines, and from that time until 1844 he was slowly but surely tending towards Rome, whose church, according to his earlier beliefs, was the Antichrist of pro-phecy. In 1832 he accompanied a sick friend, Hurrel Froude, to the Mediterra-nean and while there was himself at-tacked by an almost fatal illness. The hours of solitary reflection which were his only occupation during his convales-cence served but to increase the disqui-etude of his soul and it was upon his homeward voyage, while becalmed in an orange boat between Palermo and Ver-sailles that he wrote his pathetic appeal to Truth, the cry of a troubled soul seek-ing Faith,—"Lead Kindly Light." The Tractarian movement engaged his attention upon his return, but his belief in the doctrines of the Anglican Church were beginning to fail and he proposed a compromise or Via Media, as he called it, with the Church of Rome, arousing by this work a storm of opposition from the Anglican clergy and prelates. Finally, in 1841, he lost active interest in his work, and after two more years of preaching, followed by two of silence, he joined the Catholic Church on October 8th, 1845. Attacked by Canon Kingsley in 1863 he explained and defended his past life and actions by his famous "Apologia pro Vita Sua," a work which turned the tide of English sentiment in his favor by its evident earnestness and sincerity, and for the first time made him universally popular. Pope Leo XIII raised him to the rank of Cardinal as one of his first acts after his accession to the Chair of Peter. He lived as Cardinal for eleven years and died at Egbaston in October, 1890.

It was about the year 1850 that the revival of higher education for the Catholics in England and Ireland was commenced and the Catholic University of Dublin began to assume a material aspect. Newman was chosen for the Rectorate and he immediately stated his views as to the proper form and purpose of a University in a series of nine discourses on university teaching delivered in 1852 to the Catholics of Dublin. His task was twofold, first to win over the more advanced people and clergy and prelates of Ireland to his plan of liberal education and at the same time to fully determine the aims and policies of the institution. Taking as a basis or ground-

work of his discourses the demonstration of the incompleteness and inadequacy of any curriculum not admitting Theology, he devotes the greater part of these discourses to the proof of his statement that Theology is a science and as such demands admittance to a university, which from the very nature of its name professes to teach all knowledge or all science. Still he does not lose sight of the fact that he is also championing liberal knowledge as necessary for the inculcation into Catholic young men of the thorough principles of a gentleman, against the prejudice of bigots and the utilitarian objections of so-called practical men.

In his first discourse he explains at length his position and ideas, outlining the plan to be pursued in the following work. His second discourse establishes Theology as a branch of knowledge, ranking it among the sciences and thus giving it its passport into a university. Strengthening his position he emphasizes his ideas by explaining the bearing and necessary co-relation of Theology with other knowledge and, in the same manner, the dependence of other knowledge upon Theology, as one of the former's constituent parts, proving the incompleteness of one without the other. Then considering knowledge, liberal knowledge, as its own end, sufficient in itself, he silences the utilitarian demand for professional or commercial learning as having the greater utility and correspondingly better end. Then following in logical order he treats of knowledge in relation to Learning, in relation to Professional Skill, to Religious Duty and finally the Duties of the Church toward knowledge.

His work throughout is one continuous whole, logical in every sequence and doubly effective. His plea for Theology would win over to him the Ecclesiastics of the Church, while his second task was to convince his hearers, many almost fanatics in their adherence to things religious and their unreasoning distrust of things scientific, that a liberal education was an essential attribute of a Catholic gentleman. Addressed as these discourses were in general to a distinctively scholarly audience, Newman was necessarily academic in tone and formal in method, at times almost ponderous, always deliberate, philosophical and explicit. His work is said to be the most perfect exposition of a theory; at all times he is a perfect master of the situation. Gates says of him:—"There is something irresistibly impressive in the perfect poise with which he moves through the intricactes of the many abstractions his subject involves. He exhibits each aspect of his subject in just the right perspective, and with just the requisite minuteness of detail; leads us unerringly from each point of view to that which most naturally follows; he keeps us always aware of each aspect to the total sum of truth he is trying to help us grasp; and so little by little he secures for us that perfect command of an intellectual region, in its concrete parts and in its abstract relations which exposition aims to make possible."

He is ever ready, close student of human nature that he is, to take advantage of every opportunity, to make use of every artifice to gain the favor and good will of his audience and their consent to the projects he is exploiting. Thus, when he would reconcile them to a university modeled closely in its operation after that of his own beloved Oxford, he tells them of the earlier days when Celt and Briton were united in the common interests of learning and when "St. Aidan and the Irish monks went up to Lindisfarne and Melrose and taught the Saxon youth", and then as England in those days of intellectual need looked to them for help, so now they could and should go to England for help in their undertaking and once again unite in the common interests of education. And again, describing the system of the English school, he shows how it has produced, in spite of their deficiencies on the side of morals and with their hollow semblance of Christianity, heroes and statesmen, literary men and philosophers, men of business, of judgment, of practical tastes, men who have 'made England what it is,—able to subdue the earth, able to triumph over Catholics.' Thus he arouses the passions of his hearers, excites their religious and patriotic emotions and induces them to take the same means to restore the proper balance of the universe—liberal education.

But it is in his remarkable genius as a master of word and phrase, in his ability to choose between the delicate shades of meaning, in his power of fitting the fittest word to its proper thought, that he most excels. Listen as he tells us what he deems the Catholic idea of the Creator, note the perfect aptness of each phrase, the fitness of every word, expressing every possible aspect of the subject yet with no redundancy or tautological repetition: "God is an Individual, Self-dependent, All-perfect, Unchangeable Being; intelligent, living, personal, and present; almighty, all-seeing, all-remembering; between whom and His creatures there is an infinite gulf; who has no origin, who is all-sufficient for Himself; who created and upholds the universe; who will judge every one of us sooner or later, according to the Law of right and wrong which he has written on our hearts. He is One who is sovereign over, operative amidst, independent of, the appointments which he has made; One in whose hands are all things, who has a purpose in every event, and a standard for every deed, and thus has relations of His own towards the subject-matter of each particular science which the book of nature unfolds; who has with an adorable, never-ceasing energy implicated Himself in all the history of creation, the constitution of nature, the course of the world, the origin of society, the forces of nations, the action of the human mind." * *

* * * * * * * *

But the attempt resulted in a failure, complete, disastrous failure. The time was not ripe for such an undertaking, and when in 1860 Newman resigned his position as Rector, it was practically the end of the university. But though the institution did not succeed, Newman's work still survives, an invaluable addition to our Literature, a perfect example of the 'union of strict method with charm of style in the treatment of an abstract topic', or, as Pater says, 'of the perfect handling of a theory'. As a guide to Catholic education, and as a defense of liberal, education it deserves even greater attention, and it is perhaps for this as much as for reason of its literary merit that it will ever live as one of the greatest works of one of our greatest authors.

ROBERT E. FITZGERALD.

AN OLD STORY

By the embers glowing bright
I read my new-born verse:
How strong the lines ! how terse !
They shamed the embers' heat and light.

I read at prosy morn anew
My eve-inspired lay ;
I found to my dismay
My embers ashes—poem, too.

P. I., '10.

AN ODE TO THE DECEMBER WIND

Oh mystical, sea born, December wind
You, when the land is wrapt in sleep,
Out of the arms of the sobbing deep
Arise with a clamorous ghostly leap.
As over the world you wind and whirl,
Out of the waves that writhe and-curl
In a maddening swirl,
Yourself you hurl,
Shrieking, moaning, crying.
Oh what are the secrets you tell then,
As you whistle past dale, and hill, and fen,
Whispering, screaming, sighing ?

The heaving ocean, as you flit by,
You join your voice to his sullen roar,
And wailing together you lash the shore,
Beneath cold stars and frosty sky.
What is the dirge you two chant then,
Alone out there, away from men ?

You go where foot has never trod,
In your crazy flight, December wind,
What are the secrets dark you find,
Which none have seen but you and God ?

And when you reach the woods at last,
You lose your furious vengeful ire,
Your voice dies down like a fitful fire,
You change to a breeze from a winter blast.
What tales do you whisper then, soft breeze,
As you creep through the mute, stark, leafless trees?

Over the world to rest consigned,
When men are wrapt in soft sleep shrouds,
Beneath the scurrying flying clouds,
You chatter and clatter, December wind.
Oh tell the tales, the songs to me,
Which you cite and sing,
When at night you spring,
From the tossing arms of the restless sea.

                        James F. Twohy, '07.

"BURIED TREASURE"

"At this time there came into this valley a wicked man of evil ways, called Francis Ayes or Francis the Robber. Fear of God nor of man possessed not this follower of the Evil Spirit. Nay, even here on this mission soil, where the Post road from the south to the Pueblo of San Jose climbs the hill of the olive trees, did he secrete his treasure and monies. Within the shadow of the Church of Christ did he commit his crimes and bury his ill-gotten gains. The most part of his precious store lies buried in the orchard of the olive trees and nearest to that tree which is called the 'Robber's.' "

So wrote the Padre Esteban in his old "Chronicle of the Mission San Juan Baptista," but till this time I had not believed very seriously in the existence of the treasure which the old monk said was of such great value and which, if his chronicle were true, must be buried somewhere near my cottage.

But now with Jose standing before me talking volubly in his mixture of Spanish and English; with the old box on the table corroded by time and rotted by the damp earth; with its queer yellow parchments and unintelligible writing:—with all these then my belief in, and respect for, the old monk increased a hundred-fold.

"But yes, Senor, the little box, it was there, even at the foot of the Robber's tree. For I dug and presently my spade struck and I said 'Ah! Dios! what is here?' And then, 'madre de mi vida, the little box'—but at this point I sent Jose laway, for it was the fourth time he had repeated his story.

The box which he had found was perhaps five inches long by three wide and an inch and a half in depth. It was of plain redwood, bound with a narrow band of metal, rusted and corroded almost beyond recognition by the dampness of its earthy surroundings. In it were two parchments; on one was a curious diagram which after some study I concluded was a plan of part of the Mission land as it had been before the Mexican Invasion. There was what appeared to me to be a square field with a winding road running out of it from one corner. On either side of this road were a number of crosses placed in a line at equal intervals. In the center of the field was a prominent black mark and on the farther side of the road a rudely drawn circle. In one corner were the letters F. A.

The other parchment was to my intense disappointment partially destroyed being merely the lower portion of a larger paper. as was shown by its jagged upper edge. The remnant was all too small, not more than five inches by two, but it was very closely covered by a most astonishing jumble of hieroglyphics. There were six unbroken lines of which the first is a fair sample:

;+ | ;];+!8!]6ıoJ*?;]?!]x78;]

I sat for a long while looking in turn

at this unintelligible writing and at the plan and wondering if there was any connection between Francis Ayes, the robber of ninety years ago, and this little map with the initials in the corner. F. A. might have been the English adventurer or quite possibly some one else, but, oh no! my "*eighth*" sense told me that it could be none other than Francis Ayes and it further informed me that I was about to discover something of vast importance.

The cryptogram held even more interest for me. I had always been a lover of mysteries, and especially those which hinged on secret writings, so now I set myself to translate it into English. I said English because I reasoned that as the plan and the cipher were found together there might be some connection, and since the initials were those of Francis Ayes, the Englishman, the code, if it were his, would be in English.

Now, as is well known to anyone who has read Poe's "Fire-Bug," as I was doing at this time, e is the letter of the alphabet most used not only singly but doubled. So looking through the cipher with this in mind, I found the symbol ! used twenty-three times, and in three cases it was paired. From this it seemed probable that *e* was represented by ! The symbol] I took as indicating the end of a word, as it appeared so often and at only slightly varying intervals. If ! stood for *e*, I expected to find it repeated as the third of three characters which would stand for *the*, because this small word is the most frequently used. I found the group :+!

repeated five times in this short message, so that I had three known symbols—; standing for *t*, + for *h*, and ! for *e*.

Looking for groups containing these signs I at once found this one ;+ | ; and substituting the known letters had *th-t*, which instantly suggested *that*, and gave me | as representing the letter *a*. The next group, the-e, was undoubtedly *these*, so I had *s* represented by 8. In the next line I found the group ;+48. Supplying the values of the known symbols I had *th-s*, which might either have been *thus* or *this*. A little further on I found 84.;+, either *si-th* or *su-th*, the only possible solution seemed to be *sixth*; so I had 4 meaning *i*, and, meaning *x*.

I proceeded in this way until after much thought and reasoning I made out the cipher. As I translated it the writing, beginning with the first whole line, was as follows:

"That these may not be lost, let him who finds this dig under the sixth tree to the west from a tree which is in a direct line between the spring of St. John and the fountain in the plaza. Francis Ayes."

Now I understood the diagram; the row of little crosses represented the line of olive trees on the edge of the roadway, the irregularly shaped circle was the spring of St. John, and the black mark in the square was the fountain in the plaza.

Up to this point I had been alone in the room, but now as I glanced up I saw Bob coming across the veranda toward the French window.

"Ahoy! Bob!" I called, "come here pronto."

Bob, be it known, had been my chum ever since our Freshman year at the University. He was now my guest, for I wanted to see the pure, country air brace up that weak health of his.

"What's the row?" he asked, as he came in and dropped into a lounging chair.

"What's the matter?" Look here," I fairly thrust the papers in his face,— "look at it, man. Do you realize that I've made a great discovery? *I* know where to find Francis Ayes' treasure."

At this Bob perked up and got interested. He asked innumerable questions, wanted to examine the plan, the cipher, and the box; and when he had finished his first examination he made a tracing of the plan.

I asked what he wanted it for, and he replied "to send to a friend of mine who collects such things, and who always wants a tracing, if possible, when he cannot obtain the original." I wanted to know if his friend would like a copy of the cipher.

"Oh no! It wouldn't be any use to *him*," said Bob, "By the way, what are you going to do with the treasure?"

"I'll take a vacation and you'll come along too on your share. Just to show that I do not lose my head for a box of yellow metal, I am going to be a friend to my friends."

"All right," he said, "It's a go." For the next ten minutes we argued as to

whether we should look for the treasure at once or wait till the next morning. Bob insisted on delay, but we were cut short by Waugh, the cook, who called us to hot biscuits and coffee, so we agreed to postpone the search till the next day.

The following morning I was up at an ungodly hour and went into Bob's room to rout him out. He was asleep, but woke as I entered. He had a towel around his head and didn't seem very bright.

"Say, you Bob, get up this instant and come dig treasure," were my first words.

"No," he said, "not all the jewels of Aladdin would get me up. I didn't sleep a wink last night. That cryptogram of yours was too much for me."

So pulling down the shade, I went off to seek Jose and commence operations.

The fountain had been gone for many years, but there was not the slightest doubt as to the exact spot where it had stood. When I came to run a line between this point and the spring I found my way blocked fair and square by one of the old olive trees, the one from which I was to measure. From this tree I counted off six in a westerly direction and found myself next to the one which I have already mentioned as the "Robber's Tree."

Then Jose came up with his spade and began digging at my direction. The earth was not packed very hard and after a few minutes he had reached a depth of four feet. As he drove his spade in again it struck upon some object! Was it the treasure, or merely a stone? I wrenched the spade from Jose, who was maddeningly slow, and dug away furiously. Soon something came to light. It was—yes! it was a box, a wooden box, metal-bound and of about the same size as the preceding one. Flinging away the spade, I snatched the casket and darted for the house and Bob. But even in my excitement, I noticed the extreme lightness of my precious find.

When I reached my room I called Bob, but receiving no reply, I forced the lock of the little box with the fire-tongs and raised the lid. For a moment I was too surprised even to move. I don't exactly know what I had expected to find, but there were dim visions of precious stones and gold pieces, and instead there was—another paper.

It was extremely short and this is how it ran:

Dear Charles—

I do hope that the treasure may all come your way, old fellow, but of course the Gringos may read Padre Esteban and thus secure the booty. The unscrupulous villians! they ought to know that you are going to come. I do. Yours hunting the tall grass,

Francis Ayes.

My resentment towards Bob lasted nearly a day, but at last I forgave him on condition that he would breathe the story to no man while I lived. That privilege I reserved for myself.

R. J. RYLAND, '09·

A TRIOLET

To cultivate a smile
    Costs not so very dear,
And so 'tis worth your while
To cultivate a smile;
It may dull care beguile,
    It may dark sorrow cheer
To cultivate a smile
    Costs not so very dear.

W. B. P., '08

TRUE TO HIS TRUST

Joe hastened up stairs at the sound of his mistress' bell. Just as his hand was about to turn the door knob, however, he halted. A strange voice from within fell upon his ears. "I really cannot agree with you in this matter," the voice said. "Whether you are or not, you certainly *ought* to be afraid to have a half-crazy fellow around you." Poor Joe had sense enough to realize that he was the half-crazy fellow referred to, and his heart sank within him. But the next moment, reassured by his mistress' reply, "Why! I could trust Joe anywhere," he put on a brave face and entered.

He found his mistress engaged in sewing in company with an elderly, gray-headed, angular-featured matron, evidently the owner of the unkind voice and the unkinder remarks. As the lamplight fell upon Joe, well-built, neatly dressed, and one might say handsome, but for the reflection on his face of the puzzled, worried brain within, the visitor seemed somewhat taken aback that he should so belie her words. Joe paid her no attention, however, for he was receiving some instructions from his mistress about the delivery of a sealed note which she handed him, and soon he left the room with a parting, "Hurry up, Joe; it's important."

"Well," said the visitor as the door closed, "he seems to be a little better off than I thought. Anyway, thank the Lord! he didn't hear me."

"Didn't hear me!" If she could have glanced into poor idiotic Joe's heart, she would not have felt so much at ease. She had carelessly sown the seeds and he was reaping the whirlwind of humiliation and suffering. The cruel words, how they did keep ringing in his ears. Again and again they fell cold and distant upon his ears,—"you ought to be afraid to have a half-crazy fellow around you." But, happily, his mind was not of the most tenacious grasp, and as he hurried on through the darkness, the echo of the words became fainter and fainter and at last they died away to be followed by the sweet, encouraging reply of his mistress: "Why, I could trust Joe anywhere!" Louder and more cheery rang the reassuring words, and more sprightly and gaily hurried ahead through the mist and the gloom.

"Hands up"—He looked around startled, and saw the muzzle of a pistol alarmingly near his face. Frightened out of the few poor wits he possessed he threw his trembling hands above his head, and the highwayman proceeded to relieve him of his worldly goods. This he did in a cool and business-like fashion that spoke well for his experience. But he found only half-a-dollar and a cheap nickel watch, and he was on the point of ordering him off in disgust when he espied the note held in Joe's clenched fingers.

"You don't hold nothin' back on me;

hand over, sonny"—and he reached to take it from him. But Joe's fright was over now; the voice of his mistress rang again in his ears. "I could trust Joe anywhere," and "Hurry up, Joe, it's important." Yes, he would be true to his trust, he would show his mistress and her visitor that he was as good as anyone else; the important note would not be lost through any fault of his. Gathering all his strength, he suddenly brought down his fist on the astounded footpad's head and started to run. Only a few yards, however, had he covered when a sharp report rang out, and he was lying in the dust and another murder had been added to the city's list of crime, another murder to sell the morning papers, another murder to furnish conversation for a brief day and then to be put aside for the next novelty.

* * * * * *

It was near midnight when patrolman Downing brought in Red McRae, known to fame by at least a dozen aliases. There had been a long, hard, chase, but the measure of his evil-doing was full, and he had been captured at last. As they entered the station and Red stood blinking in the gaslight, Downing turned to him and said, "How did it happen, McRae, that you shot that fellow? Did you do it for pure deviliment, or were you as nervous as a kid on his first job?"

Red, who realized, as he himself might have expressed it that he was "all in," looked up sullenly. "The guy tried to hold somethin' back; it must be a rich deal, for when I grabbed for it, he up an' hit me with all his might. That made me mad an' I guess I lost my head."

"Well, anyway," said Downing, "hand over your booty." "I haven't got it," lied the thief.

Downing searched his pocket and took out the note, still sealed. When he ripped open the envelope, a button fell out and rolled along the floor. Red watched it listlessly until it lodged in a corner, but Downing was deep in the note and paid no attention to it.

"Well, I'll be blowed," he said when he had finished reading it to himself. Then he read it aloud.

H. Price & Co.: Please send by bearer one dozen buttons like the one enclosed, and charge to the account of Elizabeth Dorr.

"Well, I'll be blowed," he repeated, and folding up the note carefully, put it in his pocket.

MAURICE T. DOOLING, '09.

CONSOLATION

(With apologies to Malherbe)

The sorrow, my friend, thy wounded heart wrings
      —Must it never cease?
And the sigh from thy father's heart that springs
      Forever increase?

Is the loss of thy child in earth laid away
      —Fate common to all—
Some mystical maze where thy reason must stay,
      Beyond our recall?

I know with what promise his childhood was stored,
      And I would not essay
In short-sighted love one disparaging word
      Thy grief to allay.

But he was of earth where each fairest that grows
      First fails to the tomb;
And rose-like, he lived the life of a rose
      —Cut down in its bloom

Yet had thy wild vows prevailed and thy tears,
      And God should ordain,
That in silvery hair he should tell out his years,
      Where, pray, were the gain?

Thinkest thou kinder welcome to Heaven's estate
    Length of days would confirm?
Or that age would less feel the mould's heavy weight
    And the vandal worm?

No, no! my dear friend, when Death ferries o'er
    The soul from its clay,
Wrinkled age follows not to the orient shore,
    Whose morn is for aye.

Grim Death has his woes that loom up alone,
    And we fain would appeal;
But what prayer can relax his bosom of stone,
    And his fingers of steel?

The serf leaves his thatched-covered hut and his field
    To answer his call;
And the guards of the palace are powerless to shield
    The king from his thrall.

To lose then thy mind's magnanimous calm
    'Twere sinful and vain:—
To will what God wills is the only sure balm
    To heal your heart's pain.

                J. D. '07.

TENNYSON'S "IN MEMORIAM"

It is a truism that "poets are born, not made." In true poetry there is very little room for artificiality. The poet, to properly interpret life and its various phases, must feel and experience, suffer and enjoy. The real poet, true to himself and to his art, is a philosopher—a lover of wisdom. He reflects on life, religion, its mysteries, and upon himself. He expresses his thought in the language of the beautiful, yet this is his art, not his artificiality. In this brief essay we are examining the greatest philosophical poem of the nineteenth century "In Memoriam" by Lord Alfred Tennyson.

Born in 1809 at Somersly, Tennyson's early life passed in an atmosphere of music and poetry. He soon began to display the poetic power which was his. His early poems, though they are inferior to the finished product of his riper years, are remarkably sweet and graceful.

At Cambridge, where he was educated, he formed many happy friendships, some of which were with the most brilliant young Englishmen of the period. His closest friend was Arthur Henry Hallam, of whom we speak later on, for with the death of this young man, a great change and revolution of thought is experienced by Tennyson. He is confronted with a great sorrow, affecting his whole life, and changing him from a mere composer of dainty verse, to an interpreter of humanity and

truth. A new soul enters into his poetry, and it is from this period that his greatest works were written. "The Princess," his great epic on the prototype of the New Woman; "Maud" which is probably the most original of all his poems; and "Idylls of the King" were all written after the death of Hallam.

We will now consider "In Memoriam," held by many to be the most illustrious poem of the century. At least it is his greatest philosophic poem, and one of his two greatest works.

It is in memory of Arthur Henry Hallman, son of Henry Hallam, the historian, and chief friend of the poet. Hallam was born in 1811 in London. The house is referred to in "In Memoriam":

"Dark house by which once more I stand,
  Here in the long unlovely street;
  Door, where my heart was wont to beat
So quickly, waiting for a hand."

His education was excellent, though irregular, and the friendship was an equal one on both sides. Of his character we are indebted to the poem for an excellent though somewhat idealized portrayal. He was at Cambridge with our poet, and many of the earlier poems are their joint labor. His health was always delicate, and had a melancholy influence upon his character. His death resulted suddenly at Vienna, five years after he received his degree,—

"God's finger touched him and he slept."

His body was brought from Vienna in January, 1834, and buried in Clevedon Church.

The poet seems to divide the poem into eight parts, namely: I. From Death to Burial. II. Christmas Eve (1st.) III. Anniversary of Death (1st.) IV. Christmas Eve (2nd.) V. Anniversary of Death (2nd.) VI. Christmas Eve (3rd.) VII. New Year. VIII. His Birthday.

The opening lines of the dedicatory poem are among the most beautiful of the poem—

"Strong Son of God, immortal Love
Whom we, that have not seen thy face
By faith, and faith alone, embrace
Believing where we cannot prove·"

It is an avowal of faith, though somewhat cloudy and undefined; an acknowledgment of the sovereignty of God, hope of immortality, the personality of Christ, both God and Man.

In Canto I. the keynote of the poem is struck, the holiness of grief growing out of love,—

"Let Love clasp Grief, lest both be drowned."

The following Cantos express the conflict of heart and mind in the beginning of great sorrow. First, it stuns, then pain follows and memory only intensifies it. Self-consciousness, then undefined pain, then personal loss follow.

The poem then describes the homecoming of Hallam's remains, and justifies his sorrow by distinguishing between spontaneity and deliberation. The latter brings genuine love, the other often insincere.

The thread of past associations is again resumed, and he dwells upon past joys. A sense of loneliness overwhelms him, his love demands the object, or its ennobling power, else life is empty. In the solution, he decides that though his joy is dead, the nobility of love still exists.

With this discovery that joy, not love, is dead, faith is revived, and the beginning of a new and holier joy is ushered in,—

"I hold it true, whate'er befall;
I feel it when I sorrow most
'Tis better to have loved and lost,
Than never to have loved at all."

This marks the first great transition of the poem: he has risen from the personal to the universal, not discarding the personal love and individual sorrow, but expanding them to the infinite and eternal.

Here he begins the poems of Christmas. The peculiar season, its sacredness, exerts its influence, recalling scenes endeared by Hallam's friendship. The love of the dead is most precious at this time. It brings home the relationships of deepest sorrow to deepest joy.

Canto XXXI. contains a beautiful allusion, contemplating the mystery of death. Lazarus has approached the unknown, but his sealed lips cannot make it known; only faith can solve it.

A following Canto reflects and asks if there is a future life. His sorrow demands an answer. Without such a life, the world is only a riddle without a key, virtue is useless, suicide a logical remedy.

A beautiful proof he uses is, that if there is no immortality, then the highest of created natures are deceived.

He then recognizes immortality as a fact. Then he speculates as to whether his friend will know him in the other life. He knows that most earthly ties are temporal, yet he holds that a spiritual friendship, because it is a conceptual good and a truth, is eternal.

The next few Cantos concern themselves with other similar problems. He wonders if a soul mutually longs for its companion, and if Hallam waits for him and desires their reunion.

Canto L. apostrophizes the dead, appealing to Hallam to be with him in the trying moments of his life.

Speaking of the future life the poet says,—

"Derives it not from what we have
The likest God within the soul?"

He compares the higher nature of man and the lower nature of the beast, explaining why man's being does not cease with the grave,—

"I envy not the beast that takes
His license in the field of time,
Unfettered by the sense of crime
To whom a conscience never wakes."

The critical point of the poem occurs at LVI. From personal grief he reached questions affecting all mankind and finds no answer from

"Behind the veil, behind the veil."

Disheartened he lapses for the moment back to personal sorrow. Returning to the universal he conjectures as to how the old associations are regarded by the departed, a doubt assails him, yet

"Since we deserved the name of friends,
And thine effect so lives in me;
A part of mine may live in thee
And move thee on to nobler ends."

LXVI. asserts that grief affects different natures differently. The following Cantos concern the land of sleep and dreams. A little further, past happiness is mingled with present sorrow. Many of these dreams are tender pictures, and an angel consoles him when he is mocked, etc., and so in dreaming, grief becomes poetry.

LXXII. is the Second Anniversary of Death.

These Cantos deal with fame, 1, in the dead man; 2, fame in general; 3, in the poets. Hallam never lived to fulfill the promise that was his.

At LXXVIII. we note a change, like the first great change—it is a Christmas poem. Though still grieving, hope begins to dawn, growing stronger with the progress of the poem, until it is almost joy. Tainsh, interpreting this Canto says:

"The recovery consists in passing grief into hope, not in passing love into forgetfulness. The grief was love under another form; no less the hope is love. Love looking back upon loss must be grief; love looking forward to fruition must be hope. There is no loss of love, but rather its conversion into a higher form."

The sense of loss never dies, but the progress of recovery is apparent. He believes that though raised and exalted the spirit in paradise is still faithful.

He questions "Can the dead return and commune with us." He assumes they can, but only indirectly by means of the past.

He pictures 1, if Hallam had lived and he died; 2, how great their love would have grown; 3, their joy and mature death; 4, honorable public service.

There is much truth in the last verse of LXXXI. Death idealizes friendship, leaving it unsoiled, nor mingled with drossness. Death broke a happy friendship, yet

"This haunting whisper makes me faint,
More years had made me love thee more.

But Death returns an answer sweet:
My sudden frost was sudden gain,
And gave all ripeness to the grain;
It might have drawn from riper heat."

Then XCVI. deals with doubt, and how Hallam surmounted it. Of doubt, he says:

"There lives more faith in honest doubt,
Believe me than in half the creeds."

But, be it remembered, this is said only of honest doubt, not of that doubt which is due to an indifference to truth, and which is most dishonest. Of Hallam he says, "He fought his doubts and gathered strength * * * Thus he came at length to find a stronger faith his own."

The following poems of the group describe a noble man; his influence on others; the outward graces of the man; the qualities of his mind.

Then follows a contemplation of knowledge. He regards it from two aspects, as tending to the elevation of nature, and as a power. Through the knowledge God communicates to us we know Him, and are elevated; by it we act, and it is power.

"Who loves not knowledge? Who shall rail
Against her beauty?   May she mix
With men, and prosper! Who shall fix
Her pillars? Let her work prevail."

While the Christmas games in LXXVIII. are a little sad by "the quiet sense of something lost," they do not possess the hollowness they did in XXX. A realization that past and present love can abide side by side, and that past and present exist in harmony is evident. LXXXVI. returns to the what might have been, but the next Cantos depict the future, and this is good. The past, underlying the present and future, is filled with beautiful and tender memories.

We see now that the poet has made his grief a permanent influence, not a temporary overwhelming force.

From a poetic standpoint XCV. is perhaps the most beautiful canto of the poem, presenting an exquisite picture of daybreak. This canto also shows that the poet's mind is now permanently normal and healthy: still his dead friend is a great factor in his life.

"So word by word, and line by line,
The dead man touched me from the past."

Cantos XCIX. to CVII. deal with time and circumstances, depicting another anniversary of death, a change of home, a Christmas, a new year and a birthday of Hallam, the whole seeming to indicate a new era of life.

"In Memoriam" is a poem of love, in the first part it is love as grief and regret, then love as hope and joy. It adheres very closely to events and places referred to therein,—of course the reference is exceptionally tender and idealized. The lines beginning, "When on my bed the moonlight falls" are a beautiful allusion to the spot where Hallam is buried. As he leaves the church and looks out over the sea, he realizes the beauty of the scene and says,

' Sweeter seems
To rest beneath the clover sod
　That takes the sunshine and the rain,
　Or where the kneeling hamlet drains,
The chalice of the grapes of God.''

That sad tender little poem "Break, break, break," is said to have been written on such an occasion, and the lines, "But O for the touch of a vanished hand, And the sound of a voice that is still" undoubtedly refer to Hallam.

While we must admit that at times the philosophic truth of the poem is vague and misleading, still the grand nobility of the sincere sorrow and real grief which Tennyson undoubtedly felt and its magnificent expression in this outpouring of the beliefs of his heart in the grandest lyric of grief in our language, surely forces the most skeptical to acknowledge that is not a question of "Tennyson and Art" but "Tennyson and Soul." A classic on the love of immortality and the immortality of love.

LEO J. ATTERIDGE, Post-Grad.

Perhaps some would sigh
At the estrangement of fate;
Or try
To await
The turn of tide-like time;
But not I!
I hate
Those who attempt to climb
High above
An honest friend's love.

A. B. D:, '08

THE CRUCIAL TEST

"Why, that pretty little house on the hill is closed up! You don't know? Where have you been? I'll tell you the story; Lord sir, I know it too well and it has been the sorest spot in my life sir, although I did what I thought was right.

When Mr. John Fleming married Miss Dorothy Welton they were the finest couple ever tied by a clergyman. He was a big strong, fine-looking fellow, and she—well sir, I never was extra at describing, but when I say she was the prettiest girl I ever saw, why you know what that means. He had a fine job in the Eastern National Bank at the city, and taking it all in all they had very fine prospects. Then her father built the house out here for them, and as John told me one day, 'life is just beginning.' Lord, they were the most loving pair you ever set eyes on, and I tell you I used to like to see them together in their little home. A dull old fellow like me never had any thought before that two people could get so much pleasure from each other's company. I was around there a whole lot—used to bring things up from the store and the like. They were very sociable and many's the night when I've run up in the cold with a letter or a parcel from the city I was invited in to 'have a cup of tea and stay awhile.'

Well, this particular night it was blowing great guns and the rain was falling in torrents. Jack Anderson (he's the store man) and I were sitting in the back room by a cosy fire smoking our pipes, when in comes Walker, the station agent. "Say Sam,' says he to me, 'there's a telegram for Fleming; will you take it to him? I'd go myself but I can't leave the station." I didn't like the weather much but then I thought the message might be important. I got Walker's horse and made the journey safely. Mrs. Fleming came to the door. 'Telegram for Mr. Fleming, ma'am.' They were just having dinner—Mr. and Mrs. Fleming and her father who was visiting them. "Who's that—Sam? Come in, Sam, have a cup of tea, it will warm you up; horribly cold out there!" said Fleming. I came in, sat down by the fire and Mrs. Fleming got the tea for me. "The deuce! this is from Miller down at the junction—he leaves for California in the morning and wants to see me about that insurance. I'll have to leave immediately—and I won't be able to get back tonight either; last train's at 9.36, isn't it Sam?' 'Yes sir,' says I.

"Well, little girl, I hate to leave you but I must. Sam here will stay with you. And say, Sam,' says he kind of low, 'I've got quite a big wad of money in my little safe over there. You know we are enlarging our vaults at the bank, so we send all our money to the Clearing House over night. But today a lot of greenbacks came from that corporation over there on the Brooklyn side—you know the one I mean—Frank Halston your old manager's interested in it; well, as luck would have it, the money came in after we had sent the rest of the load to the House. So the cashier told me to take care of it, bring it here in the country; no one would ever know I had it, he said. So it's over there in the safe. Of course there is no danger of any one trying to steal it, but I thought I would let you know for safety's sake. So now I want you to bunk here tonight. Well, good-night little girl—see you in the morning." He kissed her and was gone.

Mrs. Fleming didn't seem to get over the fright of the telegram. After a little said good-night and retired to her room.

Mr. Welton, her father, saw what was the matter and told me about it. "She is very much afraid of telegrams,' he said, 'and always expects to hear of some death or accident in them; I don't blame her; don't like the sight of them myself."

We talked crops and politics for an hour or so, and then went off to bed. My room was a cosy little apartment partitioned off in the attic, and Mr. Welton slept in the spare room on the second floor. I don't know why, but somehow I couldn't get to sleep and laid in bed for some time, thinking; but I at last got drowsy and was just about to drop off when all of a sudden the door bell rang. I jumped out of bed and got to the hall just as Mrs. Fleming turned a switch at the top of the stairs which lit a light on the porch. The door was one of those fancy fussy kind with a glass panel in it. I tell you I was scared most to death when I looked through that glass—there on the porch were three or four men all masked. It didn't take me

long to think of what they were after—there was money in the house. I had just about time enough to get this through my head when the bell rang again. Mrs. Fleming turned out the light. "They are after the money, Sam; O! help me to keep it from them; O yes! the pistol John and I used on our trip—I'll get it."

She soon returned and gave the weapon to me. "Shoot the first man who enters," she said. The bell rang again and as we did not answer they broke the glass and came in. One of them struts up and says: "You have some money in the house, madam; if you give it to us we will not molest you." Mrs. Fleming said she could not give it to them without orders from her husband. 'I'm very sorry that force is necessary,' said the leader in a hollow voice and started up the stairs. Lord, I was scared, sir! I felt almost like running, but I saw Mrs. Fleming standing near me, and her grit made me ashamed to turn tail. I aimed the pistol at the man on the stairs, and fired. Mrs. Fleming screamed and the man kind of staggered for a minute, grabbed at the banister, and fell. The rest of them ran out. I turned on the light and started down stairs, but one look at Mrs. Fleming stopped me for a moment. She had fallen from weakness and fear, and was sitting on the stairs shaking like a leaf. She kept gazing at the black hump at the bottom with a look in her eyes that scared me. I shouted to her father to help her up, and then ran down to drag the body out of the hall. I pulled the man up so that his head rested on my arm, and then took off the mask.

My God! it was Mr. Fleming. The screams of Mrs. Fleming were something terrible and the look in her eyes drove the blood to my heart. I don't know what I did then—when I woke up they were all trying to comfort me and kept saying it wasn't my fault.

It killed Mrs. Fleming; she died a few weeks later. I got cleared; here's a piece from the paper about it. I carry it it in this envelope about me.

I took the paper and read: "The last scene in the Fleming robbery case was enacted last evening when Mrs. Fleming, the young bride of the would-be robber, died at 9.30 o'clock. She never regained consciousness since the terrible moment when she recognized her dead husband. Mr. Hampton, cashier of the Eastern National, has been severely censured by the directors for allowing such a large sum of money to be so carelessly disposed of. This has been one of the most remarkable cases in the history of crime, and had Fleming's plan not been frustrated by his wife, he would probably never have been detected. Fleming was considered the most trustworthy man in the employ of the Eastern National but, like many another, failed when the crucial test came."

MERVYN S. SHAFER, '09.

AUTUMN LEAVES

The leaves are failing with the year,
From day to day they grow more sere,
All parched is their vital sap
And turned to rust their glossy nap:
—My heart is dry, my hair is gray.

The leaves have lost their winning sheen,
No more they soothe with restful green,
Gone is their outline's oval grace,
Hard wrinkled folds have ta'en their place·
—My form is bent, my powers decay.

The leaves their wonted shade refuse,—
Farewell, my walk, thy dappled hues!
The frost has cut life's fragile thread,
And all around the leaves lie dead.
—I, useless, soon must pass as they.

A CHANGE OF MIND

Just at dusk a lone horseman crossed the ridge and entered the forest. The light faded rapidly and before he had traveled a mile it was pitch-dark. He rode easily in his saddle, the weight of his body thrown on his right leg, and his left hand resting on a roll of blankets tied to the back of the saddle.

The horse, a sturdy mountain pony, knowingly picked his way over the half obliterated trail which was coveren with leaves and pine needles. His owner urged him on and kept saying, "By to-morrow noon, old boy, we'll be in Sonora; you'll get your barley, and I—why I'll get the good time I've promised myself ever since we struck pay dirt." The horse would whinny as if in answer and stepped forward a little faster.

About nine o'clock they came to a clearing on which stood a log cabin, and as they were very tired the man thought that they might be able to spend the night there.

No light being visible, he hailed the occupants of the cabin, but as he received no reply, he dismounted and rapped smartly on the door. All was silent, so he tried to push it open. There seemed to be something holding it, and he stoop-ed and reached behind the door to re-move the obstruction. As he did so his hand rested on—the face of a dead man! "O God!" he cried, at the cold clammy touch, and starting back in fright he sprang upon his horse and spurred the faithful animal on until the cabin was left far behind.

That night-ride was one of terror; every bush concealed a lurking spectre in its mysterious shadow; every rustle of the leaves or crackle of dry branches under the horse's hoof was the footstep of some uncanny, unearthly pursuer; every moan of the wind, every cry of some belated night-bird was an ominous warning that brought the cold perspiration to his brow; even the stars themselves caught the enchantment and turned to "funeral lamps." But at last the stars disappeared one by one, the sun sent his heralding rays over the eastern hills, and our wayfarer found himself on the outskirts of Sonora.

"Well, thanks be to Heaven! here we are at last," cried he. "Now, old Boy, you'll get your fill of barley, and I— well hang it, I don't feel like a good time just now!"

HAROLD R. YOACHAM, 1ST ACAD.

The Redwood.

PUBLISHED MONTHLY BY THE STUDENTS OF THE SANTA CLARA COLLEGE

The object of the Redwood is to record our College Doings, to give proof of College Industry and to knit closer together the hearts of the Boys of the Present and of the Past.

EDITORIAL STAFF

EXECUTIVE BOARD

JAMES F. TWOHY, '07
President

J. DANIEL MCKAY, '07   HARRY A. MCKENZIE, '08

ASSOCIATE EDITORS

COLLEGE NOTES   -   -   -   -   -   IVO G. BOGAN, '08
IN THE LIBRARY   -   -   -   ROBERT J. O'CONNOR, '08
EXCHANGES   -   -   -   ANTHONY B. DIEPENBROCK, '08
ALUMNI   -   -   -   -   -   MERVYN S. SHAFER, '09
ATHLETICS   -   -   -   -   HARRY A. MCKENZIE, '08

BUSINESS MANAGER

J. DANIEL MCKAY, '07

ASSISTANTS

FRANCIS M. HEFFERNAN, '08   REIS J. RYLAND, '09

M. T. DOOLING, 09

Address all communications to THE REDWOOD, Santa Clara College, California

Terms of subscription, $1.50 a year; single copies, 15 cents

EDITORIAL COMMENT

· The unconventional editors of the College Notes and Alumni departments, have risen to such a state of subordination and disrespect of authority that we other poor department writers have to curtail our articles this month in order to give them elbow room in these pages to flourish the quill. However, in past months, we have dinned so relentlessly in their long-suffering ears the cry for "more copy," and we have applied at times such stringent pressure to obtain said copy, that it would almost seem inconsistent to blue-pencil their work now.

Somebody—not a physicist we swear—has said that "the expansion of steam varies directly as the pressure." Hence if we are responsible for the pressure we are directly responsible for the expansion too. Therefore we humbly take up that famous editorial pencil and draw a long blue diagonal over a couple of our own pages, and to the cry from our contemporaries for "more room, more room," we meekly say, "Amen, so be it."

———

As the magnet of Time is slowly drawing the spring months into its field of force, the forecasters of athletic endeavor are beginning to turn their eyes on the future. And truth to tell it is with no little eagerness that we all await the return of baseball and watch the intumescent football developments. For football has ever been the firmest prop of college spirit in the fall semester, and when this prop is ruthlessly torn away, even the artificial excitement of mock elections and boxing tournaments can hardly bear the brunt of support. And so now that three fall months have flitted by into the shadowy Past, and we are entering on the beginning of the end, we turn with eagerness to the eastern horizon and cry with the poet: "Ring in the new!"

———

With the approach of the St. Mary's series, the spirit that piloted our team to a magnificent victory last April, is stirring in its sleep and showing signs of re-awakening. And already we are beginning to hear premature whisperings of what is destined to be the great question in this 1907 series—what is to be the policy of St. Mary's and Santa Clara in the struggle for baseball supremacy? Are they going to sacrifice their sense of right and their respective reputations for clean athletics? In other and plain words are they, on account of the great evil of American colleges—the fear of defeat, going to suffer a self-imposed mark of semi-professionalism to be branded on their foreheads? Straight talk, yes, but the occasion demands straight talk. We are facing what is almost a crisis. Intercollegiate competition between the Oakland college and us is yet in its infancy, and the baseball managements of the two institutions are establishing the precedents, moulding the standards, by which future competition is to be judged. Therefore those in charge should beware lest the smoke of the present day battle blind their foresight. They are the precursors of innumerable future athletic generations, and the hands that blaze the way must be steady and true. We think that the Santa Clara management should take a firm, unyielding and unequivocal stand in this matter, and should not allow their judgments to be chloroformed A fair defeat is inestimably preferable to a triumph that may be questioned. It would be desecration indeed to weigh in the same balance an untarnished reputation for clean honorable sport, and a thousand victories. Let us all stand together on this question. We want badly to win, but we do not want to win badly. Our reputation for clean athletics may be considered as rightfully ours—our birthright. Are we going to sacrifice this right for a victory of a day, barter this birthright, like Esau of old, for a mess of pottage?

Two of our distinguished contemporaries in this state, the Sequoia and the Occident, following the big athletic meet of their respective institutions, are hurling epithets and charges of ungentlemanly and unsportsmanlike conduct at each other, and are deep in the non-uplifting occupation of mud-slinging. All of which vividly recalls to our minds, by contrast, the manly and eminently sportsmanlike treatment afforded us after our April contest, by our honorable opponents of Oakland.

Well, here is hoary old December at last; the dreariest month in the cycle of the seasons, and yet because of one anniversary in it, the brightest of them all for the sons of men. It is the last month on the calendar, the first in the story of man's redemption; the one month that was not silver in the rosary of time, and yet the one that has been turned to gold by one touch of the King. And all the world, from east to west, from the sun-kissed south to the snow-sheathed north, is awaiting the day appointed for the coming of the Guest. Let every man smooth out the path to his heart, that thorns may not cut the sacred feet of the Visitor.

JAMES F. TWOHY, '07.

Senate

The past month has been most uneventful for the Senators. With the Trusts away on a vacation, Teddie R. doing nothing more extraordinary than running down to Panama with his big stick, and with no election frauds worth mentioning, even the most enthusiastic man-with-the-rake could find little to occupy his attention. At last the Senate turned to the much abused but ever present negro, and Senator Donlon presented a bill whose substance was in brief: "That the lynching of negroes in the South is, under certain circumstances, justifiable." Senator Donlon opened for the affirmative and with a flood of impassioned oratory held his audience spellbound. At the close of his arguments, and almost before the echoes of his silvery tones had died away, Senator Casey of Sacramento arose and with solemn manner, as befitted the weighty subject, be discussed the question from an ethical standpoint, at the same time refuting many of his opponent's pet arguments. He yielded the floor to Senator Atteridge who spoke in favor of the bill, following up his col-league's line of argument. But it was Senator Budde of San Jose who exhibited the greatest display of oratorical fireworks, and it was not until several minutes had elapsed after his last sky rocket that Senator Brown, he from Napa, could summon courage to address the Senate in favor of the resolution. Senator Aguirre followed for the negative, and it was all over but the shouting. The bill failed to pass the Senate by a small majority. Another well worn question, but valuable for filling in gaps in emergencies, was the old, old resolution that the confinement at Santa Clara is too strict. It passed to the Senate from the House where it had met with a favorable reception, but it was laid to rest when it came up for discussion before the upper branch of Congress.

Negotiations for the intercollegiate debate with St. Mary's College are still under way, but unfortunately it seems that the debate cannot conveniently be held before the coming session; it is therefore too early to begin to figure out possibilities, but watch our columns later for news of the contestants.

OUR RECENT POLITICAL CONTEST

Now, dear old alumnus of Santa Clara, do not wipe your glasses and stare with renewed vigor at the above tell-tale headline. It is a fact, and we might as well confess our guilt at once—the venerable old Mission College has gone, and gone irrevocably, into the slippery, muddy, arena of politics. There is no use in getting scandalized over it as we intend to continue in our downward career; and there is no use in wringing your hands and lamenting the good old times when graft and boodling and double-tongued diplomacy and all those unmentionably numerous and edifying practices that our aspiring custodians of law and order resort to, were kept at bay without the College gates. All this has been changed in the tide of modern ideas, and during the past month the hallowed walls have re-echoed the cannonading of up-to-date electioneering warfare, and the air has been murky and sulphurous with charges and counter-charges and hissing red-hot denunciations and declamations that must have awakened the ghost of the old Spanish Major-domo and would have induced him to sally forth to check the unheard-of proceedings, had not the late improvements prevented him from recognizing his ancient haunts.

Yes! we have had an election with all its accompanying circumstances. While the portion of California situate outside the College pickets was in a buzz of excitement over the gubernatorial and other candidacies, we had our own private troupe of office-seekers, who played their mimic parts with an ability and a spirit that made us forget at times that our little college world was only a stage, and the greedy-eyed claimants for our suffrages merely players. But let us begin *ab ovo*, as our friend Horace used to say when when we were merely Sophomores.

The idea of a mock campaign and election among the students first sprang into being in no other soil than the fertile brain of our quondam friend and fellow-student, William G. Hayes. "Ric" was a genius in his way; he had a great penchant for playing the carpenter, and the cute little shelves he contrived to build into his washroom locker, for instance, were a marvel. In fact, he was a sort of two-legged beaver, never happy except when his faculties were absorbed in an accretion of some kind. Not many, however, knew that this scheming brain ever exerted its ingenuity on anything more plastic than wood, but it did. The "spirit of the yard" and the entire well-being of his fellow-students were subjects of long and anxious meditation to Willie, and an election with all its paraphernalia of parties and conventions and candidates and stump speaking and canvassing rose up before his rapt spirit as the ideal nostrum for the ennui that must seize upon the liveliest aggregation of fellows during those inevitable spells when there is "nothing doing." But alas! before the idea could cast off the slough of airy nothingness and appear in material shape, its author and owner left for parts unknown. Fortunately, however, he had generously abstained from a patent on his property, and an unpatented idea never dies—Providence transplants the mental seed into some happier soil, and thus we find Aristotle with his Plato; Johnson, his Boswell; Hayes, his Atteridge. Yes, Leo it was who nurtured the grand idea and who thus deserves most of the credit for its ultimate realization.

On the night of Oct. 31st, at 7:45 o'clock, the First Division transferred itself bodily from the study room to the Exhibition Hall. There it broke up into three parties of equal numerical strength—the Democrats, the Republicans, and Union Labor. Each party was given half an hour for its convention, during which time the two others were to be morally absent from the scene. The Democrats were the first on the floor. Caverly filled the chairman's position with much ability and his intentionally pedantic mode of speech was much relished. The secretary was R. McClatchy. H. McKenzie was nominated for Governor by L. Atteridge in the latter's well-known graceful manner. Atteridge in turn was nominated for Lieut-Governor by McKenzie, who pronounced him capable of "filling the office to overflowing." Heffernan got the nomination for Attorney-General, McKay for Sup't of Public Instruction, and Collins for Sheriff. All the nominees responded to the cries of "speech, speech" in a way

to do themselves credit. The "grateful" platitudes usual on such occasions were gratefully lacking; each one had something good to say, said it, and sat down. And the same can be said of the other candidates.

Then the Republicans pulled themselves together, and placed Aguirre in the chair, with M. Shafer as his right-hand man. August made an enjoyable address, at the end of which, after having let fly some good-natured shots at the now somewhat turbulent and hypercritical Democrats, he suggested that a Sergeant-at-Arms be appointed to keep them in order. This was done and Robert Browne had occasion more than once to look daggers at the noisy Dems. —but all in vain. In this convention, Fitzgerald in a speech to be expected from so brilliant a student, nominated J. Twohy for Governor. Twohy repaid the compliment by nominating the former for Lieut-Governor. His speech was marked by its serious tone; it was evident that he meant business and that this was no matter for trifling. The remarkable earnestness which characterized the entire campaign seems to us if not to date from that speech at least to have received a strong impetus therefrom. H. Broderick was elected nominee for Attorney-General; L. Murphy for Sup't of Public Instruction, and Aguirre for Sheriff.

Shortly after 9 o'clock, the Union Labor Party marshalled its forces, and put the redoubtable T. Donlon in the chair, with the facetious Casey at his elbow. The nominee for Governor was

Joseph Brown, who responded to the calls upon him in an impassioned speech. He was the first to outline his policy in any definite way, the other parties having contented themselves for the time being with "glittering generalities," with promises of detailed information later on. Brown laid down as some of the planks of his platform, more holidays on the calendar, more cake on the menu card, less enclosure in the yard, American labor in the kitchen. Each plank as it was announced was, needless to say, greeted with uproarious applause. Although space forbids any account of all the speeches made, it would be unfair not to mention that of Donlon, nominating Brown for Governor. It was strong, sarcastic, a trifle truculent, and lit up with some humorous touches, one of which was the demand for another Sergeant-at-Arms to keep not only the Dems. but also the equally audacious Reps. in order. Reginald Archbold was the man with the truncheon. The nominees for Lieut-Governor, Attorney-General, Sup't of Public Instruction, and Sheriff, were Schmitz, Gallagher, Donlon and Farrell. The meeting was over at about 10 o'clock, and the nominees experienced that night the uneasy couch that waits on greatness.

Next morning nothing was heard in the yard but the political situation. Joe Brown's star was in the ascendant: his tangible principles, already typewritten and on the bulletin boards, with their special appeal to the small boy's stomach, solidified him with the whole yard

immediately. In the course of the day, posters done up in our best penman's most florid style, began to occupy the coigns of vantage. Then election cards, "Vote for Twohy," done into big print in our own long unused printing-office, were put into circulation. Green with envy, the other parties betook themselves with hasty feet to the nearest up-to date printing works and there got their names into fancy type with all the modern embellishments. Progress succeeded progress in this line until at last McKay got out neat pink and white creations with his picture smiling at the voter from the left hand corner. It was impossible to go one better than this, and the other nominees gave up in despair. One of these in a subsequent speech had almost persuaded us that his party had no need and therefore no desire of making themselves known by their photos, until we suddenly recollected a story about a fox and sour grapes we had read in our youth.

In addition to these personal cards, large posters were printed in regular election fashion and were affixed to the most prominent features of this venerable institution. One of the cards that struck us as very clever, and very significant of the feeling of the parties towards each other, read as follows—

REPUBLICAN PARTY
DEMOCRATIC PARTY
Union Labor

But this was merely a fraction of the advertising ability displayed. Every few hours, some hitherto inaccessible spot in gable or tower or electric post burst into a blaze of color as some hardy sectarian affixed thereto an area of sheeting or cheese-cloth prismatic with the names and the unparalled attributes of his party.

As already hinted, there was, at least in the beginning, a certain mutual sympathy between the Democratic and Republican parties as against Union Labor. Indeed, on Friday morning after breakfast, they had a joint meeting on the handball alley, when all their nominees paid glowing tributes to their own parties and to the 2nd Division, and warned the community against Brown and his accomplices. As the vote of the 2nd Division was not pledged to any party, it was of course the objective point of all the eloquence so profusely expended. Marvelous were the virtues those orators did discover in that 2nd Division: a more manly, upright, patriotic, independent, intelligent, capable, not-to-be-led-by-the-nose-able body of voters none of them had ever seen before. Against such a bulwark of good qualities the machinations of the man from Napa would fall in vain. Fitzgerald was the last to speak. His address was one of the most rattling of the whole campaign, and he had the audience "literally hanging on his lips" as he exposed the perfidious policy of Joe Brown, and the unveiled friendship he had always shown towards the foreign domestics in the kitchen, when suddenly the tall form of that well abused individual appeared, with his suite, at the entrance to the yard. With one lordly sweep of his hand he beckoned the crowd to him, and, all at once, off they rushed helter-skelter, the whole 2nd Division and most of the 1st, leaving the Republican orator to expend his pathos upon the unfeeling cement and a few non-conformists. This was one of the most comical incidents of the election. Fitzgerald finished his speech to the bitter dregs and it is only fair to say that for wit and acumen it was excelled by no effort of the campaign.

Things went on in this way for two days with the Napaen star still eclipsing the others. Harangue after harangue were made in season and out of season by the nominees, who often sacrificed their after-meal smoke in order to buttonhole the *hoi polloi* when these were most likely to stomach anything—(no slur intended on the refectory).

On Saturday night, after early study, the Union Labor Party completely outdid its opponents by giving a phonographic *soiree* to the 2nd Division in the Hall. Of course, between the selections, which were so chosen as to put the audience into the fitting disposition, the nominees got in their little speeches.

On Sunday morning, the U. L. Party followed up its advantage by giving phonographic recitals here and there in the yard where the boys most did congregate. Things were going all their way, sure enough, and going swimmingly too, until 4 p. m. had struck and—

Heavens! What is this? What motley monstrosity is this rushing towards us through the open gates of the back yard? "Chug! chug, chug! toot, toot,

toot!" the piebald equipage gains upon us and turns out to be—Donovan's black automobile ! ! decorated with Democratic emblems on the outside, and with Democratic nominees on the inside! Round and round the yard it birred, and tooted, and snorted, with a mob of delighted youngsters in hot pursuit, until finally when it had attracted the whole college around it, when the players had quit their game, the student had dropped his book, and the scientist had forsaken his laboratory, it came to a halt before the bleachers. Down goes the cover in a twinkling, and lo ! the grave but smiling McKenzie and his confreres are up and bowing right and left and all around to the applause of the tickled and admiring throng.

Never did orarors have a more kindly disposed audience, and never did orators take more advantage of their opportunity. Atteridge was in his best form, and that is saying a great deal. He informed the boys that they had just finished an extended tour of the South, and that it had all declared for the Democrats. Luke Feeney has just telegraphed that the Gilroy vote was solid. Then Heffernan, McKay, and Collins addressed the bleachers. All were at their best, the ride through the bracing air having put them in fine fettle, and they made a very clear-cut impression on the 2nd Division. This was Collins' first appearance. He made a 'hit'—Joe's baseball tricks still clung to him—by his humorous rebuttal of the U. L.'s charge that he was a "gas pipe thug." McKenzie's speech was a masterpiece; it was

witty, good-natured, full of strong common sense, and very sincere. We are of the opinion that it was this last quality that won him the Governorship, and if so it is but another exemplifiication of the truth of Newman's advice to the orator—In the first place, be sincere; in the second place, be sincere; in the third place, be sincere. Not that we felt for a moment that the other candidates were not sincere—far from it; but in McKenzie it was so very palpable. And his good-natured humor only made it the more effective. It was then that he for the first time announced his platform, and as it was the one that "won out" we give it in full.

I. Monthly meetings of student-body, with elected delegates from 2nd Division. II. An informal gathering of the students and private entertainment once a month. III. A billiard and pool tournament twice a year. IV. An aquatic carnival and swimming tournament in college natatorium. V. A monthly boxing tournament. VI. A general invitation to the students to hear once a month the debates. VII. Support by college rooters of 2nd Division in all games with outsiders. VIII. Basket-ball in 2nd Division. IX. Petition for dismissal at X-mas two days earlier than date set. X. Band concert once a month.

The platform, as any one can see, deserves much praise. It is eminently a working platform, and meant as such, and its advent marked the wane of Union Labor. This occasion also marked the complete separation of the Democrats from the Republicans, and the formation of the former into a definite, individual, and attractive idea to the voters.

The speeches over, the top was again raised over the auto, and the bunting, etc., arranged, and then with condescending bows in all directions to the "common-people," the candidates whirred and chugged majestically out of sight. It was the first automobile ever in the yard.

Next evening, after class, we were again startled by a sudden automobile, this time a monstrous big fellow conveying the hopes of the Republicans. If they borrowed the idea of the auto from the Democrats, they were original in being 'togged out' in enormous plug hats, purloined, we fear, from the stage property-room. Their speeches were very good, but it must be confessed—and we hope no offense will be taken—that the visitation was not a great success. The auto had lost its novelty, and besides, it being after a long day of class, the boys were tired mentally and anxious to play. But the Republicans overtopped and outmanœvered their rivals in another way. It had been arranged, more or less, that the three nominees for Governor should petition Fr. Rector for an extra half-holiday. Three of the Republican candidates, knowing that "all is fair in war," elected themselves a committee, hurried off to Fr. Rector, who with a due appreciation of their ruse, promptly granted it.

That night of the 5th saw the great, final, summing-up rally of the three parties prior to the election of the following day. At 7.45 o'clock, the match was set to a bonfire the equal of which Santa Clara had never seen before, and soon the leaping flames changed night into day far and wide for many a rood around. After having basked to their hearts' content in its cheerful blaze, we all obeyed the call to the band-stand where we were to be treated to an illumination of a different order, and a display of other pyrotechnics by our politicians.

The Republicans took the stand at 8 o'clock, to be followed at 8.30 by the Democrats, who in turn gave place to Union Labor at 9 o'clock. It would be a tedious and invidious task to attempt to give any detailed account of individual speeches. They were all good, and some of them were efforts that many a time-beaten public speaker might be proud to equal. Again and again we heard members of the faculty express their astonishment and admiration. We heard also the opinions of perhaps more impartial judges on the matter, of educators and public men from outside who had requested permission to attend the rally, and whose estimate of the speeches was that they were worthy of the House of Representatives. No better proof of this need be given than that the whole crowd remained attentive to the last minute of the hour and a half occupied by the congress, and even the small boy's tired eyelids refused to close over eyes that were twinkling big and bright with interest and huge satisfaction. The utmost good feeling prevailed throughout, with just a little friction, or a "hotbox" now and then, arising from honest partisan warmth, but resulting in nothing serious. Who could blame Heffernan, for instance, for getting somewhat indignant when, just as he was about to clinch an eloquent argument by reading from some document or other, and had held up the paper for that purpose, all at once the lights went out! Some graceless urchin of Undemocratic persuasions had got at the switch. The orator was tempted to launch forth into a philippic but nobly stemmed his wrath and stopped short, just as the lights returned.

Tuesday, Nov. 6th—Election Day—dawned at last. The sun arose bright and early o'er the purple eastern hills, and his round face smiled away every speck of cloud from the sky. Evidently the old fellow wanted nothing to stand in his way or obscure his vision of the great events that were to transpire before he should seek his foamy couch in the western wave. Inspired by his example, the politicians bestirred themselves betimes, and they and their emissaries went around seeking whom they might devour and assimilate into their own party. How they did spot out their victims! What unstinted praise they lavished upon them if they were of the orthodox party! With what disinterested zeal they sought to enlighten their ignorant and besotted minds if they were not! With what convincing logic they proved themselves to be paragons—if they did say it—of all the virtues, and their opponents mere tissues of sophistical fiddle-faddle! What smiles when their efforts succeeded! What flashes of well-merited scorn when they did not! But all things come to an end. At 11.30 a. m., the box containing the votes—which, by the way, were registered on duly printed forms—was smashed in with a baseball bat—no time to wait for a hatchet—and amid solemn silence and a coterie of witnesses and tally-keepers, the Vice President began reading out the votes. The excitement was intense but suppressed. Many of the boys wrote down the votes as they were read; others made devout guesses as to the final result. At last it was over; the battle was won and lost; McKenzie and his colleagues stood radiant with the halo of a student-people's confidence on their heads; with the heavy purple mantle of honor and responsibility on their shoulders. "And his colleagues"—not all. Aguirre, the end man of the Republican party, broke through the opponents' line and secured his goal.

The defeated candidates were also successful. They succeeded in improving and developing their debating abilities; they succeeded in carrying on the contest in a manly, business-like way; and they succeeded in making our first real College campaign a grand success.

Band Concert

Gov. McKenzie's first act was to follow out an important plank in his platform. On the evening of Nov. 9th, a band concert was announced. We all went to the new social hall and found a very nice entertainment awaiting us.

Prof. Morris and the excellent Sodality band sat in the rear of the hall with their instruments tuned and waiting the word to pour forth the ever welcome waltzes and twosteps. August Aguirre, our newly elected Sheriff, first favored us with a few well written and well sung parodies and, as usual, made a big hit. Next our youthful comedians, Paul Troplong and George Mayerle, came out well besmeared with burned cork and gave us a very much enjoyed negro dialogue, interspersed with songs of Troplong's own manufacture. Then followed speeches from the newly-elected officers. Heffernan promised us that Joseph Abe R. Brown would soon be lining the inside of a cell at Folsom for his recent political misdemeanors. Aguirre warned all evildoers to beware his 'billy' and his vengeance. McKay gave us the lugubrious information that his plank of co-education was sent adrift. Atteridge had nothing special to say, but said it especially well. McKenzie rounded off the speeches. He told us that he intended to stand by all his promises, and asked for the co-operation of all parties for this purpose. He paid a generous tribute to his defeated rivals, and gave the credit of his victory to his colleagues and to his platform.

After this the meeting broke up into "most admired disorder," the benches slid as by magic to the sides of the hall, and the music and the waltzing began. A grand march and a cake walk were some of the features. Altogether it was an enjoyable evening, and we offer our sincere congratulations to McKenzie.

Mr. James' Lectures

On Nov. 20th, we were given the first of a series of three illustrated lectures by Mr. George Wharton James. The subject of it was The Grand Canyon of Arizona. We enjoyed it greatly, for it was a veritable masterpiece, but lack of space forces us to postpone our account of it.

Sanctuary "House-Warming," Junior Dramatics, and many other items have to be deferred until the Xmas number.

Mr. E. Griffith '98, who has been secretary of the San Jose Police and Fire Department Board for over two years, has resigned that office to enter the real estate business.

Ever popular Harry Wolters, ex-'09, fresh from baseball triumphs in the Pacific Coast League, dropped in on us a few days ago. Harry attended the grand finale of our political campaign and the cheers that were given him threatened to break the meeting up. He was called upon for a speech and with a few well chosen words told the fellows how glad he was to get back, and what was best of all that he is thinking of staying permanently with us. Harry has been drafted to the Cincinatti club of the National League.

Frank Farry '01 was one of the prodigal sons of last week. "Fran" has a splendid position in the American Milling Company.

Mr. Charles D. South, Ph. D. '01 has written a retrospect of College happenings which will surely interest all the students of the early eighties and recall to their minds many of the well-beloved professors and students of days gone by. I will not attempt to praise it—it speaks for itself and is written in Mr. South's usual inimitable style.

A Retrospective Glance

I. OLD SCHOOLS

As the life of any individual is, to a great extent, a recapitulation of the life of the race, so, on the old theory, "Ab uno disce omnes," it may be said that every college year is like every other college year, and that all students, according to age or class, think and act pretty much alike. They face the same requirements, experience the same restraints, enjoy the same liberties, and participate in the same exercises, sports and games.

I cannot separate myself from the idea that the young Greeks who ranged themselves on the benches in the delicious shade of the sycamore grove to hear Plato expound the philosophy of his Academy,—or those Athenian youth who trotted up and down the banks of the River Ilissus with the peripatetic Aristotle, founder of the Lyceum and inventor of the art of logic,—were, as a general rule, very little unlike the collegians who, twenty-four centuries later, are making copious notes of the arguments of Bell, Giaccobbi, Shallo and Ricard, on this, the ultimate shore of a world about which the intellectual heir of Socrates or the teacher of Alexander of Macedon never dreamed.

Imagine with what respectful deference the newly-fledged "junior" of the Lyceum regarded the lofty-browed "senior," burdened with attainments of the mind! Picture the Sophomoric brain-box puffed out partly with Hellenic lore and partly with unwarranted conceit! Then, conceive the sphere-conquering Alumnus, oppressed with the consciousness of his self-importance and prone to frown down upon both Sophomore and Freshman from his insecure pedestal of assumed superiority! It was thus yesterday; it is almost the same today.

We look at ancient times through magnifying glasses, using more powerful instruments for more remote periods; and when we direct our gaze toward the twilight of fable, things look biggest of all. Our modern heroes are all dwarfs alongside of Homer's heroes. Of Achilles, as he approached the ill-fated Nestor, the blind bard sang:

. . . . "Like a god the Greek drew nigh;
His dreadful plumage nodded from on high;
The Pelian javelin, in his better hand,
Shot trembling rays that glittered o'er the land,
And on his breast the beamy splendor shone,—
Like Jove's own lightning o'er the rising sun.".

It is a far call from Homer to Joaquin Miller; but the poet of the Sierras will bring us to our objective in a bound. According to Joaquin, California's era of giants passed with the passing of "the men of '49." He was a mere youth in

"The days of old,
The days of gold,"

And, looking back through a half-century lens, he beholds the sturdy pioneers as they seemed to his boyhood vision—all giants! Let it go at that! they were giants of enterprise and energy! But, here in California, with my quarter-century lens, I am able to discover giants of the 80's, and the particular location of the giants I find, is—Santa Clara College.

II.   THREE GIANTS

Father Joseph Bayma was a giant, intellectually and physically. By his side, big men looked small. To call him an erudite would be inadequate justice.

To the last moment of his life, he sought knowledge as a pleasure and delight. In the realm of philosophy he had few peers; in mathematics, no rival. Of music he studied both the art and the science. On the piano-forte, his playing was characterized by charming expression; and he comprehended all the mechanical details whereby the infinitude of sound-effects is produced. He simplified the formulæ of higher mathematics; was the author of many valuable treatises on geometry and trigonometry, and he found time to contribute learned historical and polemical essays to leading magazines of both English and Latin countries.

During a baseball contest, he was wont to watch intently until a fortunate stroke of the bat propelled the leathern spheroid into the atmosphere. Then his eye followed the course of the ball as it rose and fell. He knew absolutely nothing about the game; but he loved to note how unfailingly the air-cleaving globe described a parabola.

When Joseph Bayma died, it occurred to me that Robert Browning's verses suggested a fitting burial place:

"Here's the top peak; the multitude below
        Live, for they can, there:
This man decided not to Live but Know—
        Bury this man there?
Here,—here's his place, where meteors shoot,
        clouds form,
        Lightnings are loosened,
Stars come and go! Let joy break with the
        storm,
        Peace let the dew send!
Lofty designs must close in like effects:
Loftily lying—still loftier than the world suspects,
        Living and dying."

Another giant was Father Edmund Young—great of mind and body. He was both poet and orator, and his rhetorical lectures were brilliant examples of the excellencies of his teachings. Few men have been so well-loved as he.

With regard to him, I recollect a rather dramatic incident which I may be pardoned for relating. He was the College parliamentarian—president of the Senate—speaker of the House. Once during a session of the Philhistorians, an excited debater, rapped to order for using personalities, accused the chairman of partiality. The words had the effect of a shot. Never before had the speaker been assailed. Father Young sat back as if stunned. He laid down the gavel. His big breast heaved, a sob escaped him, and tears coursed down his cheeks. Recovering his composure somewhat, he rose slowly, and then in a voice full of emotion, said, "In all the time I have spent with you, I have never given cause for this. Night after night I have come here—even when tired and ill—not for my own benefit, but for yours. At last I realize that I am too old—too old! You need a younger, more active man—and so I go from you, always wishing you well!"

With his handkerchief to his eyes, the venerable old man strode through the hall, and out into the night. Then was there commotion in the assembly. The house rose in wrath against the member who had caused the scene, and had not the erring boy made immediate reparation—had he not made humble apology to the good priest—I know not to what punishment his fellow students might have subjected him. Sometimes, when justly roused, the college spirit is not a thing to be trifled with. In response to earnest entreaties, Father Young returned to his old post; but only for a short while. Alas! He was "too old—too old!"

A Titan among the giants was Father Joseph Caredda. He was frequently likened to Napoleon, for he was a born commander, and his eagle-like, steel-grey eyes flashed forth mandates that were as well-understood as if uttered in stentorian voice. For three decades he performed the duties of prefect of classes, and no student of his time ever presumed in his presence, to gainsay his authority. A wave of his hand or a word from his lips was sufficient to still a tumult and bring order out of chaos on the campus. He was a master. The student body entertained for him an unqualified respect. The guilty approached him with fear and trembling; for he seemed able to read minds. He played well on a variety of winged and string instruments, and he led the college orchestra in public concerts, after having trained the musicians in the laws of harmony. For pastime, he made clocks and mended watches. His linguistic acquirements were remarkable. He was a king of wits, and strikingly original. Naturally good-humored, his broad, shining face was seldom without a smile. His memory was prodigious; his influence amazing. No youth who ever came in contact with Father Joseph Caredda will forget the Santa Clara Bonaparte.

III. A BASEBALL RECORD.

Gazing at them over the intervening years, the students of the '80's look to be of larger mould than the student of today. The College has grown and expanded, yet it looked very much bigger then.

A record that, I venture to predict, will be equaled by none of the ball-players of this or any other day, was made in that long-ago by Robert Enright of Lawrence. The College nine was pitted against the representative baseball team of San Francisco. The score in the first half of the ninth inning was a tie—not a run had been tallied. Santa Clara was at the bat, and two men had been retired. It was then that Robert Enright grasped his trusty willow stick and advanced, like a gladiator, to the plate. (The location of the home disc has never been changed.) No matter whether the ball pitched was slow or swift—Enright hit from a gun. It sailed higher and higher, to descend on the junior diamond, bounce into the main hallway, and roll out into the Father's Garden. The College had scored a memorable trsumph, and the event was fittingly celebrated.

President Thomas H. Williams of the California Jockey Club, has changed very little in appearance since we hailed him as the champion college runner in the hundred-yard class. He was six feet and an inch in height, as lean as he was tall, and his legs were so long that he looked as if he might step across the campus. According to the student time-keepers, he covered the stated distance in a fraction less than eleven seconds. Tom graduated from foot-racing into horse-racing, and is today admitted to be one of the most successful race-track magnates in America.

A most agreeable and generous youngster was Peter Martin, now one of the crowned heads of Newport sweldom. He received more express packages than anybody else—boxes of cake, boxes of pie, boxes of candy and nuts, crates of fruit and crates of berries, and jars of jellies and jams. The young heir to millions was not merely the College epicure—he was also a pocket edition of Santa Claus. Outside of class and study hours, he seemed to be forever eating; but he never liked to eat alone, and many a valiant youth defied indigestion to assist Peter in the promotion of gastronomy. Even to-day when I see Peter's name all a-glitter in the social columns of the exclusive weeklies, it makes me think of private lunches between meals in the shadow of the old refectory.

When I registered at the institution, the poet of the College was Henry E. Farmer, who composed graceful verses and recited them effectively. Today Mr. Farmer is Chief Deputy Auditor in the United States Customs Department at San Francisco; but his prosaic and monotonously-mathematical occupation has been fatal to his old-time poetical inclination.

IV. A NOBILI WINNER.

John G. Liebert, now Deputy Auditor of San Francisco, enjoyed an immense popularity in my school-days.

He was the soul of good nature, and even went so far as to shoulder the blame and suffer the penalty for the mischievous acts of his friends. The classics he despised; no kind of study attracted him; and had a prize fallen into his hands by accident he would have swooned. Jack's case seemed hopeless—when suddenly he reformed. It was more than a reformation—it was a metamorphosis! Liebert quit the pranks of the campus; buried himself in his books; studied incessantly, and conducted himself with such perfect decorum as to dumfound his acquaintances. At Commencement, the medals awarded him covered his breast like a shield, and, for premiums, he received books enough to stock a library. To cap the climax, he carried off Santa Clara's most coveted honor—the famous Nobili medal;—for Jack, in deportment and application, had "improved" so much as to throw all competitors into the shade. He is still the same genial, lovable fellow, and everybody calls him familiarly "Jack."

The most noteworthy histrionic exhibition at Santa Clara College, within my recollection, was an elaborate production of *Richard III*, with the talented John T. Malone in the title role, and, after that, the most artistic presentation was that of the classical tragedy of "Ion," in which John A. Waddell, in the heroic name-part, demonstrated that, in all the essentials of good acting, he was the equal of most and the superior of many of the prominent actors who win plaudits on the professional stage.

V. GENERALITIES.

In our time we had no college colors save the American flag! We wore no mortar-boards! In adorning the skull we made a specialty of interior decoration! The old boys were all models, of course, and none of them deemed the root of learning bitter. Their filial affection was manifested in a monthly letter home, containing self-praise, fond wishes and a request for money.

You are tired of this—so am I, but this rambling epistle will soon be ended.

When one of Professor Huxley's pupils described a lobster as "a red fish which moves backwards," the scientist remarked that the description was good but for three things: first, a lobster was not a fish; second, it was not red; and third, it did not move backwards. But the erring pupil was quite as correct as those who intimate that, in a Jesuit institution, a student learns nothing but religion. In the higher sphere of learning, Santa Clara College is acknowledged to be the rival of the western universities.

From Alaska down to Chili—in literature, in science, in law, in medicine, in commercial and mercantile pursuits, in architecture and engineering, in agricultural, horticultural and mining enterprises, in statesmanship, and in the general patriotic endeavor to aid the progress and advancement of the land they live in—prominent in the forefront of the leaders in all these departments of world-work, particularly in the states that border the Pacific sea, are to be found the old and the new graduates of Santa Clara College.

CHAS. D. SOUTH.

Dear "old Santa Clara boys," have you enjoyed your chat with Mr. South —I have.

MERVYN S. SHAFER, '09·

Baseball

The Redwood baseball team, who uphold the honors of the college for the winter, peeled off the bark and came into the lime light for the initial game of the season. We faced Hal Chase of big league fame and his bunch of chasers, on the San Jose diamond. After nine innings of lightning like play the Chasites had the long end of a two to one struggle. It was anybody's game up to the tap of the bell, the marvelous work of Chase on the bases turning the tide of victory toward the San Jose team. Jim Twohy the guardian of the keystone sack played a brilliant game both in the field and at the bat. If he continues to bingle at his present gait the twirlers will give him a wide berth next season. Reliable Joe Collins discarded the cage and played way out in the garden. He came through as usual with his long drive, this time for three stations. Unfortunately Art Shafer picked up a mean one in the second and had to retire to rest a split finger. Watson who filled the vacancy showed up well and should develop into a very classy player. Peters of second division fame slashed out a pretty three bagger and played a nice game throughout. Pudgy Shafer took them in behind the rubber and used the head the entire game. Lappin as usual received the applause for making a seemingly impossible one hand stab of a long drive. Broderick played the first sack in masterly fashion and should make a strong bid for the positton on the 1907 varsity. Captain Kilburn served some puzzlers for four innings and such men as Chase, Brashear and Kent could do nothing with them. Joe Brown mounted the slab and pitched good ball for the remainder of the game. He had speed, good control and plenty of curves but no baseball luck. We captured six hits, San Jose five. Too much Chase on the sacks won the game. For San Jose Kent, Brashear, Freine and Chase get the lion's share. Here is the way it all happened—

REDWOODS

	AB	R	BH	SB	PO	A	E
Peters, 3b	3	1	1	0	1	0	1
Shafer, M., c....	4	0	1	0	0	1	0
Collins, rf	4	0	1	0	1	0	1
Shafer, A., ss ..	2	0	0	0	0	0	0
Broderick, 1b....	4	0	0	0	6	2	1
Lappin, lf	4	0	0	0	1	0	0
Twohy, 2b.......	3	0	2	0	4	4	0
Kilburn, p & cf..	3	0	0	0	1	1	0
Watson, cf & ss .	3	0	1	0	2	2	0
Brown, p........	1	0	0	0	0	0	0
Totals 31	31	1	6	0	16	10	3

SAN JOSE

	AB	R	BH	SB	PO	A	E
Price, 1b..... .	3	0	1	0	4	1	0
Freine, p	2	0	2	1	1	1	0
Chase, 2b........	4	2	1	0	5	3	0
Brashear, ss......	3	0	1	0	1	1	1
Kent, c..........	3	0	1	0	2	1	0
De Salle, rf......	3	0	0	0	2	1	0
Anderson, 3b....	2	0	0	0	1	0	0
McNally, cf......	3	0	0	0	1	0	0
Salberg, lf.......	3	0	1	0	1	0	0
Totals......	26	2	5	2	18	8	1

SUMMARY

Sacrifice hits—Freine. Three-base hits—Peters, Collins, Salberg. Struck out—By Kilburn 4, by Brown 2, by Friene 7. First base on balls—Off Kilburn 1, off Friene 2. Left on bases—Redwoods 5, San Jose 3. Time of game —1 hour 20 minutes. Umpire—Ed Lookalink. Scorer—A. Aguirre.

H. A. J. McKENZIE, '08.

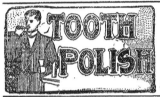

T. F. SOURISSEAU

Manufacturing
and Repairing

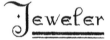

Extra Fine Assortment of Sterling Silver and Solid
Gold Jewelry

No Plate Goods—Only 10-14-18 Karat Gold

69½ South First Street, San Jose

Rooms 2-3-4   Phone White 207

Santa Clara College

THE PIONEER UNIVERTITY
OF THE PACIFIC COAST

This famous institution of learning, which is in charge of the Jesuits, has a reputation even in Europe for the completeness of its equipment and the thoroughness of its instruction. With most complete and appropriate accommodation in every department, and a full staff of professors, the institution offers uncommon advantages for the mental, moral and practical training of young men and boys.

FULL PARTICULARS MAY BE OBTAINED
BY ADDRESSING THE

Rev. Richard A. Gleeson, S. J.

Santa Clara College

SANTA CLARA   &   CALIFORNIA

SAN JOSE

Brick Company

MANUFACTURERS OF

Common and . . .
Ornamental Brick

Yards at Dougherty Station

SAN JOSE OFFICE

17 North First Street   San Jose, California

Telephone Main 594

═THE═

''Redwood''

Subscriptions are respectfully solicited
from the old boys

❧   ❧   ❧

Rates of Subscription $1.50 a year

❧   ❧   ❧

SANTA CLARA COLLEGE

Santa Clara   California

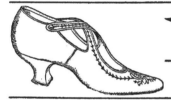

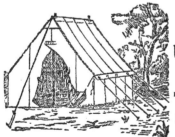

DWOOD

CHRISTMAS

THE REDWOOD

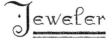

Contents.

Nace Printing Co. ◦═══◦ Santa Clara, Cal.

Monarch, enthroned in lofty state,
  Whom Angels' haloed ranks revere;
O Jesus, Lord so very great,
  We worship in exceeding fear.

Infant, encradled in the stall
  Mid courtier beasts of glebe or grove;
O Jesus, Lord so very small,
  We worship in exceeding love.

                    D. C., '07.

The Redwood.

Entered Dec. 18, 1902, at Santa Clara, Calif. as second-class matter, under Act of Congress of March 3, 1879.

VOL. VI.   SANTA CLARA, CAL., JANUARY, 1907.   No. 4.

YESTERYEAR

O ruthless Time, I cry to thee,
  Where are the friends I held so dear,
O will they ne'er come back to me,
  The friends, lost friends, of yesteryear?
Where are the days for which I yearn,
  The happy days that flew so fast;
Oh canst thou not e'en one return
  From out the past, from out the past?

Above the riot of the mart,
  The roar of trade, canst thou not hear
The cry of longing from my heart;
  Where are the joys of yesteryear?

S. F. T., '07.

CHRISTMAS RAMBLINGS

(PRINCIPALLY IN THE VICINITY OF DICKENS' CHRISTMAS STORIES)

I call the following Ramblings because I do not know exactly what the subject-matter may turn out to be. Possibly I shall end up in the editor's waste basket, but I devoutly trust that such obliquy is not in store for such good intentions as mine. Anyway, I want to say a word or two about Christmas stories.

Has the reader ever read many of them? If so, has he noticed the strong family likeness between them? Year after year they bear the same character-istics, so that to turn over the pages of bygone Christmas numbers of papers or magazines is like looking over a gallery of family portraits, in which the same features are found to do service from generation unto generation. There is our "old reliable," the proud hard-heart-ed Nob-Hill Dweller who is suddenly struck with a generous idea, and there-after cannot contain his soul in peace until he has been led by the hand of a ragged little waif up three flights of dark crooked stairs to the bedside of her invalid mother, who turns out to be an old sweetheart of his younger and better days, and by kind words and kinder coin he leaves them happy forever after. And there is his first cousin, the miser, who suddenly loses his identity or his head and scatters turkeys among the poor neighbors with unheard-of profu-sion. And then, of course, there is the rich but honest business man who sees

the golden-chained pearl necklace of his quondam daughter hanging up in a pawnbroker's window, finds out by its means her whereabouts, becomes recon-ciled to her, forgives her for marrying a poor devil of an author, and provides handsomely for her nine promising children. And then, besides, there is the prodigal son, who after a long and distressing journey over a thousand miles of unexplored country, punctuated with broken bridges and flooded tor-rents, finally, owing to unforseen delay, arrives just in the nick of time to fill up the vacant chair around the family hearth, while the heir-apparent buries his jealousy and his countenance in a generous jug of hot punch. And there are other life-long estrangements and other sudden reconciliations, and amia-ble grandparents in the green winter of their lives, and golden-haired children giving dolls to the poor children, and poor children sending a letter to Santa for money for, or conversion of, papa, and affirmative answers to the same, and holly and mistletoe over everything.

But the reader may exclaim impatient-ly: "Well, what else can we write Christ-mas stories about?" Nothing else, as far as my humble opinion goes. For there is nothing new under the sun, especially in Christmas fiction. But, as a matter of fact, we have enough to choose from; there is sufficient variety within these limits for an army of fertile pens, and, moreover, most readers are decidedly averse to innovation. Dress up the dishes in a slightly modified way, if you will; put a little more spirits in the pudding or an extra whiff of spice in the pie, but whatever you do, give us our traditional pudding and pie. We want to know beforehand what we are going to eat; we have primed our appetites for a particular bill of fare, and anything else is sure to disagree with us.

Now, I wonder if the stories in the Christmas REDWOOD will bear me out. Shall we have a helpless orphan writing a letter to Mr. Santa Claus, and the latter's answer by a wealthy proxy who adopts the orphan, having no children himself. Or shall we renew our acquaintance with the prodigal, or the miser, or the golden haired young philanthropist? We shall see. But unless we have several Thackerays and Dickens among us, my surmise will prove correct. And even they treated those very subjects aforesaid, though they were novel and original then.

Although I mention Thackeray, his Christmas stories are not Christmas stories strictly speaking. They were written to increase the sum total of man's gaiety and happiness in this workaday life, and they breathe an atmosphere of good-natured merriment that is entirely in the spirit of the season. Yet with any other date they would read almost as joyously. It is Dickens who stands out preeminently as the classic writer of this kind of literature. Before his time, it was, with the exception of Thackeray's work, genteel, formal, full of wishy-washy sentiment, and hence in a great measure distasteful. But to what literary palate could Dickens' roast goose be distasteful, and his gigantic plum pudding with its sprig of holly on the top, and his mince pie, to say nothing of the steaming hot punch. No fear that Dickens would forget the punch; it is always at your elbow when you peruse his pages and *nolens volens*, you have, if not to drink it in, at least to inhale it *ad nauseam*. But the jovial humor and thorough-going high spirits of these stories are incomparable, and though they are not very elevated in tone, they are wholesome enough in their way. They teach the pleasure of doing good, they preach the doctrine of kindness and goodwill, and they leave us all happy, and, happiness is what we were all made for.

* * * * * * *

However, I do not wish to give Dickens too much praise for his Christmas stories. He has made the world all the happier for them, it is true; and, in an earthy, unspiritual way, all the better for them, but at the same time, no one has done so much to sanction and confirm, and render classic the coarse, material, popular idea of Christmas. I do not forget that few writers have done so much to correct abuses in England,— the private school where so many children were underfed and undertaught and over-disciplined by a heartless race of Squeers'; the prison where so many debtors starved because the law had not time to attend to them; the sweat-shops where youth and slavery met; the ignorance and bigotry that found its safety-valve in anti-Catholic riots: all these were flooded with the light of his genius revealing to a shame-stricken people the degradation that had so long festered in their midst. Yes! Dickens has weeded many abuses out of England, but to plant the roses and lilies of exalted virtue in their stead is beyond his scope. The chaste spiritual mind that leads the way to elevated nobility of thought and feeling belonged not to him. He was of the earth, earthy. His idea of Christmas is happy but coarse. "Eat, drink and be merry" is the sum total of his gospel. The kitchen is the shrine where this High Priest of good cheer officiates; the savory odors of roast beef are his incense; the steaming spiced punch furnish his libations; and a turkey cooked to a crisp brown nicety is the idol which he worships on calloused knees. Even the open-handed charity which he preaches is based on no supernatural or even unselfish motives. It jars on one's nerves while he is a-merry-making to see sad, hunger-pinched faces around him; so let us feed them all, and not have a death's head at the feast.

There is hardly a spark of Christianity in these stories from beginning to end. The church bells ring out on the frosty air, but they are merely instruments of music, and we hear no divine message between their swelling notes. He alludes to our Lord as the Mighty Founder of the feast—shades of the tender-hearted shepherds of Bethlehem! He does, it is true, send the jolly family party to church, but he keeps the reader at home with Aunt George dusting decanters and with Uncle George carrying bottles into the dining-room. And moreover, when the party does return from church, he is told he has lost nothing, for a well-cooked Christmas dinner does more real good "than half the homilies of half the divines that ever lived."

The spirit of these stories is akin to that which pervades the much-lauded "Death of Little Nell," where beautiful poetic sentiment gushes out from the barren clay of mere human feeling and not from the pregnant rock of Christian faith and Christian hope.

However, we must not accredit all the blame of this to our author. Chirstmas stories as well as Christmas carols breathe in the spirit of their age and country as well as breathe it out. If they are hard and unspiritual, it is because sectarianism is hard and unspiritual. The remark about the homilies gives the clue to the situation. To how few of those divines is our Lord what He is to us and what He really is—God made man! For them His divinity was more or less of a vague undefined abstraction, and accordingly He is better out of sight during the Christmas celebration; there is no room for Him in the inn. Protestantism has banished Mary the Mother from her fireside and she has taken her child with her, It has denied her the title of Mother of God, and now it doubts or denies the Godship of the Son. The non-Catholic celebration of Christmas must thus be hollow and heart-unsatisfying; it can never be better than a play with the principal character left out—Hamlet without Hamlet.

It world be a surprising thing, indeed, if Protestantism could ever take warmly to a religious Christmas. Its extreme exponents, the Puritans, actually went so far as to banish it from the calendar altogether. On December 24th, 1652, the British House of Commons, controlled by the hard-headed Roundheads "being moved thereto by a terrible remonstrance against Christmas Day grounded upon Divine Scripture, wherein Christmas is called Antichrist's masse, and those masse-mongers and papists who observe it" passed order to abolish the feast, and to hold session on that day. And in this manner England had to keep a long sour puritanical face fourteen successive Christmasses.

Finding England too cheerful for their dyspeptic temperaments, the Puritans shipped a cargo of bigotry in the Mayflower, and came to dwell amid the gloom of the New England forests. Mrs. Hemans tells us that "they left unstained what there they found—Freedom to worship God." There is less truth than poetry in this; in fact it is the very reverse of truth. The pages of American History can show nothing comparable to the mean, narrow, cruel intolerance and ingratitude of the descendants of the 'Pilgrims.' They were narrow of head and hard of heart. The Jewisd Theocracy, with its gloom and its cruelty, was the model of their religion. They were long-faced, bilious-livered Pharisees, despising others, hating their worship, abhoring holy images, breaking stained windows, throwing down the cross. Such men had nothing but hatred for the Blessed Virgin, she whom all generations call blessed, and of course no place for the Christ-child. But while like the dragon, they waged incessant war upon the Woman and Child, like the dragon, they prevailed not. They attempted to foist Thanksgiving Day upon us as a substitute for Christmas, but Thanksgiving remains nothing much more than a social holiday plus turkey and cranberries, while Christmas keeps its honored place as the great holiday and the great holyday, *par excellence*, and the landmark of our lives' revolving years,

The last vistage of Parliamentary intolerance in England was given its quietus by Daniel O'Connell. One day a man named Thomas Massey Massey stood up in his place and called the attention of the country's representatives to the startling fact a dangerous relic of superstition, a very claw of the beast, was embalmed in their everyday speech. What was Christmas but Christ's mass— a foul piece of papistry on the face of it? It was high time to act; let the law arise in its might and banish the word from the dictionary and let Christ-tide, a decent English dissyllable take its place.

When the man had finished, big, burly, Daniel O'Connell arose· The House pricked up its ears in the expectation of hearing something good. In his sonorous and thunderous tones, Dan praised up, and expressed his sympathy with, the little man who had just manifested such anxiety for the public safety. "But," said he, in conclusion, "if he is really sincere, let him begin the reformation at home, let him purge his own name of its papistry, and let him herewith answer to the cute little name of Thotide Tidey Tidey."

The roar of laughter which followed was the loudest and longest ever heard in the House of Commons, and in its swelling waves all the little Thotides were submerged forever.

But we must finish our rather varied ramblings. However, we cannot rest without taking a passing glance at Christmas among Catholic people. How pleasant the transition! It is like passing out of the coldness and bareness of St. Paul's London, into the warmth and glory of St. Peters's, out of shadow into the sunshine, out of doubt into faith. Amongst us,. the Divine Child is the. central figure. We talk to Him, we pray to Him, we use a loving familiarity toward Him—we never once think of Him as a "Mighty Founder" of the Feast. Our churches are the chief scene of the festivities. The merry-making in Catholic countries is as intimately blended with the mass and the crib as is the perfume of the rose with the rose. In France, for instance,—poor France! O, eldest daughter of the church! "all her beauty is gone out from the daughter of Sion; the streets of Sion mourn because there are none who come to the solemnities." Where shall be your Christmas solemnities, O, Queen of the Nations, now become as a widow? —You must seek the hillside and the grove, for your own can receive you not. But to return: In France the people sing hymns, or noels for nine days preceding the Feast, and on the Night itself they put forth their best efforts, while the yule-log or *suche* is blazing brightly. and sugar-plums and all manner of sweets are rained down around the hearth. Nothing more merry than the *festin* of the light-hearted Frenchman, but when midnight approaches he gets serious, the party form into procession and singing devout hymns, make their way to the church. During the night the Christ-child himself brings gifts for the children.

In Ireland the same tenderness of devotion is found. Poor as the Irish peasant may be, and far as may be from his thoughts and his means the mince-pie and pudding, yet, Christmas is truly a feast to him. Many a weary mile, over rocky mountain or swampy bog-land, old and young will tramp to mass, and around the crib they pour forth their humble, trusting prayer. In Servia each family receives as a guest a young man to represent the Guest Divine. In Italy there is no Santa Claus, but , instead, an old woman, Befana, who had intended to travel with the Magi, but delayed too long to set her house in order. Now, in atonement, she goes from house to house seeking the Christ child, and by the way bestowing gifts on good children. In early California, prayers preparatory to the feast were said the nine days preceding, and a ceremony called the *posada*, observed, in which people went around at night looking for a place in the *posada* or inn for Mary and Joseph.

But it would be tedious to give further examples to illustrate the genuine religious feeling that animates the Catholic conception of Christmas, or to show how all its cheery light and warmth radiates from the crib. The best proof of it lies in the well-known fact that most of the faithful receive the sacraments on that day of days, and that he is regarded as hopelessly lost to the Church indeed, who, far aloof as he may have kept himself during the rest of the year, refuses to listen to the "good tidings of great joy" or to come with the shepherds to see the things "that have come to pass" at this season of grace.

I had intended to say a few words about the Christmas tone characteristic of Catholic writers, and to quote them as well as some of the carols of former days, but now that my ramblings have led me to the humble throne of the Infant King, I will rest here awhile, and I advise you to do the same, as you must certainly feel very tired.

J. D. S. '07

"GLORIA IN EXCELSIS!"

"*A Virgin shall conceive and bear a Son !*"
So spake the Prophet in the olden time—
And on this Holy Night, when; at her prime,
Yon full-orbed moon, her mighty course begun,
Rolls through Heaven's depths—this mystery is done;
Hark ! from high heaven !   how the chime
Of starry spheres and Angel choirs sublime
Sings of the Champion's Victory to be won !

Glory to God on high !   and peace on earth
To men !   the happy burden of this strain !
From distant Orient climes this new refrain
Shall woo great Princes to the Christ-Child's birth !
Ah !   blessed we, if Bethlehem's star illume
Our storm-crossed bark of life and guide us through the gloom !

B. N. P., '10.

A CHRISTMAS CAROL

(WITH SOME NOTES OUT OF TUNE)

Chandler re-read the note delightedly. "You bet I will," he thought, "it's a cinch there's no place I would sooner take a Christmas dinner."

So he picked up his pen and wrote,

"Dear Winifred, I received your kind invitation to dinner tomorrow night. It was really very kind of you to ask me and I will be delighted to be on hand. Yours as ever—Maurice C. Chandler."

As the young man was running the heel of his hand over the blotter, Spooks came in. Spooks was an old servant of the Chandler's and when the family was dispersed and young Maurice decided to hang out a shingle in Virginia, Spooks had refused to give up the ship. And speaking of ships it may be remarked that Spooks' favorite was the schooner. He had always steadfastly refused to give up, too. In fact years before the name Spooks had been given him, because his distorted vision late one night, or rather early one morning had mistaken a poor, unsuspecting lamp post for a ghost.

It was always one of Spooks' touchy points—his inebriety. He flatly affirmed that he had never in his life taken more liquor than just enough to keep his stomach in good order. And in that, he was wont to quote with glib tongue, he was only acting on the advice of the good St. Paul, who held that a little wine was good for the stomach. All of which was admirably told but only partially true. Even Spooks' stomach could not have needed all the doctoring it received.

But to come back. Chandler was just blotting his note when Spooks came in, with a large official looking envelope in his hand, and a glum, mournful look on his face.

The young attorney looked up.

"What are you looking so worried about, Spooks? You couldn't look more flustered if you were the president of the sewing club. What's the trouble anyway? That man Roosevelt bothering you again?"

Spooks loftily ignored the bantering tone and threw down the letter before his master with a gesture of deep disgust. "Read that," he snapped, "and don't blame me for looking my worst."

Here is the letter that made Spooks swear and Chandler laugh uproariously.

"Mr. Cyril Muggins. Dear Sir—

At this blessed season when all of us should be more mindful than ever of the brotherhood of man, we are making a special effort to bring some of our erring brothers out of their evil ways. Your name has been given us as a fit subject for our labors and we are going to make a plea to you. All we ask is that you will fill out the enclosed blank and that the promise to abstain for a year from intoxicating liquor which you thereby make, you will faithfully keep. Any little contribution you would feel disposed to make to help the good cause along would be gratefully received. Please put the blank and the contribution in a sealed envelope and drop it in our box at Fifth and Jackson Sts.

Yours, Mrs. Mary A. Scott,
Secretary, W. C. T. U."

Chandler looked at Spooks' sorrowful disgusted face and laughed until the tears rolled down his cheeks.

"Where is the blank ?" he asked finally, running over the letter again.

"Burned the blasted thing," growled Spooks.

Chandler laughed again and Spooks looked aggrieved.

"I don't see the joke at all," said he. "I don't think you ought to laugh at an insult offered to an American gentleman. Especially"—he added as an afterthought—"when the said gent· is your own valet."

Spooks always liked that word. Chandler bit his lip to control himself.

"Well, what are you going to do ?"

Spooks broke out. "Do?" he roared. "I'll tell you what I'm going to do. I'm going to this W. M. C. T. business and raise a howl. If she's a man I'll punch his face, and if it's a woman I'll spoil her garden, break her furniture, and walk all over her dog's tail. I'll see if a gentleman who is merely trying to keep his stomach in good order, can be bullied and bamboozled by cheap societies. I'll show them that Spooks Muggins is his own boss and don't want us help a running his own larder and drinkin' trough.

I want you to write a letter to 'em ·for me, will you?"

"I ? What'll I say? Something about how you're sorry but——"

"Not by a pipe full. Say this."

He waited until the young lawyer arranged his stationery and paused, with pen poised above the paper. Then he began slowly and thoughtfully to dic‐tate:

"You go to——"

"Wait a minute," the other interrupted, "Don't you want a heading ?"

"Nope. When they get it they'll know it's for them all right."

Then he went on imperturbably.

"You go to the devil."

"Make it thunder for politeness' sake," Chandler interposed.

"I said devil, and the devil goes," said Spooks testily.

"You go to the devil. I laugh at your note and I am going to hit up the booze worse than ever."

"Is that all ?"

"That's all. "

"Do you want to sign it yourself ?"

"No, I don't want it signed. It's the insult to manhood I object to. If there's no name at the bottom it'll look almost like a general kick to 'em."

"I see. A universal protest from injured innocents, eh? All right, Spooks."

He slipped the letter into an envelope and handed it to the man who dropped it into his pocket.

"By the way, Spooks," he went on, "Take this letter around to Marshall's. You know, third house from the corner on Turner Avenue. On your way back you might drop into the florists and tell him to send up a dozen of his best hot house roses to Marshall's tomorrow at ten. Give him this card."

When Spooks went out that night the sting was still rankling in his manly bosom.

As he dropped the envelope in the donation box at Fifth and Jackson, he grunted with satisfaction.

"That'll fix 'em," he muttered, and buttoned his coat closer about his throat.

It did fix them. The good matrons were sorely puzzled a few days after to find among the reformation letters, a note accepting an invitation to dinner.

Spooks elbowed himself through the great jolly Christmas eve throng on the streets and found his way to the Marshall residence.

"For Miss Marshall from Mr. Chandler," he told the maid and handed her an envelope. On his way home the thought of his wrongs so took hold of him that he forgot all about the florist. He must needs forget his trouble and with the simple directness of his nature, he betook himself at once to certain emporiums where forgetfulness is dispensed by the mugful.

As Chandler rang the bell the next night at the Marshall home, he fumbled at his tie complacently.

"I'm in for a good time," he thought in self-satisfaction.

He was. The door was opened by Miss Winifred herself all flustered and tearful. Chandler's jaw dropped when he saw her.

"Why, what's the matter?" he queried.

"What's the matter?" Why Maur— Mr. Chandler, how dare you come here and speak to me after yesterday? You brute, you insulting wretch how dare you?"

Poor, innocent Maurice with his eyes popping out of his head, stepped inside and closed the door.

"Why Win—" he began.

"Don't call me that, don't you dare address me by that name. So you're going to "hit up the booze" are you? And—and oh you told me to go to the— Oh Maurice !"

Her chin quivered and her lashes were twinkling with tears in the bright electric light. Chandler braced himself. She was going to cry now, sure.

But she didn't. She went on, her temper rising as her memory worked.

"And to add insult to injury, when I called you up today about the horrid note, that man of yours told me you meant every word of it. Oh you base monster ! I am glad I have found you out. I will send you back your ring and letters tomorrow, and—and—"

And then the tears came. Chandler's memory was troubling him. He remembered very vaguely something about booze, about a note, but—.

"Winifred," he expostulated, "there's some terrible mistake. I don't—"

"How can there be a mistake, sir. Your man brought the note last night. Besides I could tell your writing anywhere. Oh you can't excuse yourself."

A great flood of memory poured in on Chandler.

"Good Lord," he blurted out. "Win,

I know now. It's all a mistake. I'll call you up about it. Goodbye, dear.''

Before the tearful little slip of a girl in the doorway could move or speak, he had clapped his hat on his head and was running and stumbling down the street.

Once when he rounded a corner he ran straight into a fat, old gentleman who was pattering along all borne down with bundles. The bundles flew up and the old gentleman sat down.

"Er-er-ah Merry Christmas!" said the fat, old gentleman.

"Excuse me, I'll fix that Spooks" answered Chandler without stopping.

The fat, old gentleman, with his hat jammed down over one eye, watched the retreating form.

"Poor boy," he said sympathetically, "poor, crazy youth."

When Chandler reached home, he found Spooks sitting on the table, handsomely, artistically, gloriously drunk. The young man grabbed him by the collar and pulled him off the table.

"Look here, you blithering idiot," he said, "what have you been doing anyway?"

Spooks' eyes twinkled meditatively.

"Say," he said between bibulous giggles," some woman called up today about that W. R. M. T. note. But I fixed her. I told her we meant all we said and more, too. Lor', she banged up the phone. Ha, ha, ha! oh ha, ha, ha!"

"You consummate ass," roared Chandler, so loud that Spooks blinked, and stopped laughing so suddenly that his mouth stayed open. "Don't you understand what you did. Don't stand there with your face like a garden fence with the gate out. Close your mouth. You went and gave the wrong note to Miss Marshall, and put the other in the W. C. T. U. box."

Spooks had closed his mouth, but it flapped open again at this like a shutter in the wind.

"Holy smoke," he gasped as it dawned on him. Then he began to whimper and the tears which were very near his eyes, rolled down his cheeks.

"Oh well, don't be a baby," Chandler said uneasily, watching the tears. "It can't be helped. I'll fix it up with Miss Marshall. Cheer up, Spooks. It's Christmas, anyway." Spooks sniffled.

"I wasn't thinkin' of Miss Marshall," he sobbed. "Can't you see that after all our trouble, those Y. W. T. A. people will get your note an' there wont be nothing but love in it?"

JAMES F. TWOHY, '07·

THE FIRST CHRISTMAS

I came, mankind forlorn to save,
Thus speaks the Child in Bethlehem cave,
    At midnight hour born;
They who in death and darkness dwell,
Shall, quickened, feel the gladdening spell,
    The hopeless cease to mourn.

Lo! how the circling sky is bright
With angel choirs who sing the Light,
    Guilt's deepest gloom dispelling;
While shepherds, bidden, seek the Child,
Their God supreme, their brother mild,
    In straw strewn manger dwelling.

Strange influence the nations far
Awakes; anon, with guiding star,
    The kingly three and wise
Through desert wend and peopled ways,
Till on the Babe, with fond amaze,
    They fix their ravished eyes.

Poor fleecy gifts the shepherds bring,
With gold, frankincense, myrrh, their King
    The princes wise adore;
Who came, from error, doubt and sin,
In love mankind estranged to win,
    And Kingdom lost restore.

GEORGE MORGAN, '10

A REFORMATION

"Say, are you Santa Claus? If you are, my stocking is down stairs by the fireplace." The little white clad figure sat up in bed, and gazed at the man who was quickly going through the bureau drawers. A mask covered his face, his clothes were shabby, and his hair was matted and uncombed.

As the child spoke he turned quickly, and a revolver gleamed in his hand. He muttered something and lowered the gun.

"I was afraid you'd wake up, kid, but you want to lie down and keep quiet. Yes, I'm Santa Claus and I'm just looking for a pin here—"

"I'll get you one," and the little white gown began to crawl out of bed. I know just where they are and you don't," the little girl was on the floor now and coming toward him."

"My," she said, "how you've mussed everything. The pins aren't in those drawers; here's one."

"Thank you," said the man, "now you crawl back into bed. I'll get me a bite to eat and then I'll go."

"Haven't you had supper yet," she asked, looking up at him with wide eyes.

"No," said the man, "I guess not."

"Well, come on down stairs; I'll get you some goodies."

The burglar hesitated. Would it be better to leave the child or let her go? Would she make a noise and raise the family if he left her? She might. So he said, "All right! go ahead, but be careful, if you make any noise, I've got to leave."

"I'll go awful easy," she said, and led the way, looking back now and then to see if he was coming. In the dining room she stopped.

"Now you sit here and I'll get something to eat. It's Christmas, you know, Santy, and this is my present to you. You must be awful hungry, aren't you? My! I couldn't go without my supper like that."

"A little," he said. He watched her as she went to the pantry and brought out cold dainties for him. Every move she made he followed with his eyes. He had taken the mask from his face. It was a hard, strong face, but as he watched the little girl it slowly softened.

The hard lines vanished and his mouth took on a gentle expression, his eyes firm and steel-like lost their hardened look and became almost tearful. A vision came before his mind. He remembered a little tot that used to come and kiss him as she sat upon his knee after his day's labor. That was long ago before his wife died, and left her motherless, and when he was a good, honest laborer. Then he had sent her to an orphanage and he had— well, he had just gone wrong. It all came back to him now. He wondered where she was now, what she was doing, wondered if she ever thought of her father who had treated her so, wondered if she would enjoy Christmas as this little girl before him would. The enormity of his crime burst upon him and he realized. God! but he had been wicked. Why had he done it? Tonight was Christmas eve; he would go and do better. The tiny girl now stood before him with her present to him, not dreaming the present she was making the Little Child whose birthday came that night, when she turned that hardened soul back to His fold, restrained the sinner from his sin and sped the prodigal home.

"Why don't you eat?" she asked. Then she noticed the big tear on the man's cheek. "Are you so awful hungry it makes you cry?"

The voice startled him. He awoke from his reverie as from a sleep. He smiled at the little girl and ate.

"I must go now, little girl—"

"Alice is my name."

"All right, Alice, don't tell any one you saw Santa Claus." He placed his hand on her head. "Thank you for the Christmas present." He looked up, "So help me God," he said, "I'll do better, Won't you kiss old Santa good bye?" She raised her face and he stooped and kissed her. The door closed softly behind him, and the little girl went back to bed to dream of morning and old Santy.

IVO G. BOGAN, '08.

VIA MUNDI!

A star in the east is seen
So bright,
I ween
No other in heaven has light!
But what does the wide world care?
No comfort it brings for it to share!

A God-man is born
Of love
This morn
To open the gates above!
But what does the wide world care?
No comfort He brings for it to share!

A. B. D. '08.

AN ODE ON NEW YEAR'S EVE

Farewell, old dying year,
   Tonight thy reign must end.
You brought a smile for every tear,
   You brought a new for each lost friend,
And we will hold thy memory dear.

How cruel and mocking doth Time seem:
   When thou wert born the bells did ring,
And winter winds with gusty scream
     And icy breath
    Did hail thee King;
And now wild winds and winter bell
Do chant thy dirge and toll thy knell,
    With self same voices at thy death.

Midnight is passed; the bells ring out,
Winds scream, and man with lusty shout
   And joyful face,
   Proclaims the one who takes thy place.
But while all hail the newer year
    With voices glad and gay,
For you, old friend, we'll drop a tear;
   And mindless of the thoughtless bell
   That joyfully rings out thy knell,
    We'll think of thee and gently say
   Here was a friend : old friend, farewell !

JAMES F. TWOHY, '07

A "KRISMAS" LETTER

Deer Santy:—

i want a Krismas this yere, fer i aint had none fer to yeres an it seams auful long. mama is sik an pa is in jale an aint gilty neether. i am a gurl an want a reel doll with ise an noze an a red mouf an brown hare. i want sum stockins an shoos to. i m auful kold. good by. dont ferget.

ALVINA Y——

Such a pitiful letter! What a lot of misery is expressed in those few childish words. But such or similar is the case in thousands of homes in this vast world of ours. Many such letters are written about Christmastide, and in these letters can be seen the condition of the homes. This particular letter was written in a tenement in the worst part of that vast city, New York, in that part in which Poverty reigned and squalor and misery were the effects of its tyrannical rule.

Little Alvina's father, of whom she spoke as being in "Jale", was sent to prison for a term of three years for petty larceny in 190-. He was innocent, yet a victim to circumstantial evidence. His term expired on the then coming Christmas, but unknown to his little daughter. Her mother, Mrs. Y—, had been working hard ever since he was imprisoned, trying to keep up and earn enough to pay the meagre rent, and to buy food and clothes for her baby girl. She had taken in washing, she had gone to the sweat shops, she had done everything that she possibly could, but being a naturally weak woman she at last broke down, unable to do anything more. Her husband had been a good workman and had left her a little money. And after she had broken down and become sick, this little sum of money, which she had been trying to get along without for so long a time, had to be used. It had been two years since her husband had taken away from her. A long year had yet to pass before his term expired. Piece by piece the little sum of money gradually diminished, little amounts being taken almost daily for food to keep them alive, and twice a month the rent had to be paid. Eventually the sum was very low. But the rent was reduced after a while, because they only used one room; and Alvina was accustomed to help an old crippled man who had a small fruit stand, thereby getting a couple of oranges or apples a day. This fruit was taken home to the little room in the tenement, and she and her mother had often but a crust of bread to eat besides them. They got along this way until November of the last year of Mr. Y—'s imprisonment. It was now very cold and quite often there was snow on the ground, but Alvina had worn out all her shoes and stockings and now was forced to do without them; and so she was not only cold, but was deprived of those innocent winter sports in which children so much delight. They also had to do without a fire, coal being too high for them to afford it, and being pressed for money they sold the little stove for a small sum, and now had to go to bed whenever they were cold and wanted to get warm.

About the first of December, Alvina began to write this letter, and after many erasures and scratches she finished it without her mother knowing about it. Then she handed it to the postman one morning telling him it was for Santa Claus. He knew the existing condition in the little room in the large tenement house, and took the letter and told her he would send it. After he got away and out of sight, he read the sorrowful little missive, and the kindhearted man's eyes were filled with tears. He himself had once had a little girl of about the age of Alvina, but she had been dead about a year. And the tender memories of his own child, and the pitiful condition of this one running out barefooted in the snow and shivering there on the corner waiting for him to come, and in her childish innocence expecting the letter to be delivered,—all this caused tears to rise in the kind man's eyes and course down his rugged cheeks.

＊　　＊　　＊　　＊　　＊

That night the postman himself sent a letter. It was addressed to Gov. A— of New York, and together with his letter explaining the conditions of the mother and her child, the innocence of the father, etc., was the letter Alvina wrote to Santy. The postman explained that though there might appear to be a certain amount of boldness on his part for making this move, but that the family had no friends to whom they could

appeal. And his petition was that the man be released a couple of weeks before the regular expiration of his term, in order to provide for his family's needs.

The Governor himself was greatly affected, and immediately sent a pardon to the man. But by the time the usual formalities had been gone through, two weeks had already passed. And during this time what had become of our friends, Alvina and her mother? Indeed they were in a very poor condition. All their money was gone, and the cripple who kept the fruit stand had hired a boy to help him during the holidays, and so Alvina's few oranges and apples were no longer forthcoming. The fact is that at the second week of December they were starving! The kind hearted postman not seeing Alvina around for several days became at once curious and fearful. One morning about 10 o'clock, he went up to the little room to see if anything was going wrong, and upon reaching the door he knocked, and in a very low weak voice he heard some one from the inside say, "Come in." He entered, and saw in one corner of the dark cold room, Alvina and her mother both sick in bed. Upon going closer he observed that Alvina was yet asleep. Mrs.Y— was very thin and pale, and in a seemingly helpless condition.

The postman seeing the state which they were in, tried to encourage them and said he would send his wife over to help out in any way she could, and then, being unable to bear it longer, he left the room. His wife came soon after, bringing some food with her, and tried to console the sick child and her mother by kind words and some good warm food. For two or three days she did this, and Alvina became stronger again, but her mother kept losing physically day by day. On the fourth day under the good lady's care Alvina was able to be up and around, but her mother gradually sank lower and lower. Along towards evening she was expected to die at any moment. Suddenly the sound of heavy footsteps was heard outside the door, and a big burly man strode in, looked around, accustomed himself to the dark, and then with two steps was across the room to the bed where his dying wife lay. He kissed her on the forehead, and she opened her eyes! With a cry of joy she threw her arms around his neck, and little Alvina hurrying to his side was soon in the arms of her big father. We will now leave them to themselves for a few moments and go back to see what the Governor was doing.

He was in his private office when a servant entered, handed him a card, and waited for an answer.

"Conduct the man in," said the Governor.

And immediately a well dressed young man entered, nervously took the chair pointed out to him and began to twist his hat into various different shapes, the while looking at the floor in an abstracted manner.

"Well, young man, what can I do for you?"

"I, a– ah–, I came to speak to you on a, ah–very–ahem! important ah–matter," stammered the young man.

"You must tell me what it is if you wish any help."

"Well, ah–, I guess you remember this ah– case of petty larceny for which a certain Mr. Y— was convicted and sentenced three years ago."

"Yes, yes, what about it?"

"W– well, ah–, h– he was innocent."

"Who was guilty, then?"

"W– why I– I– I was!"

"Why do you come and tell me this now, when his term expires in a few days?"

"I– I– ah– don't know."

"Why did you do this stealing?"

"I– I– w– why I– ah– only d– did it for a lark."

"For a lark, hey? what do you propose to do now?"

"I– I, don't know!"

"Are you rich, well off, or — ?"

"Well, I– I'm worth, well! say a million."

"I'll tell you what to do then. I have pardoned the man and probably by now he is on his way home. I'll make a proposition to you; you pay that man a sum of money which would have been equal to a salary at $150 per month, for the term he served for *you*. Let's see! He served three years,—36 months; 3600 and 1800 equals $5400. No! That is too easy! Paying a man $5400 to serve a term in prison for him, and his wife and child home starving—!"

"Wh– what! Starving?"

"Yes, starving and freezing to death! Perhaps his wife is dead or dying at this minute. And—"

"S– Say! s– s'posing I give you $25,-

ooo to send to this Mr. Y—, will you do it and say no more about it to him."

"Gee, just think! Wife and children starving! The poor unfortunate! I believe—"

"S- say! I'll make it $50,000! A–and that's gettin' off pretty easy too!"

"Gosh! I'd ought to send you up for this! But—! the term is served already! And am I to make two men serve a term in prison for the same crime? No! See here! You give me that $60,000 and I'll send it to him. And listen now! If his wife is now dead or dies on account of starvation and cold you will pony up $40,000 more! D'ye see? Well! and that's not all! If something happens to him, then it's 'up to you' to take charge of the child! Now how do you like that?"

"I'm willing! It's all on my account! and whatever has happened or is to happen as an effect of this I will attend to! So here—," and writing out a check for $60,000 he handed it to the Governor and started out the door, when the servant entered again, this time holding a telegram for Gov. A— of New York.

The young fellow passed on out, and the Governor opened the telegram, and it read—"Mrs. Y— is dead!"

Signed, Mr. X— (postman.)

"Say!" yelled the Governor, "Call that fellow back."

The servant called the man back and the Governor handed him the telegram.

"H—! The poor guy! And all on my account. Here!" and he writes out another check for the additional amount, despondently rests his head in his hands,

strikes the desk with his clenched fist, abruptly gets up and walks out!

"Well, wouldn't that jar you?" from the Governor.

*   *   *   *   *

We will not return to the scene of the deathbed, but rather let us go to a newly built residence in the suburbs of the city on the eve of December 24. There we see through the window a beautiful sight! It's Xmas eve and in the corner of the room is an immense Christmas tree, lighted up with candles and decorated with all the spangles and sparklers that can be imagined, and the limbs just bending over with an abundance of toys and trinkets overloading them.

Beneath the superb tree is Alvina, and beside an open fireplace sits her father in a rocking chair, mourning the death of his wife.

"Don't cry, papa, I don't like to see you cry!"

"Well little one, we'll have to be content without a mama, so let's make the best of it. What would we have done had you not written that letter to Santa Claus, Alvina? He certainly gave you a Christmas this year, but you have to do without a mama."

"I'm awful sorry mama is dead, but I got a papa now, and Santy Claus sent us lots of money too."

The Christmas tree and its decorations, toys, etc., were a gift of the Governor himself, and Mr. Y— was very grateful to him for all he had done, and soon after had an enlarged picture made of his wife, Alvina and himself and sent it to the Governor of New York. The picture of his wife he had taken from a small tin type of her which he always had with him, and even when in prison the wardens let him keep it. This large picture seems a small compensation, but it was gratefully accepted, and esteemed more than could have been anything else by the Governor.

GEORGE J. HALL, '08

THE SHEPHERD

They blew ; soft winds sweet-laden with a sound divine—
When lo ! and from the darkness came there light
And brilliant radiance from a star all flaming bright.
Raptured, scarce I breathed—a calm intense was mine,
To see what beauty of the night could well design,
The power of the King to show, whose might
Had bidden humble Nature glorify the night,
And lay a splendid tribute at the manger-shrine.

What ! shall sages from the East with tribute rare;
With gifts that bore them down, presume to share
That joy which seemed all mine to hold, when Him I saw,
A helpless babe laid crooning in the fragrant straw?
My crook—my heart I gladly gave ; it was my lot
Naught else to give because I had it not.

F. Plank, Ex-'07.

WERE IT THE LAST DROP IN THE WELL

Oh, it 's Christmas eve and snowin', Mary,
   An' it 's chill and cold without,
An' the crops have stopped their growin', Mary.
   An' we 're poor beyond a doubt.
There beside the flickerin' coals, Mary,—
   Where it's hung so oft before,
With its toe all full of holes, Mary,—
   It can't stand many more,—
Just there close to where you 're rockin', Mary,
   Near the coals so cold an' few,
Is the little feller's stockin', Mary.
   Hangin' up beside the flue.

Over yonder in the bed room, Mary.
   On his little wooden bed,
There are many dreams a dancin', Mary,
   Through his little curly head,
Now his stockin' ain't well knitted, Mary,
   An' it ain't so very new,—
But old Santy can't forgit it, Mary,
   As it hangs beside the flue.

All our crops have failed and left us, Mary,
   Just as poor as poor can be.—
The debts they all hang heavy, Mary,
   On you, the babe an' me;
But so long 's we 've got a penny, Mary,
   A dime 'tween me an' you,
They 'll be somethin' in that stockin', Mary,
   Hangin' up beside the flue.

I. G. B. '08

OUR FIRST CHRISTMAS TREE

About a hundred and thirty miles north of Quebec, there is in the river St. Lawrence, as the reader probably did not know until now, an island which we may as well call Grandique, because that is not its name. This island is, smoothly speaking, ten miles long and seven broad. Through the center of it runs a ridge some hundred feet high, from which the sides slope gently down to the water's edge. To the eye of hawk or eagle soaring above, it must present the appearance of a monster whale lying at rest. The elevated portion of the island is hardly inhabited, but the coast line is dotted with an almost unbroken line of neat little white-washed cottages, the doors of which are painted red, and the window shutters green, in typical French-Canadian style. Each of these houses has a little barn in its company, done up in colors to harmonize, and house and barn are set in the midst of a narrow rectangular farm that runs from the shore up the slope toward the interior. These farms are, as a rule, of the same shape and size, and each is set in a white-washed picket fence as in a picture frame. And the comparison is not inapt, for a more pretty or picturesque spot is rarely to be found. The verdure of the fields, so rich and soft-colored, robes the island during the summer months, until the winter cold first turns it to russet and then covers it with immaculate white; the heavens, deeply blue, blend in the hazy distance with the lordly Laurentides, the high ridge of which sweep along in a majestic line athwart the north-eastern skies. And then the great silent river! ever flowing, flowing by, bearing little fishing boats or dories, and ships, and huge ocean-steamers towards the Atlantic or suffering them to furrow its placid bosom on their way up stream to Quebec or Montreal. It is not always placid, however; it knows how to be angry and violent, but it is ever gentle with Grandique, and never shows a very angry face within the island's miniature harbors. But gentle or rough we loved the river, it was all in all to us. We drank it, we swam in it, we fished in it, we sailed upon it. It was our communication with the outer world; it kept us apart to form a little world of our own. Many of our fishermen spend half their lives on its bosom, for the high tide brings the salt water and its finny tribes up here, and many of us, alas! were sleeping there a last long sleep. And when grim winter came with its own rough but unrivalled pleasures, what an ecstacy of delight it was to skim over the smooth ice vying with swallows in your flight.

But what has all this to do with our Christmas tree. Well, really, I don't know—probably it has nothing to do with that time-honored plant. After all, why should it? Why stick to the law of unity in this profuse season? Why not give it a vacation as we do to so many other laws and customs—the mistletoe could tell you of one of them for instance, and your own purse strings could tell you of another, I feel sure. With this understanding, let us proceed.

Though the island of Grandique is a trifle north of 'civilization,' as the word is understood by us, yet Christmas there is celebrated with a solemnity and an impressiveness that many of us can hardly realize. The crib in the church and the illuminations are such as only delicate taste and fervent piety can produce. Each family has its own little crib besides, and every house has its front windows illuminated by rows of candles. Gifts are interchanged, and as for Santa Claus, this is almost his first halting place after leaving the Pole.

But there was one thing lacking in my time. The Christmas tree was not in vogue. We had all heard of it, had read of it, and once or twice had seen it in one of the stores, where, however, its sentiment was converted into hard cash, for it was a mere lottery affair. Why could we not have a Christmas tree at home all for ourselves, with little candles and prizes and boxes and tinsel and what not? Yes! we should have one, and a beauty at that.

My eldest sister was the inventor—I had almost said the father—of the idea, and I was its champion. I always did champion her projects. She had been in the convent at Hochelaga for nearly two years and was now spending her first Christmas vacation with us.

How clever and gracious she was! I really adored her, and her bright smile was more than recompense for any trouble undergone for her sake. I thought more of her than my oldest brother was supposed to think of somebody else's sister, and that was a good deal.

So when she broke the news about the proposed tree, I was enthusiastic in its favor. I lost no time in harnessing the pony, Count; riding off to the upper end of the farm, cutting down a beautiful spruce tree, and bearing it home in triumph. Before evening it stood in its corner in the parlor, a veritable dream of beauty. All were delighted with it, with the exception of my father who took no pains to hide his contempt of those new fangled innovations.

"Gracious!" said my sister, as with arms akimbo, she surveyed the fairy creation,—"if we had only Japanese lanterns, even father would be pleased with it."

"Japanese lanterns!" I exclaimed. "Why, what are those?" After she had given me some notion of their appearance—"why," I interrupted, "I saw some of those at Le Brun's store only last week. I'll get some tomorrow."

"Well, if you're not the best little boy that ever lived," she ejaculated. And I felt more than rewarded for whatever trouble my promise would cost.

LeBrun's was the largest store in St. Anne, the largest town,—population about 700—that the Island could boast of. It lay on the other side just opposite us and was therefore seven miles away. Next morning, the day before Christmas, I set out on my journey with the intention of being back by 1 p. m. I was in high spirits, first be- cause Count was a spirited little pony and would break into a gallop on the slightest provocation, and, secondly, because it made me feel important to be on horseback. A horse was a rare thing on the island, for but few could afford to have one. The farms were small and barely sufficient to maintain a few cows and sheep. Not many of my chums had a horse in the family; fewer still could ride as well as I; and none had a horse like Count. So I felt thoroughly satisfied as my pony pranced over the frozen street of the village, and turned up the ascent towards St. Anne's.

For a while all went well. Shortly after passing the last house that sen- tinelled the road, the snow began to fall. How large and soft the flakes were! I had rarely seen anything like them. I shouted for very joy. The air had become so warm all at once; I feared lest the snow should turn to rain. But it did not. Down, down, thick fell the beautiful flakes, so soft, so noiseless— mantling road and rock and fence and tree; muffling every sound so com- pletely that I made Count pause in order that his footsteps might not mar the perfection of the death-like stillness. "Say, Count," I said, "let me drink this stillness in; I guess I'll have enough of noise all my life, but I wonder if many moments of silence like this!" I have not had any such moments since.

But Count began to snort and paw the ground in utter disgust at my senti- mental musings, and I bade him go on. Soon the snow ceased and the air got cold; but what did we care? Count capered along all the more lively. After passing the summit of the ridge, I stopped again, this time not for any purely sentimental purpose; I wanted to perform an act of charity to a fellow mortal. A little robin was limping across the road, wounded and weak, and I pursued and after some time and trouble, caught him. "Now," said I, "I'll put you into the hollow of this stump here, and I'll just close you in with these stones, and you just eat those crumbs and stay here in perfect content till I come back, and then I'll take you home and you can perch on our Christmas tree, and sing a Christ- mas hymn if your throat is in order." And bidding him good-bye, I remounted and though fifteen minutes later was glad to have fed the little bird, and to have acquired a novel and unexpected addition to the Christmas tree.

All at once, I seemed to be in the clouds--literally. Right in front of me rose an opaque wall of what appeared to be mist and snow. "Heavens," I cried in alarm, "how is it that the clouds are so near?" And I stared in blank amaze- ment—but only for a moment; the cloud rolled towards me, the temperature fell with a jerk far below the freezing point, and I found myself in a raging blizzard. Blizzards are practically unknown up there, but I had read enough about them to recognize one when I saw it.

My heart within me sank as suddenly as the temperature, and my breath came in short, hard gasps. I jumped off the horse, for I at once understood it was either exercise or death. Besides, I could not have driven Count anyway, as he danced and whinnied in mortal terror, and turned his back to the storm. It was getting colder and colder; the wind blew fearfully, and the snow, no longer in soft large flakes, but fine and hard as table salt, beat in my face with pitiless violence. At times I could scarcely see my hand in front of me, and of the horse I could see no more than his head. Poor Count! he was more frightened than I was. He had never felt a whip so cruel as this stinging, biting lash of the powdery snow. With head bowed low he took shelter behind me, and so close did he keep to me that often he actually pushed me forward. This helped me on, besides making me feel heroic by the compliment paid to my defending abilities; But it was no time for thoughts of vanity —I must hasten forward. All around me was "darkness visible" and the awful thought flashed across my mind that I might easily go in a wrong direction, and, if so, farewell hope! The fear of it froze the blood in my heart, but in a moment I saw that the violence of the wind swept the road clean of snow so that I could always see at least a step or two of it in front of me. This was my salvation. Step by step then, I pushed on, fighting my way against cutting wind and still more cutting snow, now turning around to take a long breath and to get a little respite from the cruel scourge, but Count ever forced me forward, and he seemed to feel instinctively that delay would be fatal. Oh, would the town never show near at hand? Could I hold out much longer? What made me already so tired and sleepy and my hand so numb it could hardly hold the bridle? Why not lie down and take a rest just for a moment? Fortunate for me that the fear of Count's hoofs forced me onward!

In all my life I never prayed more fervently, especially to the Infant King who long ago had to seek shelter from the cold as I was doing. As I was thus engaged, with head bent down to escape the pelting snow, I was all at once startled by a sudden cry of delight, and looking up saw a man with arms outstretched to embrace me. "Oh my Louis"—he stopped short and gazed at me in bitter dismay. "Oh my God, where is Louis? Haven't you seen my boy? He was out hauling wood." But I had not seen Louis, and the poor man, with despair in his heart and tears frozen on his cheeks, hurried on into the white darkness.

He had told me that I was not half a mile from town, as I soon could see from the more rapid descent of the road. Before long I stood before a little gate, not far back from which I made out the dim outlines of a house. Throwing the bridle over a post, I crawled up the steep pathway on hands and knees, for now I was too weak and numb to walk. It was probably only a minute, but it seemed an age before the inmates heard my knocking and admitted me into their very humble but warm and cheery abode. "See to the horse at the gate," I muttered feebly,—and—and—I want to sleep."

They found my face, hands, and feet badly frozen, and it took long and patient rubbing with snow and an internal application of stimulants before the blood returned to its normal channels.

In the late evening the wind died away and the snow ceased to fall. A clear, starlit night succeeded—a night now passed into a proverb in the island, for—thing unique! there was no Midnight Mass. The frost bound everything as with fetters of steel. The window panes were thick-encrusted with its fantastic flower work, and now and again a sharp report marked where shingle or clapboard had split under its gripping hand. Even the merry fire in the hearth had a frosty crackle, and outside—I dared for an instant, but only an instant, to open the door—the stars glittered with a steel-like frosty twinkle. What a bitter, wretched Christmas night! The thought of home sickened me. Perhaps they were in suspense about me and were even then searching for me—I felt miserable, and at the same time, rather important. Perhaps on the contrary, they were having a gay time around my tree—I felt disgusted and jealous. One thing alone comforted me. The family which sheltered me was poor, and there were no presents for the merry-eyed little children who romped about the house. Acting the bountiful Santa Claus, I gave the father all my money, five dollars, a fortune for him—and for me too—and with it he braved the cold and purchased an array of beautiful things that overfilled their hearts with delight. My timely generosity must have given the children the idea that I was Santa Claus himself, for I heard one of them say to his mother in a whisper, "Mamma, where are his long white whiskers?" to which she replied with perfect gravity, "Hush, dear; the wind blew them off." With this little gleam of humor to make me feel better, I went off to bed, wishing to leave them to their mirth unabashed by the presence of a stranger, even though that stranger were Santa.

Without taking a morsel of breakfast —it was a fixed custom in the family to go to Holy Communion on Christmas Day—I saddled the pony at the first ray of dawn and was off. How Count did want to get home! I could not hold him in. Where the snow was thin he galloped, and where it was thick he struggled and plunged impetuously. I stopped at the stump where my bird was enclosed—he was as hard as a rock. I sighed and felt guilty, and fled from the place. I saw a horse and rider coming to meet me; he stopped and halloed—it was my brother come to look for me.

They had not been in real suspense about me at home, as they felt sure that I had reached Le Brun's before the blizzard. They did not know of the bird. Still they had not kept their Christmas tree festivity.

"I was a fool for letting that child go" my father had said; "I always felt that that new-fangled notion would bring no luck to the house." And in his wrath, he took the tree, tinsel and flowers and all, carried it down to the river's bank and pitched it in. The water was fast freezing, the tree froze with it, and there it stuck a monument to my chivalry for many a day.

Next day we heard that a poor fellow had been frozen to death in the blizzard, not far form St. Anne's. He evidently must have gone dazed, for a circle of beaten track in the snow showed where he had retraced his steps around and around. He had gone out to search for a little son, who reached home five minutes after his father's departure. The boy's name was Louis.

Is it any wonder, then, that our first family Christmas tree remains ever green in my memory?

W. B. H., '10.

CHRISTMAS IN FRANCE

Oh Prince of peace! the battle old,
    Fresh-fed with hate, beats on Thy Spouse;
Foul men neath Satan's flag enrolled
    Would drag her from her Father's House,
And drive her to the barren wold.

The world's dark prince now holds the keys;
    Her own may hence receive her not;
Let her go forth—the heart's true ease
    She still may find in hillside grot
With Thee, oh Prince of Peace.

M. S. S., '09.

THE FALL OF THE MISTLETOE

The great hall was filled with people who, animated with a true Xmas spirit laid all personal enmity aside and chatted gaily with one another. The air was laden with the perfume of spruce bough, red berries and mistletoe and great yule logs burned brightly in the fireplace. The large holdings of Sir Arthur Yardly, the greatest in all Virginia, were ravaged for the spoils, and the guests made merry in the enjoyment of his hospitality.

Soon after the colony was planted Sir Arthur had emigrated to Virginia, and now at the age of sixty possessed a vast estate and, last but not least, a beautiful daughter, Lenore, not quite twenty, the joy and torment of some of the young men in the neigborhood.

The two most favored suitors were young Cleon Devereaux, a friend from childhood, and the Earl of Crawley, a recent arrival from England. No one knew which Lenore preferred for she had distributed favors impartially among them.

On a landing in the great stair case, Sir Arthur and the elderly guests played cards and occasionally watched the merriment of the young people below. Although partaking of her father's hospitality the gossip did not fail to criticise Lenore's conduct towards the young men and Miss Hightower, the Governor's sister, was heard to remark, "I don't see why she doesn't take one or the other."

At this juncture, Lenore approaching Miss Hightower said, "I've two partners for the Virginia Reel and would you be so kind as to take the Earl off my hands for I know you have had more experience with noblemen than I." The person addressed smiled sheepishly, but nevertheless followed Lenore down to the Earl who tried heroically to accept the change of partners with the best of grace.

"She is trying to catch the Earl," whispered the Governor's wife, as Miss Hightower, bowing and smiling took the proffered arm.

The Virginia Reel was danced under a huge spray of mistletoe hanging from a chandelier and many forfeits were paid as each young gallant endeavored to the utmost to catch his partner under the "tree of love." Lenore alone proving too wary to be caught. The Earl and Miss Hightower were the first couple while Cleon and Lenore were the last. The dance was an old favorite and gave excuse for much laughter and romping.

Suddenly the Earl grasped Lenore's arm and drawing her under the mistletoe cried: "Long have I waited for this happy moment." The girl screamed and young Devereaux drawing his sword cut the ribbon on which the mistletoe was suspended and exclaimed quietly: "You will have to wait still longer, my lord."

Lenore clung to Cleon's arm while

the Earl, with a face the image of shame and hate, drew his sword. But Sir Arthur, rising to his feet spoke out: "My dear friends, I have invited you here this evening for a twofold purpose, to enjoy with you a merry Christmas and to announce the betrothal of my daughter to Cleon Devereaux."

The breaking of steel marked the end of his speech, for the Earl in his agitation had bent his sword almost in two and the strain being too great caused it to break. Placing the pieces at Cleon's feet, thereby acknowledging defeat, he begged Lenore's pardon, quickly withdrew, mounted his horse and vanished into the night.

HAROLD ROBERT YOACHAM, 1st. Acad.

HOLLY BERRIES

(TRIOLET)

Heralds of joy and mirth,
　　With your vivid blushing red
You tell us of His birth—
Heralds of joy and mirth—
Who came to save the earth,
　　To crush the serpent's head.
Heralds of joy and mirth,
　　With your vivid blushing red.

　　　　　　J. A. S. '09

The Redwood.

PUBLISHED MONTHLY BY THE STUDENTS OF THE SANTA CLARA COLLEGE

The object of the Redwood is to record our College Doings, to give proof of College Industry and to knit closer together the hearts of the Boys of the Present and of the Past.

EDITORIAL STAFF

EXECUTIVE BOARD

JAMES F. TWOHY, '07
President

J. DANIEL MCKAY, '07   HARRY A. MCKENZIE, '08

ASSOCIATE EDITORS

COLLEGE NOTES - - - - - IVO G. BOGAN, '08
IN THE LIBRARY - - - ROBERT J. O'CONNOR, '08
EXCHANGES - - - ANTHONY B. DIEPENBROCK, '08
ALUMNI - - - - - MERVYN S. SHAFER, '09
ATHLETICS - - - - HARRY A. MCKENZIE, '08

BUSINESS MANAGER

J. DANIEL MCKAY, '07

ASSISTANTS

FRANCIS M. HEFFERNAN, '08   REIS J. RYLAND, '09

M. T. DOOLING, 09

Address all communications to THE REDWOOD, Santa Clara College, California

Terms of subscription, $1.50 a year; single copies, 15 cents

EDITORIAL COMMENT

To our loved President and all the faculty, to each and every individual student in the yard, to all our friends from first to last, to every man, be he friend, acquaintance or stranger, into whose hands these words may fall, we wish the fulness of Christmas joy.

The season is too sacred, the import of the season too vast, to admit of promiscuous editorial topics. There is only one theme on which at this time we can speak; and on that theme, before we close the year, before we begin another chapter in the great mystic Life book, we would say a final word. Just a few rough random thoughts on this great day which in God's beautiful order has served, for so many hundreds of years, as a noble climax to each twelve months, and we have done.

Nineteen hundred and six years ago a woman and a man, footsore and weary, bearing the greatest message of love the world could ever hear, come into their own, and were scorned, rejected. In Bethlehem that night, open doors and hands of greeting for the rich, the great, the roysterer, the sinner; no room in the homes or hearts of men for our wayfarers. In a pitiful wind-swept stable, refuge was taken at last, and there was born the Christ.

Oh the inhumanity of humanity! The first act of the greatest love draw a ever conceived, played to empty benches. The dove bearing the green bough, the message of peace, returning to the ark to beat its tiny wings in vain against barred doors. The source of succor without a friend; the God of hearths without a home. Surely the man, the carpenter with all his meekness, must have looked from the shivering Child and Child Mother, out across the snow to the twinkling lights of the merry-making city, and cried in indignation, "Oh the inhumanity of humanity!"

And today almost two thousand years later, the bells, the Christmas bells, ring out, and men, if they bear the silver chimes at all above the sordid clatter of the market place, scarcely pause to listen to the message. Year after year the bells reiterate their song, and year after year the message falls on the deaf ears of the many. And the story is so sweet, the message so divine!

The world is too grim, too harsh; the poor old world is passion-swayed and passion-swept to utter weariness. Why not cut this season off from the money clinking of the counting house, island this one day in a sea of peace and reflection and devotion? Why not stop in the rush of money madness, stop to listen, if only for a day, to the message of the Christmas bells. And the message of the bells is charity, charity. That was the great message of the Visitor on that first Christmas morn. He revolutionized the religion of the past. He ignored the grim creed, "an eye for an eye, a tooth for a tooth," and gave us that sweet doctrine, "Do good to them that hate you, pray for them that persecute and calumniate you."

The world's noble deeds are written in history, but when the hard old world smiles it is written in God's heart. Why cannot the whole world smile on this day which God has made a gift day, a day of joy? Almost all the holidays are provincial; Christmas is for the world. For pure hearts it is a day of celebration; but it is a day of forgiveness and of peace for lacerated hearts as well. The bells are calling peace to the master and the slave; peace to the saint and the sinner; peace to the publican, aye, and peace even to the Pharisee.

On this one day let a hush fall on the market place, a peacefulness on men. Let the message of the silver throated bells, the great general message of the brotherhood of man, the brotherhood of God, reecho not in the churches alone but everywhere; in the hovel of Lnzarus as in the abode of Dives; in the heart of the remorseful Magdalen, as well as in the heart of the faithful John. Let the furious race onward into the Shadow pause for a moment. Let every man, with bowed head, stop and listen to the message which the Christmas bells are telling the world.

JAMES FRANCIS TWOHY, '07·

Mr. James' Lectures

It is with real and unconcealed sorrow that we realize that we have heard the last of George Wharton James' trio of lectures. Mr. James lectured here a year ago and his appearance again - amongst us was welcomed by the boys of Santa Clara. His subjects could not have been more interesting and could not have been developed better than was done by this scholarly man who has made careful study of each. The first, that on the Grand Canyon of Arizona, was perhaps the most interesting. Mr. James has explored and lived in and near the Grand Canyon for many years, and it would be difficult to find a man who knows it as he does, and still more difficult to find a man who could tell what he knew as well as Mr. James did. Space will not allow a detailed account of all he said about any of the subjects. The causes of the Salton Sea, one of the greatest natural phenomena of our century, were explained and illustrated most graphically. We followed with interest Mr. James and his party—who were the only men who ever succeeded in making the trip—from the ill constructed floodgate out on to the waters of the Salton Sea and were sorry when he arrived there all too soon. Ramona, his last lecture, was of a different kind from the others, but equally as interesting and improving. Mr. James told us the story, and took us by means of his excellent pictures to the *real* places from which Helen Hunt Jackson got the ideas of her fictitious characters.

All the lectures were thoroughly enjoyed by all the students, and we will make so bold as to say that all who attended sincerely hope Mr. James will come again. We shall always be glad to hear him.

The Accolti Medal

In connection with Mr. James' first lecture we wish to record a very pleasing incident. Every year, a handsome gold medal is given for the best essay on the Californian Missions. Last Commencement Exercises the medal was not awarded as, for evident reasons, our jeweller in the city could not make it.

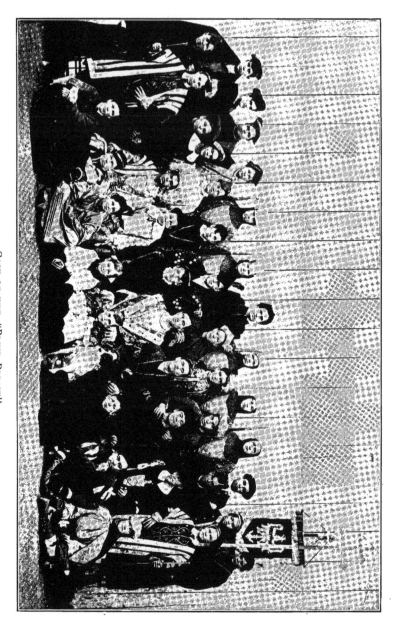

CAST OF THE "BLIND PRINCE".

Not long ago it arrived, however, and to Mr. James, the author of "In and Out of the Old Missions" was given the pleasant task of bestowing it upon George Hall, '07, the successful competitor. With characteristic grace, Mr. James added an autograph copy of his own work to the prize, and he informed us that he intended to renew the gift each succeeding year.

House

At the roll call on Wednesday evening, Dec. 12th, thirty-three Representatives responded "present." It is the largest House the Literary Congress has possessed for years. The Constitution limits the House-membership to forty, and when all who have been proposed shall have been initiated, this maximum number will be reached.

Among the new members some promising talent has been displayed. This especially has been remarked in the maiden speeches of Representatives Farrell, Dozier, McNally, Donovan and others. So that the Senators may expect a good account from the House at the next competitive debate.

Among the topics recently discussed are the following: "Are trades unions becoming a menace to public weal?" "Is more information derived from reading than from personal observation?" "Should the student who desires a university education in California enter the University of California in preference to Stanford?" "Is it of more advantage to be born of rich than of poor parents?" "Is

lynching under certain circumstances justifiable?"

If time and space would allow, a detailed account of these debates might prove both interesting and instructive. Be it said that, though held in temporary quarters unsuggestive of the forum, each of these discussions was entered upon with that old-time ambition and enthusiasm characteristic of the House. With the goodly sum realized by the Senior Dramatic Club from their late play, for our benefit, we hope soon to get conveniently and even handsomely established in our new headquarters. Hence, the dawning year presents us with a very bright outlook for a prosperous coming session.

We take this occasion to most heartily thank the Faculty for having erected so commodious a building for our use; we thank the management and members of the Senior Dramatic Club for their spontaneous support; we thank in fine, all the old alumni and friends who forwarded many generous offerings that contributed much to the financial success of the benefit drama.

Our appreciation finds expression at this happy season in the sincere prayer that each and every one of these benefactors may receive in full the blessings of the new-born Savior-King.

The Junior Dramatic Society

Owing to the lack of space, not of material, the December issue of THE

REDWOOD went to press minus the Junior Dramatics notes. But that did not discourage us in the least, for we hope to make up for lost space in this number.

The ever jealous "press-gang" of the Philathetic House once more swooped down upon the ranks of the G. S. S. with disastrous results, and carried off a few more of our choicest members. The House and Senate seem to consider us as a sort of Recruiting Agency where young debaters are nursed, and then just as they have begun to prattle intelligently within the walls of their nursery, are to be plucked from our midst to adorn the seats of the House and Senate.

Among those who were taken from us were many of the officers. But in the recent election the vacancies left by those departing were ably filled.

The return of the ballot box at the end of the election gave forth the following results: Vice-President, Jas. R. Daly; Secretary, Wm. Gianera; Censor, Robert McCabe; Treasurer, E. Watson; Sergeant-at-Arms, Seth Heney; Prompter, Chas. Brazell.

To the list of new members were added the names of Wm. B. Hirst and George Morgan, together with the other lately initiated members, promise to become famed in the art of speaking and debating.

Several very hotly-contested debates have taken place since last our notes graced the columns of THE REDWOOD, and a marked improvement is shown in the veteran speakers as one debate fol-

lows another. If a political campaign were to take place in 2nd Division, it would not have to import orators,—the J. D. S. would be there with the goods.

The President of the Society has started a series of talks on Parliamentary Law. At every meeting, after the program of the evening is completed, the members listen with attentive ears to the mysteries of the Law, so that if in the future they are called upon to don the Philhistoric gown, or even the Senatorial toga, they will be sufficiently versed in the art to let people know that they are not tyros in the rostrum.

It would hardly become us to close this year's series of notes without hailing all the members of the J. D. S. with the peaceful joys of Xmas and wishing them blessings more abounding than even those of the yesteryear.

To THE REDWOOD for all its kind attention to our little doings we say "Perge quo coepisti modo."

The Sanctuary Society

The Sanctuary room, long desired by the directors and not less by the members themselves, has finally been realized. A rather elaborate feast marked the formal opening. Mr. Brainard put forth his best efforts, and all who have been students of S. C. C. for any time know what that means. Amid the flowers and delicate bouquets loomed up dainty dishes that would have excited the most dyspeptic of students, if a dyspeptic student exists. To the other enjoyments of the evening were added a series of pleasant, good-humored toasts, all of them eloquent with gratitude for the Rev. Director, to whose efforts the Sanctuary room is due. Mr. Aguirre acted as toastmaster.

The house warming was a grand success and the christening of the new room shall be long remembered by the members of the Sanctuary Society. The need of the Sanctuary room was long felt and when first applied for two years ago, no definite satisfaction or information could be had; so the matter remained a dead letter until the memorable 18th of April, when the destruction of the old California Hotel occasioned the erection of a new building. Mr. Brainard saw his way through the difficulty and obtained a room in the new building immediately adjoining the sacristy. The room besides being fitted up with lockers for the cassocks and surplices has not been neglected in regard to the bodily comforts of the members; and it will serve as a place of enjoyment and recreation when the cold winter mornings begin to freeze the marrow in their bones. And so, to the Rev. Rector and to our Director we say "gratias."

New Statues

One of the losses sustained by the college when the earthquake came upon us was the breaking of all of our statues in the boy's chapel. The loss was keenly felt by the boys and the voids left on the side altars were noticed by them with deep regrets. It did not seem like the same old chapel with the side altars bare. It does us good now to come into the chapel in the morning and evening and see upon the altars two new statues, one of The Sacred Heart, the other of the Blessed Virgin. When the great earthquake came, with fear and death in its wake, many a mother whose boy was away at Santa Clara became nearly frantic for his safety. Two of these mothers made their way at great expense and trouble to the college on that awful day and found that God's goodness held sway and that their sons were unharmed, and these devotional new statues are the tokens of their gratitude to the "Lord of the Earthquake." They are both exceptionally beautiful.

New Buildings

The old adobe, the subject of Chas. D. South's most beautiful retrospect in the November number of the REDWOOD is, as you all know a thing of the past. Out of its ruins has risen a new building 111 feet long by 73 feet wide. The east side of this magnificent building is one long hall where the House and Senate hold their meetings. This spacious hall can be divided into four sections by large folding doors. On the west side, which faces the yard, the building is divided into four rooms. The Sanctuary has for its use the one on the south end. The trunk room comes next,—a large room fitted with racks on which to put the trunks. Mr.

Beubrer, the musical instructor, has for his studio the next room.

Last but not least comes the new social hall where every evening the boys gather and have a little time. It is a great improvement on the old social hall being much larger and having a very good floor on which we can now have a dance now and then. On cold mornings and evenings the big fire looks awfully good.

The old walk has been replaced with a new brick walk which leads from the social hall over to study hall. Around the steps of the 2nd and 1st division study halls a big brick walk has been made. A great improvement on the old boards that used to be there.

The Play

Beautiful costumes, good talent and able direction added one more dramatic success to the long list that graces Santa Claras' chronicle. The Blind Prince and the Vaudeville that preceeded it were great successes. Raymond Caverly on his frugal horn entertained the audience, which, despite the rain and severe weather, was large, in his own individual and inimitible way. Raymond is always welcome to a Santa Clara audience. No need for me in my humble way to tell you of one so famous and popular. Another feature of the evening was the performance of the Porta children on the most rare and melodious instruments, the "Marimba" or South American harp. Many times they were encored and each time rendered appreciated selections. Mr. Morris, Leo and Alphonse Ruth, and Mr. P. Perevia appeared in a novel brass quartet and were heartily received.

Percy Van Sycle, our old "rag time kid" accompanied Willie Barric who sang in his unequaled soprano, "Cheyenne," and as an encore, " Why Don't You Try."

Harry McKenzie, ever comical Harry, and the old reliable August Aguirre came before the audience as a comic team. The hit they made was stupendous—that's the word. Hardly any other result could have been expected from those two. "That ten dollars" caused many a laugh, and the fame of the owed and the ower McKenzie and Aguirre rose to its zenith. Their jokes were new and had not the odor of mildew, and their songs were fine, mostly parodies on "Traveling." McKenzie sang "Moving Day," and Aguirre sang, "A Ragtime Boy."

The Blind Prince finished up the evening. James Twohy appeared at his best, Edmund, the rightful heir seemed to fit him exactly. Jim's interpretation of the part was excellent and his action was easy and natural. August Aguirre as Oberto, the honest peasant, won the applause of the audience by his clever impersonation. Harry McKenzie as Molino, the happy-go-lucky good-for-nothing brought down the house with his clever fun making. James Daly, the son of Oberto was very good. His voice was clear and sweet and his acting was realistic. Fred Sigwart as "Rudolph" played the part of that villianous scoundrel in an unquestionable manner. Leander Murphy, the veteran villain, was, as usual, good. Every one knows Murphy was good because he always is. Edmond Lowe covered himself with glory on this his first appearance; his acting was superb, and his interpretation was also very good. He had a good part and did it justice. George Casey played the part of King Stanislaus. Did George have no other talent or did not know at all how to act his part, his fine, strong, excellent voice, full and rich, would win him applause, but George has not only this natural gift to his credit—he also played this part in royal style.

We may as well quote the following from the "Santa Clara Journal," to portray the entertainment as others saw it.

ONE OF THE BEST PLAYS EVER PRESENTED BY THE COLLEGE STUDENTS

Once again Santa Clara College hall is opened to the public, and as a people we are genuinely glad the repair work has been finished and that we will enjoy as heretofore the splendid entertainments that are presented within its walls. On the opening night the students presented "The Blind Prince."

The fore part of the program was a clever make up of vaudeville numbers that brought out musical talent and his_tronic ability that would have been a credit to actors with many more years of experience than the students of Santa Clara College. Each number was spicy, well executed and contained some nov-

elty that thoroughly delighted the large audience. Charles Barec sang in a splendidly clear soprano voice "Cheyenne" and for an encore "Why Don't You Try." The Porta children played four different times on their wonderful instrument the "Mirimba" a South American instrument of wood that proved a novelty to the audience.   *   *   *

Then followed the drama, the principal part of the program. Santa Clara College students are not new at the staging of plays, and the public is always sure of a rare treat whenever they have an opportunity of attending a performance at the College Hall. While possibly not quite so pretentious as some former productions, the piece was full of action and carried a thread of interest that held attention to the fall of the last curtain. No detail was lacking to make the play as finished and complete as if done by the professional actor, and at its completion compliments resounding the praise of its merits were on every lip. *   *   *   The scenery, costumes and stage effects were particularly fine. The same and more may be said of the orchestra selections. If there is any one thing that Santa Clara College excels in, it is the quality of its orchestra and its musical selections. The music Wednesday evening was particularly fine, better than it has been for some time past and that says much. In fact the entire entertainment on Wednesday was particularly fine and reflects much credit on the College, the student actors, and especially on Mr. George Fox, S. J. who directed the presentation.

Masquerade Ball

"Some in rags, some in tags and some in velvet gowns" in the evening of Thanksgiving day. That's the way they came, and a mighty good time they had. You should have been a student again just for that night, it was great. A big masquerade, a long contemplated and anxiously awaited happening took place. "The scene was wonderful to behold" The new hall, the future home of the debating societies, was bright with many a light, and its new and excellent floor was in fine condition for the dance. At a quarter to eight we left study hall and assembled at the social hall. There the line of couples was formed and a grand march was the beginning of one "great big time."

Professor Morris and the Sodality band furnished the wherewithal to dance by. No need to comment on the excellence of the music. To mention "Sodality band" means good music to all who know, and to those who don't well—why just take it on faith.

After a few dances the couples were formed again so that the judges could decide who should be the winners of the prizes, three in number, one to be given to the best couple in the first division, one to the best in the second, and the other to the best individual costume. The judging was a difficult operation for all were good. After due consideration, however, the prize to the first division was awarded to Harry A. J. McKenzie, a cute Dutchman, and to

Frank M. Heffernan a—my pen hesitates. I can't name it. It was something in skirts however, and it danced cleverly. It also had on blue socks. In the second division Master Cyril Smith and Mr. Frank D. Warren were the best. Cyril came as a cowboy and his make-up was excellent. In his white chaps, spurs, guns, bandana and cowboy hat he looked the typical cowboy. Frank was there with the coy look, and bashful, retiring manner of a fair little country lass His dress, procured from Lord knows where, was excellent. He leaned dependently on his cowboy partner's arm and blushed appropriately when addressed.

Geo. Mayerle was the best for the individual costume. He was certainly good. A fat Dutch policeman was his role. Naturally comical, "Dutch," arrayed in this garb was beyond description. In colloquial language "he was certainly great."

Many others were very good. Raymond Caverly, as a bashful maid of tender years, Geo. Hall and Chas. Brazell as Chinamen, the McClatchy boys as football men, were all fine. Others, too numerous to mention here, appeared in costumes that won for themselves more than one approving glance in the course of the evening. At 9:30 the bell summoned us from the scene of revelry to a warm bed, as we were rather tired from the play the preceding and the lecture the evening preceding that, we obeyed it with resignation. Although it removed us from the scene of a very pleasant 'time.'

Orchestra

Elsewhere on these pages may be noticed an eulogy of this worthy organization, quoted from a disinterested local newspaper. It was well merited at the recent Play. This praise becomes doubly grateful when we recall how disabled the orchestra was at the start of this semester. Only four of the old musicians were present for the first rehearsal last September, and among the new-comers not a single experienced performer could be discovered. The well-known energy of the director, Prof. Godfrey Buehrer, however, soon manifested itself. The boys, mostly youngsters from Second Division, responded to his efforts and as a result, we have an orchestra today which is able to render creditable music. THE REDWOOD desires to compliment and encourage these aspiring artists, and feels a satisfaction in recording their following names among the generous promoters of College spirit. Violins—Prof. August Kaufmann, Francis Cauhape, G. B. Hartmann, L. A. Calice, Robert Enscoe, Geo. Morgan, J. Lagomarsino, Arthur Navlet, Ignacio Guerra, Manuel Carrera: Violoncello—Chas. Sullivan, George Duffey: Bass—James Carroll: Cornets—Walter Schmitz, Victor Salberg: Trombone—Jos. Collins: Clarinets—Arthur Theeman, Edmund Lowe: Flute—Philip Wilcox: Drums—August Aguirre.

Second Division

The month of November saw the birth of the first Social Hall in the Second Division. It is situated where the members of the Second Academic were wont to hold their daily classes and now under the care and management of Messrs. Baird, Foster, Lyng and Sheehan, it has become the site of social gatherings in great numbers, especially in the south-eastern corner of the room where radiates in all its warmth a cheery little stove, which stoker George Broderick feeds and attends to assiduously.

A social hall in the junior part of the college has been a long felt want, but now that we have it, no more will you see the small boy standing around holding up a post on a cold morning. That is a thing of the past and the fact is appreciated by the whole division. Wherefore they tender a card of thanks to those who were instrumental in obtaining the Second Division Social Hall.

"Oh, Billiard Balls! Let's Kiss!" Only a breeze from the Junior Reading Room, where preparations are in full sway for a series of billiard games between the world-famous player Willie Hope and our own representative of the art, Norman Buck. Buck tickles the spheres to a nicety. In appearance he has all the qualities of a coming billiardist, although he has not exactly the proportions of a billiard cue, being rather robust, so much so indeed, that he complains he cannot get near enough to the table to shoot well, but he bucks the balls with such dexterity that his bucking manager, Frank Cuda, will buck him up against all opponents.

Well here we are again, after a slight absence, sitting at the old desk, quill in hand, thinking hard how we can do justice to the sumptuous table before us with its varied and tempting burden of College magazines--how we shall start.

In a few days we shall be upon the most joyful season of the year—Christmas! A time that infuses its spirit into us in such a way that we feel we should like perhaps to be lavish in our praise of all the exchanges on our desk, even the most humble. But a stern duty awaits us and one that we must fulfil, Justice only must we think of. So justice, then, to all. But we wish you a merry Christmas, exchanges, each and all of you, and may the poorest of you become as the best, and the best still better.

We have here before us the *"Notre Dame Scholastic"* for the first of December. The *Scholastic* is probably the best college weekly in the country. We have yet to see its equal. But this time we notice that the *Scholastic* has set aside its good taste. Individually each article is good, but as a whole we do not like the *Scholastic* this week. For there is no variety. Football is the one theme of each and every article. We notice an essay on football, a dialogue on a game of football, a poem on football, or rather, to be more precise, on football players; and, besides all these, sketches on the work of different football heroes. Why not give us a little variety, *Scholastic?* We believe that variety is an essential to a good magazine or paper. For if there is no variety the magazine will be a failure. Bur perhaps this is the annual football number of the *Scholastic*, if it has an annual football number. Well, in that case it might have let us "into the know" by some change in the cover, or by some outward indication of its intent and aim. However, as we said above, for the merit of the individual articles, even though they are on the same subject, we compliment our friend from Notre Dame. They are good. Mr. Bracken's comparison between the new game of football and the old, entitled "The New Game" is very forcible. His style and treatment of the subject is both interesting and convincing. We need not say that he proves to a high degree of plausibility the point he sets out to prove, for that would be super-fluous; otherwise the article would not be in the *Scholastic*.

The November issue of "*The Colum-bia Monthly*" has made its appearance —the first this year—on our desk, clothed in its new and more attractive garb. In the editorial which we found within, we noticed that the purpose of the *Monthly* is to become "bigger, broader, and better than ever before." You are to be congratulated on your first step, *Monthly*, for it is a decided improvement. We do not know whether or not there is also an improvement in the matter of the *Monthly*, for we are not acquainted with the contents of the old paper, but we do know that the matter in the present one is certainly fine. "Near the end" is a very clever sketch representing that type of man so common here on our western railways, the glib and smooth-tongued traveling man who never ends his tale. The writer merely makes him tell a story, and how his character shines through the narrative is clear to any one who reads the sketch. "The Wreck" is es-pecially well done. It is wildly passion-ate and beautiful. The Rhetorician tells us that a "composition in metrical language, produced by a creative im-agination and affording intellectual pleasure by exciting elevated, agree-able, and pathetic emotions," is poetry. "The Wreck" certainly possesses all these attributes, therefore, let us end our syllogism by saying it is *poetry*. We have seen much verse in college papers, but very little *poetry*, and this

is one of the few *poems*. We liked also "His Wife Away." This is a comical little affair done up in dialogue form, and it certainly is a grand mix-up. The editorial is written in a very forcible manner and full of good common sense and shows strength of character in the writer.

"*The Fleur de Lis*" possesses a num-ber of very good things in the first issue for November. "Beppo" is a neat little story portraying most vividly the sor-row of the small Italian boy of that name at the loss of his father, or rather separation from him. It is written in such a way that we cannot but pity the brave little fellow for his sufferings, and we feel glad at the happy ending of the tale. When a story works on our imagination as this does, it is surely a sign that there must be something in it. "Buster—a Sketch" imitates Mr. Seton Thompson too closely, we think. An imitation is all right, but it is the height of rashness to imitate too faith-fully. "The College Man in Business" is pretty well done. Forcible in style and readable. The writer shows that a college education is just the thing for the man who wishes to succeed in busi-ness. He expects the college man to correct the abuses in the present mode of business, but, as he concludes his article, "whether they will reform busi-ness, remains to be seen."

There is a scarcity of matter in the *Haverfordian's* November number. But what there is is good. "The Heidle-burg Student" is a fine lecture—for it is a lecture rather than an essay. The writer takes up the most interesting side of student life at the famous German University, and depicts it in a manner that is quite instructive, and engages our attention very closely. In every way is it above the usual literary standard of *The Haverfordian*, but at the same time it is a trifle too long to attract the ordinary reader. However, as the subject is one that requires lengthy treatment, we see no way out of it.

"The Infatuation of Ruy Blas" in the *North Carolina University Magazine* is perhaps the best essay we have seen this month. It is a defense of the infatuation, in Victor Hugo's "Ruy Blas' of Ruy Blas, the prime minister of Spain, for his master, Don Salluste, Spain's exiled prime minister. The writer defends it very well, proving that the infatuation of Ruy Blas is "true to life, to nature and, therefore, to art.' The article might be enjoyed by anyone whether he is interested in the works of Victor Hugo, or not. "The Razor" which we saw in the same magazine,

attracted us by its peculiar title, but we found that the story itself is nothing out of the ordinary, though it is written in a neat and easy style.

The *Holy Cross Purple* for November was delivered to us a few days ago. And we decided that it is most proper to review it. We like very much "Thou Shalt Honor Thy Mother." This is a very sad story of a proud and undutiful son who disowns his aged mother because she is not cultured enough to suit him. The style is simple throughout and it is written in a way that makes one realize the ungratefulness of the man. The only fault we noticed in this story is that a person can too readily guess the ending before he comes to it. "Thy Will Be Done" is another narrative in *The Holy Cross Purple*. This is also very good. We notice three poems on Autumn; don't you think, *Purple*, that one would be sufficient?

A. B. DIEPENBROCK, '08.

My fellow students will, no doubt, read this article from my goosey quill with their hard backs reclining on the soft backs of a railroad Morris chair traveling towards their dear old homes. We have had, we must admit, a very poor and dull season, athletically speaking, the college being devoid of any fall sport whatsoever. Even the illustrious H. McLane our exponent of the Lov game (tennis) deserted us, thus making our calendar a blank for the semester of '06· Of course I do not consider base ball, for as you know we will give this princely American pastime full sway after the holidays. Perhaps this protracted rest from the din and strife of athletics will put us in splendid fettle for the next period—Let us hope so!

Anyhow, fellows, we should all be happy,—even the athlete who has not had the opportunity to gormandize glory as of yore, for we are fast approaching the day which awakens the strongest and most heartfelt associations, the day we feel more sensibly the charm of each other's society, which kindles benevolent sympathies in all of us. When heart calleth unto heart and peace and good will is announced to all mankind, you can easily and rightfully forget the blank on the calendar.

Santa Claus will have a bag for the majority of you and a rattle for some of the star athletes who have been doing nothing. Don't overcrowd your Tomics (this for the athletes) eat all the red berries and white meat you can store away but come back after the holidays and try to keep the college name on top of the athletic flag pole by the same square. gentlemanly tactics that made us forge to the front last spring. If by any unforseen circumstance you should happen to slip down the pole a few—why we will still be with you. From the lean one to the stout one, from the stout one to the short one and from the short one to the tall one—we wish you a Merry Christmas and O my! what a happy New Year!

*   *   *   *   *   *

We present you with the following little packet as a Christmas present and you who have burned the nine-thirty oil while in college can figure out the dope at your own fireside on Christmas eve.

A Word From the Captain

As the baseball season is now treading on our heels, it may not be out of place for me, as Captain of the '07 team, to say a word or to about our prospects.

By winning the series from St. Mary's last term we took the State Intercollegiate Championship, and we certainly felt and still feel proud of that. However, that is past now and there is a future close at hand, at which time we want, by all means, to capture those honors again.

We will have all of our last year's team back save Wolter and Byrnes. Byrnes' departure deprives us of a clever artist at the initial sack, while in Wolter we have lost a most valuable man, one that will be hard to replace. In the box, at the bat, on the bags and in the field he was our number one man.

At the present time I can not form any new material that may come in

after Christmas; however, with the material in sight at the present time, we will have an exceptionally good team, and I have every confidence of carrying out a most successful season.

On the pitching staff we will have Joseph Brown and my humble self and possibly Chas. Freine. I am quite sure that we will be able to hold our own in the box. Brown played in but few games last season, but that is no sign that he is not a good pitcher. I feel sure that he will pitch winning ball for us this coming season. Chas. Freine has never pitched on other teams and has shown that he can hold his own in the box. The fact is we need Freine mostly in the field, as he is an exceptional good fielder, but if we are stuck for a man to pitch, it is good to have a pitcher of his stamp to fall back upon.

Our last year's shortstop, M. Shafer, will very likely hold the position behind the bat. It is not necessary to mention his ability as a catcher as you all know that he is capable of doing justice to that position. As he has a good head behind a strong and true arm, it will be a hard proposition for our opponents to steal the bags on us, even though we are going to come in contact with some very fast players.

Harry Broderick, our former right-fielder, had an excellent chance for the first bag. Of late he has shown up exceedingly well in that position, taking in different throws as though they were everyday occurrences. At the bat, well, he will very likely lead off, as he always waits for the good ones, and when they do come, he often hits them safely.

At the second bag we will have James Twohy, who played as nice a game of ball around that base last season as one would want to see. He covers lots of ground and very seldom misses anything that comes within his reach and for a lefthander he has an exceptionally true arm.

Arthur Shafer who played on different amateur teams in and about Los Angeles last season, and who made an extraordinary showing on our college team two years ago, will be our short stop. In brief I can say, "Woe to the opponents who knocks the ball within his reach."

As for the difficult corner, we have men from last season such as Lappin and Freine who could fill that position —yes, and fill it well—but they will be needed more elsewhere, so consequently very likely that base will be open for new men to seek for.

So now with a good man at third, and with the infield places filled as already stated, we will have what one may style *a stone walled infield.*

And now to the outfield.

In our left garden we will have James Lappin who made a remarkable showing in the same position, and also at bat last season, and especially in those games against St. Mary's, which were the most important. And now if we have Friene in center and Collins in right, neither of whom need introduction, we shall have a regular Gibraltar in the outfield, not only in fielding but also at the bat.

This coming year will be the second season for most of the men that will be on the team, so I think in fielding we are going to be exceptionally strong, whereas at the bat I am afraid we are not going to be quite so well off, and thereby I judge that we are going to win most of our games on small scores; however such may not be the case, for we are going to do all we can for the improvement of the batting in particular.

CLEON KILBURN, '08.

We will not bore you at any length on the recent game when the Redwoods crossed sticks with the Mountain View team, champions of Santa Clara Valley and blanked them with the odious goose egg. The game was exceedingly fast and replete with sensational plays. On whom can I place the crown of olives—well, I take the team and roll them up into one giant base ball hero and place the coveted crown on his cranium. Here is the way the new scorer received it:

REDWOODS

	AB	R	BH	SB	PO	A	E
Broderick, 1b....	3	2	0	1	4	1	0
Shafer, M., c....	4	1	0	0	10	1	0
Collins, cf	4	1	3	0	1	0	0
Shafer, A., ss ...	3	0	1	0	2	1	0
Lappin, lf	3	0	0	0	1	0	0
Twohy, 2b.......	4	1	1	2	5	3	1
Kilburn, p	4	0	0	0	3	3	0
Peters, rf.......	3	1	0	1	0	0	1
Watson, 3d b...	4	1	1	0	0	0	2
Totals 31	31	7	6	3	27	0	3

MOUNTAIN VIEW

	AB	R	BH	SB	PO	A	E
Nevens, 3b	3	0	0	0	0	0	0
Foley, ss	4	0	0	0	4	3	1
Farry, 2b	4	0	2	0	4	2	2
Graham, rf	4	0	0	0	0	0	0
Pingree, lf	4	0	2	0	0	0	0
Vargas, c	3	0	0	0	9	1	0
Shea, cf	1	0	0	0	4	0	0
Merkle, p	2	0	0	0	0	1	1
Lyons, 1b	3	0	0	0	3	0	2
Totals	29	0	4	0	24	7	6

SUMMARY

First base on errors—Santa Clara 3, Mountain View 1. First base on called balls—Off Kilburn 5, off Merkle 3. Struck out by Kilburn 10, by Merkle 9. Double plays—Farry to Foley to Lyons; Kilburn to A. Shafer to Broderick. Two base hits, A. Shafer. Passed ball, Vargas. Umpire—Atteridge. Scorer—Brazell. Time of game—1 hour and 40 minutes.

SCORE BY INNINGS.

	1	2	3	4	5	6	7	8	9	Totals
Santa Clara	0	0	0	1	0	1	5	0	*—	7
Hits	0	0	0	1	1	1	3	0	*—	6
Mt. View	0	0	0	0	0	0	0	0	0—	0
Hits	0	1	0	1	0	0	2	0	0—	4

Second Division

Following in the wake of the first division athletes, we also have felt the dire effects of this listless season. However, we have squeezed two games this semester out of the baseball lemon. The first being with the redoubtable Day Scholars' team who have taken many scalps this year, but whose baseball tomahawks on this occasion were unequal to the task and as a result they rode on the short end of the score board after nine exciting spasms.

Archbold did the morgue work in deadly style and Lyng fattened his average by catching the third strike of many who died at the plate. Foster, Peters and Watson strengthened the infield and were potent factors during the entire game. When the bell sounded the score was 10 to 4 in favor of the Juniors. A series between these two teams next spring would prove sweet candy for us all. For you who calculate the Day Scholars' ability from this one game will have to peruse the dope a little more. They have an aggregation of exceptional ability and will make any of them pedal to beat their nine.

The next and last game of the season was the struggle with the scholastics' team which was reinforced by many of the St. Ignatius fathers to be. Well, it was certainly a hair raiser; the way these nimble scholastics romped around the diamond was a caution. The game was replete with double plays, long drives and brilliant stops, and many of these were accredited to the fathers. When one takes into consideration that these gentlemen very seldom practice we must respectfully place the crown of victory on their humble heads, although the game itself resulted in a tie. Would take a small volume, if I started to enumerate the features, so we'll omit them.

Terry McGovern will occupy the box for the Angelus team after Christmas and Johnnie Irilary will don the big glove. Woe to their opponents, for Tim Flood will submerge them in regular order. The boys have selected this gentlemanly little player to lead them, with Twohy, Putman, Castruccio, McLaughlin and a few lesser lights, they have nothing but success staring them in the face.

H. A. J. McKENZIE, '08.

Santa Clara College

THE PIONEER UNIVERTITY
OF THE PACIFIC COAST

This famous institution of learning, which is in charge of the Jesuits, has a reputation even in Europe for the completeness of its equipment and the thoroughness of its instruction. With most complete and appropriate accommodation in every department, and a full staff of professors, the institution offers uncommon advantages for the mental, moral and practical training of young men and boys.

FULL PARTICULARS MAY BE OBTAINED
BY ADDRESSING THE ぷ ぷ ぷ ぷ ぷ

Rev. Richard A. Gleeson, S. J.

Santa Clara College

SANTA CLARA   ぷ   ぷ   ぷ   &   ぷ   CALIFORNIA

THE 45 H. P. PIERCE GREAT ARROW

SEVEN PASSENGERS

When we say "seven passengers" we mean seven comfortable seats. The two additional seats are in the tonneau, with backs and arms. They revolve so that the occupants can turn around and chat sociably with the three people in the rear.

The appeal of the PIERCE ARROW is made upon something deeper and more vital than a change in the form of the body. It is in the car itself.

Honest construction, adapted to American conditions and temperaments, has won for the PIERCE ARROW the enviable reputation expressed by those who know with no other motive than true conviction.

If You Want the Best Buy the
PIERCE GREAT ARROW CAR.

The Mobile Carriage Co.

762 and 764 Golden Gate Avenue

Telephone Franklin 1784   SAN FRANCISCO

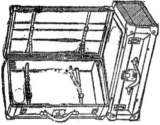

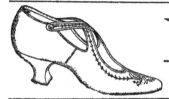

DON'T WURRY

Buzzers and bells and electric clocks,
Medical batteries with electric shocks
Everything here in the electric line,
Electric work in electric time.

Frank J. Somers
Manager

Century Electric Co.

Phone James 91   20 S. Market Street, San Joes, Cal.

THE
REDWOOD

FEBRUARY, 1907

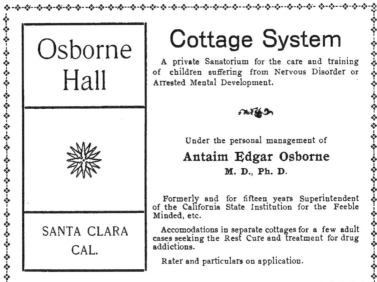

T. F. SOURISSEAU

Manufacturing
and Repairing

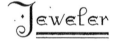

Extra Fine Assortment of Sterling Silver and Solid
Gold Jewelry

No Plate Goods—Only 10-14-18 Karat Gold

69½ South First Street, San Jose

Rooms 2-3-4   Phone White 207

Contents.

Nace Printing Co. Santa Clara, Cal.

Photo by Bushnell

OFFICERS OF BASEBALL TEAM

AUGUST M. AGUIRRE, '07, Manager; JAMES BYRNES, Coach; CLEON P. KILBURN, '08, Captain.

The Redwood.

Entered Dec. 18, 1902, at Santa Clara, Calif. as second-class matter, under Act of Congress of March 3, 1879.

| VOL. VI. | SANTA CLARA, CAL., FEBRUARY, 1907. | No. 5. |

VANITAS

The smiling rose
    Which sweetly is perfumed,
And with a glorious color glows,
    Must fade and droop away!
But wherefore must it be consumed
    So beauteous and so delicate?
Ah we would fain it were not prey
    To hoary Time's e'erlasting hate!
Stern Time, alas! the iron king of kings
    'Gainst beauty steels his cold grey eyes.
Why should he end but hateful things
    When mortal beauty's naught
But dust enrobed in godlier guise?
    To dust return
    What things of dust were wrought!
And beauty also finds its urn!

        Anthany B. Diepenbrock, '08·

THE SITUATION IN FRANCE

[LECTURE DELIVERED IN SAN JOSE ON DEC. 23, 1906, BY REV. HENRY GABRIEL S. J., OF THE
SANTA CLARA COLLEGE FACULTY]

Ladies and gentlemen: The subject before us this evening is one that has of late aroused deep and lively interest both in the Old World and in the New. The reason is that, on the one hand, most men feel that there is question of some mighty and everlasting principle, some precious and inalienable right, on the observance of which hinges the welfare and the life of nations, whilst, on the other hand, many, especially in this country, do not see how such a principle could be ignored and such a right be threatened in a state like France, whose spirit and constitution is so similar to that of our own United States. And yet such appears to be the case. Indeed, the whole measure known as the Law of Separation, is, in my opinion, so flatly contradictory and so thoroughly antagonistic to the most fundamental maxims of the republican form of government that I feel confident that every true American will be filled with astonishment and moved with indignation when he first comes to realize the odious tyranny and foul robbery which it attempts to commit under cover of a legal statute. Yes, ladies and gentlemen, here before the impartial bar of reason, before the sacred tribunal of humanity, I solemnly arraign the French Government for having violated every form of liberty—personal, civil, and religious,—

and for having transgressed every kind of justice—commutative, distributive, and legal,—by these sweeping measures lately adopted against the Catholic Church. Whether the facts which I am going to adduce will substantiate this weighty charge, I must leave entirely to your sober judgment.

Historically, the trouble between the Church and the State dates back to 1880, when, without even the shadow of a judicial trial, the Jesuits and other religious orders were forcibly dispersed, their homes closed, and nearly 300 establishments of learning suppressed. The chief promoter of this first expulsion was Jules Ferry. As Minister of Public Instruction under President Grevy, he introduced a bill for insuring liberty of education. Its main purpose, however, was to exclude the members of religious bodies from the right of teaching. Hence, Jules Simon, though himself a prominent leader of the Republicans in their political struggles with the Monarchists, and at the same time, unfortunately, a declared enemy of the Catholic Church, again and again denounced the bill as striking at the very root of liberty. But it was carried in spite of his opposition, and France ceased to be a true republic. Jules Ferry, now become Prime Minister, charged himself with applying the new law to the obnoxious congregations, while the degenerate Republicans in the Chamber of Deputies followed up their success by passing the same year another bill, for the abolition of the army chaplaincies.

However, in course of time, the Government relented somewhat, in consequence of party dissensions, and the religious quietly returned to resume their ministries for the good of the people. But again the freethinkers and infidels raised an outcry, and their animosity became more and more bitter, till, in 1901, they passed a law on association, introduced by the Prime Minister, Waldeck Rousseau, under the Presidency of Loubet, and framed in such a way as to render it impossible for religious organizations either to exercise any work of general usefulness or even to continue a legal existence. The execution of this iniquitious and despotic decree meant the banishment not only of the teaching orders, but also of the numerous congregations of men and women, devoted to the care of the poor, the wretched, the young, the aged, the sick, and the insane. All their property, movable as well as immovable, whether acquired by donation, or legacy, or purchase—colleges, schools, hospitals, asylums, homes —all was taken away by the State without any compensation, and sold at auction for the benefit of the public treasury; while the 160,000 members of these various religious communities were turned out of their own houses and deprived of every means of subsistence, after having consecratey their fortunes,

their talents, and their lives, to the social and moral improvement of their fellow-citizens.

Up till then the leaders of this anti-religious movement had repeatedly asserted, that their only object was to check the influence of these congregations, whose members, bound by vows to a life of virtue and self-sacrifice, constituted, they said, a serious danger to the Republic. But scarcely had the law on association been carried into execution, when these champions of liberty, equality, and fraternity—the motto of the French Republic—threw off the mask and began to direct their attacks against the Catholic Church. Time-hallowed processions were forbidden to appear in the streets, crucifixes and similar emblems were ruthlessly town down from public squares and buildings, and the filling of vacancies in the episcopacy was made a constant source of annoyance to the Holy See, the Pope of Rome.

In 1904, Pius X summoned the bishops of Laval and Dijon to explain their conduct in matters ecclesiastical. The two prelates proved dilatory, they consulted the Government, and were urged not to obey the summons. Yet, after some time, they both heeded the warnings of the Supreme Pontiff and went to Rome to settle their affairs. The French Government seized upon this event as a pretext to come to an open rupture with the Church. They had the effrontery of demanding an apology; the pope refused with uncompromising, yet inoffensive, dignity; the Ambassador to the Vatican was summarily recalled to

Paris, and it was officially announced that the first step had been taken towards the breaking of the Concordat.

What was this Concordat? It was an arrangement concluded in 1801 between Napoleon I. and Pius VII., by which the emperor agreed to restore to the Catholics the churches and rectories taken from them during the Revolution, and, in return for the estates which had formerly served for the maintenance of worship and the support of the clergy, to pay certain yearly subsidies to bishops and priests. It was a definitive settlement proposed by the imperial council, and though inadequate, accepted by the papacy. For these subsidies represented only a small portion of the interest due on the value of the estates appropriated by the Jacobins in in 1790. If we bear in mind that Mexico was adjudged, by an international court of arbitration, to pay full interest on the Mission Fund confiscated by President Santa Anna in the early days of the Republic, we cannot but admire the moderation shown by the Church in her dealings with France. In acknowledgment, moreover, of this scanty mete of justice, the pope granted the emperor the right of presenting candidates for vacant bishoprics.

Well, after this Concordat, this treaty sworn to by both parties, had been observed for more than a century, and subsidies been paid yearly in compensation for the property violently wrested from the Catholics, a law was proposed by M. Combes, Prime Minister, and put through the Chamber and the Senate, in 1905, annulling this solemn contract, and proclaiming separation between Church and State.

Now, this Law of Separation cannot fail to impress every unbiassed mind as a most brazen act of injustice and oppression. It entails not only the reversion to the State of the cathedrals and churches, reared in past ages by the spontaneous offerings of the faithful, and restored to the Catholics by Napoleon, but also the confiscation of all other sacred edifices, chapels, residences, and seminaries, built almost exclusively by private contributions since the framing of the Concordat, as well as of all estates and funds lawfully acquired by ecclesiastical corporations, in the course of the preceding century. Moreover, the yearly subsidies to the Catholic clergy, which, as we have seen, constitute in reality nothing but a low-interest payment on a national debt, contracted towards the Church in consequence of the unjust usurpation of her possessions;—these meagre subsidies, which up to this formed the chief means of subsistence for bishops and priests, are simply abrogated.

It is true, the Law of Separation provides for pensions to be paid to superannuated pastors and for a few years' pecuniary assistance to be given to the older members of the clergy, just as if, till now, they had been but public functionaries and mere state officials. Yet, even this niggardly and offensive concession, hedged about, besides, by a number of onerous conditions, is now going to be cancelled, on the plea that the priests and bishops have refused to avail themselves of another provision of the Law of Separation, the one relative to the foundation of associationr of worship.

For the French Government, desirous, of course, to secure to the Catholics at least the use of their own churches, now declared public propertv, had planned so-called "associations cultu-elles." The various articles, however, that embody this benignant provision of the Law of Separation, are couched in such terms as to vest the administration and control of the funds and realties originally destined for divine worship and general benificence, immediatey in boards of laymen, in whose election the Church authorities are practically to have no voice, and ultimately in the Su-preme Council of a professedly atheistic state. The property involved consists of about 30,000 sacred edifices, and of other acquisitions made by request, en-dowment, or contribution, during the last hundred years, and valued at more than $100,000,000. Without the written consent of the clergy to the establish-ment of these "associations cultuelles," and without the formal transfer by the clergy of this ecclesiastical patrimony to these lay boards, there can not only be no more public exercise of divine wor-ship, but there will also follow a whole-sale liquidation of church property.

For Protestants and Jews,—who, by the way, form but a small portion of the entire population,—this provision pre-sents not the least difficulty, since with them each congregation not merely manages its own temporal and spiritual interests, but even appoints and dis-misses its own pastors. Besides, these and similar denominations are inevitably more or less national. But the Catholic or International Church, whose founder is not a sinful man, like Luther, Calvin, or Henry VIII, but Christ Jesus, the God-Man, and whose priesthood has received the divine injunction to teach and guide the faithful, such associations of worship would be subversive of her very existence, in other words, simply inconceivable.

But this is precisely the reason why this kind and thoughtful provision was inserted by these worthy disciples of Voltaire. Hence, their ill-concealed anger and dismay, when the Holy Father, in full accord with the French bishops, proclaimed it his apostolic duty to forbid the formation of these associa-tions of worship. While loudly pre-tending to work for freedom of religion, the sole purpose of these Machiavellian tricksters had been to reduce the Church of God to a condition of utter depend-ence and hopeless servitude, under a godless State. Disappointed, but not disheartened, the French Government now began to cast about for some means or other to repair its discomfiture and carry out its impious machinations. An opportunity soon presented itself. The Cardinal Archbishop of Bordeaux, Mgr. Lecot, conceived the idea of providing for the support of the clergy, now de-prived of their former income, by means of associations formed in accordance with the laws of 1881 and 1901, but wholly and explicitly disconnected from the Law of Separation. They were to be nothing more than benevolent societies, solely dependent on the diocesan authorities, and exercising no control whatever over the conduct of divine worship. Having received the approbation of the Holy See, Mgr. Lecot proceeded to organize such associations in all the parishes of his arch diocese.

Now, Citizens of America, note the meanness of the French Government. You would undoubtedly expect to hear that this lawful and praiseworthy endeavor to mitigate the effects of the withdrawal of subsidies had been warmly welcomed and sincerely seconded by the men in power. I am sorry that I have to dispel your illusion. Regardless of truth and lost to shame, M. Briand, the Minister of Worship, speaking in his official capacity, put forward the absurd pretension that these benevolent'societies, contrary to the emphatic declaration of their founder and the well defined nature of ther object, could not be regarded otherwise than as associations of worship formed in compliance with the Law of Separation; and, hence, he expressed a wish that the example of the Archbishop of Bordeaux might soon be followed in all the other dioceses of France. It will be hard, I think, to find in all the annals of history a more glaring instance of malicious misrepresentation and disgusting hypocrisy. But again the nefarious scheme was set at nought. Mgr. Lecot immediately disbanded these benevolent societies, and

Pope Pius X. positively prohibited their formation anywhere in France.

Seeing their perfidious policy thus completely defeated, the rage of these tyrants burst forth in threats and deeds of violence. In utter disregard of the immunity of ambassadors, recognized, since time immemorial, not only among the civilized nations of Europe, but even among the barbarous tribes of America, they broke into the palace of the papal nuncio at Paris, had the secretary, Mgr. Montagnini, arrested and conveyed across the frontier, and confiscated all his letters and documents. Next day they introduced into the Chamber of Deputies several amendments to the Law of Separation, which if carried, as there is no doubt they will be, are to inaugurate a period of real persecution for the French Catholics. All pensions and pecuniary assistance will be struck from the budget; bishops and priests that attempt to hold public services will be made punishable with fines, imprisonment, and deportation; the people will have to meet for divine worship, by invitation, in private houses; and the Church will be in a condition similar to that of the early Christians under Nero, or of the adherents of the ancient faith in the reign of Elizabeth.

But you will ask, "How is it that the Catholics of France allow themselves to be dealt with so unjustly?" The answer is not difficult. While, on the one hand, illegal opposition is made impossible for them by their very religion, legal resistance, on the other hand, has been rendered impotent by the government practically establishing an anti-religious test for all public offices. For the last ten years, I mean, the ruling faction has gradually eliminated and systematically excluded every sincere Catholic from the army, the navy, the civil service, the judiciary, and the entire administration, so that the actual President and his Cabinet can count on some 700,000 salaried partisans.

The animus of the men who thus wantonly trample on liberty and justice betrayed itself unmistakably, some weeks ago, in a public speech delivered before a gathering of school teachers by M. Briand, the originator and executor of this so-called Law of Separation. Pardon me, ladies and gentlemen, if my quotation should shock your cultured feelings and wound your dearest affections. Yet, listen if you can to this piece of fiendishness. "The hour has come," he said, "to root up from the minds of the children the ancient faith, and to replace it by the light of free thought. We must get rid of those time-worn ideals. We have already driven Christ from the schools and from the hospitals, from the prisons and from the courts, from the ships and from the barracks; it remains for us to drive Him out of France." *

Who could ever have believed such a thing possible? Here is a servant of the people's interests, a member of the President's Cabinet, openly flinging threats and hurling scorn at the August Person of Him, whom the vast majority of his own countrymen and hundreds of millions of believers all over the world

adore, invoke, and love, as their Crucified Redeemer and Lord Divine. Fancy for a moment what would happen in this country if one of our officers of state, for instance, Mr. Elihu Root, were to proclaim the destruction of Christianity as the grand program of our administration. This atrocious insult, this horrible utterance, brands the whole movement, not simply as anti Catholic, but as downright anti Christian. And this estimate is shared even by such distinctively Protestant publications as the London Saturday Review. "Pius X.," it wrote, "is fighting the battle of Christianity in the twentieth century."

In fact, no unprejudiced person, that has followed the course of events in France since the expulsion of the religious orders in 1880, can have failed to recognize signs of a carefully plotted, firmly organized, and widespread conspiracy to make the nation, which first and foremost of all the Teuton Bar-

---

*Since M. Clemenceau lately told a newspaper reporter that these words had not been uttered by M. Briand as Minister, it may be well to subjoin a no less significant quotation from a speech made the other day by M. Viviani, Minister of Labor, and posted up by order of the Senate, in all the communes of France—"We have given ourselves to this work of anti-clericalism; we have plucked from the souls of the people all faith in a future life, all belief in delusive and phantastic visions of eternal bliss. To the man that pauses at nightfall, crushed under his daily toil and weeping over his misery, we have said that behind these clouds on which he sadly gazes, there is nothing but pious chimeras, and with one bold stroke we have extinguished in heaven the lights that will never be rekindled."

barians embraced the Apostolic rule of faith and the Christian code of morals, now become first and foremost in the profession of atheism and naturalism, in the worship of human pride and sensual indulgence. You want to know who are these conspirators? Judge for yourself, ladies and gentlemen. It is surely a curious fact that the majority by whose solid vote these oppressive statutes were carried, both in the Chamber and in the Senate, is almost entirely, if not exclusively, composed of Freemasons. Again, it is an open secret, vouched for by the official publications of Masonry, that these infamous laws were eagerly advocated and their adoption confidently predicted in the Masonic conventions even before they had been so much as proposed in the Legislative bodies. And has it not been cabled all over the world, that the latest maneuvers of the French Government had called forth expressions of hearty approbation and triumphant congratulation from hundreds of lodges in and outside of France? I know full well that in this country there are numbers of Masons that look upon their organizations simply as a benevolent brotherhood, and who would immediately sever all connection with the order the moment they were to discover, that it had taken an active part in these dastardly and persistent attempts to destroy the liberty of conscience and freedom of worship of millions of loyal citizens and French Catholics. Just as it would be manifestly absurd and wicked to saddle the faults and vices of any individual Jesuit on the whole Society of Jesus, so it were no less unreasonable and unjust to hold every single member of a secret society accountable for the impiety and criminality of one or more of its divisions in distant countries. No, we must be fair towards all, whether friend or foe. Yet, it is nevertheless but too true, that the Grand Orient of France, already several years ago, formerly rejected all belief in God, our Almighty Creator and Sovereign God; and that, since then, the very name of the Deity has been expunged from the readers and manuals in the schools; while, under pretense of diffusing knowledge and popularizing science, an army of diabolical lecturers has been kept constantly at work to destroy in the heart of the nation every glimmer of faith and every seed of morality. Such, ladies and gentlemen, is the anti Christian campaign and such are the detestable tactics carried on by French Masonry against the Catholic Church, in keeping with the blasphemous boast of that rank Minister of Worship and rabid infidel, M. Briand.

But let us return to the main issue. You remember my contention at the outset was, that the French Government, by its recent proceedings against the Catholic Church, had violated every form of liberty and transgressed every kind of justice. I trust, ladies and gentlemen, that I have said enough, not only to prove to your satisfaction this momentous charge, but also to make it clear to you that the very foundation of popular liberty has been undermined and the chief bulwark of human justice has been shattered by this benighted and frenzied power of Antichrist. The Church, on the contrary, stands out before the world as the custodian of liberty and the gonfalonier of justice. She is ready to accept separation, but cannot subscribe to spoliation, and will never submit to oppression.

A few words, if you allow me, in conclusion. Severe as the present trial may be, it is sure to turn to the advancement of the true religion. Already now, there is a noticeable increase in the attendance at Holy Mass. What French Catholics need especially, is political unity and energetic action, and nothing, perhaps, is better calculated to bring about these happy results than the actual stress of persecution. Besides, it not the first time, even within our own recollection, that the followers of Christ have been assailed by the sectaries of Satan, and have come forth victorious from the long and painful conflict. Witness the imprisonment suffered by several bishops in Brazil, about forty years ago, because they resisted the profanation of consecrated temples by certain powerful fraternities of laymen; and again, somewhat later, the hardships, fines, and sentences of exile, inflicted on thousands of religious and ecclesiastics in Germany, who could not in conscience submit to the caesaro-papism, or the claim to state supremacy, of Bismarck. It is, then, not without reason, that our Holy Father, Pius X., expressed the other day his confident hope that this fierce outburst of hostility to the cause of Christ in France would prove but the prelude to a glorious triumph. But even if, according to the inscrutable designs of Providence, the contest should turn out otherwise, even if it should result in utter disaster and complete destruction, yet our trust in the perpetuity of the Catholic Church will ever remain unshaken. Indeed, we are convinced that long after these anti Christian states shall have disappeared from the roll of nations and vanished from the map of Europe, the work of Jesus Christ will still stand, and spread, and flourish; since it has for its Supreme Overseer the successor of that devoted fisherman of Galilee, who, in reward for his faith, received from the Son of God this infallible promise: "Thou art Peter, and upon this rock I will build my Church, and the gates of hell shall never prevail against her." In this divine assurance let us pray, dear Christian friends, and pray earnestly, for our persecuted brethren as well as for their persecutors; while yet remembering that "Blessed are they that suffer persecution for justice' sake, for theirs is the kingdom of heaven."

TO ARCHBISHOP MONTGOMERY

Pastor, faithful, good—well done !
Early though fell the gloaming, early set life's sun.
As melancholy night
A world conceals,
Yet a full orbéd universe reveals,
Whose rays, blessed pilgrims in the darkness, cheer
our sight;
So when death's shade
On what of thee was earth
A pall had laid,
There was another birth;—
A clearer vision of thy myriad worth.
Joyful hope and faith serene
Shine there in varied sheen;
Holy zeal, thy soul fierce-burning;
Fortitude, each stay o'erturning
Single eye, earth's wisdom scorning;
Lowly heart, earth's honor spurning ;
Slight of gold, the earthling's treasure ;
Bounteous hand, ignoring measure ;
And charity, of all the radiant host the queen.
Yet while the star-lit depths we fondly view,
Steals down our cheek the chill night's silent dew.

J. R., '08.

THE SHATTERING

The train whistled long and dolorously and the big man reached under the seat for his grips. So did the little man and their shoulbers bumped. They both sat up and laughed.

"Fairville?" queried the little man, good naturedly.

"Yes," answered the other," and you?"

"So am I. I stop there twice a year. Travelling man, you know. You don't live there, do you?"

"No, I never saw the place."

The little man flicked his cigarette out of the window into the darkness.

"Well, it ain't much to look at." He consulted his watch.

"About ten minutes," he calculated. "We're running ahead of time, too."

The train lurched and rounded a curve. The big man thrust his head out the window and watched a few straggling, winking lights grow out of the darkness.

"No," he decided, musingly, "It aint much to look at, Fairview! I'm anxious to see the place though."

The little man leaned back in his seat complacently

"Tall us the story," he said.

"It isn't exactly a story," the other said, regarding his cigar meditatively. "Only an old friend of mine whom I haven't heard from in a long time used to live there. Years back I went to college and fell in with a young fellow namee Rempt—Bob Rembt. Of all the men I met at school I think he was the most brilliant and the most popular. I took to him at once, and oddly enough he seemed to like me. We both played varsity football and that threw us together a great deal. He came pretty near to being my ideal in the student line. He was a splendid athlete, but he never lost himself in athletics as I did. His class work was a marvel. I was a frcshman when he was a junior, and he finished two years ahead of me. He carried off all the honors and was offered an Oxford scholarship. About that time his father died, thongh, and he couldn't take it. He drifted out west and I lost track of him. I tell you that man's got a brilliant future before him. He has brains and he has the moral sense to back it up. I think—"

The big engine chortled and threw itself back on its haunches. The cars reeled and slowed down, the lamps swinging.

The little traveling man looked out the window. "Why, here we are," he chattered, and gathered up his magazines and grip and overcoat; "Come on."

They alighted at the little red lonesome depot. A pale young man in the office was sitting nnder the lamp tapping a telegraph key.

The little man shrugged his shoulders. "Awfully lonesome," he told his companion.

Somebody waved a lantern and the long train trembled.

The two men stood and watched it pull out, throbbing and rocking through the darkness like a comet.

Then they turned toward the quiet street that led up to the town.

"Go on with your story," said the traveling man, taking his companion's arm with an air of good comradship.

"Well there isn't much else to go on with. Bob used to tell me that he would come back to Fairville some day when he would be worth enough to buy up the little town. So every year I sent a letter here for him with the usual injunction about, 'if not called for in five days, etc.' The letter always came back.'"

They plodded along in silence for a few moments. Once the big man stopped to light a cigar, and they both could hear the scraping of a fiddle in a little saloon a short distance ahead. When they started the little man did not notice that his hand had been shaken from the other's arms.

Finally the traveling man picked up the thread again.

"I suppose your friend settled down and married in the west and has forgotten all about Fairview and his ambitions," he said.

His companion did not answer. When they were passing the saloon the little man stopped.

"Let's have something," he suggested, "I know this place."

The traveling man found a seat for his companion at a table, and then pushed his way up to the bar to order.

The big man looked about him and blinked. The walls were rough, unpapered, and unpainted, and covered with coarse prints. A few lamps in tin cases on the wall burned murkily, and down in the other end of the room on a rough stage, a man in an extravagant darkey make-up was reeling off a song.

The little traveling man returned and sat down.

"A little rough," he said affably, "but characteristic."

Then the bar tender came up with filled glasses in hand. The big man looked up at him and his face went gray.

"Bob," he whispered, dazed. A glass from the bartender's hand shattered on the table and the liquid radiated to a brown map on the rough table.

"You'll have to excuse me, gentlemen," the man said in a low tone, and sopped up the liquor with a cloth.

"Bob," from the big man again, unsteady, and a little hoarse.

The bartender turned to go, but his foot slipped and he lurched against the table. He straightened and laughed harshly.

When he had gone the traveling man said, "Pretty insolent fellows, sometimes—these barkeepers."

The negro on the stage was bawling doggerel, and the big man watched him with swimming eyes.

His companion spoke louder, "That fellow ought to be fired," he laughed, "he's about half shot, you know."

The big man smiled faintly. "Yes, I know," he said slowly, "I know."

J. F. T '07.

THE BEGINNING OF THE END

The native postmaster had sneered when he had handed him the letter; even to him it seemed strange that a neat, dainty missive should have been addressed to a "beachcomber," and such a miserable one. Lack-luster eyes gazed from a dissipated face; and hair, —long, sandy-colored hair, gnarled and twisted, evidently had long since been innocent of comb or brush. His clothes were scant, dirty rags that merely emphasized the half-starved frame. A hacking cough, at little intervals, denoted that his suffering was nearly over.

He almost ran to the beach, grasping the letter as though he was afraid someone might take it away from him.

"It's from her," he muttered òver and over again. He passed the natives who gazed at him wondering, and significantly tapping their foreheads. "Loco," one said.

Sitting there in the shadow of an upturned boat, he tore the envelope open with feverish haste, and read:

Dear Jack:

I really do not know how to write this letter, as I know it will embitter you. Listen—When you went away eight years ago to-night, you promised a speedy return. You said that you only wanted to make a stake, enough to buy a cozy little home for us, a vine-covered cottage with a wide front porch and a garden [of roses] encircling it. Do you remember, Jack?

And I wanted you to stay, arguing that we could be happy together until we could buy it, and without going away could make the money. I knew it would take longer, as the wages were poor then, but as an alternative I offered to go with you. You were obstinate then, Jack. You little knew how heart-broken I was at losing you, for believe me, boy, even then I had a presentment that I would never see you again.

And then your letters, first cheery and full of courage, and coming often; then at long intervals——letters that spoke of discouragements and failures. I wanted you to come home, knowing full well in my woman's heart that stakes and money count for naught if we lose or even delay our happiness, yours and mine, dearheart! But you were still obstinate and finally the letters ceased.

The cottage, as we had pictured it, and our happiness as we had planned it, kept alive that love for a long, long time, Jack; but at last it gradually died because it had nothing to feed on. That memory served to hearten and cheer me while waiting days, long, weary days, for word from you.

It is two years since your last letter, boy, and I have given up hope. Christmas I am to be married to William Vinters, a most honorable man and one who has been very kind to me. I don't know why I am writing this to you, but in my mind it is the only thing to do. So if you think of me at all, do not grieve for what might have been, but console yourself with the thought that I wasn't worthy, etc., and sing Annie Laurie, a song about a broken promise.

I am sorry, but please do not answer this, as it is hardly the proper thing for a married woman to receive letters from any man, save her husband. And if you should happen to wander through this little town, forget that I ever existed, even as a friend—it will be better so, and safer. For, who knows?—we are both human, and he has been very good. While—

*   *   *   *   *

Gradually the sun, now a huge red ball of fire, sank from view. Darkness deepened, and still the "beachcomber" sat there repeating word for word her letter, until it had seared itself into his brain, and even when it had become too dark to read, he sat there mumbling incoherently, unconscious of his surroundings.

Finally, the cold, night air roused him. He drew his ragged coat closer about his shivering form, and gradually, mechanically, tore up the letter into the smallest possible bits and cast them into the water—cast them back whence they came.

Dully, stupidly, his mind worked. But, even then, he realized that it was the beginning of the end.

EDWIN MCKENZIE, Specl. '11.

A PRAYER

O God, I ask Thee not to lift my load,
Nor pray that Thou wilt clear the thorny street;
If Thy great hand but makes more rough the road,
I'll bless and kiss the stones that cut my feet.

Only to know, Lord, that I need not fear,
As though the dark my weary footsteps plod;
Only to feel Thy silent Presence near,
Only to walk each day with Thee, O God.

With humble heart myself I will resign
Unto my cross, my crown of thorns, my pain:
Only to feel Thy great calm Hand in mine,
As on I walk through darkness and the rain.

J. F. T. '07.

PLIGHTED

Let the poet's brains still grind out strains
 In praise of the eagle's whirring flight,
And the nimble steed whose vaunted speed
 Vies with the viewless winds of night ;
Can they match our song as we dash along
 Down through the night like a shooting star,
  With many a lightsome thump and jar;
  My jolly old reckless Motor-Car !

Oh, there be who laugh and who lightly chaff
 When I praise your ribs of steel and zinc,
But I love each screw and each washer too,
 And I simply dote on your fragrant—odor.
So I sing you a song as we dash along
 Down through the night like a shooting star,
  Mocking what men call near or far,
  My jolly old reckless Motor-Car !
    * * * * / / / * * * *

Ah, I loved the life and the spunk and strife
 That throbbed in your pulse's iron beat ;
I adored each bolt and each playful jolt
 As we rattled and rolled on the cobblestone street ;
And never was troth since time began
 Like the troth I'd have pledged as a faithful man,
  Had kindly fate but steered us straight
From the spleen of yon up-turned oyster can !
      G. J. H., '08.

THE SPELLING REFORM

The Spelling Reform is no more. It died a violent death at the hands of Congress. But, like a certain feline, it may have other lives besides that which received its quietus from the outraged dignity of the Law, and we should not be much surprised to find the idea of reform alive and—recalcitrant throughout the English-speaking world for many a year to come. For ourselves, we hope that such may be the case. The reform proposed by the Simplified Spelling Board may have been ill-conceived and inadequate; it may have been prematurely developed by forced and abnormal methods; its advocates may have been more zealous than discreet in endeavoring to foist it upon the public nilly-willy, as if it had no merits of its own to stay it, but these things are merely accidental blemishes to be entirely dissociated from the idea of reform itself. They should in no wise make us forget that the anomalies of our spelling demand the sacrifice of one or two of every child's school years, that they mean a waste of intellectual effort and even of time all through life, and that they present a desperate difficulty to foreigners, thus preventing the spread of the language.

Clearly, then, a more simplified and regular mode of spelling is desirable, if we are to look at the question from a common-sense and unsentimental point of view. But aye! there's the rub! Who cares to look at it from a strictly unsentimental point of view—always excepting Mr. Carnegie, whose confessed *summum bonum* in education is book-keeping? Our words, spoken or written, are our dearest friends, who hold an intimate place in our affections, for out of the abundance of the heart the mouth speaketh. If we are not always thinking of them, we at least are thinking through them. But they are not merely the vehicles of thought; they modify the thought, they have acquired an objective independent existence of their own which reacts on our thought and our ways of thinking. Thus they have come to be part and parcel of our intellectual selves, and to change them seems like changing the very fibre of our minds. We have become used to them, they are one of those habits which are second nature, they are our familiars who know all our humors, and we will no sooner part from them than we would from our right hand, which clumsy as it may be, is yet more accustomed to our way of doing things than the most skilful hand that could be given in exchange.

Hence the storm of indignation which the President's mandate to his printer aroused. England was naturally the centre of the whirlwind. President Rosevelt was called all sorts of hard names, and America was thrust outside the pale of civilization. The English language was declared in jeopardy. Punch took a hand and came out with a cartoon in which the English Language under guize of a stout old oak tree has been attacked by President Roosvelt, who is standing in the foreground with an axe in his hand. Father Time is examining with a microscope the almost invisible dent made by Teddy's vandal strokes, and inquires the cause thereof. "I kan not tel a li," says young America, "I did it with my litl ax."

To be candid about the matter, one can hardly blame England for feeling "put out" by the President's action. The English language belongs to her as much as, if not more than, to us. The language originated with her, and it would be absurd to deny that by far the chief bulk of our literature is due to her genius. The language is stamped with her name, and accordingly he would be a narrow-minded American indeed who would not sympathize in large measure with the almost personal sense of injury experienced by Englishmen at the Spelling Board's linguistic Declaration of Independence. But beyond this national spirit manifested by the English press, it has other grievances in common with ourselves, against the Reform purely on its own demerits. It sees, as we do, that if the plans of the Board were feasible—as they certainly are not —the result would be a complete split-up of the world-embracing English tongue, and whatever be the mutual sentiment of John Bull and Uncle Sam, they at least wish to understand each other.

However, it cannot be gainsaid that England is not above a little narrow jealousy on this point: Take the ending or, for example Webster, as is well known, was the first lexicographer to substitute or for our and this ending has been universally adopted in America. In England, before Webster's time, either spelling was used. In confirmation of this, let us look over a book published in 1683. Its author is Samuel Johnson, not the Doctor, but a Protestant divine; and the work which is entitled: Julian's Arts to Undermine and Extirpate Christianity, is a "well of English pure and undefiled." On page 59, then, he has *governor*, and on the page following, *governour*. Three times on page 60, and also elsewhere, do we find *emperor*, though *emperour* is more usual with him.

Let us appeal to another author, Sir Thomas North, whose translation of Plutarch's Lives served Shakspeare in the composition of his Roman plays. I have before me a photographed reproduction of this work made by T. A. Leo, London, 1878. Opening the book at random, I find on page 973, *honor;* page 236, *dictator;* page 784, *favor*, etc., etc.

So the spelling fluctuated between *or* and *our* until Webster came to declare in favor of *or*. Whereupon England espoused the cause of *our*, which even Dr. Johnson's dictionary could only partly enforce, so that today those endings are badges of nationality.

However, my main object is not to convict englishmen of antagonism just for the principle of it to everything American, but rather to show that some of the changes advocated by the

Spelling Board are not American innovations but, on the contrary, a return to the way of the ancients. But leaving all national views aside, let us consider the Reform in itself, the difficulties it would have to contend with, and its own inherent defects.

While we all acknowledge the need of more law and order in our spelling, a need that the ridicule of foreigners is ever bringing home to us, yet the thought of change causes a painful tug at our heart-strings. The greatest modern English writer says that the world is moved by sentiment. We are used to silent letters and to misleading letters just as we are used to the ivy that clothes our ancient oak trees. Take the word *oak* for instance. Who would care to spell it *oke*? No one surely who has seen oak trees and learned to love them. I can hardly fancy an Englishman feeling complimented on hearing his country's Tars called "hearts of oke" and I can fancy a dame of literary "nerves" losing half her pride in her antique *oken* furniture along with the loss of the letter *a*. Again, what suitor would be so rash as to address his adorable Dulcinea as "sweet-hart," even with a host of reformers directing his quill? 'Tis hard to picture him "sighing like furnace" or writing "a woful ballad to his mistress' eyebrow" who could forbear the tribute of a silent *e* to her charms.

Yet it is the fact that *oke* and *hart* were the modes of spelling in vogue before and even during the time of Shakespeare. We need not be surprised at

this for they are perfectly in every way, and they correspond more to the basic principles of English orthography, namely, that the spelling must represent the sound without introducing foreign and disturbing elements, and that the long sound of a vowel is indicated in writing by the addition of a mute vowel, as every schoolboy knows. In North's Plutarch's Lives, which bears the date 1589, we find *oke* and *hart*. Whether Shakespears adopted the spelling of his historical guide, I am unable to say, not being able to lay hands on a First Edition of the immortal dramatist, but it would not be surprising if he did. Two of the great English versions of the Bible prior to that of King James use *hart*, and in good father Chaucer we read, "The bilder oke and eke the hardy asshe." In Ellacombe'e "Plant Lore and Garden Craft of Shakespeare" we find five authors cited, four of whom wrote *oke*, and the fifth *oake*. The latter alone wrote after King James' Version, and this leads one to suspect that this Authorized Version gave vogue to the more arbitrary at the expense of the mose reasonable spelling.

So we are enabled to judge of Punch's cartoon at its true worth. If Father Time finds it difficult to discover the nick made by Teddy's axe, it is because the tree is furrowed with cuts and cross cuts of reformers and counter-reformers back to the time when the stout tree was a mere sapling. And moreover it is not to the mark to call the tree the "English Language." There is about as much difference between the English language and its spelling as between a man and his portrait. If the language were identical with its spelling, what language did North write, or our Samuel Johnson, or Spencer, or Shakespeare? Taking up the first of these again, we find such unenglish words as *outragious*—outrageous enough, i' faith —*uucoutroulable, logick, judg, imploying, shal, odly, lyon* and so on without end, all of which cannot belong to the English language as they find no place on the leaves of Punch's oak tree.

Which goes to show that the appeal made to tradition and to the genius of the English tongue, and to the hallowed laws of etymology—wonderful what a respect we have suddenly acquired for these laws, you and I, who never deigned them a thought before!—that these appeals are simply a mask for our fond attachment to the spelling we have learned in the impressionable days of our childhood. As for the etymological value of the present system, the philologist assure us that it is a negligeable quantity.

Prof. Cleary of Fordham University, who writes his views on the situation in the Fordham Monthly with an acrimony that is evidently begot of personal disapproval of the reformers and their tactless and aggressive methods, which he believes, require reform more than their spelling, says that the written word primarily represents the idea. Where would the facetious Professor lead us to?—to the days of the pyramids with their hieroglyphics and ideography? We are sorry to differ

from him, but surely the primval function of the written word is to portray the spoken. We grant that in silent reading we do not consciously advert to the sound of the word, but unless we have been pupils of the Deaf and Dumb Schools, we do so subconsciously. This half unconsciousness, however, is sufficient to confirm our dependance upon and rivet our attachment to the written form, and to increase the difficulty of reform.

Apart from the extrinsic obstacles offered by the natural dislike of dispossessing our familiar friends, and by our repugnance to unlearn what in the learning required so much pains both from application of mind and of birch, the scheme of improvement has enemies nearer at home; it is a house divided against itself; it is inconsistent. It creates more irregularities than it removes, and its list of 300 words is really another burden for our overworked memories. Why is *ed* retained in *spelled* and not in *heapt?* Why one *p* in *chapt, clapt,* and two *c's* in *succor?* We could pick out a dozen of such anomalies. Why is *c* allowed in *scepter* and a moment later dismissed from *similar?* Why have we *kist* and not *hist?*

Perhaps Professor Matthews would say in reply: "Oh well! leave that to us. Rome wasn't built in a day. You learn that list now and later we will give you new words to spell." That's the very difficulty, we should always be getting new words to puzzle us, and always be at the foot of the class. We should never know whither we were tending or what was ahead of us; spelling would be in a state of anarchy, and what was the proper thing today might tomorrow be as ridiculous as the fashions of last year. One of the most patent indices of a good education would be done away with, and Uncle Si, who writes in an instinctively phonetic way, would be on a level with Macks Muller who has just received a raise of salary as proofreader for the Boston"Daily Philologist." Our written language would be subject to perpetual change, the dictionaries would go to the wall of our archives, there would be no norm to follow save the good pleasure of Messrs. Carnegie, Matthews & Co., and all would be confusion worse confounded.

Again, whence were the guarantee that, even if we could agree among ourselves, the rest of the English world would follow in our wake. And if it did not follow, then disruption of the language would be the gradual but inevitable result. Whence also the guarantee that the difficulties of reform might not be shown by hard experience to be altogether beyond our sanguine speculative calculations, and eventually prove insuperable, and that we should not be forced to return to the port from which we so rashly sailed without rudder or compass?

The present scheme of the Spelling Board is then entirely unworkable. Its self-confidence has lost it the confidence of the people, and its indiscreet zeal their good will. Let it first obtain for itself the authority to dictate to us; let it not

be a provincial committee of self-appointed teachers, but a Parliament representative of all the English speaking countries, and composed of men desirous of safe-guarding all interests and endowed with a learning that will make their pronouncements as final as such a subject-matter will permit.

Mr. Archer, an English philologist, writing in the Fortnightly Review of such a conference, or Witenagemote, as he calls it, says its main duty would be not to "produce a report on the principles and methods of spelling reform, but to get out a spelling book of the entire English language; that is, if it saw, after careful consideration, that the advantages of such a reform compensated for the difficulties to be overcome. Such a step would put the whole question on a new footing; it would bring it from the abstract to the concrete, from the speculative ts the practical, from mere possibility to accomplishment. People could see for themselves that the innovation is desirable and feasible, and the spelling book would win adoption in all the schools. The older generations could be gently habituated to its use by having the newspapers devote to it some ol its columns. The change, at best, could be but gradual, but bearing the seal of a linguistic parliament fully representative and as authorative as experience and learning could make it, and backed up by the good will of the people accruing fram a clear knowledge of its practical advantages, it could not fail in the long run to attain to universal usage.

Among many objections wherewith President Wheeler of California University has put himself on record against the reform is this, that "phonetic writing would involve imitation of the various dialectical forms of the spoken language." I cannot see the justice of the objection. Surely the reformers did not advocate the phonetic system when they declared it "absolutely impossible." A moderate phoneticism is all that is required, a phoneticism that would remove such exasperating anomalies as *cough, rough, though, through, bough;* that would give a uniform spelling for identical sounds as, to take Mr. Archer's instance, in that class of words ending in *ieve, eive, eave, eeve.* It seems incredible that the Simplified Spelling Board would authorize each individual, Yorkshireman or Cockney, Scot or Kentuckian, to stereotype his own peculiar pronunciation or mispronunciation in the written form, and thus break up the language at once into uncouth jargons that would render adjacent counties unintelligible "barbarians" to each other. Even the most matter-of-fact reformer could hardly take Josh Billings for his guide.

J. D. '07.

SLANDERED

Two words were whispered: one, with deadly aim
    Sped from the black depths of a bitter heart;
The other from Love's sanctuary came
    With balm to soothe the smart.

Alas! the years have proved that Love is vain,
But Hate—how mighty! Lo the victim there
Crushed 'neath a ruined life creeps on in pain,
    The nursling of despair!

F. H., '09.

MY BROTHER'S MEMORY

Twelve times, dear Brother, winter dread
    On thee its snowy pall has thrown;
    Twelve times spring's tearful smile has sown
The violets on thy lowly bed.

Yet let me close mine eyes awhile
    And lo! thou stand'st before my gaze
    Just as thou wert in other days—
The youthful grace—the winning smile.

Still sparkle in the dark-blue eye
    The gifted mind and generous will;
    The tempered laugh is playful still,
And thoughtful still the forehead high.

The voice yet echoes in my ears;
    I hear thee ask in wistful tone
    How fares it with me, as alone
I wander through the darkened years?

The proffered hand I fain would seize,
    And feel the thrill I felt of yore,
    And all my heart to thee outpour;
But ah! what idle dreams are these?

Though dark and lone the way I trod
    When set thy day in morning's glow,
    Dear Brother, yet 'twas better so,
—What sweeter than the ways of God?

True, we had built on years to come,
    Had placed afar the final goal;
    But He who loves the virgin soul
Sent thee an early summons home.

Evanish, then, a grief so blind
    As grudged its treasure to the tomb;
    Let faith shine clear amid the gloom,
And sorrow's cloud be silver-lined.

A ship sets sail the world to round,
    The lessening shore the seaman spies,
    And e'en when ocean mocks his eyes,
His looks are ever homeward bound.

The antipodes are passed, and now
    His darkling west is orient fair,
    Hope breaks the lengthening chain of care,
Love shifts her watch from helm to prow.

E'en so to Love, O, Brother mine,
    We wed strong Hope, and grieve no more:
    Life's west we leave, and wait the shore
Empurpled in the dawn divine.

                      C. D. '07.

THE MAN WITH THE MASK

The sun was just sinking behind the western hills silhouetting the outline of a silent figure holding his wiry Pinto by the bridle. With a slap on the pony's back, the man mounted. "Well Spotty," said he, addressing the horse, "Uv all the holes we ever struck, this beats the bunch. By jingo, the prospect uv it's enough to freeze the whiskers of hope, aint·it?" He turned wearily from his survey of New Mexico's lonesome scenery and made his way towards the town, there to bury his troubles in a "jolt of moonshine."

New Mexico in 1880 was not a very thickly populated country, and the town I speak of was situated in a wild and desolate part. The mountains were well wooded with stunted trees and brush which gave a wild and forbidding look to the country, and its situation among the precipitous and rocky gorges obtained for it the name of "Lost Canyon." "Road agents" were numerous and scarcely a night passed that some saloon was not robbed and the contents of its cash-drawer removed.

The rider, like most westerners, wore a broad felt hat turned up in front and his face was tan and haggard. As he turned his horse's head towards town, a hand caught his bridle and a hearty voice exclaimed "Hello Bronch, yer forgotten yer old pal? Who the dickens u'd a thought to see yer here?" "Huh," exclaimed Bronch, returning the clasp.

"Glad to see yesh, old king. What got yuh out inter this hole?" "Why, what's the matter? yesh look grumpy, what's up?" 'Aw, nothin', I jis' been admirin' yer scenery. It's rather jolly, nit." "O you'll get used to it," chuckled Pete. "Yer sheriff I see, said Bronch, noticing the star on Pete's shirt. "Yep, and yesh can bet yer hat it ain't no pipe by a darned sight. It's a pretty rough town. Come on over and have a tip of Kentucky; yuh looks all. done up." "Heard yuh had a reward for the capture of a certain Black Pete or Jack?" said Bronch. "Yep, yer right. There's a reward all right for Black Jack. Everyone's tried for him but no one got back to tell the tale."

By this time they reached a long low adobe building which served as a prison and home of the Sheriff and Deputy. Around it lay the town—all small buildings with tiled roofs and adobe walls. They entered the town hall, if it may so be called, by a small iron-bound oak door. The walls were about threè feet thick and supported a roof of tiles arranged on oaken beams. "Do yuh know, Bronch," said the Sheriff when both were seated, "that it's the mos' ticklish job to be Sheriff uv this country that this respectable puncher ever thought of takin'?" "I'd buck the job right away if it wasn't for finishin' Black Jack and some uv his pals that have been holdin' up the stages between here and Las Vegas. And seein' I've got yuh ter help, I guess we oughter be able to have a little success."

Black Jack was a bandit of a peculiar character. He never robbed women, towards whom he was alway polite; but for men he had no respect. During the last month the U. S. Mail had been relieved of its valuables and Wells-Fargo lost two drivers and three boxes. It was no use to go in pursuit of the marauders after the crime was committed, because they were possessed of the happy faculty of concealing their tracks.

The excitement over Black Jack's latest depredations had finally subsided and everyone in town was under the impression that he had left the country. One night while some cow punchers and miners in the vicinity of the town were assembled in Flynn's, a man quietly walked in, covered the crowd with his guns, and from a position behind the bar relieved everyone of cash and valuables. Finally, with a crash the light was extinguished and a simultaneous rush made for the door. A few minutes afterwards a figure calmly opened a window and sprang out into the night. The next morning Flynn found that he was minus fifteen hundred dollars, and another of Black Jack's dare-devil deeds was recorded in the history of Lost Canyon.

"Say Pete," said Bronch the next day, "call that posse business off till tomorrer night." "What do I want to do that fer? Yer not going to back out, are yuh?" "Back out? I wouldn't back out fer the best or worst man in the country, pard. I want to try a little plan uv my own to git this gentleman." "No hard feelins, Bronch old king, I was'nt tryin' to throw yuh down. Course, we'll call it off. If yuh need anyone jus' talk." "Guess six tomorrer night'll do. The stage leaves Cimarron at nine, don't it?" "Yep." "Well, that's all the time I want."

The stage departed from Cimarron the next night in good time with but two passengers. One was Bronch, the newly appointed Deputy, the other a Mexican A short distance along the road a few more were taken on, so that the capacity of the stage became taxed to the utmost. One was an Englishman on his way to Santa Fe, and the others a Bostonian and his family, and two miners. The Englishman was a typical Londoner with exalted opinions and delicate hands. The Mexican evidently was ill at ease and now and then cast suspicious glances at the other passengers from under his bushy eyebrows.

Up and down the grades the stage rolled and pitched. There was a full moon and the wild and rocky landscape stretched far off to the right and left. Suddenly the calmness of the night was broken by a sharp report and the stage came to an abrupt halt. The miners were up in an instant only to be ordered back to their places by the Mexican who covered them with his revolvers. "Hand over your guns, all of you," he exclaimed in a savage voice. By this time his confederate from without was on the spot and took part in the disarming of the passengers. "I'll see the British Consul at Santa Fe," exclaimed the Englishman, "this orrible violence is houtwageous." "Aw shut up," growled the bandit "or I'll fill yuh so full uv holes that yu'll never reach Santa Fe nor anywhere else. Now, young feller up on the seat, make the collection fer my pard and I. Move along, er I'll help yesh." The person referred to promptly descended from his seat and taking the Mexican's hat went around the circle of bewildered passengers. The miners were already relieved of their belongings and the Bostonian threw in his watch and pocket book with an evidently forced laugh. The Englishman however believed in standing up for his rights. "Aw fawncy," he exclaimed, "this is a bwutal attack." "Throw in yer lump," shouted the bandit "and stop yer protestin'; and that precious bay winder uv yers too." "Addwessing me, suh? I pway what do you wish?" "Show him Gomez, we're wastin' time." The Englishman needed no further persuasion and promptly dropped his gold monocle into the hat.

When the collection was taken, the unwillingly appointed collector handed over the proceeds to the Mexican. Then withdrawing in the shadow of the stage, he suddenly whipped out a gun and the next instant "Black Jack" was looking down the barrel of a 44. "Drop yer gun Jack," shouted the passenger, "I've got yer this time." He had scarcely finished, however, when there was a flash and the daring passenger fell to the earth in a pool of his own blood. "Git," said the bandit to the driver, and when last seen, the two highwaymen were making their way into a neighboring forest.

When Broncho came to he was lying by the roadside under a blanket. He tried in vain to raise himself and called out but no one heard him. As the light mist that pervaded the atmosphere cleared and the dawn appeared in the eastern heavens, he found to his surprise that he was but two feet from the hitching post in front of the jail. How he came there and who conveyed him he could not tell. Finally he revived enough to make his way to the door of the prison but that was all. A passerby awoke Pete and both of them set about to find out the extent of Broncho's injuries. The bullet was found to have entered his body just below the shoulder and penetrated the right lung. The following note was found pinned to his shirt.

This feller is the gamliest devil in Pecos—he tried to take me single handed and almos' got me but my pard got the lead on him, I hope he pulls through becuz he's one of the mos' reckless devils that ever pulled a gun. Ye'll find an ole Mexican Doc at Flynn's, mebbe he can help him.   BLACK JACK.

Bronch had a long and hard siege before he fully recovered and it was due only to the care and untiring labors of the faithful old Mexican doctor that he was able to resume active duty again. One afternoon as he was sitting down in front of the prison enjoying the sunshine, a stranger rushed up and called for the Sheriff. "Watcher excited about," asked Bronch. "Didn't ye hear? we got him." "Got who? exclaimed Bronch. "Why, Black Jack," replied the excited stranger, "and if ye don't believe it ye can come and see for yerself. It happened this way. Royce, Gibbons, and myself wuz goin' over to the old minin' camp and we met him on the road. He whipped out his guns and got behind a boulder and the way he pumped the lead at us was enough to rattle the teeth in a Mexican mule. He pierced ole Gibbons' digestive organs the first crack. After that we got in a place where we could see him and I noticed Royce runnin' up towards him calling us fellers along. Jack had run out uv ammunition and couldn't get one way er the other without some uv the fellers gettin' a bead on him. When we got within a good view uv him Jack was calmly rollin' a cig and his two guns were layin' on the ground in front uv him. Royce covered him and he made no attempt to get away. 'Lookin' fer yer pard?' said he, 'he's down there in the gulch somewhere with his toes turned up.' After that the fellers bound him and got him on a horse and sent me in the lead to let Pete know what wuz doin'."

It was not long before the party arrived at the prison, and as Pete was not around it fell to the lot of Bronch to take care of the prisoner and see that he did not escape. "Comfortable?" asked Bronch. "Yep" came the answer, "Well, I guess you don't remember me?" "Nope" replied the prisoner, "never saw yuh before." "Well, I've got a painful recollection uv the meetin'. Maybe yesh remember the night yesh held up the stage and came near gettin' taken by un uv the passengers?" Jack jumped to his feet. "By jingo, yer not the man, are yuh?" "Yers truly the same," answered Bronch, "Are you the feller the Mexican shot?" "I am," returned Bronch, "and if there's anything yuh want done, yuh better speak, fer yer time this side of the divide is gettin' short now." "Well, take this note," answered the bandit eagerly, "and send it to my folks in Montana." "Montana!" exclaimed Bronch, when he had recovered from his surprise "what wuz yer name and what part did yuh come from?" "My name" replied Black Jack slowly "was Bill Williams and" . . "My God!" exclaimed Bronch jumping up suddenly, "don't yuh know me?" "Yep, George, but I tried to keep it from yuh as long as I could. I knew yuh the night uv the hold up when I sawn yuh layin' on the ground and I thought yuh were done fer, sure." "Where did that Doc come from," asked Bronch, or rather George, weakening a little. "I never saw him around these parts before. He fixed me up great an' if I ever see him again he's got somethin' comin' to him." "Well," said Bill, "that would be tellin' but if yuh insist, seein' it's yuh I'll tell yuh." "I insist" returned George. "Well I guess I got tew own up to it then; it was me that did the doctorin', an' I guess yuh never knew how yuh got back ter the prison that night?"

"Put it here, Bill," cried George, "I'll see yuh over the border ter night." "No yuh won't, returned Bill, "I'm goin' ter stay right here." "Yer a fool ff yuh do," returned the other "fer you'll be shot sure, as yuh were taken while resistin' arrest." "No" replied Bill, "I tol' yuh I waizn't going." "Look here, Bill, yer goin' if I have ter tie yuh to a hoss and take yuh. I'm tryin' ter do yuh a turn fer ole times' sake." "George, I'll go; but I tell yuh yer true blue, yer doin' too much even fer a friend."

"Gome on, Bill," said George. "Guess it's dark enough."

It was near seven o'clock and the moon was just commencing to rise over the hills. "We got ter try it now er never. Come on." They started along in the shadow of the buildings and did not dismouut until they got a little ways out of town. "Wait a minute" said Bill, 'somethin's comin' our way." By this time the pursuers came within sight around a slight bend. "By Jingo" said George, "it's Pete with two other fellers." They spurred their horses and took a path leading up through the Bigfoot Canyon, with the pursuers gaining on them at every step. The canyon became more rocky and difficult the further up they went, and with the pursuers gaining rapidly on them it soon became evident that something had to be done and done quickly. Letting George continue along up the canyon. Bill quietly got to one side and waited until the posse passed some distance ahead. Then suddenly several shots rang out in the air and Bill sent his horses at breakneck speed down the canyon, while he stepped aside to await developments.

Not long after, he heard the posse returning and when they had passed he continued his way up and found his friend. "Better camp here, Bill" said George. "I'll keep watch fer a while and call yuh when I get topheavy." Bill tied the remaining horse to a scrub oak and then rolled himself up in a blanket under the shade of a large rock. In a few minutes all was silent except for the deep breathing of the outlaw and the occasional screeches of owls as they flew back and forth through the canyon. "Bill! Bill! Oh Bill!" whispered the sentinel, "wake up." "What's the matter?" "Sh—There's someone comin'". "Wait a minute while I go and look, By jingo! ten uv 'em" he said running back a few seconds later. 'Better be movin', eh? If it wazn't fer yun, I'd fight 'em right here and either them er me ud never see to-morrer. They're never goin' to take me alive, that's a cinch."

In the meantime the moon was high in the heavens and revealed George standing silently and evidently meditating. A battle was going on within him between two powerful motives; one was friendship and the other duty. There before him stood his boyhood friend and companion; one who had seen him through thick and thin and whose life was now in deadly peril. What should he do? "Good-bye, Bill" said he stretching out his hand "I can't, I can't." Bill took the hand and grasped it fervently; with this George departed and made his way slowly up the canyon. When he had advanced some distance, he turned and looked around. There was Bill crouched down behind a rock with a gun in hand awaiting his chance. Suddenly there was a flash and a loud report and then another and another. A minute later he saw Bill stagger to his feet and press his hand against his head. "I'm a comin' Bill" said the over-generous George, "are yuh badly hurt?" Bill made no reply, but toppled over mortally wounded.

His friend stooped down to examine the path of the fatal bullet, which had crashed its way through the temple. As he was in this posture, an exclamation "Here's one for you," came from a near-by bush, followed instantly by a bullet that drove through Bill's breast and laid him over the body of his ill-starred companion. He lingered for several hours, and was conscious long enough to make an honest avowal of his temptation, his crime, and his sorrow. "Put no mark over my grave," he begged, "for, boys, I want ter be forgot by everybudy, for I wuz more trew to me frien than ter me honor."

CYRIL J. SMITH, '06·

OLD AND FORGOTTEN

(TRIOLET)

What now does the old world care
For such as you or I ?
Men's love we once did share
What now does the old world care ?
For the fire was but a flare
And long ago did die;
What now does the old world care
For such as you or I ?

A. B. D., '08.

THE TURFMAN

Slowly raising his eyes from the fire, Norman Parker let his gaze rest for a moment on the picture upon the mantle, and then sank his head despairingly in his hands.

Without, the night was clear and cold, and the great round moon looked down from a cloudless throne, flooding her realms with a silver brilliancy, Within the leaping blaze set fitful shadows dancing on the wall.

About him was peace and calm, but within was a heart torture-torn, and every glance at that picture drove deeper into his soul the arrow of despair. She loved him, but alas! did she realize his suffering? Did she see the financial difficulties staring him in the face?

Norman raised his head suddenly from his hands.

"I must do it," he cried. "Harvester runs tomorrow for a stake of twenty thousand. If I win, I canpay my debts and be a straight man once more. But God! suppose I lose—impossibl e! I will not lose!" As he spoke he put on his coat and went out into the night.

The large office seemed unnaturally dark and still as he cautiously entered it and approached the safe in the corner. He knelt before it and after glancing furtively about, set to work to open it. A few turns, a click, and the big door responded to his touch. He fumbled around and from the darkness drew out a roll of bills, put them in his pocket, set the combination, and left the office unseen.

As he hurried along, almost running in his fear, his excited imagination peopled the silent night with hundreds of eyes to see him, and hundreds of ears to hear him. The pale flare of a street lamp focussed all its rays on the star of an officer and this gleaming star seemed to point him out through the darkness. At length he reached his door and in due time strove to soothe his racked brain by sleep.

The dawn broke bright and clear. The cheerful day augured well. Norman was up early and soon with high hopes started for the track.

The grandstand was filled to its greatest capacity. The fences along the track were fairly black with people. As the boy rode Harvester to the barrier, thousands of men and women burst into cheers. Queen followed and then Stanford; each was greeted with a wild burst of applause. In the crowd there was a young man with a feverish brow and trembling hand, who staked his six thousand dollars on Harvester. He returned to the rail but the din of the shouting and then the Sabbath stillness of that great crowd thrilled his heart until it beat in usison with the clattering hoofs. It was too much; he must retire and, hidden, await the issue in trembling suspense. To brace himself he leaned in a half-conscious way against a post with his hand clutching desperately something beneath his coat.

At last the race was over. A deathlike pallor shrouded his face as the teller mounted the box and commanded silence. "The first race," he cried, "for the twenty-thousand dollar stake was won by Queen and"—Bang! Bang! echoed and reechoed across the place. A wave of human beings rushed from every side and beheld Norman Parker lying on the floor already dead. When his body had been removed and all was again quiet the teller resumed, "The first race was won by Queen and Harvester. Being a dead heat the bookmakers are prepared to pay the double amount."

HAROLD HOGAN, 3rd Acad.

THE BEGINNING OF THE END

Hurrah! the goal is almost won!
The object of my sighing;
And the weary course is nearly run,
And the toilsome task is nearly done,
—My student-lamp is dying.

But why the disappointed gaze
To the past is ever shifting?
Why is enchantment's fairy haze
Gathering round the bygone days,
And from the future lifting?

Ah, let the truth prevail—the blue
To homely brown is changing,
And the happy groves far off that grew,
And the sunny gleams made glad the view,
Fond youth's horizon ranging

Are not in fee of man's estate.
No tempting dream of beauty
May lure him to the good, the great;
His steps obey a nobler bait
—The stern, strong voice of duty.

Senior.

The Redwood.

PUBLISHED MONTHLY BY THE STUDENTS OF THE SANTA CLARA COLLEGE

The object of the Redwood is to record our College Doings, to give proof of College Industry and to knit closer together the hearts of the Boys of the Present and of the Past.

EDITORIAL STAFF

EXECUTIVE BOARD

JAMES F. TWOHY, '07
President

J. DANIEL MCKAY, '07   HARRY A. MCKENZIE, '08

ASSOCIATE EDITORS

COLLEGE NOTES - - - - -	IVO G. BOGAN, '08
IN THE LIBRARY - - -	ROBERT J. O'CONNOR, '08
EXCHANGES - - -	ANTHONY B. DIEPENBROCK, '08
ALUMNI - - - - -	MERVYN S. SHAFER, '09
ATHLETICS - - - -	HARRY A. MCKENZIE, '08

BUSINESS MANAGER

J. DANIEL MCKAY, '07

ASSISTANTS

FRANCIS M. HEFFERNAN, '08   REIS J. RYLAND, '09

M. T. DOOLING, 09

Address all communications to THE REDWOOD, Santa Clara College, California

Terms of subscription, $1.50 a year; single copies, 15 cents

EDITORIAL COMMENT

The discursive people of the United States are watching and discussing two events which at present are the leading topics of interest. One, the intumescence of the antipathetic feeling entertained for the Japanese by the dwellers on the Pacific Coast; the other, the controversy between church and State in France. The Japanese question has really two heads. One is the Japanese immigration, the coolie trouble. The other is the education of Japanese students in San Francisco. The former case we do not propose to treat except in so much as it may be intertwined with the latter. But we are more intimately connected with the educational difficulty and will state our view presently.

The educational question is simply this. The people of San Francisco through their board of education, deeming it a grave evil for their girls and boys to have grown Japanese as school companions, undertook to segregate and centralize this obnoxious element. In so doing they were justified and acting perfectly within their rights. It was not only absurd, it was a menace for young children to have as school mates these Japanese young men with their years so disproportionate to their low class standing, and national ignorance of, and disregard for, our own standard of morals. To remedy the evil it was resolved to conduct a school solely for Japanese students, in order to give them the educational benefits to which their citizenship entitled them, and to remove the menace to the white children in other schools. It was a logical, legitimate and perfectly innocuous solution and would have been effected quietly but for a few impeding circumstances.

First of all, action was blocked by the Japs themselves. Misinterpreting the change, they imagined that they were being deprived of some inalienable rights and immediately complained. Their complaint reached the ears of the Japanese consul and in time its echo floated across the Pacific to the imperial courts of the Mikado. Thereupou Japan, flushed, nay a trifle inebriate with success, bristled at the imaginary indignity.

About that time, as a surrogate to this, the Americans added their little share to the general discord. Their action needs but little explanation. Probably the most dominant feature of this young country is the intense racial feeling. In the early sixties differences and incombatability of races rent asunder the nation, and divided it with a stream of blood At present racial antipathy between the whites and blacks is called a very grave evil, and as further evidence, there has been passed the exclusion act to circumvent the yellow peril. And so when race feeling was involved in the San Francisco trouble, the Californians, who had felt none too friendly towards the Japs anyway on account of economic reasons, became very bitter on the subject. Already the whole affair had been given undue notoriety and then Mr. Roosevelt stepped in.

President Roosevelt has had a remarkable vigorous and laudable term, but in this case, for once, he made a grave and culpable blunder. We do not pretend to approve or condemn the President's interference in the immigration trouble, but we think that his action in the educational difficulty was a large factor in linking the two problems together which would otherwise have been distinct. And by the combination a more cumbersome and dangerous resultant was produced.

A national treaty is outside of its province when its terms tie the hands of State legislators or in any way hinder them in a free enactment of their state laws. California is constitutionally justified in deciding her own problems, and in purely local and state question like education, she and only she has the authority to direct. From unreliable sources Mr. Roosevelt gathered that the Japs were being excluded (not segregated) and with characteristic impetuosity, he constituted himself judge and jury and strongly condemned this state's action in his annual message to Congress. Too, his arguments were objectionable. He tells us that we have as much to learn from Japan as she from us. Are we to be called self-sufficient, blind to our own attributes, if we object strenuously to being classed with these people but lately raised from social barbarism and as yet unweaned from pagan immorality? Californians think Mr. Roosevelt should allow the state to act within its constitutional rights and work out its own problems without interference. The flames of racial discord are bad and menacing enough in San Francisco without the President trying to extinguish them by blowing on the fire.

————

The passing of the old year marks also a kaleidoscopic shift in REDWOOD affairs. The February number represents the last efforts of the outgoing editors. To-morrow the college monthly changes hands. This month sees the first working of a clause added to our constitution last year, to the effect that the staff be elected for each semester, and furthermore that in view of the coming final examinations, no senior remain on the staff after January. We do not propose to lose time by making a number of closing comments. It is fit and congruous that our valedictory should be as short as was our reign. It always happens and it seems a trifle ironical that ever in life the action that pushes back the curtain for an entrance must hold it back for an exit, too. But rules of Life are unyielding even to journalists. Like all mortals they too must bow to the inevitable. To the incoming editors we the outgoing can only say, with hat in hand, "exituri salutamus." We did our best to uphold Santa Clara through her official organ, and we feel confident that the work entrusted to us we are committing to faithful hands. If the handling of your college paper is a pleasure, remember it is a responsibility as well.

And so without more ado about nothing let us draw down the cover of our desk, and turn out the editorial lamp. Let us close and lock the sanctum door and for to-night leave the room in shadow.

Tonight rings out the old,
Tomorrow will ring in the new.

JAMES F. TWOHY, '07.

Passion Play

It has been announced that the Passion Play will be produced this year. Martin V. Merle, author of the "Light Eternal," which has made a tremendous "hit" in the East, is now on his way from New York to stage the performance. The parts have not as yet been assigned but Mr. Fox, S. J., who will have the direction, has the cast made out and ready.

Last year we were on the point of producing the play · but the earthquake effectually prevented. Beautiful new scenes had been painted and no labor or expense had been spared to make the pruduction a grand and unprecedented success. Mr. Merle worked hard and conscientiously in drilling his men and in devising stage effects. No need to say that everything will be right when we simply say "Mart" is going to stage it. He comes fresh from the East with new ideas and improvements on the old ones.

Many of the old boys who covered themselves with glory are to be with us again and take their old parts. John J. Ivancovich will play Judas. All who have ever heard of the Play have heard of this wonderful part, which, according to Mr. Ashton Stevens, John himself to a large degree created. Others of the old favorites who will again grace our boards are Gerald Beaumont, W. J. Mc-Kagney, J. B. Shea, M. Griffith, Jos. Farry, and last and far from least, J. Bacigalupi.

Bishop Conaty's Visit

On the afternoon of January 31st Rt. Rev. Dr. Conaty, Bishop of Los Angeles, was given a very impromptu, and hence rather unpretentious, reception in our college hall. As James Twohy said in his graceful little speech of welcome, distractions as a rule are best away from the college student, but such a distraction as is the visit of a man eminent for virtue and ability is always welcome and beneficial. It certainly did us good to hear his Grace tell us stories of his old college days at Holy Cross, and to find before us a living, breathing, proof of the fact that a boy may get "lines" now and then, and even sometimes be put "on soak" for talking in the dormitory, and yet turn out a great and good man. Other remarks of our kindly, genial guest will also be treasured by all his hearers, and none of us but was moved by his cheery words to a resolve of being a more diligent student, a more vigorous athlete, and an all-around better man.

The thanks of the boys are due Edgar Nolan and Raymond Caverly for the sweet music they discoursed for us, and James Daly for his spirited piece of declamation.

Students Attend Arch-Bishop Montgomery's Funeral

The Senior and Junior classes gladly responded to the invitation of Rev. Fr. Rector to represent Santa Clara College at the obsequies of onr late beloved Coadjutor Archbishop. Archbishop Montgomery had a paternal heart for all his spiritual children, and his unvarying thoughtfulness towards us in presiding at our annual commencement exercises, in visiting and addressing us from time to time, shows that we were not the least in his affections.

Condolence

The students offer their sincere sympathy to Mr. Wm. Shepherd, S. J., of the Faculty, in the loss of his mother, who died on January 25th. She had the extraordinary privilege of being the mother of five Religious—three daughters in the Congregation of Notre Dame, and two sons in the Society of Jesus. A consolation of such a substantial value as this is, needs no words of ours to supplement it.

Examinations

The final examinations of the first semester were held on January 28th, 29th, 30th. Giving an account of one's stewardship is not always a pleasant task, especially when one's affairs are not just in the condition they ought to be in, but gracious! they do feel pleasant when we get over them.

An Expected Treat

It is very likely that Mr. Seumas McManus, the noted Irish writer, will regale us with a lecture or two in the course of the month. In case he does, one of his subjects will be "Irish Wit and Humor." The Lecturer and his subject will prove rival drawing cards.

Lloyd E. Allen, ex '07,—last year our Baseball Manager, and a member of the business staff of THE REDWOOD, and a general good fellow always, was a visitor during the past month. Lloyd has registered at the University of California. To his ability is largely due the brilliant success of the baseball team last year and the winning of the championship. He was popular with everybody and THE REDWOOD feels sure that it voices the sentiments of the entire student body when it wishes him all success in his University career.

THE REDWOOD desires to express its deep and heartfelt sympathy to Charles Laumeister in his late bereavement. The loss of a mother is indeed a mighty one, but how much comfort there is in the thought that she had led an exemplary Christian life and that her edifying death was in keeping with her life.

William Maher, '05 Com., is in the employ of the California Northwestern Railroad at Tiburon.

John Parrott, ex '07, is with the Union Trust Company of San Francisco. John is a recent graduate of Georgetown.

Carl Fitzgerald, '01, stole a march on us. He was married last month right under our very noses and without the knowledge of a single student. Perhaps he foresaw the reception that would be his had he made it a public affair. "Prof." is a little bashful you know. The bride is a well known Santa Clara girl—Miss Lillie Ruth. She has a host of friends who join their congratulations with ours and wish the young couple a long and happy period of married life.

John Riordan, A. B. '05, and A. M. '06, is in Attorney Heney's office, San Francisco, and from all accounts must be kept pretty busy, as his employer has been doing some rather strenuous work lately, to say the least.

Thomas Blow, ex '06,—one of our '05 football stars, has registered at Stanford. Tom visited us last week accompanied by Harry Gulling, ex '08, who is making a tour of California.

Edward S. Kirk, ex '06, was another visitor. Doc is a Deputy Tax Collector at Oakland. While here he paid his Redwood subscription for the present year. Not so bad for a politician. Thanks, Doc.

A letter has been received from John Regan. John is naturally modest and said little or nothing about himself, but we hear from other sources that he is doing very well. He is managing several mines for his father in Idaho. John was one of the most representative students that Santa Clara has had, and he will long be kindly remembered by both the boys and the Faculty.

M. R. O'Reilly, '06, Santa Clara's petit business man, is now battling in the commercial field, for his own benefit, and from all accounts the entries in his ledger have been mostly on the "gain" side. He has located in Los Angeles and is the junior partner of the firm of Aldrich & O'Reilly, Real Estate. THE REDWOOD owes much to O'Reilly —more than it can ever repay. He improved the paper in more ways than one—increased the advertising, increased the subscribers—always had heart and head working at full pressure in its service, and, in a word, was the key that fitted the lock. "Mike" held many other offices of trust and wherever he was, there was prosperity. We hope that prosperity will continue to follow him and that his conquests in the realm

of dollars and deeds may be as "pronto" and as—well, we hope he may have a regular "veni-vidi-vici" time of it.

Santa Clara College had a representative among the editors of the State who took the trip offered them by the Southern Pacific Railroad to the Salton Sea. He is a young man for an editor —in fact, he had the distinction of being the youngest man in the party. Gerald P. Beaumont, ex '07, head of the "San Jose Mercury," has been making the literary stars of this section "sit up and take notice." They are surprised that such a youngster holds so important a position, but when they take a good square look at his work and his methods, their surprise changes to admiration and wonder. And he isn't swelled up about it either—he still wears the same size hat and is still the same Beaumont we knew here at Santa Clara. If you don't believe it, just knock at the door of the "Editor-in-Chief, San Jose Mercury," and if it isn't true, why, I'll take the responsibility. We all rejoice in your success, Gerald.

We have been singularly fortunate this semester. Not a single death has so far been chronicled in the Alumni columns of THE REDWOOD, but now Divine Providence has seen fit to call to our minds the serious side of life by summoning one of us. The lesson has cost us dear, the price being one of Santa Clara's truest, brightest, and most virtuous sons. When John J. Burke, A. B., '97, graduated from his

Alma Mater he was watched with more than ordinary interest by his Professors and fellow students. One so competent in his studies should make an enviable record in life later on, they hoped, and their expectations were fully realized. They heard of his entering the offices of Snook & Church, and of the brilliant examination he passed to qualify for an attorneyship. Then came his election to the Assembly for two successive terms, together with the presidency of the Young Men's Institute, Pacific jurisdiction. For one so young his future indeed looked bright. But death "froze the genial current of his soul" and closed a life full of great and useful achievement and of promise of greater to come. Upon these we need not dwell; every newspaper in California has reviewed them at length during the past few days. To his bereaved relatives and friends THE REDWOOD joins with the Faculty of Santa Clara in offering their heartfelt sympathy.

A very interesting and interested visitor among us lately was Mr. Robert Williams of San Francisco, who was a student here not less than 46 years ago. Such an opportunity is altogether too good to lose, and accordingly, we did not fail to notify Mr. Williams that a letter from him about ye olden days would be strictly in order.

*   *   *   *

Mr. James A. Douglas, grandson of Sir James Douglas, first Governor of British Columbia, dropped in not long ago to see his old prefect and friend, Fr. Neri. Mr. Douglas was here in the 70's; at present he resides in Victoria, B. C.

*   *   *   *   *

Not all his important legal business can make Mr. Delmas forget his Alma Mater, whose interests he is ever eager to further. He spent some hours with us a month ago.

MERVYN S. SHAFER, '09.

·IN THE LIBRARY·

Some weeks ago we received from the publishing house of Benziger Bros. a circular in which a strong appeal is made for more extensive support_ of their magazine. Benziger's Magazine is an illustrated monthly of over fifty quarto pages, with a special department for women and another for children. Its present subscription price is $2.00 a year. Considering that it is the most varied and entertaining periodical of its kind in the language, the price is far from being exorbitant; it is in fact quite modest. The object of the publishers is not money-making; all they want in the financial line is that the paper should pay its own way, and not as heretofore round up each year with a snug little deficit. The purpose of the paper is something infinitely nobler than income; it is the diffusion of Catholic truth and the safeguarding of morals, especially in the case of the young. This it does in such a taking, interesting way that we would fain say of it what a German critic said of Wiseman's Fabiola,—"It is a good book with all the success of a bad one." May good Benziger's Magazine have all the success of the cheap, sensational, irreligious magazines that flood our scribe-ridden land!

The magazine is all it claims to be—popular in all its features; it is full of interesting stories, and articles on all manner of topics; it is profusely illus-trated and its religious art pictures in large, extra size, some of them in colors, are the best we know of in any publi-cation; and its departments already mentioned are attended to with the most painstaking care. There is not an uninteresting line or commonplace illus-tration in the whole book, and its typog-raphy and general execution is what anyone acquainted with the work of Benziger Bros. might be led to expect.

The Benzigers, then, have surely done their share in the spread of Catholic lit-erature, and we hope and pray that the Catholic public will show their appreciation. Catholic parents whose means allow it, are in duty bound to give their children such sound, clean reading matter as may serve for an antidote against the poison of the irreligious and indecent newspaper that attacks them in every street car and on every street corner. Parents ought to know that the daily paper that does not offend against Christian modesty is a rare thing indeed—its value is as of a thing from afar. And the secular magazines are too, as a rule, very injurious in their influence—they are materialistic and sensational. Accordingly those parents who do not supervise their children's reading, fail—as our catechism does, and common sense ought to, tell us—most gravely in their duty. For they, in fact, allow their children to mingle with all sorts of company, good, bad, and worse—because the reader is in the author's company, and the latter does all the influencing—with the usual result that they are too knowing in things where ignorance is bliss, or, at least, security. The parent who sees his or her child absorbed in such a book as Benziger's Magazine can feel assured that he is with a companion who will do him a great deal of good. We hope, then, that the heads of Catholic families into whose hands the REDWOOD may fall, will give a little thought to this matter, and that, unless they are well supplied with Catholic periodicals already they will lose no time in getting acquainted with the magazine we are recommending. They will lose $2.00 by the transaction, it is true, but they will have gained a bright, sunny, cultured friend who will visit them once a month, and who will leave the whole family all the better and happier for his coming.

NOT A JUDGMENT

BY GRACE KEON—BENZIGER BROS.—
$1.25

It is said that Miss Keon is quite a young writer, but no one would ever suspect this from her charming books, which have all the elegant ease of mature experience. The story is interesting from beginning to end, though we think that if Nonie McCabe had been left undisturbed in her cradle instead of being forced out into the bleak night just to serve as an introduction to the novel it would have been an improvement. The conversational parts of the book—and conversation forms the bulk of it—is very cleverly managed throughout, though we think its merit reaches its climax in the chapter, 'The Charity Seance.' The story is woven around a poor and superficially unattractive girl, Mollie Farrell, who however is endowed with much cleverness and great force and independence of character. She becomes acquainted with a young doctor who in the goodness of his heart devotes a large amount of his time and wealth to the poor of the East Side slums. He is of an as equally pronounced individuality as Mollie herself, and the result is that after a series of repulsions they at last come to understand each other, and of course, got married. The book has some very common-sense criticism of the untactful and unintentionally unkind methods used by rich folks who with motives often curiously mixed, spent their spare time in "slumming."

THE WESTMINSTER LECTURES

B. HERDER, ST. LOUIS

The lectures were primarily intended for Cathedral Hall, Westminster, but so valuable have they proved and so much appreciated have they been by the public, that they are published as they come out, both by an English and an American Company. They deal with fundamental, theological and moral questions in a way that is at once thoroughly sound and at the same time interesting and intelligible to the average Catholic layman. Certainly no educated Catholic who desires to be able to give a reason for the faith that is in him, should be without this valuable series of popular treaties, and we think moreover that the students' libraries of our Catholic colleges are incomplete without them. Among those we have received lately are: The Witness of the Gospels, by Monsignor Barnes, M. A.; The Existence of God, by Mons. Moyes, D. D.; and The Immortality of the Soul, by Rev. F. Aveling, D. D. Very neatly printed, they cost in paper 15 cents each; in cloth, 30 cents.—B. Herder, 175 Broadway, St. Louis.

Among the best of our exchanges is our latest arrival—*The Nassau Lit.*, for Xmas. It is attractive in form—nicely covered and gotten-up—and what is more important, it possesses interesting matter of a good literary quality. The historical sketch, "The Rittenhouse Orrery," we liked very much, not that we are particularly interested in any orrery but because the article is written in such an easy, flowing, simple and natural style. The verse though exceptionally fine and of sufficient quantity, has not a variety of subjects. "Girl" an ode, proves to be the best verse in the *Lit.* "My Lady Nicotine," "The Dance" and "The Quest" also struck us favorably. "The End of the Year" however, is not so good. It is a hackneyed theme and seems to have a little of Bryant and Byron in it. Here and there we notice that it becomes a little prosaic. In a recent novel, we read that we should always write new things in an old way, old things in a new way or new things in a new way, but never old things in an old way. "The End of the Year" seems to be an old thing written in an old way.

As to the prose, it is well done, from beginning to end. "Golden Apples" is clever, but in places the conversation verges on the pedantic. "The Dreams" pictures the wretched condition of the poor in some of our big cities very well. "The Edge of the Forest" is a most fanciful little sketch.

The *Touchstone* for January is extremely interesting. "Cub's Assignment" keeps one in a worry of suspense until the end when the hero awakes and he and we find it has been all a dream, and he and we feel a trifle cheap. "'Tis Worth While" is full of wholesome sentiments but there is not much rhythmical ease about it. "In the Wind" is rather unique, being in negro dialect, a rare thing in a college publication nowadays. "College Fraternities" should have been called "College Fraternities at Lafayette," we believe, for not all college fraternities are like those described, far from it,—they are just the opposite. Many college fraternities do "foster a spirit of exclusiveness," many college fraternities do "break up the natural bonds of fellowship between students of the same institution or the same class." And because you "do not find it so at Lafayette" is no good reason why it is not found to be so at other colleges. Of course, however, the fraternities have done a great deal of good, but in many colleges this good was done to a bad end, and therefore, it was not good but bad. The means do not justify the end any more than the end justifies the means. "It would seem to me absurd" writes the author "to suppose that any group of average young fellows, not to say chosen fellows, would deliberately combine and make a secret bond to promote immoral ends." Let the Professor argue as he may, the fact remains that there are many fraternities that do "promote immoral ends," taking the term, of course, in its widest sense.

In the course of his address, Prof. Owen says:

I will maintain optimism, therefore, against all who come, basing my belief upon this one truth of human nature, that we rise to a better life with a thrilling sense of strength and victory; and we sink to a worse life stung with a sense of moral defeat.

Yes, the sanguine Professor does maintain a very pronounced brand of optimism, but, while not advocating any dumpish pessimism ourselves, we think that virtue lies in the mean. If Mr. Owen believes that men will do good and avoid evil merely because of a thrilling sense of victory or a stinging sense of defeat, he certainly has great faith in human nature that is vitiated in its source. We think that everyday experience, to say nothing of Revelation, is all against him.

The Exchange editor of the *St. Ignatius Collegian* picks out what he terms "The Six Best Sellers," and naturally we feel highly gratified that "THE REDWOOD" is among these six, for it makes us realize that our work is not in vain. The *Collegian* speaks as follows:

It is not an easy task to set oneself down before a table heaped high with college journals —magazines in scarlet, blue, buff and gray, newspapers with crowded columns—each containing something of true merit, and all crying for a hearing, and to attempt to select from all the pile six exchanges—"The Six Best Sellers" —that represent all that is best in amateur journalism, and the standard set by them all for the quarter, after much reading, re-reading, sorting and weeding, however, we have selected the half-dozen and trust that we do not err in presenting THE REDWOOD for November, *The Georgetown College Journal*, for November, the *The Williams Lit*, for November, *The U. of Virginia Magazine* for October, *The Red and Blue* for November, and the *Labarum* for November, as the best of our exchanges received since we last went to press.

Many thanks, *Collegian*, for putting us in such select company. We'll have to look out ourselves hereafter, for *noblesse oblige*. But, frankly, it makes us feel just a trifle dizzy to find ourselves in Abou Ben Adhem's situation—our name at the head of the list.

In the St. Mary's *Collegian* for January there are a number of very well written articles. "Glimpses of France" is timely and we found it well worth reading. It gives us a clear idea of the religious and political condition in that enslaved nation. The treatment is good but in places we observe the lack of proper connecion between paragraphs. "Socialism" is a worn-out theme but it is necessary at times to treat of it in order that the absurdity of it be kept in our minds. The writer, however, has the knack of handling an old thesis in a new way and so we found the article not at all uninteresting. Probably the best of all, though, is the brief sketch on the life, character, and genius of Washington Irving the founder practically of *belles lettres* in America. This we found interesting as well as instructive. Of course the writer has for his ulterior end in view the purpose of instructing, but he svoids nicely the usual pedagogical style so often met with in such articles.

The editorials in the *Collegian* are usually very excellent matter to read. They are brisk, snappy, and always dealing with lively topics. The other departments—always excepting the "Josh" column which should really be in the waste-basket—though local and interesting mainly to S. M. C. students are also readable to outsiders, on account of their spiciness.

However, good things are sometimes commingled with bad, as the January *Collegian* illustrates. The bad here is in the form of a so-called poem which is thoroughly vulgar throughout, even to the subscribed *nom de plume*. We refer to "Hanging to a Strap", a performance we deeply regret to see in such a high-toned magazine.

A. B. DIEPENBROCK, '08.

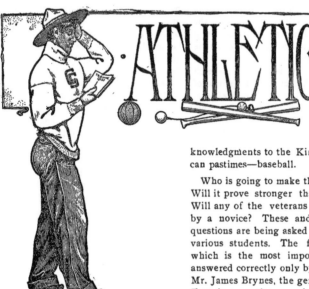

Now comes the college pet, the darling sport of Santa Clara. Every college, whether it be primary or secondary, has her favorite pastime. The majority place the football on the imperial throne of sportdom; a few, aquatically inclined, sacrifice to the god Neptune; others serve other idols. We of Santa Clara College are staunch admirers of all clean, manly, athletic sport, but where one has a collection of good things, he usually takes the one which looks the best, and so it is with us. At this time of all the year we bow acknowledgments to the King of American pastimes—baseball.

Who is going to make the first nine? Will it prove stronger than last year? Will any of the veterans be displaced by a novice? These and many other questions are being asked constantly by various students. The first question, which is the most important, can be answered correctly only by the teacher, Mr. James Brynes, the genial little San Francisco gentleman who will act as coach this season. It would cast a reflection on you dopeisters, baseball fans etc., if I should give here at length smiling Jimmy's record (with apologies to Mr. Byrnes for naming him thus), but for those that have not followed baseball suffice to say that Jimmy played in the coast league, made good from Alpha to Omega and by mixing plenty of brains with his playing as that famous artist Sir Joshua did in mixing his colors, he attracted the practical eye of Connie Mack of the Philadelphia Americans. His wardrobe was shipped east, followed by Jimmy himself on a fast flyer. These easy going people of the Quaker City are not very easily satisfied, but genial Jim made it easy for them by making good. Mr. Byrnes is made of that kind of ginger which bubbled over at Kingston and which is now rebuilding that stricken city. Like all loyal sons of the Golden West, he has come back with us for a short time. During this interval, Jimmy will whip over youthful collection of college tossers into a rattling good outfit who by their performances on the diamond will make their fellow students howl with glee. Jimmy may, as our instructors do in the various classes, answer some of these difficult questions. "Father Time" will certainly answer those that Coach fails in, and Augie Aguirre will very gratiously give out the dates to the over-zealous students.

Yes, the first practice brought out the usual troop of aspirants. Chaseites, Lajoieites, Wagnerites and even the suggestion of Waddellites were visible to the dreamy book worm on the bleachers. After Jimmy tried them all, the weeding-out process was quickly concluded, and out of the valuable remainder there might possibly be produced a player of the above caliber before the curtain falls on this semester's play. Just a word or two of colloquialism, friend reader, to express my idea of the captain—"Well, Cleon Kilburn is the candy and he won't be very sweet when the opposing batsman try to lick him—see." You all know how that infield works better than any Waltham.

From Pudgy M. Shafer behind the rubber, doing perfect pegging to the sacks, down to Broderick, a daisy from last year's outer garden, doing perfect duty at the first station, then to Flash Twohy, the fastest keystone sacker of all collegians, from there to Charles Friene on the puzzle corner who keeps the league magnates at a distance with a college education, on again to Cousin Art Shafer at short, making sensational plays, I say that Mr. Byrnes will have to wire Connie Mack to send his bunch here if he expects to eclipse or even penumbra that infield. Jimmy McGlyn, our molecular philosopher wisely says, "Gee! der ayre certinly pippins."

Joe Collins, the premier batsman of college balldom, will probably hook them in out in right. Joe caught last season, but has shifted to the field in order to sting them harder. Little Jimmy Lappin, the baby of the team, needs no introduction; my pen refuses to spill its thoughts, but this baby is a Ball Baby, believe me. He has everything except mass or volume—head, nerve, speed, good eye, nice arm, never drops them and hits hard all the time. He has everything that makes a good ball player. As to who will get the coveted vacancy in center field left open by the departure of Byrnes to Georgetown and Capt. Wolters, '06, to the big league; nobody knows. Of course Captain Kilburn will do the mound work together with his compeer, Big Joe Brown, who should prove his mettle to be of good quality this season if his recent workouts count for anything.

The work of Peters, Foster, Salberg, and Watson certainly deserves mention.

These ambitious students have been running neck and neck for the coveted vacancy. It is really a shame and we can blame the Fates that there is not a place for every one of such a Trojan quartet. They all play gilt-edge ball. It looks like a toss-up to me. Give it to the boy that sticks the best—that is the only solution.

Father Morton might be complimented for the masterly way in which he is handling the athletic affairs; as also Augie Aguirre, who is pulling on the rope of success to a nicety.

New suits, coats, caps, and other baseball paraphernalia, will shortly make their debut. Won't bore you with descriptions—watch for the outfit. Start the new uniforms out right, fellows, by placing a victory in the coat pocket.

George Casey will handle the second team this year. What of it? Ans.— Successful season, first-class team, everyone satisfied. Harry Wolters, last year's captain, has kindly consented to pick the team. After this is done the chosen few will elect a leader. The student body will lend financial support to the team this year, and rightly so, for this is merely the Prep. school of the first nine. Shafer and Lappin were taught in this school. Watch George and his nine grow. He will have a natty bunch with such men as Archbold, Gilfillan, R. Twohy, R. Brown, Bogan, Meyer, McNally, Jones, Donovan, Hartman, McLean, L. Wolters, Pierce, Gallagher, McConnell, Hubbard, Strohl, Mainguaneau, Duffy, and Lyng. "Don't wurry," watch them play.

Basket Ball

Thos. Donlan will manage the basketball interests this year. Tom is dickering with teams in the near vicinity and promises the quintet a lively season. Eastern football coaches are urging the game upon their pupils, as it improves their passing, stamina, wind, and perfects their handling of the pigskin. It is not a ladies game—yes, it is when ladies play it—any more than is baseball, football, or any other sport.

This game is now taking the west by storm; in the east it is already established, all the colleges having crack teams. Although the team has not been selected, here is the way the first squad lined up last week. Center, Aguirre; Forwards, Twohy, Bogan, McKenzie (capt); Guards, Murphy and Schmitz.

Tennis

We have noticed with much gratification the opening of the tennis season, celebrated a few days ago by a game played amid much enthusiasm. It is a good thing that such a healthful sport has devoted adherents in the school. The officers of the tennis organization have worked very hard to make a good court, and we are glad to say their efforts have been successful.

With a few applications of pulverized gravel and many tiresome rollings the court has been put in good condition. A tournament will be held some time in February, the date being as yet uncertain. Everyone who likes tennis should turn out for this, as all will have an equal chance; competent judges will give handicaps according to experience and skill.

Treasurer McLane, when approached on the subject of the tennis outlook for the year, was very communicative. "Now look here. We've got a good fast court here in good condition. We've worked hard on it, but are satisfied by the thought that it will benefit many. See? There's lots of fellows in the yard who do not like baseball and tennis provides them with a healthful, manly sport, one that makes the muscle grow."

"Now we want a bunch of members. There are many that want to join, but are held back by the thought that they do not know how. Now, my boy, we all had to learn and everyone will be willing to show you. Don't wait until you get on to the game. Come around and see us—the more the merrier."

Santa Clara 9—San Jose 1

The above sentiments cannot rightfully be taken back, for the team showed the skeptics from Missouri that they were certainly deserving of all the good things said about them. In their baseball debut Jimmy Byrnes' pupils played rings around Amy Mayer's professional leaguers, even though they did have the famous Hal Chase as their Napoleon. Hal's team reproduced "The Comedy of Errors" in elegant style, having ten black marks in the mistake column when the whistle blew.

What proved the undoing of such a quintet of stars as Chase, Stricklett, Strieb, Arrellancs, and Hickey, only the score books can tell. Captain Kilburn had the leaguers at his mercy; it was one big fishing party for him with the opposing batsmen biting every inning. M. Shafer held Kil up splendidly the entire game and cut them off regularly at the plate.

The entire infield worked like a brainy man with a good watch, while Collins and Lappin in the outfield were never affected with dropsy. Peters and Watson broke in for the first time and made good, the former by a clean bungle and the latter by his work on the sacks. For the visitors, Chase secured two hits and Arrellanes pulled down a pretty drive which looked good for two stations. It is not necessary to describe the throng present at the slaughter, except that it was unusually large and did not expect to see the College boys trounce the Big Guns. All of us seould rejoice in this victory because it shows what we can do when we try. It starts us right—this winning of the initial game. We have tasted the victory, and we shall taste it again. I will not bore you with an itemized account of the victory, but here is what happened, in a general way. The College secured eight safe hits, to San Jose's four, two of which were secured by Chase. They made ten errors, we made four and purloined eleven sacks to their six. Kil fanned five and their trio of twirlers fanned—nobody. We made it nine tallies to their one.

In a sentence: "Santa Clara outplayed them at every stage of the game." San Jose never had a chance, but that is not saying that they won't come back at us. Sure they will; Mayer is a good loser and Santa Clara College does not have to sing, "Why Don't You Try." Mayer simply said after the game, "You won O. K., but then we'll have another one."

Since writing the first part of the athletic news, the tryout for right field has been decided, and Peters is the lucky ninth man, with Watson as substitute.

Second Division Notes.

(BY WILLIE GIANERA, '09)

Although baseball has not taken hold in Second Division so far, that does not argue that it is not going to do so. Our Leagues have been formed, but the rain of the past few weeks has kept us from the field. But now everything seems to have turned our way again and the little League is in full blast. Among our last year youngsters of the League, Harry Curry, Nolting, Kerns, Wilson and a host of others have returned to make the coming season a successful one. Fr. Galtes, the President of the League, has put up a medal for each member of the coming team. The fellows are working hard for it, and at present it is difficult to tell who has the best chance, as the teams are very evenly matched.

As to our big League, I must say that this part of athletics in Second Division is on the down grade. However, we have plenty of material for a good League if all the members would only pull themselves together. I hope that by the next issue we will be able to give more encouraging news. Now to come to the large fellows of the Division. Our Junior team was dealt two hard blows during the last month that has all but taken the last remnant of hope out of us. On our return after the Christmas holidays our best player, Reuben Foster, swelled up so much that he was sent to First Division, and our fast little catcher, Howard Lyng, crossed the boundary also. The absence of these two will materially weaken our team unless there be a few stars among the new comes. Let us hope so!

H. A. J. McKENZIE, '08.

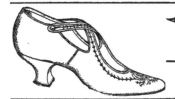

THE
REDWOOD

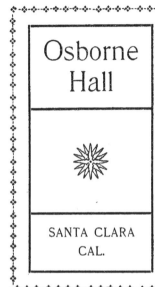

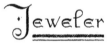

Contents.

Nace Printing Co. ⬥ Santa Clara, Cal.

The Redwood

Entered Dec. 18, 1902, at Santa Clara, Calif. as second-class matter, under Act of Congress of March 3, 1879.

| VOL. VI. | SANTA CLARA, CAL., MARCH, 1907. | No. 6 |

CLOUDS

White sheep that wander o'er blue fields ethereal
   Led by the shepherd south-wind's cheery cry;
Or, massed in serried ranks a host imperial,—
   All day the clouds flit through the changeful sky.

What true heart could behold, unstirred to extasy,
   Their myriad-mooded loveliness when day,
Slow-dying scatters round his flaming legacy
   Of richest gold on field and hill and spray.

Yet have I often watched with raptured wondering
   Their sullen passions when the storm-kings wrath
Had summoned his embattled hosts, loud-thundering,
   To hold high orgies in his wreck-strewn path.

For in such scenes, I thought, was imaged truthfully
   A lesson for man's fitful life below:
My soul ten thousand storms might harass ruthfully—
   Each storm a glory for the after-glow!

                       F. H. '09

WILLIAM MAKEPEACE THACKERAY

Of recent years, Thackeray's fame as a classic English novelist seems to be on the increase. The reason of this is not far to seek. For besides that brilliant style, the firm tone of which would wear well in any age, he has the advantage of being in the highest meaning of the word, an historical novelist. Not that he has tarried so long or so lovingly in former epochs, as many others, particularly Sir Walter Scott has done—though in this field also he has produced very remarkable work—but I mean that his descriptions of his own times form a most precious historical bequest to posterity, and that his clear-cut, and faithfully realistic pictures of life among the higher classes in the England of the forties, are an ever-growing inheritance for all time to come, to be placed in the same category with that of Smollett or Fielding.

What gives these works even already this historical interest, and invests them with that atmosphere of enchantment that ordinarily comes but with the distance of centuries, is that the age in which our author wrote is an age much further removed from us than mere dates would indicate. The changes that have since taken place have done the work of centuries for it. It was a period of a distinctly peculiar character. It immediately preceded or it saw the birth of many of the great inventions that have changed the face of the modern world. When Becky Sharp made her exit from the hated old school at Chiswick, there was no iron-horse to bear her away from the great stone gates into the world that lay before her. But if Sambo and his coach proved a slower vehicle, they certainly left a more effectual distance behind them, for, in those days, towns forty miles apart were almost foreign to each other. Becky knew full well, accordingly, that in flinging Johnson's "Dixonary" out of the window right in the teeth of the whole awful establishment, she was perfectly safe, and would run across her school-mates or school-marms no more. The wonder-working wire had not yet come to enrich the earth, and to tell us in a breath of the ravages of famine in Russia, the heavy crops in New Zealand, the ravings of the Mikado in Japan, or the aches and crimes of the Sick Man of Turkey. Rummum Loll could then come to London and there pose as a prince of the bluest Brahmin blood, and have the "old dowagers crowding around him," and the fair sex "sniggling up to his india-rubber face," and no telegraphic operator in distant India to expose him. These conditions are passed away forever; the times are changed and we have changed with them; and the England of fifty years ago is as distant from us, as it was from that of Queen Anne of whom our author so loved to speak. That age is historical and its most vivid historian is William Makepeace Thackeray.

His greatest portrait in this way is, it almost goes without saying, *Vanity Fair*, and after it, *Pendennis* and *The Newcombes*. And here let me make a digression. It is often said that *Vanity Fair* is the greatest novel in the English language. It seems to me that this is a very unmeaning compliment. Novels vary as their subject-matter, and accordingly some are so specifically distinct from others as to afford no sufficient common ground for comparison. The decision must ultimately be left to the cultivated reader's individual taste; in other words, no decision can be arrived at. As a realistic portrayal of fashionable life, where the characters live and breathe and walk before your very eyes, where the style of the language combines grace and ease, and sweep of periods with extraordinary pithiness and dash and vigor, *Vanity Fair*, it is true, has probably no rival. But there are others. For instance, in detail and vividness of historical knowledge, in titanic conception of plot and character, in luminous portrayal of bygone men and manners, in thrill of interest, it is difficult to believe that any novel can quite come up to *Kenilworth*. And by the author himself, *Vanity Fair* was not regarded as his best work.

However, *Vanity Fair*, and its companion novels, though yielding in epic grandeur to the creations of the wizard of the North, and to other works besides, have one great merit over these in that they are more true to life. "Paint me as I am" was the spirit that guided his pen. Nothing too bad or too good for the ordinary bounds of human possibility entered within his field of vision. Heroes and heroines he has never met with, and accordingly he leaves them alone. His novels are, as a rule, novels without heroes. All this, of course, is of "malice prepense." Our author's matter-of-fact mind was ever in arms against the magnifying and idealizing that distorted the men and women of fiction out of all likeness with their prototypes of flesh and blood, and shut out the vision of human life in order to disclose a Utopian dream. Especially did he revolt against the maudlin practice of—to put it strongly—painting the devil as an angel of light, investing murderers and criminals of every species with a halo of sentiment such as Lytton places on Eugene Aram, or Goethe is said to put on the ignoble brow of the libertine. In *Catherine*, a disgusting story of disgusting people, Thackeray combats with great fierceness this foolish tendency of dressing vice in romantic qualities. He says satirically:—

"This is the proper end of fiction, and one of the greatest triumphs that a novelist can achieve; for to make people sympathize with virtue is a vulgar trick that any common fellow can do; but it is not everybody who can take a scoundrel, and cause us to weep and whimper over him as if he were a very saint."

And again:—

"Some of our novelists have compounded their drugs in a similar way and made them so palatable that a public once healthy and honest, has been well-nigh poisoned by their wares."

This, then, is Thackeray's distinctive merit, that he is true to life. His people are real people, whom we have met with, or feel we may meet with, in flesh and blood. Stripped of all praeternatural qualities as they are, they have only gained in human interest; they compel our attention and they force themselves into the circle of our acquaintance. Who that has been introduced to Becky Sharp has not projected her into real life, and found some reminder of her in the workaday world around him?

The best proof of his truthfulness to nature is that the author himself, as Miss Mallock informs us, felt the objectivity of his brain-children very strongly. Once he thought he recognized Captain Costigan holding forth, naturally enough, in a tavern. On another occasion he found it impossible to go to sleep "with Colonel Newcombe making such a fool of himself."

In all English fiction perhaps, there does not exist a character that is at once so entirely selfish and heartless, so mean and so unworthy, and that so engrosses our attention and extorts a measure of admiration, or at least, of sympathy as Rebecca Sharp. It is a marvel of art that while our author paints her to the life in all her unloveliness, he yet forces our fascinated gaze to mark her every footstep. And much the same interest clings to Osborne, Lady Kew, Pendennis, Beatrice, Barnes Newcombe, and others.

Even in his historical novels this fidelity to the lifelike is equally marked. His principal work of this nature is *Esmond*: It was regarded by himself, and by his critics, as his masterpiece. Dealing here, as he does, with Queen Anne's time, the period he loved the most, Thackeray has revived the dead past. He gives not a history but a reproduction. His tale is that of an eyewitness. At the touch of his magic pen the curtain of time swings back, and there on the stage before us pass the men and women of two hundred years ago, kings and generals, statesmen and soldiers, gay wits and fair ladies, the ill-fated Stuarts; Malborough, Eugene, and Blenheim, Dicky Steele, Addison, Swift[1] a troop of others less known to fame, but all acting equally well their parts. Each is dressed in his proper costume; the knights are brave with wigs and and ruffles and swords, scarlet and gold; the ladies have their flowing trains and their high headdresses of lace. But the crowning triumph of the book is that its language is entirely that of Queen Anne's reign, and throughout it all rings the Addisonian cadence, the easy, musical and agreeable, but somewhat incorrect style of the great essayist, whom to appreciate is to avow purity of literary taste. The following sentence is taken almost at random, but may serve to illustrate his imitation of the 17th century writers:—

"At length, on the third day at evening, they came to a village standing on the green with elms around it, very pretty to look at; and the people there all took off their hats, and made courtesies to my Lord Viscount, who bowed to them all languidly; and there was one portly person, that wore a cassock and a broad-leafed hat, who bowed lower than anyone—and with this one both my lord and Mr. Holt had a few words."

Leaving aside the considerations of particular works of our author, we shall henceforth deal with more general aspects of him. A trait of his that strikes one at first sight is his penchant for preaching. He manages to get a little—or a big—sermon into nearly every chapter. Every now and again he interrupts his reader to invite him to take a good look around, size up his company, and derive some useful lesson therefrom. Mr. Whibley, his biographer, censures him severely for this, and compares him to the tiresome chorus of elders in a Greek play. Yet on nothing did Thackeray pride himself so much as on his preaching: he looked upon it as his special vocation. Of his writings, the sermons were the parts he liked best, and the part we fear his readers usually vault over with a clean leap. Yet it cannot be denied that they are sometimes excellent reading. For instance—

"I never could count how many causes went to produce any given effect or action in a person's life, and have been for my own part many a time misled in my own case, fancying some grand, some magnanimous, some virtuous reason, for an act of which I was proud, when lo! some pert little satirical monitor springs up inwardly, upsetting the fond humbug which I was cherishing—the peacock's tail wherein my absurd vanity had clad itself—and says, 'Away with this boasting! I am the cause of your virtue, my lad. You are pleased that yesterday at dinner you refrained from the dry champagne; my name is Worldly Prudence, not Self-denial, and I caused you to refrain. . . . . You hug yourself because you resisted other

temptation! Coward, it was because you dared not run the risk of the wrong! Out with your peacock's plumage! walk off in the feathers which Nature gave you and thank Heaven they are not altogether black.''

Truth to tell, however, the reader is justified in 'skipping,' for there is a hesitancy and a mawkishness about the sermonizing that makes it irritating and unsatisfactory. It is quite plain that our author has "not been sent,," he does not speak as one having authority; he is ever uneasy of his premises; his ideas of religion and hence of right conduct are nebulous. He ever yearns for better things in himself and in his neighbor, and he would fain guide us upwards. But his wrist is weak; he is is fearful of appearing too dogmatic; he is always looking behind him; and his sermon usually dies away in an apologetic laugh.

He destroys with the left what he builds with the right, and the sum total of his message seems to be: We are all snobs; you and I are snobs; the greatest snob is he who thinks he is not a snob. We are all sinners; the blackest has some white spots to redeem him; and the whitest has his share of sable. Saints and sinners, we're pretty much alike. Put the saint in the circumstances of the sinner, and he is a sinner. We all live in glass houses, so let us not throw stones at one another.

However, in spite of the unsatisfactory apologues to his sermons, let us hope that Thackeray has done much good. He is always on the side of virtue, and he ever ridicules vice and hypocrisy. He applied the lash of his satire only to what deserved it, and the good, wherever found, had in his noble, manly heart a sincere admirer. The warmth and generosity of this heart it was that saved him from becoming a cynic. It is unjust to associate such a word with the name of Makepeace Thackeray. An editor who could hardly bring himself to inflict the pain of rejecting even the most outrageous contributions, and who, when forced to be thus cruel, would pay the contributor out of his own pocket, such a man was scarcely the stuff of which the cynic is made.

Still, it must be owned that he is somewhat morbid in his fault-finding. At the commencement of his literary career, he had written for *Punch* a series of sketches on the snobs to be found in the different classes of society. These *Snob Papers* were so popular that their number was stretched to forty-five, and to secure a sufficient string of victims, he had to keep a suspicious, satirical eye on everybody he dealt with. The natural result followed—he soon came to regard every child of Adam as, *ipso facto*, a snob. His eye became accustomed to look for the dark side of human nature, and his native melancholy accentuated the blackness. According to his own confession all the characters in *Vanity Fair*, excepting Dobbin, are 'odious.' What a sad confession, and what disappointment and heart-aching it betrays!

Such being his state of mind. it is only to be expected that in depicting virtuous people he should be an utter failure. He is absurdly ill at ease with them; he does not know what to make of them at all, and the upshot of his good intentions is to make them unreal, wooden, or else weak and silly. All his good women, save the refined and devout Catholic Madame Florac, are mere wax-dolls, poor silly fatuous creatures whom the author himself heartily despized. "How is it," he was asked, "that you draw all us women as either wicked or silly?" "Madame," he replied, "I know no others." His good men fare scarcely better. The unselfish, faithful Dobbin must wear a ridiculous name and a ridiculous face, and be kept in the obscure background. And his grand specimen of nature's highest nobility, dear old Colonel Newcombe, is at times a veritable Don Quixote, whom we must not wonder at if his honest but unwisely hot indignation, and his child-like ignorance of practical affairs, and his unselfish bull-headedness cause his brain-father to pass a sleepless night. If Colonel Newcombe brought a decade of sleepless nights to Thackeray, we should more readily forgive his faults.

Another irritating feature of Thackeray's satire is that it is too refined. When not overdone, this kind of satire, it is true, is the most telling, for the sensitive soul, unlike the body, seems to feel the touch of the finger-tip more than the blow of the clenched hand. No satire is more exquisitely delicate than that which Newman used against Kingsley. But the average reader is not as delicately organized as the author of *Hypatia*, and Thackeray's pearls are quite thrown away on him. In *Barry Lyndon*, for instance, our author has depicted a very demon incarnate, a professional gambler, liar and debauchee who, however, is made to pose throughout as a man of high culture and noble ideals, and who persuades us almost of the dignity of the gambler's calling. It is, of course, all satire, but the ordinary reader will shrewdly detect the satire only when it is pointed out to him in a footnote. Again, it is annoying to find heinous crimes constantly alluded to as peccadilloes, and a youthful course of immorality as merely "sowing his wild oats."

Though of a melancholy turn of mind, Thackeray's humor was never-failing. It lights up every story he tells. Several of these are professedly humorous. He was wonderfully skilful at parody, and in his *Novels by Eminent Hands*, he hit off the style of Disraeli, Lytton and others so well that these novelists mistook his stories for some forgotten product of their own pens. His *Rebecca and Rowena* is a glorious burlesque on *Ivanhoe*, and *A Legend of the Rhine* on tales of romance in general. His broadest piece of fun is *The Tremendous Adventures of Mayor Gahagan* wherein an Irish warrior exercises the—according to Thackeray—national prowess for boasting upon his adventures in hazy, far-away India. It is a rare occasion indeed, and the doughty major certainly improves it; Baron Munchausen has to retire to a back seat. Who but Gahagan could ever have so pointed that gun as to lop off the trunks of one hundred and thirty-four of the besieger's elephants at one shot? or could calmly descend the hill, pick out a tolerably small and plump elephant of about thirteen feet high, throw it over his shoulder, and make off for the fort and his adorable starving Belinda? or could have the discretion not to fight seventy men, but run away.

"I was running—running as the brave stag runs before the hounds—running as I have done a great number of times before in my life, when there was no help for it but a race."

In this connection, it may not be out of place to remark that Thackeray's treatment of the Irish was invariably unfair. He was fond of making them play the ridiculous parts in his stories, and his *Irish Papers* are certainly not over-friendly. But he manifested the same narrow-mindedness towards Germany, which in his hands cuts a grotesque figure; and also towards France, a nation he regarded as a huge practical joke. Of the French Revolution he claimed that not Carlyle should have written the history, but the jocose Dickens.

The following is taken from the *Yellowplush Memoirs;* it is a hit at Bulwer Lytton, and seems to smack of a little personal ill-will—a rare thing with Thackeray. Bulwer is advising a footman of a literary turn not to take to writing.—

"Bullwig was violently affected; a tear stood in his glistening i. 'Yellowplush,' says he, seizing my hand, 'you are right. Quit not your present occupation; black boots, clean knives, wear plush all your life, but don't turn literary man. Look at me. I am the first novelist in Europe. I have ranged with eagle wing over the wide regions of literature, and perched on every eminence in its turn. I have gazed with eagle eyes on the sun of philosophy, and fathomed the mysterious depths of the human mind. All languages are familiar to me, all thoughts are known to me, all men understood by me. I have gathered wisdom from the honeyed lips of Plato, as we wandered in the gardens of Academus; wisdom, too, from the mouth of Job Johnson, as we smoked our 'backy in Seven Dials. Such must be the studies, and such is the wisdom, in this world, of the Poet-Philosopher. But the knowledge is only emptiness; the initiation is but misery; the initiated, a man shunned and bann'd by his fellows. 'Oh,' said Bullwig, clasping his hands, and throwing his fine i's up to the chandelier, 'the curse of Pwometheus descends upon the wace. Wath and punishment pursue them from genewation to genewation; Wo and thrice bitter desolation; Earth is the wock on which Zeus, wemorseless, stwetches his writhing victim,—men, the vultures that feed and fatten on him. Ai, Ai; it is agony eternal—gwoaning and solitawy despair; Aud you, Yellowplush, would penetwate these mystewies; you would waise the awful veil, and stand in the twemendous Pwesence. Beware; as you value your peace, beware! Withdraw, wash Neophyte! For heaven's sake—O for heaven's sake!'—here he looked round with agony—'give me a glass of bwandy-and-water, for this clawet is beginning to disagwee with me!"

In general, Thackeray's fun is broad; all it aims at is to raise a jolly, good-natured laugh, and with that it is satisfied. The exquisite agony of mirth which Dickens knew so well to evoke, often by a mere word, is quite beyond the rival novelist. To cite an example. Mrs. Clippins is giving her testimony in the famous Bardell vs. Pickwick suit.

After assuring the judge (who advises her not to try it) that she does not intend to deceive him, she goes on to explain why she was listening at the keyhole, and puts the best face on the matter in this wise:

"I walked in, gentlemen, just to say good-morning, and went, in a permiscuous manner, up stairs."

That *permiscuous* belongs to Dickens alone: Thackery's humor was not exquisite enough for such a touch.

Of Thackeray's religious opinions little need be said. Upon the greatest and most momentous of all questions, he knew not what to think. Like Tennyson he stretched faint hands into the dark, and hoped that good would somehow be the final goal of ill. He speaks thus on the death of one of his characters:

"Let us hope that Heaven may have some regions yet accessible to James, which Dr. Mc-Craw's (Presbyterian) intellect has not yet explored. Look, gentlemen! Does a week pass without the announcement of the discovery of a new comet in the heaven? . . . So let us hope divine truth may be shining and regions of light and love extant, which Geneva glasses cannot yet perceive, and are beyond the focus of Roman telescopes."

The answer springs up spontaneously: "Who does not hear the Church, etc.,"—but perhaps Thackeray was not to blame. He had been reared in the Anglican "City of Confusion."

Towards the Catholic Church, violent as he dealt with it at times, he showed great respect and even yearning. He makes Clive Newcombe say:

"There must be moments, in Rome especially, when every man of friendly heart, who writes himself English and Protestant, must feel a pang at thinking that he and his countrymen are insulated from European Christendom. An ocean separates us. From one shore or the other one can see the neighbor cliffs on clear days; one must wish sometimes that there were no stormy gulf between us; and from Canterbury to Rome a pilgrim could pass, and not drown beyond Dover."

He showed his sympathy for the Catholics in the troubled times of 1851–'52 by atttending Dr. Newman's sermons. And it is noteworthy that Catholic clergymen fare better with him than those of his own denomination, for whom he reserves his keenest shafts of satire.

In conclusion, then, we love and admire Thackeray. He always advocates the good and rebukes the evil, though the mists of religious doubt obscured both the beauty of the one and the ugliness of the other. He drew vice in plain colors but never so as to allure, and in this he stands without many rivals among novelists. He always showed an unswerving regard for the truth, and novelist though he was, he would never sacrifice honesty to effect. A keen observer of men and manners, he has, in a style more easy than Stevenson's and more vigorous than Kipling's, given us vivid and reliable portraits of English life in the forties, portraits that can never obscure with age. While bewildered in his religious opinions, his was a religious soul, and a spirit of reverence is about him. We will part from him in his touching description of the death of our beloved Colonel Newcombe, who after meeting with sad reverses, dies at the hospital of the Charterhouse:—

"At the usual evening hour the chapel bell began to toll, and Thomas Newcombe's hands outside the bed feebly beat time. And just as the last bell struck a peculiar sweet smile shone over his face, and he lifted up his head a little, and quickly said, 'Adsum'! and fell back. It was the word we used at school when names were called; and lo, he, whose heart was as that of a little child, had answered to his name, and stood in the presence of The Master."

J. D. '07.

TO YOUTH

Thy voice is the clearness of stars in the night,
    And reaches as deep in my soul ;
And lustrous thine eyes—a whole springtime of light
    In their grey depths unknowing of dole.
Thy features are rounded in virginal round,
    And tinted in virginal hue,
And thy heart has a joy, and thy laughter a sound,
    There is naught in the whole world so true.
And every lithe motion is passion and grace
    And thy breathing is sweet as the air,
Thou art pure, and divinity dwells in thy face,
    And O, thou art wondrously fair.

Ah, be so forever in bud and in blow;
    No death shall thy beauty enfold!
Nor lose of thy light, nor lose of thy glow,
    Nor the virginal round of thy mould.
The God that hath made thee a vision of grace
    That dwells in thy soul and thine eye,
Would keep thee forever immaculate, trace
    Thy pathway when danger is nigh.
Ah, breathe unto Him all the sweets of thy breast!
    To Him leap thy passion, and dare
To love as thou canst, God's own love and best,
    For O, thou art wondrously fair!

                    P. J., '91.

WHERE IGNORANCE IS BLISS

I

The grim, cold front of the prison struck a chill into the breast of the young man as he went up to the massive door and placed his finger on the button at the side. The tinkle of an electric bell came faintly to his ears from far within, and then a door banged and he heard someone approaching with slow, shuffling step. Nearer and nearer came the footsteps until at length they stopped and the great door swung slowly back on its creaking hinges.

The young man stepped hastily inside. "I'm James Randall," he said, "and I came to see my brother Bob."

"Follow me," the gruff-voiced guard replied as he slammed the door shut, and started down the corridor.

The guard led him through long lines of cells to the end of the corridor, down a steep flight of stairs and into another corridor much darker than the one above. Here he took out a bunch of keys and fitting one into a door on the right, unlocked it and flung it open. A bare cell was disclosed with a dark figure huddled on a bench in one corner.

"Bob," cried the young man, springing forward. "Bob."

The crouching figure jumped up and with a cry of "Jim," rushed across the room and seized his hand.

"Bob," said the young man, "why did you do it?"

The other buried his head in his hands and sobbed.

"Oh God! my father," he cried, "my father! It will break his heart, and I just wrote to him yesterday that I was doing so well. Jim, you'll have to go home and tell him this. My God! the blow will kill him."

II

The crimson flush along the western sky had given place to an ever-deepening shade of purple. The first faint stars were twinkling in the east. A gentle breeze swept over the valley and rustled among the leafy tree-tops, and now and then a faint protesting chirp came from the birds at rest among their branches.

The old man sat longer than usual, this evening, on the bench before his cabin, musing in the twilight and breathing in great draughts of the refreshing air. For he was supremely happy. He had received a letter that day from his boy Bob in the city, telling how well he and Jim were getting along, and promising to pay him a visit sometime very soon. It was the first letter the boy had written for a year, but then he was so busy and worked so hard! Oh no! he had not forgotten his old father. How kind and cheerful the letter was—the old man stroked it tenderly with his hand, as if the dead page had life. They were two such fine boys, Bob and Jim, and the old man was proud of them both, but somehow Bob had always been his favorite. He remembered how as a little fellow Bob had always gotten the best of Jim by some trick. Yes, he was always full of little tricks, little harmless tricks, the old man thought.

As he sat thus musing in the twilight —was it the twilight that flushed his cheeks so?—the gray head sank lower and lower on his breast, and his breathing grew gentler and gentler, until at last he slept.

A dusty stage coach came jolting and lurching down the valley and drew up with a flourish at the gate. A well dressed young man stepped out and came slowly up the path towards the cabin, while the stage, at a crack of the driver's whip, lurched and jolted on its way.

The traveller approached the old man, and seeing him asleep, called softly to him, "Father, father!"

The old man paid no heed, but slumbered on with a smile upon his face.

"Father," the young man called again, this time louder, with a sinking at his heart as he thought how that smile must fade from his father's face when he heard his story.

"Father!"—but still the old man gave no heed. The young man bent over and placed his hand on his father's shoulder. Then he straightened up with a start.

"My God!' he sobbed, "he's dead, my father's dead.!" His eyes fell upon the letter in the motionless hand, and he added, "thank God, it's better so."

MAURICE T. DOOLING, JR., '09.

BONAPARTE

When you, in haughty pride,
Through slaughtered hosts did ride
 Midst universal hate,
  Midst sigh and groan,
 In pompous state
  To gain a throne,
   Was that success?

Or did there rest,
 Some hidden smart,
Within your breast
 O Bonaparte,
  To turn it all to bitterness?

    M. T. DOOLING, JR., '09.

RUSKIN

(VILLANELLE.)

O painter of the earth and sky,
Of rarest gifts this gift was thine
All nature's beauties to descry.

For thee violets' dewy eye
Was hallowed beauty's blissful shrine,
O painter of the earth and sky.

You soared about the mountains high;
You sailed upon the foaming brine;
All nature's beauties you descry.

With nature's vivid hues you vie.
You paint the rainbow's fair design,
O painter of the earth and sky!
You tell us how the snowflakes lie
A crystal robe on lofty pine:
All nature's beauties you descry.

The mound and mount you sanctify,
You clothe God's work in garb divine:
O painter of the earth and sky,
All nature's beauties you descry.

L. J. P. '08.

THE CALL OF THE SPIRIT

Old Mecheto sat down and a hush fell on the tribe. The crackling flames crept starward throwing a red glow on the painted haggard faces about the circle and reached with long wavering fingers into the black recesses of the forest behind. Somewhere from the purple tangle of the stark trees came the long low plaint of the whip-poor-will.

Then arose No Tongue, the Chief. He wrapped his blanket tightly under his chin, standing erect, symetrical.

"My brothers," said he, "always in the council is No Tongue silent because he has not been given the power to talk. But now my soul is sad and the words flow to my lips from a full heart. For a thousand moons has our tribe lived on this island, and brought our food out of the soil and forest. We have never left it; all our brothers and fathers are buried here together. Here did our fathers build their houses and here did they fall in honorable death defending them. But now a famine has come. The soil no longer produces fruit of our labors. The great spirit has laid his hand upon us."

An aged squaw broke in with a low moaning and the chief waited until she was silenced. A dog of the tribe pointed his muzzle upward and howled lugubriously. His frosty breath floated wraithlike above his head. No Tongue went on.

"Tomorrow the ship will come and take us away for the pale face chief has promised. Our tribe will be scattered and the time will be when no man will know his own children. We will be put as slaves to the pale faces because their coming is greater than ours. It is the will of the Great Spirit. He has laid his hand in wrath upon us, and we must submit. Our tribe will be dispersed throughout a strange land and here our homes will crumble, and the bones of our fathers will be out there"—with a sweep of the hand toward the burying ground—"forgotten. I cannot go on. My heart is sore with grief. Get to your homes and be prepared for the morrow."

Slowly and in silence the tribe arose, and in twos and threes were swallowed in the forest. And all the time the flames snapped fitfully in the cold air, and the whip-poor-will mourned plaintively. For some time neither Fleetfoot nor Cloud Daughter moved, or spoke. The young brave gazed dreamily into the fire and his companion watched his face. At length he roused himself.

"Cloud Daughter, when we got the promise of the paleface to take us away in his boat my heart was not lightened, nor was my grief lessened, for I knew that it only meant slavery for all of us, and I determined to stay. Death I preferred to servitude. But I cannot have you go into the life I would shun, and you cannot stay with me. Your life is too fair, too beautiful to be snuffed out like a brand in the fire. And so this have I done. For four days have I saved my share of corn, and I have stolen the share of Sharp Knife. When the ship comes tomorrow you will hide in the deserted hut of Macheto near the burying ground where I have stored away the provisions. In five days I will I be back in a small boat to take you away to the land of plenty. I can escape, and I can row a boat from the land. My arms are strong, and when they fail my heart will lend them strength. For my heart is strong with love—full of strong love for you, Cloud Daughter."

She arose and spoke simply,

"Your will is mine, Fleetfoot. To-morrow will I stay. In five days I will be awaiting you in the hut of Macheto. Goodnight and farewell."

She held out her arms and he took her to him. For love is the same in the hearts of all men. After all civilization is only a crust with the best of us and a little scraping will show the savage underneath.

*   *   *   *   *

Shortly after the boat left the island, a young officer came on deck.

"Captain," said he, "that last Indian that came on board has gone plumb daffy. He's as crazy as a loon."

The Captain swore.

"We'll have to put him off," he said. "If those other Indians find out he's crazy there'll be the deuce to pay. An Indian has a superstition and a terrible fear of a crazy man. I have it, we'll put him off at the mission here. That new missionary hasn't got any liveried help waitin' on him, and he may be able to use your loon."

Thus Fleetwood, the noblest of the tribe, was hurried off the vessel like a thief, and handed over to Father Francisco, of the little mission.

*   *   *   *

The change had come on Fleetwood suddenly, almost instantaneously. Nineteen years had slipped by and Fleetwood, or Simple Joe, as he was called in the rough mission village, had toiled happily and contentedly, year after year for Father Francisco, his hands strong but his eyes vacant, his mind a blank. And then one night he had wandered down to the shore.

He turned his gaze away from the little chapel on the hill bursting at the window and crevice with yellow candle light, with its tiny cross on the top limned black in the white moonlight, and watched the tossing ocean dreamily. And as his ears were filled with the deep-throated crying of the waves, his satisfied contentment, as it always did when near the ocean, slipped from him like a cloak, and a restlessness, a great indefinite yearning took hold of him. His eyes fell on that tiny speck, the island away out there in the water, and his benumbed brain and dormant memory stirred uneasily. And then at the psychological moment, there came the cry: Clear and sharp and distinct as words or a written page, the long low plaint of the whip-poor-will. And the mists of the years faded like smoke, the darkness was lifted from him. The flood of memory was flung open, but the stream pouring through was not roaring, chattering, hysterical, but swift, silent, deep. Without a glance backward, unhearing or unheeding the low shout of the worshipers in the chapel on the hill, Fleetfoot ran swiftly along the shore to row a boat lying on its side on the beach. Not mechanically or like one in a daze, but quietly and methodically he pushed the rough craft into the water and stepped in. Sea and sky were calm, a study in purple and silver. With steady, powerful strokes the savage sent the boat reeling and leaping through the water glancing up at the cold white moon, wrapt in a haze circle, which swam through a frosty sky and was reflected a hundred times in the restless water throbbing under his feet, and a great joy took hold of him. He alone in the night was driving himself back to the island to Cloud Daughter. He forgot or was ignorant of the years between the promise and fulfillment. His savage strong nature measured motion not like ordinary mortals by time, by the rising and setting of a sun, but by the thoughts which is love's way, the way of the angels.

He glanced over his shoulder at the island which had grown from a speck to a splotch in the green waves, and the rough oars strained with the pull of his strong shoulders. As the boat, propelled by one strong stroke shot up to the shore, Fleetfoot leaped on to the sand. A silence that almost spoke hung on the trees and all the land, a solemn silence that would have stricken fear into the heart of a caucasian, but which filled with a fierce joy the heart of a red man, the fledgling of nature. With swift, noiseless steps he made his way unerring over the faint trails heading straight for the old grave plot of the tribe. Then quite suddenly he emerged into the open space of the burying grounds and the shadow of the trees into the flooded clearing, and for the first time he paused. The hut which he had expected, the hut of Macheto was gone and a pile of rotten debris lay where it had been. Fleetwood stood with one hand pressed against his forehead in a puzzled way, then behind him came a scraping, a sudden rush of feet and he wheeled around. The moon was at his back and he eyed dully the face and figure standing before him in the broad white light. It was Cloud Daughter. She must have been on her hands and knees for she was just rearing herself to her feet. Her face framed in matted hair was sown with a thousand wrinkles, her hands, face, and form were distorted, hideously, pitifully. But Fleetfoot was blind, he flung out his arms. "Cloud Daughter," he cried, and his heart was in his voice. She did not answer at once. He stood there with arms outstretched, a statue, and the woman threw two claw like hands above her head and fell to laughing wilder, worse than one in hysteria. For a space Fleetwood stood terse, across his memory flooded a cloud of remembrance, a faint recollection of the boyhood time when he would be awake and listen, somewhat awed, to the wild mirth of the hyena. Then he sank to his knees and grasped her two mis-shapen hands roughly.

"Cloud Daughter," he cried, again it was wrung from the soul. She drew one hand away and passed it curiously through his hair.

He knelt there motionless. From the mystic trees he could hear the whisper-ing ghostly voices of the night, woven with that the sobbing of the waves on the seashore. This was undistinct, an undercurrent, a dream, and above it cruelly like a human face on a painted back ground he heard the gibbering of the thing before. His head fell forward on his bronze chest. Somewhere out of the night came the long, low plaint of the whippoor will.

JAMES F. TWOHY, '07.

Yes! it is peace
　　To flee from gain's ignoble strife;
In humble ease
　　To lead the simple country life;
To breathe the air
　　Made sweet by brook and flower and tree;
The joy to share
　　Of smiling valley, hill, and lea;
On moss to lie
　　Lulled by the song when song-birds woo;
To view the sky
　　Where cloudlets float in dreamy blue.

A. M. DONOVAN, '10.

TENNYSON

(Villanelle.)

Sweet minstrel of the fair and bold,
 O Tennyson, all music thine!
Thy theme was braver days of old.

For thee brave feats in legend told,—
 For thee pure friendship's love divine,
Sweet minstrel of the fair and bold.

Thou sang'st of knighthood's fealty sold,
 Thou sang'st of loyal faith's decline;
Thy theme was braver days of old.

Thy pages Arthur's deeds unfold;
 Restored, his former glories shine;
Sweet minstrel of the fair and bold.

And vanishes oblivion's mould:
 Love's genius daunts its ruin malign;
Thy theme was braver days of old.

And now with them thou'rt balmed in gold
 Of thy own song at poesy's shrine;
Sweet minstrel of the fair and bold,
Whose theme was braver days of old.

                    G. A. W., '08.

MY NOVEL

CHAPTER I.

[In which the Reader and the Hero are Introduced.]

On the 1st of April, 1887, in the charming and romantic suburb of San Francisco, well known to the fashionable world as the Potrero, Jack Chesterfield made his first appearance and surely never alighted upon this orb a more delightful vision. We shall not dwell upon the details of his infancy when he was mewling and so forth in his nurse's arms, and displaying all the infantile cussedness to which every child of Adam, even the hero of a novel, is subject. Suffice it to say that at the age of seven he lost both his immediate ancestors, who died of broken hearts, and was placed in charge of a maiden aunt of three score and three summers. As is common with sentimental young ladies of her age, this demoiselle was much given to novel reading—I'd have dedicated this one to her, only that she has come to a premature demise—and in consequence neglected her young ward sadly. Fortunately this latter was of a wonderfully hard, unyielding, unconquerable character, and was well able to take care of himself. He was his own papa and mamma and spinster aunt into the bargain, and he cared not a rap what the "old guinea"—as he wittily termed his guardian—did or undid to him. He loved himself dearly and, truth to tell, he had as yet no rival. Naturally, therefore he grew up as all heroes do, entirely free from, and superior to, the little laws that enslave the sheepish bulk of mortals who always must do as others do; sublimely careless of others; full of fine craft that marked him as a future diplomatist; and most overbearing or rather commanding in his ways. As he was blest with a heroic appetite, which he never failed to satisfy by frequent inroads upon the pantry, kitchen and passing pedlars, his blood became so generous and rich that it could not be contained within the limits of veins and arteries, but broke out into common pimples and blotches over his face. Inconsiderate persons, of skin-deep perceptions, may regard this as a blemish, but such forget that a hero of a novel is invariably a paragon of beauty. A paragon was Jack Chesterfield. He had a parabolic Roman nose, that a geometrician would have gazed upon with delight; curly hair as black as a tinker's pot; and a mouth so small and pouty that it did not afford room for the free use of his tongue, thereby rendering his articulation rather indistinct. This, I confess, was a defect and the only one of which he was himself conscious, but so manfully did he fight against it as almost to obliterate it in the vehement and even frantic gesticulation, and the inconceivable grimaces which supplemented his efforts to render himself intelligible.

CHAPTER II.

[In which Our Hero Takes a Journey.]

The reader has perused the foregoing chapter to very little purpose if he does not clearly discern that Master Chesterfield is just in the most seasonable condition for Claratas College. Accordingly let us escort him thither.

On the morning of January 4th, 18—, the sun rose. Over the crest of the long-stretching eastern hills galloped the golden chariot, with Phoebus in the box-seat, bathing the mountain tops in a sea of luminous glory, shooting his winged rays at one altitude after another, until peak and spire and tower had all submitted to his royal rule and put on his glorious livery. At last his eagle eye discovered the Potrero, and directing a flaming glance right through our hero's bedroom curtain, struck the crest of his Roman nose just as it was in the throes of a stentorian effort—and Jack Chesterfield awoke.

"Gee whiz," said he—it was a special charm of his that he used the simplest language—"Gee whiz, I've got to stawt this mawning for Clawantas. Wondah what soht of a dump it is!" And he jumped up, donned a bran new suit, putting over the vest a sweater, black in the body, and black and yellow stripes in the sleeves, which looked like the legs of a zebra. On the breast of this garment he had sewn with his own hands a large yellow C to signify his intention of patronizing Claranta's athletics.

We shall draw a veil over the parting scene. The spinster aunt, who never arose before 10 a. m., had bidden her darling nephew farewell on the preceding evening. "My heart shall count the hours till I see my little boy again," she had sighed. "Be a good boy—never fight with boys bigger than yourself; be careful of your property—never lend or give anything to anybody. Never play at any games lest you break your neck or your limbs—write to me once the term—see that you do not spoil your clothes, and—though of course you will get an allowance out of your father's money, here's a quarter out of my own purse. Don't spend it extravagantly now—and learn all the poetry you can. Good bye"—smack, smack!

And the good creature retired to her room and her novel. Next morning when her maid brought her at 9:30 a. m.—long after Jack's departure—her usual breakfast of chocolate and other eatables, she found her dead!! She had died of grief!

[To be frank with the gentle reader, there is not a word of truth in the last paragraph. I put it there for the sake of effect. It's quite the thing among us novelists to put people to death in that way—it shows in an instant the intensity of the grief we speak of, and saves us a deal of description. The bare fact is that the spinster aunt is dead,—when she died I know not, but it was not from grief but from gout. Anyway I wash my hands of the old lady forever.]

At 9 o'clock that morning, Jack settled himself comfortably in his seat in a chair car of the south-bound flyer, his brown-paper parcel, and suit case and telescope basket disposed snugly at his feet. As soon as he was ready, the train started. On it went gathering force and fury at each moment; on, on —up grade and down grade, snorting and steaming and puffing like the very demon, spitting out red sparks and black cinders—whirling clouds of dust from the earth—on, on past bridge and trestle, creek and cataract, past town and country, hills and hedges, until the panting monster hardly seemed to touch the rails, until it seemed a winged thing possessed, until the whistle blew and with a shriek and a hiss and a jerk it stopped at Clarantas Junction.

CHAPTER III.

[In which Knowledge Makes a Bloody Entrance.]

Many and multifarious were the thoughts that pervaded our hero's mind as he stepped on the sacred soil of learning. His chest heaved under his yellow C as he drank in the first draughts of the pure air of Parnassus, his ultramontane nose snorted as if he had already started to climb to its lofty summit, and visions of future fame floated before his eyes. Even the old college buildings, done up as they were into all manner of gaudy colors by a nomadie troop of extempore Italian artists wore to him a solemn gray aspect. His overawed imagination idealized persons also. For—

"Well, young man, what is your name?"

"Jack Chesterfield, suh!"

"Well, Jack, I'll examine you in your studies tomorrow. In the meantime, come and see the Vice-President—he will look after you for the present, and make you feel perfectly at home. By the way, what branches do you want to study the hardest?"

"I like novel-weading very much, but I wish to devote myself entiwely to poetwy and owatowy, suh."

The Prefect of Studies smiled and left him to wait outside the Vice-President's door.

Waiting outside the same door were two other boys, whom our stranger looked at through his roseate fancy. One a smooth, oily chap, with a long sharp nose that ended in a blue pinch, was evidently a coming Rockefeller. And it was equally evident that the other lad, a pale-faced mannikin with a scraggy crop of red hair, and who looked like the genius of famine eloped from a cornfield, as Irving says, was of a highly spiritual temperament, and might turn out a second Peter the Hermit, and lead a crusade against Chinatown. He had barely time to arrive at this conclusion, when the Hermit addressed him.—

"Say, Greeny, got any dope about you?"

"Any what?"

"Any rope—anything in the line of 'baccy, you mut? If so, hand it over!"

"Gee whiz! I didn't think you weah allowed to smoke! I've got lots in this suit-case. Let's show it—I'll sell it duth cheap foh"—

"Sh! you dub! Hide it—we're on soak; close that—" But the warning was too late. How could it be otherwise—does not a hero always do things in the most critical nick of time? Else, how could the novelists get their dramatic situations? As he was exhibiting the cheroots, the First Prefect suddenly loomed over him.

"Well, young man! coming here to break the rules and make others break them? We'll have to instil some notion of order into you."

"But—but," blurted, or rather, spoke our hero calmly," those fellows thweatened me with cawpowal punishment if I did not give them up. They wote to me a week ago to bwing them. Anyway, I— I meant them for the Pwesident," he added, in a stroke of diplomacy.

"I'll see that he gets them," replied the V. P. with an ambiguous smile." And summoning a prefect he put our hero into his hands, to direct his own attention to the two young smokers. When he got through, they were shedding copious tears and breathing fire and vengeance on the newcomer.

After supper they lured him into the 'gym', and incontinently the Hermit fell upon him with his fists. The boys were apparently well matched, and a deligted circle formed round to see the fun. Jack bent down his head and struck around like a windmill. But the Hermit kept his eyes about him and hardly got a blow, while he managed to give now a jab in the jaw, now a poke in the eye, now a tap on the nose, until soon that organ emitted a crimson stream. Horrified at the sight of blood, and fearing defeat, or death, our hero resorted to a *coup d' etat*. Throwing himself upon his

back on the floor, and raising his legs, he nimbly kicked at his cowardly antagonist. The Hermit dared not go near him in front, and tried to circumvent him from behind and fall upon him, but Jack revolved too quickly on the hub of his back, to allow the stratagem. What more dramatic situation could we discover to end up the present chapter?

CHAPTER IV.
[In which Jack woos the Muse.]

No doubt the reader is in a state of extreme suspense and agitation concerning the fate of our rotary hero. But calm yourself, gentle soul! Who ever heard of the hero of a novel dying or being disabled in the fourth chapter? The idea is preposterous. Why, it would be simply taking the wind out of my sails; or leaving me standing high and dry, a laughing-stock to the whole world. Accordingly, then, Jack issued from the fray completely victorious and triumphant, and though covered with dust and gore, covered with glory. Who else, finding himself deficient in arms against his enemy, could have put him to rout by using a little headwork and converting himself into a revolver?

But now came into play his real and best self. After lying flat for an hour on his stomach upon a bench in the yard, he got up, looked around with a fine frenzy in his eye, and made a bee-line for the first prefect in sight.

"Fathuh," said he, "do you know anything about poetwy?"

The Father confessed to the soft impeachment.

"Then put it heah! Say, would you believe it?—I've wote fohty-foah lines of poetwy! Heah, wead it."

The prefect was incredulous, but on having the paper thrust into his hands, read as follows:

In the Potrero I first saw the day.
Its situated on the south of the bay.
And of all the fair spots I ever did know.
The fairest of all is the fair Potrero.

I've got all the brains that's coming to me.
I've got strength in my arm, and grit in my [eye.
And my looks   .   .   .   .   .

Here he broke off. "Well," said he, "of all the wonderful!—You don't mean to say this is your first production!"

"My fust pwoduction!—'pon my soul, it is! Pwetty good, eh?"

"Well, young man, congratulations! You've certainly got a future before you. Now, let me advise you, Just hand this to the editor of our College paper, The Gooseberry Bush, and charge him 15 cents a line. But look out! he'll try to cheat you. Those rascals are over their ears in money—why, their ads. alone bring them a clear profit of $300 a month. However, if they want to be mean, well, come down to 5 cts. a line, but not a cent less! Anyway, you will make you will make your reputation this time, and for the future you can dictate your own terms. But, honestly, now, did you write all that yourself?"

"'Pon my soul, cwoss my heart, I did. Pretty nifty, eh?"

"All right, then—be off. There's the Editor—that fellow with the long hair, who looks as if he owned the earth."

CHAPTER V.
[In which Greek meets Greek.]

Freighted with his precious manuscript our hero hied over to the Editor of the Gooseberry Bush. The mighty man wore a far-away look; his gaze was intent on some distant elysian field, or, perhaps, the summit of Olympus. So that when our poet stood right in front of him and said: "Hello! I presume yu'uh the editah of the Goosebewy Bush," he actually paid him not the slightest notice. The editor stared at vacancy; the poet stared at the editor. For the first time in his life, Jack was overawed by the presence of greatness; he shivered with nervousness and his tongue balked not only at the r's but at every letter in the alphabet.

"Mistah," he managed to blurt out, "Mistah," pawdon the intwusion, but if yu'uh looking for poetwy, heah's the dope fuh you." And he thrust the paper into the editorial hand.

"What's this, sir?" cried now conscious greatness.

"A poem for the Bush, suh. I'll give it for 15 cts. a line, nothing less. You can't bluff me."

"Fifteen cents a line, caitiff! Begone! —but stay, let us read! . . . . Stuff! trash! nonsense! Why little Flavio McGlynn could write better poetry than that by throwing an ink-bottle at a sheet of wrapping-paper!"

"Well, the Pwofs. ought to know! Mr. Vaepouh told me to chawge that much."

"Oh"—a light broke over the journalistic brain. "Let us see!—Why, our wits were a wool-gathering! Of course, we'll sign a cheque for five dollars."

And forthwith "we" wrote out a draft on the Bank of the College Commercial Department, and telling him to present it to Prof. G. at 11.30 a. m. the following day, bade his contributor farewell.

"Yu' uh sutainly a gent, Mistah Editah, and I'll tweat you to a bag of jelly-beans, see if I don't," and our hero took his way, his heart overflowing with joy and gratitude.

CHAPTER VI.
[In which Greek meets Turk.]

On the following day, at 11.30 a. m. Prof. G. was perspiringly propounding to his class the mysteries of posting. The Prof. was warmed up; there was fire in his eye; his mustaches struck out right and left in a frantic effort to challenge all-comers; his voice was high and menacing. In a word, Prof G. was dissatisfied with his class and was mustering all his elements for a storm.

All at once a loud knock at the door!

Now I hear the unsophisticated reader exclaim: "How can that be? Does not the whole world know that at 11.30 at Clarantas, the boys are in study hall? How, then, could Jack be free to wander around?" I reply: College rules were made for, and bind, only the vulgar; and anyway, is there no such thing as a "drag"?

"Come in," said the Prof. "Well, what do you want?"

"Please, Prof. G., cash this cheque for me."

"Cash this cheque! What do you take me for, sirrah?—A runaway Hibernian Bank? There's the door!"

"Now theah, Pwof., don't twy that gag on me! Nothing doing! I've wote a nifty poem, haven't I—and now shell out the dough." And he slapped the Prof.'s vest-pocket with perfect familiarity.

"Hands off, you lunatic." roared the astonished dignitary. "Poem, eh? Do I look like a poet? Here goes your cash"—as he tore the cheque in pieces, a treatment he would evidently like to extend to its owner.

Our hero turned white with red spots. "Mistah," he burst out," You'll woo this highway wobbery! I sweah I wote that poem. I'll see the Pwesident; I'll sue the whole blamed joint for this; I'll take it out of youh salawy! See if" . . .

During all this, the Prof. had been visibly swelling with rage. His eyes bulged out in a manner frightful to behold, his mustache squirmed around like live electric wires, and his chest sucked in a cubic yard of air at a gulp. The reaction was immediate—a frantic gesture towards the door, a hissing escape of steam, and a thundering explosive

"Git!"

And our hero got.

CHAPTER VII.
[In which our Hero Uses his Handkerchief.]

The reader feels sorry for poor Jack. He wants to know if he melted into tears, or swore at poetry, or turned despondent. Oh no, not he! A hero, reflect, is by nature irrepressible. Like the dolphin, if he is always going under, he is always bobbing up. The sun of adversity—to vary the figure—may crack the fine clay of which he is made, but can never melt it.

Michael Buhlkonn was perhaps the worst boy in the yard. As president of the Sanctuary Society, he had the use of several keys; and as censor of the 'gym,' he had a few more. These, in his vanity, he always jangled in his hand in such a way as to excite our hero's curiosity. On his asking what the meaning of it all was, he was told that Buhlkonn was insane, and often so violently so, that unless all the keys of the place were given him, he would burst the doors open. It was added moreover that the fellow had a diabolical grudge against Jack Chesterfield, whom he suspected of trying to steal his keys, and that he had designs upon his life.

Of course there was very little truth in this, or what there was was grossly exaggerated. But our hero being of a noble upright soul, naturally believed it to the letter.

Accordingly he kept a steady eye on Buhlkonn, and kept at a safe distance from him. For instance, when the lunatic approached the handball alley, Jack would quit the game on the plea of having cramps. When Buhlkonn showed up at the tamale-stand, Jack would not even wait to get the tamale he had paid for. When Buhlkonn stalked in the south end of the yard, Jack would make for the north. For some days they kept thus at opposite points of the compass, until at last the lunatic brought matters to a crisis. Seeing his victim engaged in conversation with a stoutish prefect, he swooped upon him from the rear, uttering a horrid cry, and brandishing a penknife in his hand.

Around and around the prefect they scurried, This official lost his head completely, and stood helpless and unhelping. Finding him deaf to his cries Jack shot off at a tangent and flew to the First Prefect's office.

The First Prefect was at his desk, engaged in drafting a milder code of rules for the college, when his door was flung open, two arms were flung around his neck, and a warm breath gasped, "Oh Father, save me!"

Now the Prefect had seen what was going on; in fact it looks as if he nearly almost half connived at the affair. He poohooed the danger.

"Just show him a white handkerchief! That will quiet him."

That evening when the students were seated at the groaning supper table, quietly but earnestly engaged in plying knife and fork, and listening to the droning from the reader's stand, all of a sudden everything was thrown into consternation by a boy jumping upon his chair and frantically waving a white handkerchief!

It was Jack! He had caught the malevolent eye of Buhlkonn fixed upon him from a neighboring table.

CHAPTER VIII
[THE DENOUEMENT]

Novel writing is not nearly so diffi-

cult as I thought at first. Just get a
good interesting introductory chapter
that will button-hole the reader, then
keep on adding others as they come,
and make them all tend to the denouement. After all the denouement is the
thing! Get a sensible denoument, and
all's well that ends well. Then, of
course always be at your ease. Remember once you are a novelist, you
know everything; you can read right
into your· reader's heart, and consequently it is he who should feel uneasy. There is really nothing to worry
over. For myself, I did lose my breath
at the first plunge, but now that I see
the opposite bank with a gilded *Finis*
stuck up on a sign post, I breathe freely
and strike out mightily.

Just after penning the above who
should walk in upon me but Prof. Blare
of Cambridge, my dear chum at the
village school, my dear chum at college,
where he led our class. It is eight
years since last we met and we embraced long and lovingly. And in an
outburst of friendly feeling and confidence, I thrust my manuscript into his
hand, asking for a frank, candid
criticism.

"It's my first novel, Hugh, you know,
and I expect some defeats. So don't
be afraid to speak out."

He spoke out. "For God's sake,
man," he exclaimed at the end of
Chapter VII, "you don't mean to publish that thing! Why, your hero is a
fool and a liar! My dear Veale, it's a
string of impossibilities! Those incidents could not have taken place at

Clarantas! A prefect allowing helpless
boys to be duped! Absurd! A prefect
drawing up milder rules! Who ever
heard the like? Why they seem to
have no rules there at all! And the
groaning supper-table! and the sighing
spinster aunt! and—why everything
is so unreal, so-so—"

Thus far I had treated him with the
silence of contempt, but now flesh and
blood could stand no more. "Enough
of that," I shrieked," enough!" Keep
your infernal claptrap for your pupils,
if you have any. How dare you judge
of a novelist? Unreal! unreal! What
have I got to do with reality? have I
been working day and night," I brought
my fist down upon the table, "and
toiling and moiling, and boiling with
fever, and shivering with ague, and—"

But it is not necessary to finish the
period, for my friend had taken his departure ere I began it.

Of course, I feel a little put out by
the scene. It is sad to see a life-long
friendship thus destroyed by green-eyed
jealousy.

As for my novel, truth to tell I do not
esteem it so much myself, but then I
was always considered over-modest, and
it is probably better than I· think it.

But I must not forget the denoument.
When the boys understood the why and
the wherefore of the white handkerchief, they yielded to the most uproarious expressions of hilarity, entirely
regardless of our hero's tender feelings.
Not only that! returned to the yard,
they besieged him with a volley of jibes
and jokes, and to add insult to injury,

waved a white handkerchief at him when he showed temper. This led him to fear that he was getting insane himself, and though the crowd soon desisted and dispersed, the fear kept working within his soul. Seeing a little fellow blowing his nose with a handkerchief that had once been of a candid color, he fell upon him at the first opportunity and punished him most severely. A hasty prefect, not understanding the provocation, chid Jack in most undignified terms. "Gee whiz," thought our hero, "they ah all down on me—I'll go clean cwazy if I don't make twacks wight away."

It was a beautiful night. The full moon bathed her chubby round face in the dark blue depths; the stars blinked and twinkled and winked with a levity that old age seems not to diminish; the owl and the bat held high revel among the sombre trees. Through the dim silence of the yard stalks a stealthy figure, flanked by a suit-case and a basket. It gains the clothes-room—always left open, of course, being run on the honor system—it stuffs Buhlkonn's clothes into the basket, excepting the white handkerchiefs; it throws Buhlkonn's overcoat—all's fair in war—over its shoulder; it steals back and climbs to the top window of the Scientific Tower; opens it; shudders at the awful, gloomy, depths beneath; stands on the dizzy ledge; slips one arm through handle of suit-case, other arm through basket; seizes overcoat with teeth; then with a swing and a lurch it gets a hold of the frail drainpipe, and down, down, it slides to the street,—and safety and freedom are won!

Bravo! my hero—first and best beloved! Shake well the dust of Clarantas from your feet. She was not worthy of you, and many a moon shall wax and wane before she shall look upon your like again.

FINIS.

S. J. C., '09.

THE WINDS

Fitful the winds to-day!
Away, away,
And never to stay,
  They come and they go,
  They fly to and fro,
    Here, there,
    And everywhere!
Racing, chasing,
  Vying, flying,
  Sighing, dying,
Oh fitful the winds to-day!
      ANTHONY B. DIEPENBROCK, '08.

THE MISTS

    Slowly
From dew beds lowly
  Mists arise;
    Creeping,
And upward sweeping
  To the skies.

    Straying,
And quaintly playing
  On their way;
    Lightly
They form in sprightly
  Disarray.

    Whiteness
Of fleecy lightness
  To the view;
    Shining
In silver lining
  'Gainst the blue.
      M. T. DOOLING, '09.

THE NEW YEAR'S HANDICAP

It was New Year's Day. A great crowd had gathered at the race track to see the handicap run. Many crack horses were entered, and among these were Daisy L. with Walman in the saddle; Yellowtail with Thornton up—Thornton was better known as "the Kid;" and Therbot with Thieman doing the honors.

The New Year's Handicap was to be the fourth race. Many of the jockeys who were to ride in the main event rode also in the preliminaries. The third race was just finished when a great hubub broke out among the crowd. A horse was cutting up and was trying to throw his rider. He at last succeeded in landing him against the fence and everyone was asking who was the jockey? was he hurt? how did it happen? and the like. Murmurs arose that the Kid had been thrown. He was to ride the handicap. Who would act as substitute? All of the best riders were engaged to ride the race. There was no chance of Yellowtail winning unless the Kid rode him. Bets began to change. Those who had backed Yellowtail now changed to Daisy L. who became the favorite. In the betting ring all was confusion.

In a jockeys' room of the C. J. C. a different scene was taking place. Mr. Wills, the owner of Yellowtail, and a doctor with his assistant, are bending over the couch on which a boy is lying, with face ashen pale, scarcely more so,

however, than that of Mr. Wills. The owner of Yellowtail depended a great deal on the boy, even more than on his horse.

The doctor who had been examining the boy stood upright. "The boy can not ride this race," he said, "I will not allow it. It would perhaps prove fatal." "But I'm all right," pleaded the boy. "I'm going to ride." And he made a movement to get up but the pain caught him and he sank back with a suppressed groan.

"He's hurt rather badly, Mr. Wills, yes, pretty badly, I'm afraid." The Kid glanced at Mr. Wills and saw the despairing look that came across his face at the doctor's words. "Say, Doctor, I'm going to ride this race and win too," he said, with a brave smile. "See if I don't." A knock at the door called Mr. Wills away for a few moments. As he went out the Kid said to the doctor, "Say, Doctor, don't you see I've gotter ride. My God, you know what I'm trying to tell you — he'll be ruined if that horse doesn't run. I don't care what you say—I'm going to ride."

The doctor, seeing it was no use trying to stop the determined boy, turned, and as he went out the door said, "As you will, but don't say I did not warn you."

The Kid was soon dressed with the help of the stable boy and valet, and was ready as Mr. Wills entered. He saw what the Kid had done. Neither spoke for a moment. The Kid's eyes dropped to the floor, but he raised them and asked cheerily, "Hello, Mr. Wills, how does Yellowtail look?" Mr. Wills did not answer his question.

"Kid! my boy, maybe you had better not do it." "But I'm all right," the Kid said. "I'm going to ride that race and show Walman that he's an old lady in the saddle." He spoke clearly, but there was something that made him hold his sides as he spoke.

The bugle sounded, and with the help of the stable boy the Kid mounted Yellowtail. There were eight horses in the race, and Yellowtail was the first out, his saddle marked I. The crowd were all standing up to get a glimpse of the boy who was to ride and fill the Kid's place.

As his trim little form came in sight dressed in the blue body, white sleeves and cap—the color of the Wills stable—a mighty cheer went up and even the judges clapped for the game little fellow.

The horses were some time in getting into their places. The people in the grand stand all watched the start with great interest. The start meant everything for the horses. Meanwhile the Kid was watching the horses with one eye while the other was on the starter. He was very faint; there was a mist before his eyes; he fell to thinking. Could he win? He kept thinking of the doctor's words, "It may perhaps prove fatal." Suddenly he was brought back to his surroundings by the sharp voice of the starter, "Where in the deuce are you bringing that horse, Kid?" The

Kid saw his chance. All the other horses were ready. He wheeled his steed and dashed for the ribbon.

"They're off!" came the cry from the grandstand. Yes, they were off with Walman in the lead and Winton close behind, then came the Kid. He kept repeating what the trainer had told him, "Keep him to the side away from the bunch." He worked his way slowly but surely to the side. When he got there he was almost last.

But the spirit of the race was upon him. He forgot his pain, forgot the doctor's words, forgot everything but the mad desire to win—to beat Walman.

The horses were half way around when the people in the grandstand saw a horse leave the bunch and go to the front. From the colors it seemed to be Walman. Quickly he drew away from the bunch. If the people who looked so intently at this horse did not see another horse coming along, it was because he was on the side away from the bunch.

The Kid saw Walman take his horse to the front and resolved to follow. He gave Yellowtail a taste of the whip and the horse responded with a marvelous increase of speed. Past one horse—riding even with another the Kid kept his horse at it. Now he was riding high on the animal's neck. Yes, the Kid was riding—riding as he never rode before, and gaining at every jump. Could Yellowtail keep it up? Could he hold that awful pace? The leading horse was not far ahead. Although

Walman heard the Kid coming he dared not look around. Walman had a faint idea that it was the Kid but he could not see. The two were all by themselves several lengths from the others. Already they could hear the confused yells that came from the grandstand. The wire was not far ahead and the riding was now in earnest. The Kid was alongside of Walman who, try as he might, could not draw away. Riding high on the horses' necks and whipping almost in unison they strove for supremacy. Now they were in the stretch. The yells in the grandstand were plain. "Come on Kid." "Give him the whip." "That's the way, Walman, you got him," fell upon their almost unheeding ears.

The wire loomed straight ahead; the Kid threw his whip away and began to urge his horse. Would he respond? Yes, with one magnificent effort he leaped forward, with one bound he had passed his rival, with another he was over the wire. The Kid had outridden the famous jockey, Walman.

Deafening cheers arose for the game little youngster, but he did not hear them. He was unconscious on the ground and beside him stood Yellowtail, the other winner of the New Year's Handicap.

FRANK D. WARREN, 2nd Acad

DEATH

Oftimes, I seem to feel thy tread,
And turn to view thy visage dread,
A gliding shadow wakes the fear
*   That thou art near.*

Among the wood thy voice I find,
I feel thee in the moaning wind,
In rustling leaves a step I hear,
*   And think thee near.*

I turn me where lone vigils keep
Pale crosses o'er my loved one's sleep;
Then from my heart the cry sincere:
*   Kind Death—draw near!*

George Morgan, '10.

The Redwood.

PUBLISHED MONTHLY BY THE STUDENTS OF THE SANTA CLARA COLLEGE

The object of the Redwood is to record our College Doings, to give proof of College Industry and to knit closer together the hearts of the Boys of the Present and of the Past.

EDITORIAL STAFF

EXECUTIVE BOARD

ANTHONY B. DIEPENBROCK, '08

President

FRANCIS M. HEFFERNAN, '08   MERVYN S. SHAFER, '09

ASSOCIATE EDITORS

COLLEGE NOTES - - - -	MERVYN S. SHAFER, '09
IN THE LIBRARY - - - -	GEORGT J. HALL, '08
EXCHANGES - - - -	MAURICE T. DOOLING, '09
ALUMNI - - - - -	HARRY P. BRODERICK, '08
ATHLETICS - - - -	CARLOS K. McCLATCHY, '10

BUSINESS MANAGER

FRANCIS M. HEFFERNAN, '08

ASSISTANT BUSINESS MANAGER

JOHN W. MALTMAN, '09

Address all communications to THE REDWOOD, Santa Clara College, California

Terms of subscription, $1.50 a year; single copies, 15 cents

EDITORIAL COMMENT

And now it is that the new staff toils under the editorial lamp. And greatly in its now dimmed light do we miss the friendly faces of some of the former literary editors and business managers. For they were men who by their fluent pens had ever kept up THE REDWOOD to its high standard, and whose busi-

ness ability had given it the most prosperous year it has yet seen.

It seems to be the irony of fate that three of the best men in their respective departments that have yet been REDWOOD editors should simultaneously end their term of office.

James F. Twohy, '07, the former editor-in-chief and President of the Ex-eeutive Board, is one of these. In him we lose, undoubtedly, one of the best all-around writers that has ever guided the destinies of THE REDWOOD. His poetry has been very excellent, and his prose has always been read with the keenest enjoyment. But not only this—we of the staff who have worked with him last semester have lost a valuable helper and one whose kindness it will be hard to forget.

Another is Harry A. McKenzie, '08, editor of athletics and member of the Executive Board. He succeeded in making the department of athletics so pleasing that it was read not only by students, faculty and alumni, but also by the exchanges and by outsiders into whose hands THE REDWOOD happened to fall. The delightful humor of the style in which he wrote served to give the articles a value entirely independent of the information they conveyed.

And last but by no means least—know that the order in which these names is taken is not that of merit, for their spheres are far too different to allow even the possibility of compari-son—is Daniel J. McKay, '07, the ex-head of the business staff, whose energy in that department was the main cause of the prosperity THE REDWOOD en-joyed last semester. Under him we saw the subscriptions double and the advertising become most successful.

Also do we miss the genial editor of College Notes, Ivo G. Bogan, whose stories from time to time were exceed-ingly good; as well as Robert J. O'Con-ner '08, whose pressing studies compelled him to seek retirement from the Li-brary department after five months ser-vice.

So here, then, old staff! we tender you our congratulations for the faithful and efficient work you have done for your College magazine. You have the best wishes of all on the present staff-and may your successors exhibit all the good will and enjoy a large measure of the success that was yours!

It is no small credit to Santa Clara College that she should have been the literary mother of the now famous Mr. Delmas. Whatever college education he received, he received it here. It was at Santa Clara that he became ac-quainted with the rich treasure of Roman and Grecian classic thought, and that he conceived for the ancient masterpieces that love which has found its expression in a life-long daily study of them, undeterred by stress of work or other obstacles. This constant devo-tion it is that has given Mr. Delmas' oratory such a lofty, finished style. Anyone well acquainted with Cicero can at once detect his influence with his untiring student—the vivid coloring; the full rich sonoriousness; the musical smoothness; the majestic sweep of the periods, all bring us back to the days when the greatest orator of imperial Rome stood up in the rostrum of the Forum, and before a spellbound multi-tude scourged the evil-doer, defended the oppressed, or made or marred mighty rulers as armies could not have done. Besides the classics, however, Delphine M. Delmas had living models of style to form him. Notably among these was Fr. Young, S. J., his English teacher, a most finished and elegant scholar, to whom his most famous pupil has ever paid his acknowledgments of indebt-edness and gratitude.

ANTHONY B. DIEPENBROCK, '08.

Lecture

The announcement of a literary lecture to the college student who has an aversion for such a means of education is generally productive of a few words of discontent, some of them to say the least not at all complimentary to the lecturer. But Mr. Seumas McManus, the noted poet, novelist, and patriot, treated us to an agreeable surprise the evening of February 12. From the very outset his lecture on "Irish Wit and Humor," commanded attention and fostered laughter. Mr. McManus was introduced by the Hon. Frank Sullivan of San Francisco who acted as chairman of the evening. One of the eminent Irishman's purposes was to dispel the prevalent idea that the average Hibernian's humor is of the bungling kind, and does not consist, as many people imagine, merely in the Irish Bull. He showed that the joke was generally on the other fellow and that the son of the sod usually comes out on top of the heap. Mr. McManus painted a vivid word picture of the life in the lowly Irish cabins and gave some laughable sam-

ples of the wit that existed in them. He developed his subject by proving that people are deserving of freedom who through all the trials and troubles of war and famine still preserve their hearty laugh and good natured jest. The lecture was unique in every way and its novelty made it doubly enjoyable.

Medals

Several of the medals which are awarded annually were announced by Rev. Fr. Gleeson on the First Wednesday. The first of these is the Archbishop's medal, a prize of $50, for the best paper on Christian Doctrine—only Academic students eligible. The Barchi Medal, a prize of $25, is for the best paper in mathematics. The classes qualified for competition for this medal are from First Academic to Senior. The Congiato Medal, a prize of $50 open to Post Graduates, Juniors, Seniors, is awarded to the best defense of the following thesis: "The Hylmorphic Theory of St. Thomas Aquinas and the Scholastics not only does not conflict with the recent data of a sound and solid Philosophy, Physics and Chemistry, but agrees most amicably therewith, supplying a legitimate explanation of the main and fundamental phenomena of light, sound, heat, magnetism and electricity as well as of affinity, proportions, volumes and the rest of the laws of the combination of substances." Last is the McCann Medal, a prize of $25 for the best poem on the San Francisco Disaster, open to all students.

Redwood Story Contest

At the monthly scholastic exercises held in the Hall on the first Wednesday of February, the winners in the RED-WOOD story contest for the first semester were announced. The competitors had been divided into three sections to which equal prizes were awarded. In the philosophy classes the winners were: 1. James F. Twohy; 2. Ivo G. Bogan; 3. George J. Hall. In Sophomore and Freshman: 1. Cyril J. Smith; 2. Mervyn S. Shafer; 3, Maurice T. Dooling. In First and Second Academics: 1. (not awarded); 2. Harold R. Yoachim; 3. Frank E. Warren. Besides these a special prize was awarded Harold Hogan, 3d Acad.

Return of Martin V. Merle and the Passion Play

Martin V. Merle of "Light Eternal" fame and fresh from triumphs in the East is with us once again. With Mar-

tin to stage it, the Passion Play should be a success indeed. And his presence is not the only good omen. There seems to be plenty of talent and the cast promises to be "the best ever." It will be composed of almost the same members who were rehearsing prior to the seismic rattle of last April, and at that time Mr. Merle was enthusiastic over the showing made. There are a few changes in the minor parts. The cast in full will be announced in the next issue of THE REDWOOD.

Division of 2nd Academic Class

On account of the increasing roll of the Second Academic the Prefect of Studies has found it necessary to split that class into two sections. Mr. Charles Walsh, S. J., the original teacher of the class, has one division, Mr. John Gearon, S. J., the other. Both divisions are on a par with each other as regards class work and at the completion of the semester will be fused, forming the First Academic.

Sanctuary

The Sanctuary, like the rest of the college organizations, began the semester by the election of officers. Mr. Brainard, S. J., took the Director's chair. The new officers who will guide the destinies of the Sanctuary for the next six months read as follows: President, Robert O'Connor, Treasurer August

Aguirre, Secretary Reginald L. Archbold; First Division Censor Ernest Watson, Second Division Censor Thomas Lannon, Reading Room Censor, Alexander Oyarzo, M. Shafer.

The House

We "of the House" have had very little to say—our efforts have been mostly of the "doing" order. The first regular meeting was held February 6th, Speaker Fox presiding. We at once proceeded to the election of officers with the following results, which by the way looks like a good start for the coming year. H. P. Broderick, Clerk, Joseph M. Collins, Librarian, Robert J. O'Connor, Corresponding Secretary, Ivo G. Bogan Sergt. at Arms, Committee on Entertainment, James Lappin (chairman), John Maltman, Reginald Archbold.

Junior Dramatic Society Notes

The same familiar group of faces met the gaze of the president of the Junior Dramatic Society, as he gave the call for order and opened the first meeting of the New Year. The repetitions and examinations which just recently came to a very welcome finish, were the cause of our dropping things, dramatical and oratorical, for the the more inexorable duties of class work.

The meeting was strictly a business affair, in which the election of officers

was the principal feature. Mr. Heney, who at present lies ill at his home, (we hope not seriously) was, by a large majority, elected to the high position of vice-president. Although he is not expected to fill his vice-presidential chair for some time, on account of his illness, still, as soon as he does appear on the scene, he will be ushered with a glad hand into his duties.

Mr. Daly, who for some time past has very creditably filled the office now in the possession of Mr. Heney, was elected by acclamation to the office of Secretary. To have this department of the J. D. S. properly looked after, it is necessary that the holder of the honor be a talented and energetic man, and we feel sure that James R. will supply the demand.

The heroic duties of Treasurer first hovered over and then rested on the devoted head of Mr. McCabe. Although, as he himself says, he is rather *gauche* in the art of pulling purse strings and depriving unwary members of their hard-earned pocket cash, yet even at the sacrifice of his feelings it is his sworn intention to keep all graft from within the walls of the J. D. S.

. The officers of Sergeant-at-Arms and Censor, which, until the last meeting was held by two members, are now combined and are taken care of by Mr. Brazell.

It was with tingling ears and face all aglow, that Mr. Barry heard the glad news of his election to the office of Librarian and Promoter. So pleased was he with the result of the balloting that when called upon to make his little speech of gratitude and acceptance— well, as he confessed himself, he was rather weak in the knees. But this sensation, which causes the knees to seek each other in time of nervousness, is a negligible quantity in Willie when the time comes for debating. It is easily seen that Mr. Barry is a comer in the speaking line, for his ambitiousness sticks out predominantly over all his features.

In the near future, the chair of Mr. Watson is to be vacated, owing to the fact that he is soon to be called to the House. Like all others who have pre-ceded him in this upward step, he goes to the best wishes of the J. D. S.

Several members' names are expected before long, to be placed on the roll call of the Junior Dramatics, so that soon our quarters will be filled if it were not for the watchful eye of the House, which seems ever on the alert for good debaters. But there is one good quality in the House, we must admit, and that is, that whenever they run short of good speakers and debaters, they realize that the Junior Dramatic Society is the place to look for the wherewith to supply the vacancy.

MERVYN S. SHAFER, '09.

· ALVMNI ·

Chas. J. Grisez, A. B., '03, is in the real estate business in San Francisco, representing D. Coffin & Co., at present the largest realty company in that city.

Angelo F. Quevedo, A. B., '05, the celebrated minstrel of Santa Clara during his days here, is now managing the Hotel Sanz in the City of Mexico. This enterprise is right in Angelo's line, and news of his success was not slow in reaching us.

At the recent elections held last November, John E. McElroy, B. S., '90, A. B., '91, was elected to fill the office of District Attorney of Oakland. He received the nomination of the Republican, Democratic, Union Labor, and Independent parties, a thing seldom heard of. Our old friend "Doc" Kirk, ex-'05, had the pleasure of proposing Mr. McElroy's name before the Democratic party. This makes the fourth time he has been elected to this office.

Among the visitors of the past month was Leo J. Hicks, ex-'05. Leo graduated A. B. from Georgetown University last year and then entered the law course at Harvard. On account of failing eyes he was forced to take a leave of absence, but hopes to be able to resume his studies when the next semester begins. Not only was Leo a bright luminary in his classes, but he also attained fame in athletics. He played on our varsity eleven of 1903 and his propensity for the gridiron was well established. While at Georgetown he succeeded in obtaining a position on the 1905 eleven.

James A. Bacigalupi, A. B., '03, and Joseph Curley, A. B., '05, broke away from their law studies in San Francisco, and spent a few days with us last week. Jim and Joe have a failing for the pure air of the Santa Clara Valley and consequently their visits to the Alma Mater are frequent—but, however, less frequent than welcome.

We hear that Charles Byrnes, ex-'07, and first baseman for the Champions of '06, is a candidate for Bachelor of Arts at Georgetown this year After graduation he intends to enter Princeton to take up the study of law. We have no doubt of his success, for his reputation as a serious student is known to us all.

Robert Y. Hayne, ex-'08, and Alumni editor '04, has entered the Law Department at Yale.

Welcome back into our midst! Sennett W. Gilfillan, Com. '06, has returned to college and is registered in the class of '09. By the way, he jumped into prominence at once by pitching for the second team and holding down his opponents to one lonely single.

Notice comes to us that Roman J. Lacson, M. A. '01, and later Ph. L., Ph. D. and L. L. B., at Georgetown, is practicing law with the firm of Hartigan, Rhode & Guttierrez, Santo Tomas, Manila, P. I. It does not require a prophet to predict the most distinguished success for Mr. Lacson.

We have word that "Bobbie" Keefe, A. B., '02, and the greatest pitcher our nine ever could boast of, is to return to the New York Americans this year at a large salary. "Bob" joined the Highlanders last year, being drafted from the Pacific Coast League, where he led in the amount games won, having an average close on to 700 per cent. He was not with New York more than six weeks when he was attacked with appendicitis. An operation was necessary. It was successful, but it left him in a weakened condition. After a long rest he joined the Montreal Club of the Eastern League, and during his short sojourn

with that team established an enviable record. As a result he is down as one of Clark Griffith's twirlers this year. The boys of his Alma Mater wish him all success, and it is the universal opinion that he will make good from the start.

Cupid with his golden bow that never rusts has once more come into the ranks of the Alumni. Pierre V. Merle, Com. '03, he of the smile "that won't come off," brother of our "Mart" of Light Eternal fame, and a prominent member of the Santa Clara College Alumni, was married recently in San Francisco to Miss Beatrice Josephine Beretta. While on their wedding trip Mr. and Mrs. Merle dropped in and spent a few hours with us. A base ball game between the first nine and Stanford happened to be in progress at the time and Pierre was right in his glory. For two years "Smiling P. V." as we called him, played on the varsity nine. He caught "Bob" Keefe, now of the New York Americans, and the way he received "Phenom Bob's" delivery often electrified us. After graduating, Pierre was given the position of manager in his father's clothing establishment in San Francisco, and as he was in base ball, so was he in business, "always in the game." The Faculty, the members of the Redwood staff, and the entire student body extend to Mr. and Mrs. Merle their heartiest congratulations.

HARRY P. BRODERICK '08.

THE RIDINGDALE FLOWER SHOW

Among the new books laid before us for review, one of the most attractive is this tale of English country-life, by Fr. David Bearne, S. J. It is a story of the sturdy, healthy-minded village lad, whose character comes out all the more clearly by contrast with a cousin from London, a highflown, flighty youngster who is going to show his ignorant rustic relatives "a thing or two." But alack! he finds that in all real, manly, ennobling accomplishments they have left him far behind. They are all well versed in the classic English authors, while his literature has mostly been taken from "The Boy's Ripper." Very charming descriptive passages are to be found in the book, and the conversation is very sprightly and interesting, and altogether calculated to fascinate the attention of the young reader, to whom it is particularly addressed. The title of the book is misleading, however; only three chapters, and these disconnected with the bulk of the story, are given to the "show." A more vigorous title would have been better. Benziger Bros—85 cts.

THE SOGGARTH AROON

One of the most delightful books we have read for many a day, is the series of sketches of Irish country-life as viewed through the eyes and the heart of an Irish curate. It is the daintiest gem from the pen of its gifted author, Rev. J. Guinan, C. C. While unequal in sparkling wit and masterly delicacy of touch to "My New Curate," it has a ring of sincerity about it and a pathos that cling tenaciously to the memory. The book leaves a sadness behind it,— the sadness of injustice and enforced poverty and oppression, but it teaches many a lesson of the nobility and heroism that reside under a peasant's tattered coat. Benziger Bros.—$1.25.

GEORGE J. HALL, '08.

We approach our exchanges this month a little hesitatingly, for we have not yet reached that degree of familiarity with them which is needed for a true appreciation of their merits. But we will try to criticise them as fairly as possible and to use our ax only when we deem it absolutely necessary. We may make mistakes but our criticisms will be sincere.

The Yale Lit.—a new arrival by the way—is an admirably well balanced magazine. Even the cover of the *Lit.*, which would be out of place on another college paper, is very appropriate for this venerable patriarch, breathing as it does an air of dignified antiquity. But the cover is not the only thing we like about the *Lit*. Its fiction is all first class. "The Country Girl" is what one finds so rarely in college magazines, a truly humorous story, without any trace of silliness. The writer has a sure touch and a facile pen and although his sense of humor is very keen he keeps it always under control. "Clancy's Boy" is a pathetic little story of the bravery of cowardice. A little sketch, "The Emigrant," struck our fancy, not because it

is pleasant, for it is far from that, but because it is true to life.

Like most of our exchanges for this month, *The Lit.* is rather short on poetry, "The Artist," a frenzied rhapsody of disappointed love in blank verse, has an easy flow that shows its author to be proficient in metrical composition. It contains several beautiful descriptions which, however, might well have been put to better use. "Chords" is undoubtedly the best poem in this issue. Strongly imaginative, it is written in an easy style that pleases the ear as well as the mind.

The discussion of the action of those at the Jamestown Exposition, in making it a great military and naval celebration, is a very timely one. After summing up the whole matter and showing how in a year's time the purpose of the exposition has changed from a display of the arts of peace to a grand spectacle of war, the editor concludes, "We must . . . . realize that the government's million and a half appropriation can be expended in glorifying our natal day— more fitly and more advantageously than by its evaporation in the luridity and glitter of war,—on its furtherance, and may American sentiment so desire it, of a more effectual peace." With this sentiment we heartily agree. Did President Roosevelt gain the Nobel prize for naught?

An abundance of fiction, some of it very good, marks the *Xavier* for February. We especially enjoyed "A Victim of Fate" and "Rigby's Luck." Between these two there is little choice—both have good plots, both are well written, and both are interesting. In the former story the accidental exchange of two valises, one of which contains sixty thousand dollars, and the subsequent arrest of everybody in sight by a blundering detective, serve to keep the reader's interest at fever heat until the very end. "Rigby's Luck" is, as its title indicates, a story of Dame Fortune's smiles, in which that fickle goddess, after seemingly deserting him, combines a practical joke and a midnight ride to land a thousand dollar prize for her fortunate favorite. Of a character far different from the other fiction in this magazine is "A Purchase of Genius." The author's style is good and the story seems to end happily—two points greatly in its favor surely—but after all what is it all about? Perhaps the writer knows, but if he does he has succeeded admirably in keeping the secret from his readers.

In its verse the *Xavier* is not so good. "Eventide" is the only poem that rises above the commonplace. Among the *Xavier's* editorials we noticed an excellent defense of the college magazine under the heading "Why We Exist." From the frequency of such articles in our recent exchanges we begin to wonder whether a few practical suggestions on how to exist would not be more to the point.

With the January number *The Bowdoin Quill* "begins"—we quote from its editorial column—"the second decade of its existence." *The Quill* celebrates this event by giving us a very small issue, even smaller, perhaps, than is usual with this diminutive publication. Its pages display, besides the departments, one essay, three poems, and a single story. One of the poems, "The Isle of the Blest," shows a true poetic fancy and is extremely rhythmic and melodious. The sonnet "Evening" pleased us because of its evident sincerity. The essay gives a picture of university life in newly awakened Japan and is written in an entertaining and interesting way.

"The Honor of France," the only contribution of fiction, is not, as one might imagine from its title, a story of the swashbuckling type, thickly sown with flashing swords, fresh-spilt blood, and the sparkling eyes of fair damsels. Although a king is introduced we find him but a man and our awe of royalty is lost in our sympathy for a dishonored father. It is a well told tale, and wonder of wonders! the author has miraculously avoided the use of even a single French word. As usual, we regret to lay this magazine aside, and is this not the greatest praise which we can give?

We admire the cheerful disregard of the seasons shown by the editors of our latest visitor, *The Amherst Lit.* While we who dwell in the Golden State, with its much vaunted glorious clime, are shivering over the editorial stove in a vain attempt to keep warm, this magazine comes to us replete with stories of summer, sketches of summer, summer pleasures and summer fancies while there is not even a verse to the King of storms to let us know that this is the dread time of his rule. Perhaps there is a lack of propriety in this but nevertheless we are pleased with it and we honestly envy a man who can sit indoors when the mercury is hugging the bottom of the thermometer and write, cheerfully and with never a trace of bitterness or regret, about the gay, glad, carefree summertime. Surely they are a cheerful lot, those students of *Amherst*, and enjoy that peace that the weather cannot give.

The only fault that we can find with *The Lit.* is the scarcity of good verse—any verse for that matter. The essay on "Wordsworth's Theory of Poetry" is ably written and serves to offset the lightness of the other articles. The little sketch "Truant Hearts" deserves notice for the refreshing picture of boyish life which it presents. "On Desperate Seas" is a very pleasing story woven about a conventional plot.

The obituary of Archbishop Montgomery in the *S. V. C. Student* for February is a fitting tribute from our sister college of the south to that great and good man who always took such a paternal interest in the education and training of Catholic young men. It shows a sympathetic appreciation of his life and work and a true sorrow at the death of one whose life was a blessing to so many.

A Song From "Moonflowers"

Under
The sombre hills of wonder
Far away
Lie the Gardens of the Nights
Breathing rest and quiet lights
All the day.

Fountains,
In the shadow of the Mountains,
Rise and fall,
Waving slowly to and fro
As the night winds come and go
And sigh and call.

Rivers,
Where the willow waves and shivers,
Wander by;
Silver stars above them lean
Towards their waters deep and green,
From the sky.

Nightly,
From these Gardens rising brightly
I may see
Waters leaping with delight
While the minstrels of the night
Herald me.

Morning
Eastward now has given warning
With her stars;
Fallen lies the Dome of Night
And the stars are taking flight
Wide and far.

Higher
Fly the shafts of crimson fire;
Hasten we
Now to shadow-haunted caves
Where the slumbrous cypress waves
Silently.

—Tallifer, University of Virginia Mogazine.

MAURICE T. DOOLING, JR., '09.

Stanford 4, S. C. C. 3

The opening game of the intercollegiate series with Stanford was played Feb. 7, on an ideal baseball day. The sky was without a cloud and old Sol reigned supreme in all his glory. The recent playing of the College team seemed to prophesy victory for us but we possessed an oversupply of confidence which coupled with a few costly errors served to lose the game. Although we are sorry to have been defeated, we should be, and are proud of the pluck and gameness our team showed. Never for an instance did they give up but after a seemingly hard rebuff, came back as strong as ever.

Collins was missed very much on account of his wonderful fielding and reliable hitting qualities. If Joe had been in the game with one of his long hits the score would probably have read differently.

Kilburn pitched for the College and put up a good game puzzling many of Stanford's batters with the twisters he threw to them. Mervyn Shafer on the receiving end put up probably the best game of the team, though Lappin was not far behind. Shafer is a very heady player and Stanford found that it is somewhat rash to try to steal second on him. In the eighth inning three of these venturesome youths had to walk crestfallen to the benches from the unattained second. In addition to this, Pudgy had to account to the scorer for a tally. Husky Lappin played an exceedingly good game, hauling in many difficult chances and procuring a run. Peters led the team in batting, securing a two-bagger.

In the last of the ninth, with three

runs against our clean sheet, Pudgy Shafer slammed the ball to center field making first, took second on the third baseman's fumble and was forced home by Stanford's pitcher walking three men. With the bases full Peters was equal to the occasion. Catching the ball full on the nose he drove it to left field; good for two sacks and sending Lappin and Twohy home. Then Kilburn hit to short and was thrown out, thus ending the game.

Stanford 4, S. C. C. 1

The second game with Stanford was played February 9th on the Stanford ball grounds, with quite a large crowd in attendance, our own team being accompanied by nearly all the students of the College. The bleachers at Stanford were filled with a gaily cheering throng and conspicuously through this were strewn the gay colors of Stanford feminity—a great help to the home team.

Spider Brown did the mound work for the College and acquitted himself very creditably, though at times he was a trifle wild. He was not given good support. Our nine this game did not show their usual good team work and were evidently very nervous. Twohy more than compensated for any bad plays he may have made by getting three hits out of four and bringing home our lonely run. The first time Art Shafer secured the only two-bagger.

Stanford 2, S. C. C. 2

The clear and sunny day of February 12th seemed to augur good fortune to us in our baseball game with Stanford, but signs and prophesies are not always to be relied upon although this one half-fulfilled her cheery promise. We hoped for victory but were disappointed though we had the satisfaction of not losing. It was a hard fought game, bitterly contested to the end of the thirteen innings, and it was regretted by both sides that the darkness came to stop the even contest, without either side being able to make the much coveted run which would decide the game.

Captain Kilburn pitched for us and deserves much credit for the way he held out during those tiring innings, never lagging and ever sending the balls over with the same swift speed. Although a little wild in the earlier part of the game, he warmed up to his work and after the fifth inning pitched perfect ball. The wildness of Kilburn at first, the poor support given him and a few errors were the causes of allowing the two runs to be scored, one in the first and one in the fourth. After the fifth, Kilburn settled down and following his example the team braced up and gave him good backing. They found no difficulty whatever in holding Stanford down to its two unearned runs.

In the seventh inning, resolved at least to equal the performance of Stanford, the irrepressible Friene hit the spheroid out to centerfield and reached the initial sack in safety. Twohy followed, securing a beautiful hit to right garden and while the fielder was recovering the ball Friene raced home, leaving Twohy on third. Twohy's long drive was the second three-bagger of the season. Broderick then stepped to the bat and after carefully judging the ball drove it to center field bringing Twohy home and thus tying the score.

SANTA CLARA

	AB	R	BH	SB	PO	A	E
M. Shafer, c....	6	0	0	0	12	5	1
A. Shafer, ss ...	5	0	1	1	8	0	0
Lappin, lf.......	4	0	1	0	2	0	1
Friene, 3b......	5	1	1	0	1	1	0
Kilburn p	5	0	0	0	0	0	1
Twohy, 2b	5	1	1	0	3	5	0
Broderick, 1b...	5	0	1	0	13	2	1
Peters, cf	3	0	0	1	0	0	0
Salberg, rf.......	4	0	0	2	0	0	0
Totals........,..42	2	5	4	39	18	4

STANFORD

	AB	R	BH	SB	PO	A	E
Scott, 2b.......	4	1	0	0	1	4	0
Stott, c	4	1	1	0	13	0	0
Fenton. 3b.......	4	0	2	0	1	4	1
Presley, 1b	5	0	2	0	14	0	1
Owen, lf.........	3	0	0	0	4	0	0
Dennis, cf	5	0	0	0	2	0	1
Witmer, p....... .	4	0	0	0	2	1	0
Gore, rf.........	4	0	0	0	0	0	0.
Cadwalder, ss.... .	5	0	0	0	2	3	0
Totals........ 38	2	2	0	39	12	3

HITS AND RUNS BY INNINGS.

```
            1 2 3 4 5 6 7 8 9 10 11 12 13
Santa Clara 0 0 0 0 0 0 2 0 0  0  0  0  0 —2
      Hits  1 0 0 1 0 0 3 0 0  0  0  0  0 —5
Stanford    1 0 0 1 0 0 0 0 0  0  0  0  0 —2
      Hits  1 0 0 0 0 0 0 0 0  1  0  0  0 —2
```

SUMMARY

Sacrifice hits, A. Shafer; Three base hit, Twohy; First base on balls, off Kilburn 4, off Witmer 6. Hit by pitched ball, Kilburn 1, Struck out by Kilburn 11, Witmer 9. Left on bases Santa Clara 6, Stanford 4.

California 2, S. C. C. 2

Tuesday 19th saw our first game with California this year, played at the University ball grounds. The day was not a good one for base ball, being cold and disagreeable, but our team warmed up and played an excellent game. Twelve innings with a tie score of two runs is certainly a good game, although a few mistakes did occur. Kilburn occupied the box for the College, pitching a perfect game. He had all kinds of speed, and plenty of puzzling twisters that baffled the Californians. With their reputed heavy hitters they were only able to secure two hits off Kilburn and those were a result of chance. The little twirler had them at his mercy and had it not been for a few unlucky plays the Californians would have been blanked. Art Shafer was responsible for our first run, making two bags by a long drive to left field. Friene followed and duplicated the performance sending Shafer home. In the fourth inning we made our second run, Lappin walked, went to second on the second baseman's error and crossed the plate on Broderick's bunt.

Friene should be complimented on the way he takes care of the intricate corner. He takes in everything and his peg to first is like a shot from a gun. Art Shafer's playing was also noticeable for its good qualities. He secured three of the five hits made. Watson in the right garden is a good fielder though not so reliable at the bat.

Pudgy Shafer on the receiving end of the battery is a good team mate for Kilburn. It is interesting to watch the little midget study the batter furtively, signal Kilburn the result of his observations and then receive the ball which has sent some baffled batsman to the bench.

The game was a long fought battle bitterly contested to the very end by both sides, without either being able to secure the needed run.

S. C. C. 3, California 2

In the best game of the season California went down to defeat at the hands of the Red and White by a score of three to two in eleven close and interesting innings. The result was very uncertain to the last moment although the College outplayed California at nearly every point of the game. In this game it was quite noticeable that the College had better team work than in the other games. It worked like a machine, everything in its place and exactly fitting that place, no cog slipped or caught. The wheels moved quickly and easily, and that is why we won.

The first run was made in the second inning by Watson, who played an exceptionally good game. He took first on balls, stole second and was sent home by Kilburn's two bagger. California worked hard to secure a run but was unable to do so until the seventh inning when Schaefer made their first run.

Now came the interesting part of the contest when a little mischance meant the loss of the game. Broderick was the first man up and connecting squarely with one of Jordan's twisters sent it out to center field where Sweezy was unable to reach it in time with the result that the runner trotted to third. But alas! he got no further.

During California's turn at bat in third on a wild throw. Wultzen then came up and hit the ball into Lappin's hands who made a good throw home but overtook Causley too late.

Though a little dismayed the team worked as hard as ever. Twohy stepped to the bat and hit the ball over second, took the next sack on an overthrow and was sacrificed to third. Shafer up next, hit to first base beating it out. Pandemonium now reigned. The chance of tying California was at hand and those not in the game helped the good cause along with their voices. With Lappin at the bat Jordan threw one over which Berkeley's catcher failed to hold. Siezing the opportunity Twohy sped home tying the score. The following batsmen retired in one, two, three order.

Kilburn held the Californians striking out two men and allowing the other only a pop fly which was easily caught.

Salberg who was substituted for Peters slammed the ball to Causley. Causley threw wild and Salberg took second. Pudgy Shafer took his turn and made a beautiful hit, through third to the left field, Salberg raced home and ended the game.

The feature of the game was the collegeians' very hard hitting. With two exceptions everyone secured a hit. Kilburn pitched his best ball. The hits he allowed were scattered and only three men received tickets to first.

Shafer on the receiving end caught a good game, pegged well and his timely hit spelt victory for us. The rest of the team in their respective positions played well and certainly if they keep on in this style there will be nothing to fear from either California or Stanford.

CALIFORNIA

	AB	R	H	SB	PO	A	E
Reed, 2b	5	0	2	1	2	2	0
Causley, ss	2	1	1	0	3	4	0
Herster. 3b	6	0	2	0	1	4	0
Wulzen, 1b	4	0	0	0	11	0	0
Jordan, p	5	0	0	0	0	3	0
Miller, rf	5	0	0	0	1	0	0
Smith, lf	4	0	1	0	1	0	1
Schaefer, C	5	1	1	0	11	2	0
Sweezy, cf	2	0	1	0	2	0	0
Totals....	37	2	8	1	32	15	1

SANTA CLARA

	AB	R	H	SB	PO	A	E
Twohy, 2b	4	1	1	1	2	3	0
Shafer, ss	4	0	2	1	3	2	0
Friene, 3b	4	0	1	1	1	1	2
Lappin, lf	4	0	0	1	1	0	0
Broderick, 1b	5	0	1	0	13	1	0
Peters, cf	4	0	0	0	3	0	0
Watson, rf	3	1	1	3	1	1	0
M. Shafer, c	4	0	1	0	8	0	1
Kilburn, p	4	0	2	1	0	7	0
Salsberg	1	1	1	0	0	0	0
Totals......	37	3	10	3	32	15	3

HITS AND RUNS BY INNINGS

	1	2	3	4	5	6	7	8	9	10	11
U. C.	0	0	0	0	0	0	1	0	0	1	0— 2
Hits	1	1	0	0	1	2	2	0	0	1	0— 8
SantaClara	0	1	0	0	0	0	0	0	1	1— 3	
Hits	1	1	1	1	1	0	0	1	1	1	2—10

SUMMARY

Sacrifice hits, Causely, Wutzen and A. Shafer. Three base hit, Broderick. Two base hits, Kilburn, A. Shafer and Watson. First base on balls, off Jordan 6, off Kilburn 3. Double play, Friene to Broderick to Shafer. Hit by pitched ball Jordan. Struck out by Jordan 7, by Kilburn 9. Passed balls, California 4. Wild pitches, California 2. Left on bases, California 9, Santa Clara 7. Umpires, Collins and Eagan. Scorer, H. J. McKenzie. Time of game 2 hours aud twenty minutes.

S. C. C. 8—San Jose O.

The above score tells how the College beat or rather whitewashed the San Jose league team. Wolter and Jimmy Byrnes formed our battery. Wolter is pitching in his old style. Anyone who has ever seen him in action needs no further account. Byrnes caught a good game. His pegging was especially fine. Collins was at his old place in center field and played his position perfectly, besides securing a few hits.

San Jose 7—S. C. C. 5.

Spider Brown occupied the slab for the College but was a trifle wild allowing three runs to be made in the first inning. The support given him by the team was very poor. At the end of the fifth inning, Friene twirled them over, Lappin playing third, Collins left and Peters center. In the third inning Twohy and Art Shafer were on the bags when Friene's two bagger brought them home. Friene stole third and crossed the plate on Collins' hit. Joe Brown and Lappin were responsible for our other two runs.

Second Team.

Next in importance to the 'varsity team in baseball comes the fast little second team that can hold its own with anything of like size. Under Manager Casey's able direction, they should have plenty of games to play and with the advice and assistance of Coach Wolter they should win these games. A large squad tried for the places on the team with the result that Wolter picked the following: Pitchers, Gilfillan and Archibold; catcher, R· Twohy; 1st base, McNally; 2nd base, Foster; 3rd base, Donovan; shortstop Salberg; Fielders, Lyng, Strohl and Sheehan Salberg, Foster, and Strohl are the Phenomena of the team, although all are exceptional.

On February 7th., the, second team met the San Jose High School and drowned them by an overpowering shower of runs. Everybody had a pass for a free ride and many of the tickets were round trip. Little may be said of the game as it was entirely too one-sided to be interesting. Gilfillan pitched a good game.

February 13th, the team met the Santa Clara High School team and showed them a little of real baseball. S. C. H. S. may play good ball for a High School but they are hardly in the second team's class. Their pitcher had plenty of steam but his shots proved an easy mark for our batters. Archbold pitched in great style allowing very few hits. Foster and Strohl played in their usual good manner. Strohl noted for his hard hitting powers was good for a few bingles. Another hard-hitting youngster on the team we must not overlook is Joe Sheehan, lately a convert to the national game and fast becoming an

adept with prospects of rivalling the old "vets." Of the two pitchers, Gilfillan and Archbold, it is hard to determine which is the better, but as both are so deserving we will leave better dopesters to figure out that question.

Junior Team 9, Santa Clara High 5

The crack Junior Team has once more reorganized and although the ranks of the old timers are sadly depleted the team has so many fast and clever ball tossers that the outlook for a successful season is more than bright, especially with such a coach as Joe Collins. With this promising material, with careful training and guidance he should turn out a team that though small, should hold its own with teams of like size and over. They are especially endowed with hitting qualities as shown in their first game with Santa Clara High on Feb. 19.

The line-up and batting order in the game was as follows:

Nolting	l. f.
Irilarry	c.
Gianera	s. s.
Brown, R.	1st b.
Hartman, J.	2nd b.
Watson, A.	3rd b.
Ford	r. f.
Lohse	c. f.
Jones	p.

At all times of the game they showed themselves superior to their opponents and especially distinguished themselves by their frequent hits. Captain Gianera and Brown accounted to the score for two hits apiece. At a critical stage o the game, with two men on the bagsf and runs badly needed, Ford secured a two-bagger and brought home the desired runs. Nolting made a very spectacular catch that almost seemed impossible. The ball came way out over his head. Running backward he jumped in the air and caught the fly one-handed, the force of it carrying him over. In the sixth inning Barry and Flood exchanged places with Lohse and Ford and made a very good showing.

Jones is rather wild but with time he should gain control. Irilarry caught a good game.

Games are being arranged with the following schools and it is very likely that they will be secured: San Jose High, Hoyts Academy, Anderson, and St. Ignatius College.

Basket Ball.

The followers of the throw-and-chase-the-ball game are busily engaged in hard practice at present,—a preparatory step to defeating their opponents by overwhelming scores. We think this the proper place to say a few words in defense of chasing that inflated bladder around. Many modern Herculean athletes express the opinion that it is a game for those physically incapacitated or, as they term it, old women. Now the only way to cure these oracles and wise men is to give them one dose of basket ball, equivalent to one game, and that tired all-in feeling will materially change their opinions.

The best player of the team is undoubtedly McKenzie, whose quick passing and accurate basket throws place him in the lead. He is always moving in the game and when he and Aguirre commence to work the ball down the field it is nearly impossible to stop them. Aguirre will probably play center since he puts up a good quick game. Murphy is another of the probabilities. Leander's specialty is also quick passing with very creditable throwing. Schmitz is taking off superfluous avoirdupois and will play the same good game he played last year. Bogan and Twohy are about tie in the race for honors. Both are fine players and put up a strong game.

CARLOS McCLATCHY, '10.

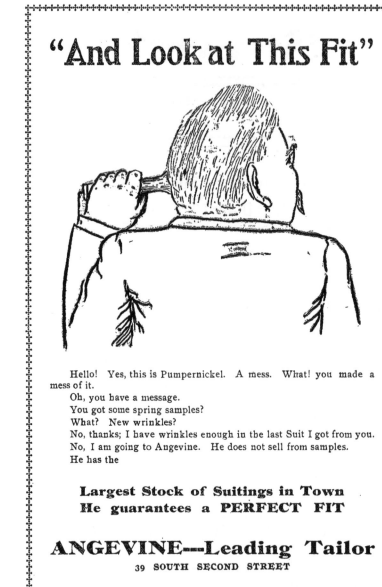

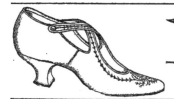

Santa Clara College

THE
REDWOOD

APRIL, 1907

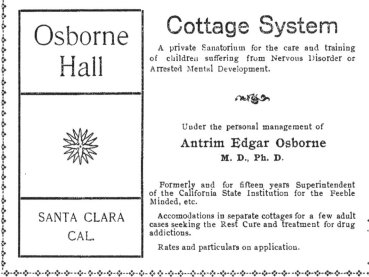

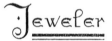

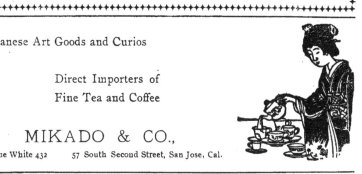

Contents.

Nace Printing Co.　Santa Clara, Cal.

The Redwood.

Entered Dec. 18, 1902, at Santa Clara, Calif. as second-class matter, under Act of Congress of March 3, 1879.

SANTA CLARA, CAL., APRIL, 1907.　　No. 7

THE BUILDER

uild well thy Spirit House,
　With many rooms; give space
joy and truth and hope and gentle sympathy,
t leave no space for fear;
　anger bar the door, and o'er the window
　thy soul when hate is nigh,
ifold the curtain of a loving thought.
　ild in the inmost valleys of thy heart
　temple to the God of Love,
ith stone hewn from the Hills of Harmony,
sed in thy work the scented wood
hat grows in Freedom's Land,
nd place within its halls
he Shrine of Peace.
pon the walls hang tapestries
ve from the threads of Kindly Thought.
ll all the vases of thy dreams
ith buds that bloom from noble impulses.
ien hast thou builded 'gainst the ravages of time
　work of infinite achievement—
eval with Eternity,
　dwelling place of Truth.

　　　　　　　　　　Harry T. Fee, S. B., 1891.

A MODERN MIRACLE

[THE PICTURE OF OUR LADY OF SORROWS IN THE JESUIT COLLEGE OF QUITO IS SEEN
TO MOVE ITS EYES]

As the result of an astounding prodigy, a picture of Our Lady of Sorrows has lately been exposed to public veneration in the capital of Ecuador. Until the miraculous event I am about to relate, it had hung upon the walls of the boys' dining-room in the Jesuit college of that city. It can hardly fail to prove of interest to students of Jesuit colleges all over the world (and of other catholic colleges as well) to learn of the extraordinary favor bestowed by the Blessed Virgin upon their fellow-collegians in far-off Ecuador. My account of the matter shall be taken mainly from the process gotten up by the ecclesiastical authorities to sift the facts of the case.

Rev. Fr. Andrew Roesch, S. J., Prefect of Discipline of the college, being called on April 27, 1906, before the Vicar Capitular of the Archdiocese of Quito, Rt. Rev. Dr. Perez Quinones, and his secretary, and the Chief Notary, deposed in writing as follows:

"On Friday, April 20, 1906, the following event took place in the Jesuit College in this city. The boarders had nearly finished supper, when at about 8 o'clock, I entered the dining-room and, contrary to established custom, and much to the students' surprise, I gave 'Deo Gratias,' that is, permission to talk.

"I related at several of the tables what had happened in San Francisco, California. This gave occasion to the boys occupying the first table (who had made their first communion on the previous Holy Thursday) to make some reflections upon the disaster and to enter upon a conversation concerning the Blessed Virgin. One of these, Jaime Chaves, raised his eyes to an oleograph of Our Lady of Sorrows hanging on the wall at a distance of one metre and half (five feet). He was astonished to see the picture shut its eyes. Filled with fear, he covered his own eyes with his hand, and told his neighbor, Carlos Hermann, who perceived the same marvel. Beside themselves with terror, they knelt between the table and the bench and recited an Our Father and Hail Mary. Then they called one boy after another, until at last one of them hastened over to me and begged me very earnestly to go and see what was happening. At first I pushed him away telling him to quit such nonsense, because it seemed to me a hallucination of the boys, but finally, pressed and called upon by those who were looking at the prodigy, I approached the table nearest the picture, with the set purpose of dispelling the illusion. I ascertained carefully whether the lamps moved, or any ray of light was reflected upon the image: nothing of the kind appeared.

"Placing myself in front of the picture, surrounded by the boys, I fixed my gaze steadily upon it, and saw the Blessed Virgin slowly shut the eyelids. Not yet believing it to be certain, I withdrew from the place. Brother Alberdi, who was even nearer to the image than I had been, surprised at my action, called out to me: 'But, Father, this is a prodigy! this is a prodigy!'

"I returned to the place I had first taken, and I felt a cold shiver run through me as I saw, without being able to doubt of it, the image shut and open its eyes. While this was going on, all the boys who were present at the scene, kept shouting with one voice: 'Now she shuts them! Now she opens them! Now the left eye!'—for it must be remarked that sometimes she shut only the left eye, or at least more plainly than the right, and it seemed more tightly closed. This was repeated several times and lasted fifteen minutes more or less. When, however, I gave the signal for quitting the room, as it was late, and I feared besides to excite the boys too much, it ceased. The boys, nevertheless, did not leave the room willingly, but wished to kneel down and pray. I refused to allow any demonstration, as I considered that if the fact was wonderful, there were not wanting witnesses to prove it.

"All this do I testify to and affirm in Quito on the 27th day of April, 1906.— Andrew Roesch."

Then follow 39 other narratives written in presence of the same tribunal, each one apart from the others, no inter-communication having been allowed. They were written by Br. Alberdi and thirty-four of the boarders from ten to seventeen years old, and four servants, who, called by duty or attracted by the noise, had come into the refectory. All of them are unanimous in essentials, to wit, that the picture of the Blessed Virgin shut and opened its eyes very slowly several times during a period of fifteen or twenty minutes, and that it closed the left eye more frequently than the right.

It is worthy of note that the permission to speak in the refectory was given on Friday, and that those who first saw the prodigy were at the time speaking about Our Lady, and, moreover, that all were biased against rather than predisposed towards the likelihood of such an event. For it is plain from all the accounts that the first to see it were branded as visionaries, fanciful, and feverish, although in the end they had to be believed in view of the reality of the facts.

After each witness had written his report, he was subjected to a cross-examination in which he declared under oath what he had written to be the truth. He was given the opportunity to make any modifications he wished, and had to answer under oath the following questions:

1. Whether he thinks it possible that deposers could be mistaken.

2. Whether he had heard or read about that time any accounts of similar events.

3. Whether there was sufficient light to see clearly what was going on.

4. What effect it produced in his soul and on his conduct.

5. Whether at the beginning of the occurrence he was afraid and troubled and afterwards remained in peace and tranquility.

Noteworthy modifications of the several accounts there were none.

With regard to the answers, that of the boy George Merizabal deserves quotation. Replying to the first question, he speaks thus: "For me any mistake was impossible, because not being able to see standing on the floor, I climbed up on the bench and saw clearly from a distance of less than one metre (about three feet). When some of the boys said that the appearance was caused by the reflection of a kerosene lamp, this was put out, but the movements of the eyelids continued as before."

Another boy, Carlos Samaniego, adds a special detail: "And the Blessed Virgin remained very pale that night."

To the second inquiry, all answered that they had not heard or read any revelations (*relaciones* in the original— probably a misprint for *revelaciones*) or visions.

To the third, the unanimous reply was that there were four powerful electric lamps, so that the light was more than sufficient.

But where the hand of Mary is more clearly revealed is in the answers to the fourth query: "What has it produced in your soul or in your conduct?" Here is Fr. Roesch's reply: "The effect pro-duced upon the boys has been highly beneficial; they have formed a league or association for the purpose of com-bating evil conversations, and as a re-sult no complaint has come to me on that score during these days. In this they acted of their own free-will. There has been much increase of fervor and good conduct. On the day following the occurrence, more than half the boys came to confession. All the Fathers re-marked an extraordinary change in the boys, which I believe will be lasting. Another league has been established to promote good behavior among them-selves and for mutual correction. As for myself, I believe I have grown in fervor."

Of the two boys who were the first to see the marvel, Chaves says: "I have improved in conduct;" and Hermann, "I feel more devotion toward the Blessed Virgin and am behaving better."

Carlos Samaniego says: "I am better as regards piety; I love the Blessed Virgin more and pray more to her. I go to communion more frequently and more fervently. I have likewise im-proved in conduct, for I used to be rather disobedient to the Fathers, and now I obey them readily."

This is how Master Carlos Donoso Lasso expresses himself: "I have been converted somewhat, because before I did not pray at all, but used to go go to sleep at Rosary time. Now, how-ever, I do pray, and I pray also to the Virgin of Sorrows, which before I did but little, now, however, more. So also

I find some improvement in my conduct."

Finally, here is what Victor Manuel Medina says: "I have remained more devout and with the desire of always seeing the picture of the Blessed Virgin. and from that day I pray with more devotion. Before I did not care much to hear Mass every morning, but now I get up just to hear it every morning with more devotion."

Not to repeat, I pass by many other beautiful depositions, in which those happy boarders lay bare with ingenuous simplicity the renewal of soul that they experienced along with the heavenly visit, and the good desires to which it had given birth.

One only witness, a boarder of twelve years old, says: "I remained as if I had seen nothing; very little impression was made on me."

And in truth he was not well disposed to receive extraordinary graces, as may be seen by his own statement. Thus he says: "I was engaged in bad conversation when the First Communion boys came to tell Fr. Roesch. I did not believe it and went on talking filthily, when I saw all the boys get up from their seats, and in the midst of all the noise, I saw the picture of the Holy Virgin of Sorrows open and shut the right eye, and I remained as if I had seen nothing; it hardly made any impression on me."

The same pupil in repeating his testimony explained further: "Only once did I see her shut the right eye, but even that was not entirely clear to me.

I heard the boys say that they saw it, but cannot affirm the fact although I have good sight and there was sufficient light in the dining-room."

Of the author of the above relation and explanation says in its report: "There is a pupil who declares he did not feel impressed, but there are good grounds to doubt whether he fully perceived the reality of the phenomenon."

With the exception of the boy already referred to, all, even the First Prefect, answer to the fifth question that they felt fear and terror, especially in the beginning, "because we did not know," says Fr. Roesch, "whether or not this manifestation of the Blessed Virgin is a presage of some divine punishment." "When I was convinced of its reality," says Carlos Hermann, a boarder, eleven years old, "I was afraid, thinking there was going to be an earthquake, but now I feel very happy." The same thing happened to most of the students. The fear they felt in the beginning was turned into happiness or content—*gusto* as Carlos Albornoz calls it. "I feel in general," he tell us, "a wish to pray and begin a new life."

One witness more to confirm what has been said. A boarder, Carlos H. Alcaron, says: "I was fearfully frightened, as at something terrible. That night I knelt down in my alcove to invoke the Blessed Virgin, for I had never thought to see such a great miracle, and on the following morning woke tranquil and beaming. I have improved completely, and have left off doing things which I did not wish to leave off, and I have made a resolution never to say an immodest word."

To the steps taken by the Very Rev. Vicar Capitular to ascertain the facts, we must add those of the illustrious Commissions of Physicists, Medical Faculty, and Theologians. The first two, composed of enlightened laymen, the most eminent and distinguished in Quito, affirmed that considering the place where the phenomenon occurred, and the sound health and constitutions of those who saw it, it is impossible to explain on natural grounds an event so extraordinary.

The special commission of Theologians added that in its judgment so prodigious an occurrence could not be attributed to any diabolical agency.

In view of all that had been said about the matter, a commission of Theologians, formed of various Canons and Religious of all the Orders existing in Quito, excepting the Jesuit, met in that city under the presidency of the Very Rev. Vicar Capitular, and drew up their opinion, which the Vicar published in the final decree as follows:

"1. The event that occurred on the 20th of April in the college of the Jesuit Fathers is proved as historically certain.

"2. This event, considering the circumstances under which it took place, cannot be explained by natural laws.

"3. This event from its antecedents and consequences cannot be attributed to diabolical influence. Therefore it may be believed with purely human faith, and for the same reason the vene-ration permitted by the church may be given to the picture which has been the instrument of it, and recourse may be had to it with special confidence."

Sunday, June 3rd, was appointed for the translation of the miraculous picture. The venerable image was borne in procession by a great concourse of people, religious societies, the Jesuit community, the Seminary and chapter. "The streets," says an account from Quito, "were handsomely decorated, and the assembled crowd behaved piously; all looked upon the act with respect, and upon the 'Sorrowful Mother of the College' with the most heartfelt affection and piety."

When the procession arrived at the church, the picture was received with a solemn *Magnificat;* the Very Rev. Vicar addressed the people from the pulpit in a short and fervid exhortation, the crowd filling every foot of available room in the spacious building; and the *Te Deum* was sung before the Blessed Sacrament, which was exposed.

The miraculous image remained exposed to view, and the faithful poured in to honor it on this and the three following days, June 4–6th, during which most solemn services were held.

The fervor of the people has kept on after the triduum, so that a compact multitude is constantly gathered round the Blessed Virgin, and the miraculous movements of the eyes have been re-peated upon different days and in presence of witnesses of every condition, with the result that the widest publicity now attaches to the prodigy. The ecclesiastical authorities have already taken down the evidence of several gentlemen on the matter.

The detailed description of the picture has been juridically stated and is now on record. Among other details it is stated in the legal document that "the picture is a chromolithograph 42 centimetres long and 40 wide (15½ inches by 15.)"

Considering the miracle and the salutary effects that have come from the loving glance of Mary, I cannot better finish my plain narrative than by repeating the words of the Very Rev. Vicar of the Archdiocese of Quito in his pastoral allocution concerning the event: —"God has willed to make it clear on this occasion that the oft repeated prayer with which we are wont to call upon the loving heart of Mary, 'Turn thine eyes of mercy towards us.' is not only not in vain, but heard in very deed and literally granted. She has cast upon us her eyes tearful and tender, she has shown herself a mother."

Translated from the Spanish of F. X. Hoyos, in *Paginas Escolares*, Gijon, Spain.

THE GAMBLER

Most fascinating vice,
I own thee king
Of my poor soul ;
To thee I sacrifice,
To thee I bring
My humble toll.
Ah, how thy charms entice,
Thy fetters cling—
Thou hast control,—
Until my life—a paltry price—
I'd madly fling
Away, to roll
Once more the fatal dice.

M. T. Dooling, Jr., '09.

THE LAST WORDS OF CHRIST

On Calvary's hill were crosses three,
    The sun shone in the middle sky,
The murmuring city thronged to see
    Our Lord between two robbers die.
Men round His cross their mockings made
    Their scoffing with His sorrows grew
"Father, forgive them," thus He prayed—
    "They know not what they do."
Hark the coarse jest !   Behold and see
    Man's cruel mirth—His agony.

II

Mark the wracked frame, the bleeding brow,
    The torments in His anguished eyes ! – —-
Hark the soft accents—"This day thou
    Shalt be with me in Paradise."
Hark to His words, O mother dear,
    And deign to aid this suppliant one,
From Jesus' lips didst thou not hear—
    "Woman, behold thy son !"
I am thy son; ere life had fled
    "Behold thy mother, son," He said.

III

The light that lit the path He trod,
    A moment failed. His misery
Gushed forth in words, "My God, my God,
    O, why hast Thou forsaken me?"
His voice wailed down the breeze and died;
    A solemn stillness reigned. Then burst
A moan from parched lips; He cried
    In bitter woe, "I thirst."
O, Heart, consumed with raging fire,
    Teach mine to thirst with Love's desire.

IV

O cruel thirst, O bitter woe !
    'Tis o'er. God's pitying mandate came.
O hearken, "It is finished.". Lo !
    He sees the end of Death and Shame.
With one last prayer the veils descend,—
    "Into thy hands," aloud he cried,
"Father, my spirit I commend."
    Bowing His head, He died.
Thus Jesus died my soul to save
And snatched the Victory from the Grave.

                        H. L., '08.

THE COMING OF THE DAWN

Abraham rubbed his bloodshot eyes. Far down the road a great multitude was creeping towards him, a brown sinuous serpent on the white dust of the road. He listened intently and to his ears was wafted the deep murmur of many voices. He stood in the road, the sun beating down on his massive disheveled head, reeling drunkenly in his tracks. And as the din swelled and the mob approached, above the maze of clubs and bobbing spears and helmets, he caught sight of the stark ungainly arms of a swaying cross. Then he remembered. It was the day set for the execution of the Nazarene. So he stood there with his hands resting on his broad hips and waited.

When the man was passing, Abraham was caught up by the surging crowd and swept in so close to him that he could feel the warm breath of the panting victim. And just then the cross-bearer stumbled and slipped weakly to his knees. In Abraham's sottish brain the frenzied shrieks of the mob fanned his sordid brutishness into flame. For an instant the patient face was upturned and Abraham struck out at it madly. A fleeting glimpse of a crimson stain on the bearded lips, and then he was swept back, far out on the skirts of the crowd. Once the shoulder of a Roman's horse struck him and he fell. He arose, brushed the matted hair from his eyes, and cursed.

As the freighted cross dropped with a thud into the hole, a deep murmur ran through the crowd. The sullen copper sun was gone and the white bruised body on the cross was sharply outlined against a black sky. And then across the firmament from one horizon to the other, there flamed a great jagged shaft of lightning. A wail of terror went up from the people.

Abraham stood stolid, indifferent. In all his life he had never known fear and he was fearless now. At his elbow an old man was breathing thickly. He turned and eyed him dully. The man's hand was unsteady, his face splotched with fear.

"What think you of the man?" he asked tremulously, with a shaking wave of the hand towards the sacrifice.

Abraham shrugged his shoulders and moved on. He pushed his way through to the innermost circle of the crowd, curious to get a better view of the crucifixion.

His eyes roamed about. In the sea of ashen faces he caught a glimpse of Malchus and over Malchus' shoulder the face of his father. He laughed senselessly. His father's lips were working in terror, and the cold sweat was rolling down his face.

And then quite by accident his roving eyes rested on the woman standing at the foot of the cross. At the same instant her eyes were turned towards him and their gaze met.

All the blood surged from the hot

brain of the young Jew and he fell back a step. The face was wonderful, and the eyes—in them he saw what only he and one other had ever seen, and a great wave of understanding swept over him. The woman's eyes reverted almost instantly to the upraised Form, and Abraham's gaze followed hers. Through the gathering gloom he looked again at the naked Figure. And he noticed that the blood was welling from the lacerated lips, and something hot, unbearable, stabbed through his heart and seared it. He himself had struck the blow, back on the road.

He stood there a moment, motionless, with blinking unseeing eyes. And then, as the fact slowly dawn on him, all the strong intensity of his passionate nature flamed out. He broke through the crowd and fell on his knees before the woman.

"Forgive me, O Lady, forgive me. I am the man that struck, I struck Him in the face. See, His sacred blood is on my hand. Oh, wretch that I am. Forgive me, pray Him for mercy. I dare not go to Him for I struck Him on the mouth when He had fallen. Tell me, is there any hope, any hope for me?"

His frame was quivering, and the chords in his strong neck stood out like rope.

The woman turned her face to him, a patient face, but stamped with agony. She tried to speak, but her trembling lips made no sound. So she pointed mutely to the One on the Cross, closing her eyes to hide the anguish in them.

Above the riot of the storm,

"Father, forgive them for they know not what they do," said the Man.

Abraham bowed his great tousled head.

A young Jew, running wildly through the dark, before the lash of terror, stumbled over the kneeling figure and spat out an oath.

Abraham did not move. Around him night and chaos had gripped the world. But in his heart dawn and a great peace had come.

JAMES F. TWOHY, '07.

THE TIE THAT BINDS

It is strange, when you come to think of it, what a great influence even our most common acts often exert over the whole course of our future lives. We repeat an action once too often and the whole machinery of the Fates, which we had before considered so stable, is disturbed. The great wheels slip and turn, bearing us whither they will, and when they cease we are amazed to find how great a change has been wrought by so slight a cause.

It was no more unusual for John Morrison to beat his son, than it was for him to be drunk. In fact the one followed as a natural consequence upon the other and both were of such frequent occurrence as to have become well established customs. Yet if John Morrison had refrained for only a single evening from this customary diversion he would have saved himself from a year's term in prison, he would have kept his son from much pleasure and much pain, and above all this story would never have been written. But the psychological moment had arrived and he did beat him, as usual, on the steps of their tenement home. Beat him to such an accompaniment of drunken curses that the attention of a well-dressed passer-by was attracted, and this passer-by being an energetic young man, promptly interfered. He sent the drunken father reeling and cursing inside the doorway with one well directed cuff, and then turned his attention to the son.

"Don't cry, sonny," he said, bending over him, "he won't hurt you now." Then as the boy glanced up, with a pitiful attempt at a smile, the young man showed his genius for diplomacy by asking that opening question among all boys, "What's your name?"

"Jimmy Morrison," sniffed the boy.

"Why, that's funny," replied the young man, "my name's Jimmy, too, Jimmy Kendal. Jimmy," he continued, "that wasn't your father beating you just now, was it?

"No, sir, he's only my uncle," lied the boy. For the pride of the poor that allows whole families to starve rather than ask for aid, was strong within him. Then, too, he loved his father in a way.

"And, Jimmy, what did he beat you for?"

"I asked him for something to eat and he got mad."

"Why, Jimmy, are you hungry? Then come with me."

James Kendal displayed another master stroke of diplomacy by taking taking the urchin to a nearby restaurant and giving him his fill. After that the boy was his.

*   *   *   *

"I understand," said Bobby Harding to his crony, Jimmy Kendal, during their after-dinner game of billiards, "that you've adopted a kid."

Jimmy Kendal missed an easy carrom shot and fell violently to chalking his cue. He did not answer for some time and then he said slowly:

"Yes, I did take a kid. A little fellow with a brute of an uncle. He's been at my house for nearly a week now and he's the most grateful little cuss I've ever seen. Poor little devil! his uncle used to beat him every day. But I saw to it that the old man got a year for being drunk and disorderly, the day after I took the kid. He won't bother the little fellow for a while now."

"Well, you old philanthropist," laughed Bobby, and then seeing his friend's embarrassment, he fell to discussing the latest yacht race.

* * * * *

As for Jimmy Morrison he seemed to be well satisfied with his new home.

A few days after Jimmy's adoption, James Kendal had had a long talk with him in which he had explained that Jimmy's first duty was due to his parents.

"But you see, Jimmy," he had concluded, "that since both your parents are dead, I shall take the place of your father and you shall owe your first duty to me, just as you would owe it to him if he were living."

He wondered at the strange quietness and reserve of the boy after this, buf he never thought of connecting it with his last words.

While he was silent the boy's mind was in a turmoil. So he owed his first duty to his father he thought, and here he had come away and left the old man alone with no one to take care of him, no one to bring him home when he was drunk, and the next day he had been "jugged." Now if he's been there, he could have steered his father from the "cops" as he had always done. You bet his father had never been "pinched" when he was around. But now it was too late. All he could do was stay with Mr. Kendal.

These thoughts grieved Jimmy for two or three weeks but after that he seemed to forget them and grew cheerful and happy again. He started to school and, strange to say, he liked it and did well in his studies. He knew the pleasure of being clean and well dressed, of good meals and a warm bed. He grew to love James Kendal with a love that was almost worship, and Kendal in his turn loved the boy as his own son. Thus they went on for a year, each day carrying Jimmy farther from his past, and the bond between them grew and strengthened.

Then one day on his way home from school Jimmy stopped and stood still, thoughtlessly swinging his books by his side as he watched a drunken figure reeling down the street, stopped and stood watching it as it staggered towards him. Then his heart gave a great bound for he knew it was his father. His father came on and on, and Jimmy's heart stood still as he reeled unsteadily by him. He stood there gazing at the retreating figure for what seemed to him an age and his whole world was tumbling about his ears. Stood and gazed with his books hanging idly by his side while he fought his silent battle with himself. Then he shouldered his books again and deliberately turning his back on the retreating figure continued slowly on his way.

The sight of a policeman standing on the corner brought him up with a start. He stood for a moment wavering uncertainly. Then with a sudden fierceness he flung his books from him into the street and disappeared in the busy throng.

MAURICE T. DOOLING, JR., '09.

THE FADED FLOWER

(TRIOLET)

Only a little faded flower,
Yet stirs it the heart of the brave.
Why does he fond kisses shower
On that little faded flower ?
Ah ! 'twas plucked from the fragrant bower
That shadows his little one's grave.
Only a little faded flower
Yet stirs it the heart of the brave.

W. I. L., '09·

THE CITY BEAUTIFUL

They speak of a city beautiful
　To rise on the ruins of the old,
With temples and towers and palaces,
　And marvels manifold:
And the streets shall run wide, artistical,
　With never an alley or lane;
The rocky hills shall be terraces,
　The valleys become plane ;
And all shall be fair and precious,
　As in dreams we are wont to behold
In that wonderful city utopian,
　That shall stand on the grave of the old.

But I muse over a city beautiful,
　Not builded of mortar or stone,
Where the temples are incensed with suffering
　And the streets are hushed and lone.
'Tis reared by sweet faith, strong fortitude,
　On faith's foundation broad,
And the garnered wealth of its palaces
　Are valued alone by God.
In the hearts of our patient refugees
　My City Beautiful stands,
Begotten of trial borne manfully,
　Not builded by human hands.

　　　　　　　　　　J. D. '07.

HIS CONFIDANT

R–r–r–r–r–r–clang, clang!

Now this is not a fire alarm, nor an earthquake, nor anything of that sort; it merely means that Mr. Watkin's telephone rang out upon the silence of his down town office. But it did sound as loud as a fire alarm and as vexing as an earthquake to this exceedingly busy gentleman who was endeavoring to do two hours work in one.

"Say Henry," he called to his clerk, "for heaven's sake, answer that phone." But seeing the phone standing right at his elbow on the desk, Mr. Watkins suddenly concluded he might as well attend to it himself and let the clerk hear but one end of the conversation.

"Hello."

"Oh! it's you, is it, Laura?"

"Home at 5:30—an hour earlier—Impossible!"

"Absolutely impossible, I tell you."

"Dinner, dinner—I'm in no hurry; I'm not starving."

"Good Heavens! how long does it take me to dress? Don't you know we're married now and I don't have to be quite so particular as I used to."

"Don't have to be quite so particular, I say."

"A minister! Great Scott! Why, I've turned Dowieite."

"Well, I suppose it's no use talking."

"All right, I'll be there, but I'll take it out of your new Easter bonnet. You'll see. Good bye."

"Well, Henry," said Mr. Watkins, "I've got to go home at once to be present at some confounded dinner where Mrs. Watkins entertains some professional gormandizer or other. If this isn't slavery to fashion, well—I'd like to know what is. Here look over this bunch of letters, hunt up that one from the Stock Exchange and put it on file."

Mr. Watkins flung the letters at his clerk in anything but an amiable mood, put on his overcoat and hat and strode out of the office, muttering something like a cuss-word about society and all its charms.

A few moments later found him boarding a car headed for Ocean Park. The car was quite well filled, but luckily he was invited to a seat at the side of a kindly-looking elderly man who wore greenish spectacles and bright red side-whiskers.

"You see this is the very last seat," the man explained, and I suppose you deserve it as much as anyone else."

"Thank you," replied Mr. Watkins, "I am a bit tired, I'll admit, and hanging to a strap would hardly be congenial just now."

It was not long before the two men were on fairly good speaking terms with each other, and it was then Mr. Watkins began to pour out his tale of woe.

"Say, are you much of a society man?" Watkins inquired.

"Very little—I dislike its ceremonies. They're a waste of time."

"Bully for you, sir! Why, would you

believe it—I had this very night to leave my office where I am a week behind in my work, two hours earlier just to accommodate society. You see I've got to get home and dress for dinner, just as if dress had anything to do with a man's appetite! Just as if I were some little maiden's wax doll preparing for a tea party."

"Well, I sincerely hope the dinner will prove worth it all!"

"Oh yes! No doubt or that. Laura—that's my wife, you know; we've been married two years now—Laura's crazy on society, but she knows how to get up a good dinner, just the same, and I'm sure that hungry good-for-nothing minister will enjoy it."

"Minister, what minister?"

"Well, you see the whole affair is in honor of some lean-sided druid whom Mrs. Watkins regards as an oracle. He's the guest. I don't begrudge him the dinner, of course, but why the d——, what right has he to rob me of my office time and my own private home pleasures? Why doesn't he get off to the desert, and live on locusts and wild honey?"

"Well, that's pretty hard on the minister," said his companion.

"Not at all, not at all. Not half hard enough! My wife, although the best little woman in the world, is simply society-mad, gone plumb daffy on it, don't you know, and she wants me to be as far gone as herself. Then here comes along this fakir, this sentimental preacher to encourage her in her nonsense. Why, it's enough to make a

man turn his back on religion forever."

"But perhaps they are old friends, perhaps he has been away and has just returned," stammered Mr. Watkin's fellow passenger.

"Well, here's my street; good bye sir."

"Good bye," and the two men separated in the throng that poured off the car.

* * * * *

Mr. Watkins arrived home safely, and after a gruff, but not really unkind salutation to his wife, went to his room to dress. Having been a confirmed bachelor for many years, he was able to dress himself without any foreign help, and collar buttons, ties, cuffs, etc., found themselves in the right place without dint of the strong language said to be fashionable on such occasions. He emerged presently from his room arrayed in all the glory of a Roman breastplate, as he termed his immaculate shirt-front, cut-away dress coat, and the rest. A protracted glance at the mirror had shown him a rather nice-looking middle-aged gentleman indeed, and it was with feelings greatly mollified, in fact, with much more satisfaction than he cared to admit, that he went down to help his wife receive the guests.

"Norman dear, let me introduce you to my old school friend, Mr. Spurgeon. He has just returned from . . ."

But Mr. Watkins heard no more. His heart died away to a mere nothing beneath his breastplate, for before him stood a man with green spectacles and red side-whiskers.

JAMES V. CARROLL, 1st Acad.

TO A BUTTERFLY

O you gorgeous butterfly !
　　Gaily dight,
Flitting here and flitting there,
Not a sorrow, not a care—
　　Only pleasure
　　　　Without measure
　　Is your plight.
Passing idle, sunlit, hours
Midst the flowers'
　　　　Fragrant bowers,
Whose varied beauty you outvie.
With the richness of your dress;
　　You art fairest,
　　　　Yes, and rarest
Of all creatures, I confess.

　　Yet with all your brightness,
　　And your joyous lightness,
With all your splendor in mine eyes,
　　No matter how gay
　　You seem today,
You are only a worm in gaudy disguise.

MAURICE T. DOOLING, JR., '09.

RUSKIN IN "A JOY FOREVER"

After reviewing the works of the writer, who, as he said, "has left a deeper stamp upon the language than any other Englishman of the century," Van Dyke was moved to exclaim: "He has taught several generations to see with their eyes, think with their minds and work with their hands." No better eulogy could be written than these few words of praise expressing better than volumes could have done, the good accomplished by the life-work and writings of John Ruskin, Poet, Artist, Art Critic, and Political Economist. Hardly a line of work was left untouched by him during his many years of active life.

Ruskin was born of Scotch parents in 1819. His early training was very strict, forming the influence that guided him throughout the remainder of his life. Educated privately at first, he was later sent to Oxford where he graduated at the age of twenty-seven. Having acquired an early taste for painting, his inclinations naturally turned to art and his graduation was marked by the publication of the first volume of his greatest and most forceful work, "Modern Painters." Its subject is manifold; it deals with the "object and means of landscape painting, the spirit which should govern its production, the appearance of nature and a discussion of what is true in art as revealed by nature." It is remarkable for its many poetic description and "pretty passages,"

which Ruskin afterward complained excited more comment and received more attention than did the real purpose and idea of the book. The writing and publication of these volumes extended through a space of twenty years and naturally contained many contradictions caused by the broadening and changing of his views during that period. Too forcible and eloquent at times for cool deliberation, the work is lacking in philosophical merit and its value as a criticism is lessened on the same account. Nevertheless the volumes still remain as one of the greatest works of the day, valuable for their very positiveness of statement which invites deeper thought by compelling contradiction, for the richness of their observations on nature, and the brilliant poetry of their prose. Perhaps the greatest result of the work was in that it tore aside the mystery that had surrounded art and placed before the people in the plain terms and expressions of the day what had hitherto been understood only by the "high priests of the craft." The period of this production was also lavish in its publication of a multitude of various works ranging in subject from poetry and art to religion and political economy. About 1860 his interest in art began to wane in favor of the more pressing needs of the British workingmen. Naturally of a sympathetic disposition, he had here a task to his liking and suitable to his natural

talent and ability for strength of denun-
ciation and invective. He began to
send out letter after letter upon the
intolerable wrongs of the laboring
classes, and from that time until the date
of his retiring from active life, he devoted
his strength and his fortune toward
this chosen cause, unfortunately losing
both in the hopeless struggle.

He still, however, found opportunity,
from time to time, for further writings
on his earlier subject, Art. "Sesame
and Lillies," "Arata Pentilici," "Ariadne
Florentina," "Mornings in Florence,"
"The Bible of Amiens," and "The Art
of England" followed each other in close
succession, but in most of them we
notice a change of treatment from his
previous writings on the same subject.
A more sober and subdued style char-
actizes these later efforts. Such a work
is the essay entitled, "A Joy Forever."

This was written and delivered first
in the form of two lectures at the
opening and dedication of the Manches-
ter Museum of Art, in July, 1867, and
later revised and printed in 1880 with
supplementary notes by the author. Its
title was taken from the words of Keats
which had been inscribed on the cornice
of the Exhibition building at Manches-
ter, "A Thing of Beauty is a Joy Forever," and it is throughout a plea for
the recognition of the element of Political Economy in Art, in so far as it regards its production, accumulation and
distribution. It is characteristic of the
man that he should begin his first lecture, which deals with the production of
art, with a short discussion upon pover-

ty and wealth, but he soon connects it
with the subject in question when he
explains that the art treasurers of the
nation are among its greatest wealth.
After delaying for a few moments upon
the theories of Political Economy in regard to the employment of labor, he ap-
plies these same principles to the production of the young artists and their
employment and application to easy,
various, and lasting work, that the best
results, namely, the best pictures or
statues or architecture as the case may
be, may be obtained. Having thus
dealt with production of art, good, living art, he speaks in his second lecture
of the accumulation and distribution of
the art already produced. And here
Mr. Ruskin calls attention to a fact that
merits considerable notice from the true
lover of art.

He speaks in no gentle terms of the
men who would pose as patrons of art at
home, furnishing rich castles in the
height of magnificence and luxury,
copying the art and architecture of the
famous masters of the continent, while,
at the same moment, they through neg-
lect are allowing those priceless treasures, the original works of these
masters, to be ruined by want of care
and the ravages of war. It is in
keeping with his usual style of denun-
ciation that he should compare the people of the continent, the natives of the
cities where the most priceless art
treasures are to be found, the artists
and art professors of the day, the art
dealers and the people in general, to a
den of mischievous monkeys, fighting

and quarrelling among a set of priceless pictures and either wantonly or unknowingly destroying them, but destroying them nevertheless. But let Ruskin himself relate the comparison. He says in the course of the lecture: "I assure you in the course of fifteen years in which I have been working in those places in which the most precious remnants of European art exists, a sensation whether I would or no, was gradually made distinct in my mind, that I was living and working in the midst of a den of monkeys:—sometimes amiable and affectionate monkeys, with all manner of winning ways and kind intention, more frequently selfish and malicious monkeys, but, whatever their disposition, squabbling continually about nuts and the best places on the barren sticks of trees; and that all this monkey's den was filled by mischance with precious pictures and the witty and wilful beasts were always wrapping themselves up and going to sleep in pictures or tearing holes in them to grin through; or tasting them and spitting them out again, or twisting them up into ropes and making swings of them. . . . . And see how. . . The professors repaint the old pictures in all the principle places (liking their own work the best) leaving a bit of background to set off their own work, as the monkeys who tear holes in pictures to grin through. Then the picture dealers cannot sell the old pictures in its pure state, all the good work must be covered with new paint to resemble the professorial pictures in the picture galleries . . the

monkeys who make ropes of the pictures to swing by. Then every now and then in some old stable or wine cellar . . . . somebody finds a fresco of Perugino's or Giotto's, but doesn't think much of it . . and so he whitewashes the fresco . . . and these sort of people come generally to be imagined as the sort of monkeys who taste the pictures and spit them out, not finding them nice."

Mr. Ruskin's command over the English language is not the least of his attainments. An almost limitless vocabulary, melodious rythm and flow of sentence, and a brilliancy of illustration and description mark the greater part of his writings, though found indeed principally in Modern Painters. He himself used to say regarding his facility of expression, that his work was "always done as quietly and methodically as a piece of tapestry. I knew exactly what I had got to say, put the words firmly in their places like so many stitches, hemmed the edges of the chapters round with what seemed to me graceful flourishes, and touched them finally with my cunningest points of color." It is true, however, that his very facility in expression and the limpid flow of his words often "ran away with his sobriety," and led him into rambling sentences which were the "pretty sentences" that he himself complained that they spoiled the effect and purpose of his writings. But granting for a moment that they are at variance with the general direction of his ideas, they are still valuable as examples of the effect of the pen wielded by the master hand and guided by a master mind. For instance, what wealth of thought is contained in the few lines in his first lecture at a period where he has digressed upon the subject of extravagance in woman's dress; and how well the poetic thought is expressed. He says, speaking of the amount of work spent at times for a single dress, and of the amount of good the same labour expended in another direction would have accomplished. Listen—" . . . they who wear it have literally entered into a partnership with death; and dressed themselves with his spoils. Yes, if the veil could be lifted not only from your human sight you would see—the angels do see—on those gay white dresses of yours, strange dark spots and crimson patterns that you know not of —spots of the inextinguishable red that all the seas cannot wash away; yes, and among the pleasant flowers that crown your head and glow on your wreathed hair, you would see that one weed was always twisted which no one though of —the grass that grows on graves."

But the very frequency of beautiful passages in Ruskin's works makes quotation and illustration difficult. The writer is overwhelmed, as it were, by a sea of poetry, and he emerges with but a few of the luckily caught waves of color, very probably inferior in poetic quality and literary merit to many others of the multitude that have confused him. Ruskin should be read slowly and well, and be viewed from the many different phases of his work, from its value as regards economics, and finally and above all, as an example of Literature, for whatever may be said by vindictive and revengeful artists, and whatever may be the opinion of the world at large concerning his merit in the field of Political Economy, Ruskin is always pre-eminently a master of English, and his works have marked an epoch in the history of our Literature.

R. E. FITZGERALD, Post-Grad. Course.

FRIO TOWN BILL ON THE STYX

No wonder we moved up to the camp fire. There was a double reason for doing so. The weather was stormy and cold, and, besides, Cyclone was going to tell a story. When Cyclone told a story, he told it well, and the cattle-camp that had him was to be considered lucky. So, near the friendly warmth of the fire, we forgot the storm, and appreciated Cyclone's remark that "there war'nt no storm within twenty feet uv a camp fire, so why not come in an' be soshuble."

"Bill wuz the mos' onery cuss I ever seen," he began. "He wuz as shrivelled up as a prarie-hen in a blizzard. But one thing Bill could do, an' that wuz shoot. Shoot! Why that feller could shoot the hair off'n a billy-goat's jaw, with his gun upside down. Mor'n once Bill kicked into a scrape, drew an' squinted 'long the gun like a streak of greased lightenin', and shot the spokes out uv the other feller's machinery 'fore he cud draw. There wuzn't 'nother feller in Frio Town as cud shoot anywheres near Bill. There wuz only one time Bill drew an' found the cards against him."

"How wuz that, Cyclone?" asked Pony Rawlinson, the foreman, as he leant forward and dug a stick into the coals for a light.

"Wuz back 'bout seven years, an' Bill an' I wuz workin' the range an' brandin' for the Circle S outfit up at Dry Creek way. Me an' Bill an' 'nother feller had pretty much the run uv the roughest, brushiest, an' cussedest hard ridin' country on earth. The day we struck the Galloway Roughs, Bill balked. Tom an' I took the Big Mountain trail that afternoon an' left Bill in camp, sour as a lemon, an' slingin' the almightiest bunch of profanity aroun' as ever blued the air of the Bear Paw. We rounded some calves up, an' with a couple uv misdirected prayers, we got 'em down ter the corral 'bout 4 o'clock. As I come roun' the camp I smelt trouble brewin'. I knew Bill. I guessed what wuz comin'. He met us at camp, grinned sourly, gave a hitch ter his gun, spit a couple uv times, an' opened up. He said as how he wuzn't goin' ter ride in that kind uv a country for the best this and that that ever walked the earth. He said if we didn't want ter come with him we didn't need ter, an' he said he didn't give a damn. He walked away in the direction uv his broncho, an' I saw the last uv Bill punchin' the breeze up the dusty road.

"Tom an' I cleared up the bunch from the Big Mountain range, 'bout a hundred head, an' cleared fer Pine Canyon an' the Sugar Loaf. But we wuzn't agoin' ter come through so easy. We had some 'bald-faced' bulls in the bunch, an' if they didn't raise partikler ruckshuns, I donno what yuh'd call it. Well, we just camped 'bout half way 'tween Pine Canyon an' the Cedars. We wuz pretty done up 'bout night, so we druv the bunch into an' ole sheep corral, an' built our fire, an' turned in. Must ha' been 'bout an hour er so after, we heard the darndest rough-house I ever heard. I got ma gun, an' guessin' it wuz some maverick as had no business roun' here, I wuz preparin' ter pepper his carcass with forty-fours, when inter camp stumbles Frio Town Bill. He sutonly wuz a picter fer a Dutch weddin'. His hat wuz gone, gun, chaps, an' sense. I reconed as how Bill must ha' been shakin' it up with a bunch uv hoss thieves, becuz in the long time uv my experience on the range I never saw a wuss specimen uv humanity.

"Well," sez I, kinder icy, "what's the game now?"

"Water," sez he, purty thick.

I got sum an' sot down waitin' to see his next throw. None seemed to be comin', so I lead off.

"Well, what's up?"

"Been ter hell, Cyclone," he sez, solumn as an owl.

That floored me. I saw through the hull thing as clear as day. Bill was loco, plum luny.

"Now look here, Bill," sez I, "you jes' take a rest," an' then by way uv humorin' his imagination, I mos' naterly remarked that "it must ha' been hot in hell at this time uv the year."

Bill looked at me and groaned. "Hot! It wuz hot 'nuff ter make the rattle-snakes squeal, an' so all-fired rocky that a timber wolf cudn't back track himself if he tried."

This took the starch out uv ma gun hand, an' I wuz reckonin' what kind

uv chances I'd ha' cleanin' out uv camp with a hull skin, an' gettin' out uv the unpleasant presence uv the darndest nut-factory that ever wore a hat, when he cumes aroun' the fire an' sez:

"Cyclone, yuh jes' listin ter what I'm agoin' ter say, an' then yuh can make yer conclusions after. I see ez how yer thinkin' I'm crazy. Get that spook out uv yer noodle, and listen. I've got as much sense uz yuh er any man that ever wore hair, Cyke, ole boy."

I saw there wuz no gettin' roun' the business but ter let the win' run out, an' I said I'd listen ter his yarn, an' in the meantime I'd plan my escape. I'd have ter either make fast tracks fer the timber er take chances uv crackin' his countenance which I didn't like ter do, even ter a lunytic, an' then, besides, Bill wuz purty clever with his bones, but this wuz only a—well, another question.

"Cyke," sez Bill, "when I left yer an' Tom th' other day, I mosied off ter the O. B. place, an' got a job, that I thought wuz goin' ter skin this all ter pieces. I thought I'd hit the real thing in a han'-basket, fur sure. Next morning, the foreman come over ter me, an' sez, "Frio, we're got sumthin' fer yuh ter do. You an' Mooney 'ill have ter go over ter Fryin' Pan Ridge an' get sum cavves that's chasin' 'roun' there. It'll be easy, but it's kinda lonesum.' 'Leave that ter me, Lizzy,' sez I, 'I got the best blame remedy fer lonesumness yuh ever heerd uv.'

"Mooney an' I left camp early an' I tuk my little brown bottle. When we got ter the Fryin' Pan, we got ter know how it felt ter be baked pertato. Dust wuz thick, an' the win' wuz hot, the san' wuz hot, the air wuz hot, an' wust uv all, I wuz hot. I saw I'd been hashed inter a — mean job, an' I can jes' tell yuh I used langwige that made blue streaks in the horizon. I showed Mooney a few tricks in cussin' that he wuz a stranger ter, an' the way he kep' out uv my reach wuz a wunder ter see. We finally had to separate so ez ter get the bunch between us. That's where our troubles started in. I got along fine till one little red cuss uv a calf as full uv pure cussedness as a mule, started up a ravine that ran straight inter the middle uv the Fryin' Pan. I jabbed the spurs inter ole Sioux, an' went for 'im.

"The calf kep' right on ahead runnin' like the devil bent on an election, straight along through the ravine. I cudn't head 'im off, an' I cudn't get 'im by chasin' 'im, so I got the rope, an' made a throw fer 'im. Surprisin' things happen once an' a while, an' I bit off one uv the biggest I ever saw. I threw an' missed and before I cud get breath, ole Sioux slipped an' sprawled on the slippery stones. Off I come with a jolt that rattled my grinders like dice. Sioux scrambled up and started up the cache with me in tow hangin' ter the stirrup like a dead coyote ter a rope. If I had a nickle fer every time I hit the earth that day I cun uv bought out Rockefeller a dozen times. Then I stopped but Sioux kep' goin'. I was too darn near dead ter care much what happened then, an' so I lay still, I felt fer the little

brown bottle, an' pulled it out an' took a swig. After that I felt better, an' gave vent to some surprising statements an' cuss words that I didn't think I had the talent ter invent. I took another swig uv the little brown bottle, an' then it wuz I began ter see things on the landscape that wuzn't there before. Most all kinds of things appeared, some I'd seen before, an' some that I didn't. Things get twisted sometimes, and so thinkin' my imagination wuz out uv whack, I took another eye-opener out uv the bottle, and got up. Then the hull bunch uv things I saw and didn't see began ter start up a reg'lar buckwing dance. "Bill," sez I ter myself, "it's up ter yuh, yuh gotter get out uv here sum way." So I started. I must ha' got 'bout twenty feet when I made a slip, an' went down, down, down, till I guessed I wuz goin' straight ter Hades on the fast-mail.

"I landed with a jolt that wud parerlize an ox. When I got my neck inter joint again, I found I wuz in the water, an' goin' down stream lickety-cut. I tried to stop navigatin' at sech a lively rate but wuz no use, I jes' kep' goin'. There wuz a kind uv moonlight on the river, and I cud see some kind uv a boat ahead, an' so I let a yell that echoed all over creation. Things happen fast an' the next thing sum'un grabbed me by the neck an' jerked me onter board. There wuz a great commotion in the cabin, an' in 'bout a second a big Dago run on deck an' grabbed the guy that caught me. "Charon," say he in a deep voice, "I ha' told thee many times to let these mortals of the upper world alone, and . . " "But dear Nero," sez Charon, lookin' scared, "he wuz floating, and I helped him, "and besides he may be a good slave." "See yuh here," sez I, lookin' at Chrron ez fierce ez they make 'em, "the quicker yuh get that idea out uv yer head, the better fer yuh, sabe?" "Huh," sez Nero, "so yuh are one uv those barbarians they call Irish. Olly Cromwell speaks of yer nation ez one uv beasts. Is it not so?"

"This was too much, an' so I began ter throw the lead at Mr. Nero. An', Cyclone, that bloody Dago jes' caught 'em colts forty-fivers in his hand, an' when the gun wuz empty, he threw 'em back ter me, an' sez, "wonderful, wonderful! almost as good as a javelin!"

" 'Bout a half-an-hour after, they got me down stairs, an' tole me ter get busy on the culynery department. I got busy so blame quick that I hit Charon on the head with a rollin' pin. Nero butted in next. "Nero," sez I, "bunch the breeze, an' do it quick, er I'll hit you on the kettle with a fryin' pan " He didn't take my gentle hit, so I give him one that he took, and it wuzn't nuthin' easy neither. This wuz a reg'lar declaration uv war, an' Nero took it up fast. I scooted for the deck, an' jes' got there when Nero came up, an' this time he had a bunch. Charon wuz in back and Nero wuz in front. Now I wuz in a fix.

"Say, Charou, ole boy," sez I, "yuh got me inter this, so see ef yuh can get me out; ef yuh don't, I'm goin' ter slip it ter yuh, sure." He took the hint, an' tole me ter follow, an' we hustled along to the hindquarters uv the blame ole scow. He pointed to a boat an' tole me ter get in. I did, an' we shoved off. Nero saw us, an' yelled like—oh, yuh bet he yelled, but I looked at Charon, an' he saw I meant biz an' he kept goin'. The ole boat started to get the current, an' we wuz goin' ter beat the band, when all of a sudden I seemed to be fallin', an' the last thing I remember wuz bein' carried sumwhere. I came ter myself, looked up, an' saw ole Charon standin' beside me. "Hello, hello!" I sez, "fast trip, wuzn't it?" Charon whinnied in answer. I looked up again, an' rubbed my eyes. Sure ez day it wuz Sioux. I put up hand an' thet wuz him. I tried ter get the little brown bottle but it was empty. I got up an' found I wuz jes' where I wuz that mornin'. Well, then, ter make a long story short, I got out uv the bloomin' place ez fast ez Sioux cud go, an' here I am. That's the end uv my story."

I waited fer a minute, and looked at Bill. "Bill," I sez, gettin' up from the fire and kinkin' a box at him, "yu're a d— liar; yuh've been on a spree, and yuh made this up fer a poultice."

Bill reached fer his gun, but it wuzn't there. "How'd yuh guess," he grinned.

"Because Lodi Wassar saw you yesterday with the Cain bunch, an' yuh got cleaned out even ter spurs an' gun."

"What did yuh listen ter the yarn fer?" he asked.

"Oh," I sez, "I wanted ter see if yuh wuz ez crazy ez you looked jes' now. They say," sez I ter get him riled, "they say Lodi got the drop on yuh,"

"He did," sez Bill, "I wuz drunk. Let's turn in, there's work tomorrer."

CYRIL J. SMITH, '09.

The Redwood.

PUBLISHED MONTHLY BY THE STUDENTS OF THE SANTA CLARA COLLEGE

The object of the Redwood is to record our College Doings, to give proof of College Industry and to knit closer together the hearts of the Boys of the Present and of the Past.

EDITORIAL STAFF

EXECUTIVE BOARD

ANTHONY B. DIEPENBROCK, '08
President

FRANCIS M. HEFFERNAN, '08   MERVYN S. SHAFER, '09

ASSOCIATE EDITORS

COLLEGE NOTES	MERVYN S. SHAFER, '09
IN THE LIBRARY	GEORGE J. HALL, '08
EXCHANGES	MAURICE T. DOOLING, '09
ALUMNI	HARRY P. BRODERICK, '08
ATHLETICS	CARLOS K. McCLATCHY, '10

BUSINESS MANAGER

FRANCIS M. HEFFERNAN, '08

ASSISTANT BUSINESS MANAGER

JOHN W. MALTMAN, '09

Address all communications to THE REDWOOD, Santa Clara College, California

Terms of subscription, $1.50 a year; single copies, 15 cents

EDITORIAL COMMENT

Once again the time of commemoration for one of the most stupendous series of events that the chroniclers of the world's history ever recorded, has come with its joys and blessings, and gone to join the past. On the first Easter Day, nearly nineteen centuries ago, the independence of mankind was proclaimed by the resurrection of Him who is Life itself—independence from the slavery of sin and Satan, and independence from the sad exclusion from the Heaven of Adam's race, and certainly an Independence day is a great day indeed. Many a nation has a set day on its annals when it remembers and celebrates its freedom from some tyrannical conqueror, on which day the whole nation rejoices and makes merry. So is it not a great day which is the monument to the Independence, not of one nation or two, but of all nations? Satan had blinded our first parents to their destruction, had by his diplomacy, if we may so call it, deceived them and made them his slaves. That slavery had been transmitted, as a most precious heirloom might have been, down through the ages to the time of the freedom of mankind. The paradise of man's human nature had been blighted, weeds had grown everywhere and the tree of knowledge gave forth a bitter fruit. It almost repented God that he made man

But as night cannot last forever, neither could the gloom that overcast mankind; and an ever-brightening ray of hope penetrated even the dark corners of the earth. The star of promise of a Redeemer to come, could always be found shining in the firmament for God's chosen people.

But at length the prophecies were fulfilled—those things which had been foretold by the inspired seers in the dim ages before now actually came to pass. The seed of the woman crushed the serpent's head—but not without unspeakable suffering and even death. No! He trod the wine-piess alone and no sorrow was like unto His sorrow. But the sorrow and suffering He claimed for Himself, while the joy of his glorious Resurrection, He has given to us.

Of course it is not to be expected that there will ever be a golden age when the race of fools will become extinct. From the time of Adam thousands of years ago until the present date, 1907, A. D., the race of fools has increased and multiplied. "The multitude of fools is infinite." And even as their number is the number of their achievements. The latest achievement of this race has been accomplished by six Massachusetts physicians, who being men of integrity and great intellectual abilities should be believed by all their compatriots. They have been experimenting for six years, they say, to determine whether or not the human soul is "an actual material thing"; and to-day, that is, the tenth day of March—they have announced their conclusion, which is that the human soul is an actual material thing. And moreover, wonderful to behold! it is affected by gravity, to the extent of half-an-ounce. Is this not marvelous?

Hence we may draw a conclusion which gives us much hope. For some day when science has reached its height, and men by means of some wonderful scheme or ingenious device are able to penetrate into the bowels of the earth, nay, even to the center of gravity, there they will find the souls of the friends they loved here upon earth. And will it not be a joyful reunion? Of course the soul will be attracted there unless bound by the property of impenetrability. But it is evident that such is not the case. The soul vivified the whole body and therefore is in the whole body. Hence in that case it compenetrates the whole body, and is coexten-sive with it. Now if the soul can com-penetrate the body, it can also compen-etrate the earth for the body is no less matter than the earth. So there will be no resistance to the force of gravity, and eventually the soul will be drawn down by the huge spider gravity.

This weighty discovery suggests a whole troop of questions. For instance, does the soul of a pot-bellied alderman not tip the scales at a more decided angle than that of a scraggy, skinny starveling? Does the soul of a dys-peptic out-weigh that of a comic editor? Have political bosses and Frenchmen any souls at all? Why does a dead fish weigh half-an-ounce less than a live one?

But having settled the main question to their own satisfaction, the learned doctors will dispose of these minor matters in due time.

In another page will be found an ac-count of a wonderful miracle that hap-pened at the Jesuit college in Quito a year ago, and that, as we read in *Razon y Fe*, has been since repeated in full view of thousands of people in that city. To our Catholic readers we offer no apology for the article. We who are the children of that Church whose long existence amid the unceasing persecu-tion of the world is in itself a stupen-dous miracle to those that have eyes and see, who believe that the church is the coming of the unseen world into this, who have been habituated from our childhood to regard God, not as a vague,

far away *Deity*, ruling us by general laws, and sacrificing the individual to the general mass, but as a kind, personal Father who holds each of us in the hollow of His Hand and who reckons as naught the most fundamental physical laws of creation in comparison with the salvation of a single soul, we, I say, will find no more difficulty in believing this miracle than we do in accepting any other perfectly authenticated historical fact. To our non-Catholic readers we beg to submit the following from New-man, who surely cannot be accused of gullibility:

. . . we affirm that the Supreme Being has wrought miracles on earth since the time of the Apostles . . . . We affirm it on a First Principle; they deny it on a First Princi-ple. . . . . Both they and we start with the Miracles of the Apostles, and then their First Principle, or presumption against our miracles, is, "What God did once, He is not likely to do again;" while our First Principle, or presumption for our miracles, is this: "What God did once, He *is* likely to do again." . . . They do not say, "St. Francis or St. An-thony, . . . did no miracles, for the *evi-dence* for them is worth nothing;" or "because what *looked* like a miracle was not a miracle;" no, but they say, "It is *impossible* they should have wrought miracles." Bring before the Protestant the largest mass of evidence and testimony in proof of the miraculous liquefac-tion of St. Januarius' blood at Naples, let him be urged by witnesses of the highest character, chemists of the first fame, circumstances the most favorable for the detection of imposture, coincidences and confirmations the most close, and minute, and indirect, he will not believe it; his First Principle *blocks* belief."

And again.

"Suppose you yourselves were once to see a

miracle, would you not feel that experience to be like passing a line? should you in consequence of it declare, "I never will believe another if I hear of one"? would it not, on the contrary, predispose you to listen to a new report? would you scoff at it, and call it priestcraft, for the reason that you had actually seen one with your own eyes? I think you would not; then, I ask, where is the difference of the argument, whether you have seen one or believe one?"

The great Cardinal is, of course, arguing with Protestants; as for unbelievers the argument goes back further than we have time to follow at present.

But what's the use of arguing? The cry of the world has ever been and ever will be: "Oh the chicanery, the wholesome fraud, the vile hypocrisy, the conscience-killing tyranny of Rome!"

———

Not many weeks ago, the President of a certain university not a thousand miles away, was standing in the fierce limelight of public criticism. Many things kind and unkind were said of him, many things true and untrue. His enemies threw mud too freely in his direction, while others were too servile in their adulation. One enthusiastic devotee went so far as to call the President in question the greatest man that California could boast of, the only man whose word had weight in the councils of the wise men of the East. This drew forth some stinging comments from the Sacramento *Bee*, which we read with great delight, though, as we have not the article at hand just now, we are unfortunately unable to quote. The *Bee* reminded the sycophant that there had been great men in California long before the university President saw its coasts, men in comparison with the depth of whose learning and wisdom, he is but commonplace shallowness. That is true; we could name some of these men ourselves without racking our memories. And we think the editor of the *Bee* is rather a greater man than that President, and exercises a greater and healthier influence on Californian opinion!

ANTHONY B. DIEPENBROCK, '08.

Death of Father Traverso

On the morning of March 25th, an honored and well-beloved guest of the college since nearly a year, passed away in the person of Rev. Sanctus Traverso, S. J. He was born in Genoa, on All-Saints Day, 1825, and entered the Society of Jesus in 1843, being hence at the time of his death in the 82nd year of his age, and the 64th of his religious life.

Fr. Traverso came to this country early in 1856 shortly after his ordination to the priesthood, and was at once appointed Professor of Latin, Greek, and other branches, at Santa Clara College. Here he remained until 1880, with a short interruption of two years, 1860–62, spent at St. Ignatius, San Francisco. In 1880 he was made one of the assistant pastors of St. Joseph's church, San Jose, and in that capacity he labored until, through old age, his strength deserted him.

Owing to the battered condition of St. Joseph's residence after the earthquake, Fr. Traverso came to spend his last days in the college where he had labored for over twenty years. As he was very hard of hearing, none of us boys came into personal contact with the venerable old man, although he a was very accustomed figure around the garden and vineyard. But though unacquainted, we were greatly edified nevertheless, for the Rosary in the fingers and the wonderfully sweet and serene expression on the face told us that he was a man whose thoughts were habitually in heaven.

He took to his bed on St. Joseph's day, March 19th, and quietly prepared for the end which he clearly saw was at hand. Almost his last words were: "Yes, Fr. Rector, I am going home this time."

Death of Father Sullivan

Another aged Jesuit Father, who had also been sent to Santa Clara by the calamity of last April, has breathed his last among us. Fr. Florence John Sullivan, S. J., was born in Frederick, Md., in June, 1823. In that famous old town he attended the Jesuit College of St. John's, where he made his preparatory studies. His higher studies he made at Georgetown, though he took no degree. When about nineteen years of age he entered the Jesuit Novitiate in Maryland, but after a stay of some months was compelled to leave on account of ill health. After this heavy disappointment he came to California as a pioneer, bringing his own stock and wagon over the plains. He located near Stockton, purchasing a farm there, and becoming in course of time, a successful and well-to-do farmer.

So highly was he esteemed by his fellow-citizens, that in appreciation of his worth, they elected him Judge. This office he held from 1850 to 1858. In the meantime, however, the old love for the Society of Jesus was strong within him, and reviving health revived his hopes of yet being counted among its members. To his great joy he was readmitted, and in February, 1858, began anew his noviceship at Santa Clara. The two years of noviceship over, he taught and perfected here for several years.

In 1864 he was ordained priest in St. Ignatius church by Rt. Rev. Joseph Alemany, O. P., first Archbishop of San Francisco.

Thence until 1866, he taught at Santa Clara, when he was transferred to St. Ignatius, San Francisco, where he labored until old age compelled him to quit active service. R. I. P.

Absence of the Fr. Rector

On April 1st., Rev. Fr. Rector left us for a five weeks tour in the East. He is accompanied by our former President, Fr. Kenna, S. J. The Reverend gentlemen are to visit the principal catholic colleges and universities in the Middle and Eastern States, as well as the most noted secular institutions of learning, such as Harvard, Yale, the University of Pennsylvania, and others. From all of these they will gather new and practical ideas about boarding colleges, which we hope before long to find materialized in the New Santa Clara College at Mountain View. The plans drawn up over a year ago were in San Francisco at the time of the fire and were, in consequence, entirely destroyed. But the earthquake had already impaired their value, as it necessitated many important changes both in the materials of construction and in the style of the buildings. Work will begin upon the new plans immediately after Fr. Rector's return, and it is hoped that the year 1907 will see the corner stone laid. In the meantime, the work of grading, laying out roads, etc., is going on vigorously.

St. Patrick's Eve Entaintment

The extraordinarily large crowd—so large that many people had to be refused entrance—that gathered in our hall on St. Patrick's eve, was treated to an entertainment of which the worst criticism that can be made was that some of the numbers were a trifle long-drawn-out. It consisted of several short numbers, followed by a one-act sketch, "The Kid," written by Martin V. Merle for the occasion. The Senior Quartette opened the entertainment in a skit entitled "A Little Bit of Everything," This was followed by a medley of Irish selections, stirringly rendered by Professor Austin Morris' Band. James R. Daly gave a recitation appropriate to the occasion. Walter Schmitz, in an illustrated song, was one of the features of the evening. Harry McKenzie and August Aguirre had the large crowd laughing with a clever melange of songs and jokes. The ever-welcome Porta trio, with their unique but beautiful instrument, the marimba, furnished a very satisfactory musical number. Mr. Geo. D. Schaffer followed with some well rendered selections on the mandolin. The main feature of the evening was Mr. Merle's "The Kid." This is a very powerful and cleverly written little episode of Arizona's cattle ranch life. Like all of Mr. Merle's dramatic work, the piece conveys a striking moral lesson, and in this respect is as good as a sermon, or better. The author was ably supported by those who took part James A. Bacigalupi as "Jimmie Oliver" was easily the star of the evening. James Twohy in the title role played a very difficult part and played it well. Harry McKenzie—"Shorty Jones," gave a happy rendition

of the happy-go-lucky cowboy. Leander Murphy as "McComas," the villian of the play, was "there" all the time, and Ivo Bogan, last but far from least, acted a natural college man as "Joe Randall." Music furnished by Professor Buehrer's Orchestra relieved the monotony of the intermission in a very agreeable manner.

The Weather

The memory of the proverbial oldest inhabitant would search in vain for a stretch of weather similar in quantity and quality to that which we have been enduring for the last three months. Twenty-four inches of rain tells the tale, when one reflects that 13 inches is about the average in this valley for the whole season. And the end is not yet. The perverse old weathercock is, at this moment of writing (March 24th), facing his brazen bill towards the sour and sunless South, and beckoning another wind-and-rain storm this way. Our games have been utterly deranged; the elements seem not to have a shred of respect for the dates we had solemnly laid down with Stanford and Berkeley, etc., and the only notice they pay them is to be more particularly violent on those days. Holidays without number, so to speak, are things that "might have been." However, things might be worse. The troop of bodily ills in the way of colds, fevers, etc., that generally come in the train of such weather as this, are notably absent, and though some of the Faculty were somewhat indisposed for a few days, yet, on the whole, we have been remarkably fortunate in this regard. And the Reading Room President tells us that of late there has been a wonderful run on the billiard tables, with a consequent swelling of his purse. " 'Tis an ill wind," etc.

"Passion Play"

The play will be presented on the following dates: Monday evening, May 13th, at 8 o'clock; Tuesday afternoon, May 14th, at 2 o'clock; Wednesday evening, May 15th, at 8 o'clock; Thursday evening, May 16th, at 8 o'clock; Saturday afternoon, May 18th, at 2 o'clock; Saturday evening, May 18th, at 8 o'clock.

Nothing will be left undone that can make this third production of Santa Clara's Passion Play eclipse its predecessors. New and elaborate scenery has been painted by Michael O'Sullivan, gorgeous costumes and new armor are being prepared, and magnificent light effects have been designed by the presiding electrician, Rev. Richard Bell, S. J.

The music will be a special feature. Mr. Buehrer, the director, recently spent a year in Europe, where he made a study of religious music appropriate to this dramatic masterpiece. The singing will be rendered by a double quartette of trained voices, with chorus, and accompanied by a large pipe organ and orchestra.

The following is the personnel of Senior Dramatic Club, which is giving its best efforts to the successful presentation of the play.

Geo. Golden Fox, S. J., president; Martin V. Merle, '07, stage director; August M. Aguirre, '07, stage manager; J. Walter Schmitz, '07, assistant stage manager; the Rev. Richard H. Bell, S. J., electrician; C. Kilburn, '08, assistant electrician; J. Daniel McKay, '07, business manager; H, George Casey, '07, Floyd E. Allen, '07, assistant business managers; Lester Walter, '09, property-master; Frank Cuda, '11, Daniel Tadish, assistant property-masters; Harry A. J. McKenzie, '08, press agent; James F. Twohy, '07, Robert E. Fitzgerald, '07, Harold R. Yoacham, '11, press agents.

CAST OF CHARACTERS

The cast of the play, which is in ten acts, follows:

Sadoc, Shadrach, Zorbiel, Shepherds of Bethlehem—George H. Casey, Harry A. J. McKenzie, Ivo G. Bogan.

Angels of the Lord—Lewis Byington Ford and Frank J. Warren.

Ammon, Dathian (emissaries of King Herod)—Floyd E. Allen, Joseph Farry.

A Hindoo; an Egyptian, a Persian (three kings or wise men from the East) —Jose Gazton, George J. Hall, Charles Bercht.

First Citizen, Second Citizen, of Judea —George Mayerle, James Carroll.

Thamar, Captain Palace of King Herod—John B. Shea.

Archelaus, Son of Herod I—Gerald P. Beaumont.

Athias, a Rich Young Publican—James F. Twohy.

Jechonias, His Father—James Bacigalupi.

King Herod I, Ruler of Judea—Michael Griffith.

An Old Man—Paul Troplong.

An Officer in Herold's Palace—Cornelius Mullen.

Joshua, Captain Caiphas Palace—Bernard Budde.

Caiphas, Nathaniel, Annas (high priests of Jerusalem)—William McKagney, Edmund Lowe, Harry Birmingham.

Boas, Esrom, Abiron (merchants of the temple)—Harry A. J. McKenzie, Frank Heffernan, H. George Casey.

Matthew, Judas, Thomas, John, Andrew, Peter, James the Less, James the Greater, Philip, Bartholomew, Thaddeus, Simon (the twelve disciples)—James F. Twohy, John J. Ivancovich, Cornelius V. Mullen, James F. Daly, Edmund Simard, August M. Aguirre, Edgar Nolan, James Whiting, George Duffy, Mervyn M. Shafer. James Carroll, Harold R. Yoacham.

Pontius Pilate, Roman Governor of Jerusalem —Lee J. Murphy.

Priests, Shepherds, Soldiers, Angels, Populace, etc.

Junior Dramatic Notes

The by-gone month of March has watched with interest and complacency the meetings held within the walls of the J. D. S. The zeal and devotion of the numbers were evidenced by the fact that when Cyril J. Smith was dis-covered stuffing the ballot box it was moved that he should be arraigned before the tribunal of Justice.

The "Society" placed its cause in the hands of the clear-headed and cool Ernest Watson, while the accused sought refuge in the fluent and witty Robt. McCabe, closely seconded by Joseph Sheean. The jury impaneled, the witnesses were called and recalled to the stand whenever the prosecuting attorney or defending entertained the slightest hope of extorting further damaging evidence.

The trial was extremely one-sided,—the odds favoring the prosecution. The attorneys for the defense had no positive proof whatever to work upon, their only hope being in leading their witnesses through a labyrinth of pointed questions, and thus endeavoring to show the jury that their testimony was nothing but wheedle and barrican.

They tried hard to convince the jury who remained firm and staunch in their convictions. Mr. Marcel Lohse was appointed foreman of the jury, who returned the verdict of "Guilty," but recommended the clever Cyril to the mercy of the Court.

Mr. G. G. Fox, S. J. was called upon to grace the trial with his presence and act in capacity of Judge. His Honor expressed himself highly pleased with the proceeding and said it caused him deep pain to inflict punishment on the guilty party. But Cyril received it like a man and still bobs up serenely

A recent debate, "Resolved: That Phonetic spelling should be universally adopted," has proved to us that into our midst we have admitted a very valuable member in the person Mr. Hirst. Assuming the negative half of the question, seemingly the worst side, his wealth of knowledge and facileness of speech brought him out of the mixup with glowing colors: and now in our opinion Phonetic spelling should be universally adopted.

"Resolved: That the Japanese Immigration to these United States should be restricted," was a debate so cleverly and masterly argued that the Society has yet witnessed nothing its equal. And what Californian could remain phlegmatic and indifferent in such a sanguine question? On this occasion two newly admitted members made their debut, Mr. M. Lohse and Mr. L. Ford. The former speaker was pointed, trenchant and filled with pectus. But he met his equal in the person of Mr. Ford. His man's manner, logical conclusions, and ready eloquence made it difficult to decide which of the two was the better.

Sad to state that the month of March could not travel on its way without robbing us of two members. The alluring magnetic power of the House of Philhistorians was too great a strain for such seasoned members as Mr. Watson and Mr. Daly. With a few words of gratitude and devotion to the J. D. S. they took their leave. By the departure of Mr. Daly the office of Secretary was vacated, but without much ado a plebiscitum put Mr. Barry in the position.

By this move the office of Librarian was left without an incumbent. It was, however, soon filled by Mr. Robt. Flood. The fact that "Jim" does not take bookkeeping will not lessen our confidence, for we have discovered in him a knack for keeping things straight.

Besides the above mentioned Messrs. Ford and Lohse we enrolled Messrs. E. Nolting, C. Degnan, and L. Newton, all of whom, we have the highest hopes, will fill creditably the positions of those who have left us with a God-speed and gone over to the Philhistoric majority.

MERVYN S. SHAFER, '09.

It was brought home to me lately that there is a special advantage in being an alumnus of a Jesuit College, and one which we may be perhaps inclined to overlook. The advantage consists in this, that when one is closely connected with one Jesuit institution, he is in a way allied to them all. A graduate of Santa Clara, for instance, cannot possibly feel that he is a perfect stranger, or entirely an "outsider" when he visits St. Louis University, or Georgetown, or Fordham. And if he were to feel that way, the warm reception—in the best sense of the expression—that he should receive when it were discovered that he was a Santa Clara "boy," would teach him better. During the past six months Mr. Merle, A. M., '06, had been travelling throughout the Middle and New England States in connection with his play, The Light Eternal. He says that in the Jesuit colleges on his route, he felt almost as much at home as he does at his favorite Santa Clara. Again and again he would be visited in the green room by Jesuit alumni or under-graduates who just dropped in to see him, they said, as he was a Santa Clara boy, and to offer him their congratulations. On the strength of this bond, the Sodality Association of St. Francis Xavier's, New York, sent him an invitation to their annual banquet. As Mr. Merle was editor of THE REDWOOD for two years, we take a special pleasure in thanking our fellow collegians for their kindness and courtesy.

It is with pleasure that we note the re-election of John G. Covert, B. S. '91, as Superior Judge of King's County, California. Mr. Covert has already held this office for six years, which is a distinct proof of his ability.

Joseph Carey, A. B. '92, M. A. '93, for a number of years attorney for the New York Life Insurance Company in Chicago, is now in Tonapah, Nevada, engaged in large mining interests, besides attending to a very extensive law practice.

James V. Comerford, ex-'05, who after leaving here joined the ranks of the

pedagogues, is now principal of the Virginia City High School, Nevada. Whilst this information was slow in coming to us, our old friend having received the position about a year ago, still better late than never are our congratulations. Light fall upon him the trials of the schoolmaster!

James Flynn, Com. '99, A. B. '01, and James P. Ennis, Com. '88, are also in the Sage Brush State. Mr. Flynn being employed in Virginia City by the C. and C. Mining Company, and Mr. Ennis at Gold Hill by the Yellow Jacket Mining Company.

The Alumni editor had an interview not long ago with Hon. J. J. Barrett, Com, '90, B. S. '91, in his elegant Law offices in the James Flood Building, San Francisco. Mr, Barrett, noted for his persevering efforts while at college, carried his stick-to-it-iveness with him to the outside world with the result that it was not long before he attained a wide-spread reputation and an exceptionally lucrative and extensive practice.

When the duties of Mr. Barrett are less arduous, it is the Alumni editor's intention to trouble him for a retrospect of the days spent within Santa Clara, and also of his achievements after leaving his Alma Mater.

John O. McElroy, S. M. '05, found time to break away from his law studies to make the Annual Retreat at his Alma Mater. John is at present in the office of the ex-District Attorney of San Francisco, Lewis F. Byington, B. S. '84,

and is also attending Hasting's College of Law.

Thomas Ena, ex-'08, is now in Reno, Nevada, employed as draughtsman by the Reno Mill and Lumber Company. While at Santa Clara Tom came into enviable artistic prominence by his clever sketches for a little hand-written newspaper that used to be pasted up weekly upon the First Division bulletin board.

With delight do we note the rapid advancement of Louis Magee, ex-'08. Not long ago he secured a position with the Sparks-Humphrey Meat Co, at Beckwith, Nevada. By hard work he soon became Assistant Manager of the office, and from recent reports promotion is to fall to him again.

"Louie" for three years was the star quarter-back of Santa Clara, and it was principally on account of his generalship that the famous 1902 eleven achieved such great success. He has best wishes from us all and we hope that he may keep going toward the top with the same speed as he often circled an end on a quarter-back run.

The following "old boys" were numbered among the visitors at Santa Clara during the past month:

Rev. William Fleming, A. B. '97, now at Sacred Heart Church, San Francisco.

Joseph Farry, A. B. '97, practicing law in San Francisco.

William J. Maher, Com. '05, bookkeeper for the Mahon Jewelry Company, San Francisco.

HARRY P. BRODERICK, '08,

If we are to judge of the literary merit of a college by the magazine which represents it—and what could constitute a better test?—the standing of Columbia University must be very high indeed. For there is not a single article in *The Columbia Monthly* for February which we did not read with the greatest interest and pleasure. The prose is particularly fine, and we consider "The Road to Yesterday" to be the most interesting essay of the month. Although in its poetry *The Monthly* falls a little below the high standard set by its prose, yet even this is what we style good verse.

"An Idyl of Late Autumn" has a rather common-place plot but the charm and novelty of its setting lend it an attractiveness which the most novel plot in the world could never give. The greatest though not the only charm of "Rococo" lies in the delicately hinted comparison between the poor street fakir and his more fortunate companion. We have been following "The Further Adventures of Baron Munchausen" with the keenest interest, and although we were exceedingly sorry to learn of the unfortunate accident which cut off so valuable a life, nevertheless we must congratulate Mr. Hawley on the unusual and startling manner of his character's demise.

"The Question Of His Influence" in *The Dartmouth Magazine* for March contains the plot for a fine story. If it were only condensed about one-half, this would easily be one of the most readable stories of the month, and even as it stands it merits attention. "The Catching of the Mail" is the same old story which we used to enjoy so much in our childhood. The "Kid's" only chance was to catch the mail and of course he caught it. We felt sure he would. As for "Atwood's Love Affair," well, it is just about twice as silly as its title would indicate. We are glad of one thing though, Atwood didn't get her. "The Camper's Joke" is probably the best bit of fiction in the magazine. It is a little story but it contains a great deal. If some of the idiotic practical jokers who infest every school could read this it would surely do them no harm and might—though we confess we doubt it—result in a great deal of good.

We have met nothing in our recent

exchanges which created such an interest among the members of the staff as the first of the "Letters From an Undergrad to His Dad" in *The Georgetown College Journal* for February. This letter is written in a delightfully slangy style which George Horace Lorrimer has made so well known in his "Letters From a Self-Made Merchant to His Son" and contains more solid fun in a page and a half than many a humorous story of a more pretentious character contains in a dozen.

"Caxton," in the same magazine, is a good detective story with a real thrill at the end in the form of an unexpected surprise. The murdered man wasn't murdered at all. We have only one fault to find with it. The criminals leave a battered corpee lying around and nobody takes the trouble to tell us whose it is or where it comes from. In fact nobody seems to care.

"A Valentine for Two," in *The Tattler* from Randolph-Macon Woman's College is a strong, well-written love story. We had come to think that a woman's hero was a paragon of manly virtue and that her heroine was constructed with a thousand flaws. Yet here we have a real man with a man's weakness and a real woman with a wsman's strength. The writer, who does not sign her name, handles her characters with the snbtlest skill. Decidedly this is the best article of any kind in *The Tattler*. The authoress of "A Fable For Alumnae" does well to apologize to Carolyn Wells for her work falls far short of its witty model. "After College—what?" is a rather long winded

love story told through the medium of a girl's correspondence. The writer—she signs herself "L. '06"—makes her hero who is a doctor, write, "I'm needed here, but pshaw! what's a day off, a dollar or two and *even a life or two* compared with the pleasure of seeing you?" Don't you think this is going a little too far, Miss "L. '06"? We're sure we do.

The opening number of *The Columbia*, published by the American students of Fribourg University, demands our recognition. This visitor from over the seas is a very creditable production, and its verse especially is to be admired. "Light Of Light" is so good that we would like to quote it if its length allowed. As it is, we have contented ourselves with a little poem which we found at the head of "Alumni Notes." The reader can judge of its merit for himself.

Congratulations, Columbia, and success.

May this New Year with kindly hand
Bring sunny days and golden hours,
And round thy heart with magic wand
Wreathe virtue's noblest, sweetest flowers.

May this New Year with heavenly art
Repress the sufferer's restless sigh.
And cheer the fevered, lonely heart
And waken hopes that never die.
> L. A., in *The Columbia.*

THE EXILE

No one to call thy countryman, no home
Whither to roam;
No flag to call thy nation's and no strand
Thy native land;
Nothing in common with those round thee, save
The waiting grave.
LaFayette Lentz Butler, in *The Nassau Lit*

MAURICE T. DOOLING, JR. '09

Santa Clara 2—California 1

The third game with California was played the 28th of February on California's diamond. Both nines displayed good form, playing consistently and well, but the Red and White played a much superior game both in fielding and head work, in both of which elements, especially the latter, can be seen the thorough training given them by Coach Byrnes.

Santa Clara found Ghirardelli, who in this game made his first appearance against us, no harder to hit than Jordan.

We secured quite a few safe bingles off his delivery. He was given very good support by his team-mates and if the Californians could hit as well as they field they would have a larger percentage of games won.

On our side Kilburn pitched a good game. He had nearly perfect control, and in one or two tight places extricated himself in the best possible manner. To add to his good record he allowed no stolen bases. He was given fine support, Broderick and Mervyn Shafer predominating in this respect.

California held the Red and White down until the sixth inning when Lappin led off with a healthy souse which the pitcher unluckily got in the way of, or rather couldn't get out of the way of, thus robbing Husky of first. Broderick was hit by Ghirardelli. Later Ghirardelli overthrew to first in his anxiety to dispose of our first baseman, with the result that he meandered to second. On Salberg's drive, Broderick scored. The two men following were retired by the good fielding of the Berkeleyites.

In California's part of the inning, Causely hit to Salberg and was forced to second by Heister walking. Wulzen slammed the ball to left field and stopped running on second. Causely scored.

Lappin was the author of the second run which was made in the ninth. He hit to left field and was sent to the next bag by Broderick's hit and scored on the error of California's third baseman. Watson and Mervyn Shafer were retired on flies to third base and center field.

California gathered all her energies for a last effort but was unable to tie the score.

SANTA CLARA

	AB	R	H	PO	A	E
Twohy, 2b.	4	0	1	.4	1	1
Shafer, A., ss	4	0	1	4	4	0
Freine, 3b............	4	0	0	0	4	0
Lappin, lf	3	1	2	1	0	0
Broderick, 1b........	2	1	1	10	1	0
Salsburg, cf..........	3	0	1	1	0	0
Watson, rf...........	3	0	0	0	0	0
Shafer, M., c	4	0	1	7	2	0
Kilburn, p...........	4	0	1	0	0	0
Total.......	31	2	8	27	12	1

CALIFORNIA

	AB	R	BH	PO	A	E
Reid, 2b........	4	0	0	0	1	1
Causley, ss	3	1	2	2	1	2
Heister, 3b	3	0	2	2	1	2
Wulzen, 1b..........	4	0	1	11	0	0
Miller, lf.............	4	0	0	2	0	0
Smith, rf	2	0	0	1	0	0
Schaefer, c	4	0	1	5	1	0
Sweezy, cf..........	3	0	1	3	1	0
Ghiradelli, p	3	0	0	1	5	0
Total.......	30	1	5	27	10	5

RUNS AND HITS BY INNINGS

Santa Clara 0 0 0 0 0 1 0 1 0
　　　Hits 1 2 0 1 1 1 2 1 0
California 0 0 0 0 0 1 0 0 0
　　　Hits 0 0 0 1 0 2 1 0 1

Two base hits, Wulzen. Stolen bases, Santa Clara, 5. Left on bases, Santa Clara, 9; California, 2. Base on balls, off Kilburn, 2; off Ghiradelli, 4. Struck out by Kilburn, 4; by Ghiradelli, 5. Hit by pitched ball, Broderick. Umpire, McKenne. Scorer, McKenzie. Time of game, one hour and forty minutes.

Santa Clara 12—All Stars 5

Santa Clara met and defeated the renowned California All Stars on the college diamond on March 3d. The All Stars had men of great reputation in ball circles, the names of such celebrities as Joe Nealon, Cincinnati's big first baseman, "Heinie" Kruge, Shimpf, Heitmuller, Eagan, and Bliss gracing their line-up.

Kilburn pitched in good style for the college, and for the most part he only allowed the All Stars hits that were easily fielded. He was given good support by his mates who played together with perfect team work. Pudgy Shafer played second base for Twohy who was out of the game with a bad ankle and he put up a good consistent game.

Eagan made the first run ot the game in the fourth inning. In the fifth the All Stars managed to cross four men over the plate making the score five to nothing in their favor. But though a little discouraged, we set our jaws determinedly and picked up the bat. A regular shower of hits was the result. We counted up to seven before we got out of breath, and most of them were good generous souses. Broderick, the first man up, walked. Soon after he was brought home by a hit by Byrnes. Following this good example his teammates by various means raced around the plates. From a baseball game it degenerated to a joyous merry-go round with the All Stars furnishing the music. When the merry-go-round stopped the scorer counted the tickets at the home plate and found them to amount to seven—a run for each hit.

In the seventh inning the merry-go-round again started, but this time the scorer collected only five tickets. This ended the runs.

ALL STARS

	AB	R	BH	PO	A	E
Smith, cf	3	1	0	1	0	2
Eagan, ss	2	1	1	3	2	1
Heitmuller, lf	2	0	1	2	1	0
Nealon, 1b	4	0	1	9	0	1
Kruge, 3b	4	0	1	1	4	0
Bliss, c	3	0	1	4	2	0
Shimpp, p	2	1	0	0	3	0
Widdkerr, rf	1	1	0	0	0	1
Miller, 2b	3	1	0	0	0	0
Totals	24	5	5	20	12	5

SANTA CLARA

	AB	R	BH	PO	A	E
A. Shafer, ss	5	1	1	5	1	1
M. Shafer, 2b	5	1	1	1	2	0
Friene, 3b	4	1	1	2	0	0
Collins, cf	3	2	2	3	0	0
Lappin, lf	4	1	1	2	0	0
Broderick, 1b	1	2	1	6	0	1
Salsburg, rf	4	1	2	0	0	0
Byrnes, c	4	1	2	4	1	0
Kilburn, p	4	2	3	5	1	0
Totals	34	12	14	28	5	2

RUNS AND HITS BY INNINGS.

All Stars 0 0 0 1 4 0 0
Base hits 0 0 0 2 3 0 0
Santa Clara ... 0 0 0 0 7 0 0 0
Base hits 0 0 0 0 7 0 1 6

Stolen bases, All Stars, 2; Santa Clara, 2. Double plays, Friene to Kilburn to Broderick. Hit by pitched ball, Friene. Struck out by Shimpf, 3; by Kilburn, 2. Umpire Knell. Scorer, H. McKenzie. Time of game, one hour and forty minutes.

Santa Clara 4—Stanford 3

March the 9th saw the first game of our second series with Stanford played at Santa Clara. It resulted in a victory for us, although the team was weakened on account of Twohy's inability to play because of a sprained ankle. Little Salberg filled the vacant place very satisfactorily.

Stanford started the ball rolling when Owen made a run in the first, whereas it was not until the ninth inning that the Red and White succeeded in scoring. With two men out, Broderick knocked the ball into the trees and raced home. The tenth and eleventh were unproductive of any runs for either side, both Santa Clara and Stanford playing close ball.

In the twelfth inning, Ganong, catcher for Stanford, was able to get around the four sacks and make a tally, and Thiele soon after duplicated the performance, making the score three to one in Stanford's favor. Scott luckily was retired.

Of our performance at the bat this inning, the score above has already hinted the story. Salberg walked, and later took second on an overthrow to first. Peters retired on a fly to left field. Twohy batted for Pudgy Shafer. Thiele gave Twohy first as a compliment. Kilburn laid the ball down to Cadwalder who juggled it too long to catch him, at the same time allowing Salberg to cross the rubber. Twohy on second from Kilburn's drive stole third and tallied on Arthur Shafer's hit. Kilburn took second and third on a wild overthrow to first. Lappin brought him home on his hit to left field. Lappin was later caught off first. Here is the tabulated performance:

STANFORD

	AB	R	BH	PO	A	E
Scott, rf	5	0	1	0	1	0
Owen, lf	5	1	0	4	1	0
Presley, 1b	5	0	2	20	1	0
Fenton, 3b	4	0	1	1	4	0
Samson, 2b	5	0	2	3	4	0
Wirt, cf	5	0	0	2	0	0
Ganong, c	3	1	0	5	3	0
Goodell, p	2	0	0	0	.1	0
Cadwalder, ss	3	0	1	0	9	1
Thiele, p	1	1	0	0	3	1
Total	38	3	*7	35	27	2

SANTA CLARA

	AB	R	BH	PO	A	E
A. Shafer	5	0	2	4	2	1
Lappin, lf	5	0	2	1	1	1
Friene, 3b	5	0	1	4	5	1
Watson, rf	5	0	1	0	0	0
Broderick, 1b	5	1	3	10	0	1
Salberg, 2b	4	1	1	5	1	0
Peters, cf	5	0	0	1	0	0
M. Shafer, c	3	0	0	9	2	0
Kilburn, p	5	1	2	2	5	0
†Twohy	0	1	0	0	0	0
	42	4	12	36	16	4

RUNS AND HITS BY INNINGS

Stanford ....1 0 0 0 0 0 0 0 0 2— 3
Base hits ...3 0 0 0 2 0 0 0 0 2— 7
S. C.............0 0 0 0 0 0 1 0 0 3— 4
Base hits ...1 1 1 2 0 1 0 2 1 1 1—13

SUMMARY

Three base hits, Friene. Home run, Broderick. Sacrifice hits, Goodell, A. Shafer and Lappin. Stolen bases, Presley, Samson, Cadwallader, A. Shafer (2), Broderick. Innings pitched in, Kilburn, 12; Goodell, 7; Thiele, 5. Base on balls, off Kilburn, 5; off Thiele 1. Double plays, Owen to Presley. Struck out, by Kilburn, 9; by Thiele, 4. Wild pitches, Kilburn. Hit by pitcher, M. Shafer, Scott, Goodell, Cadwallader. Umpires, Collins and Sales. Scorer, McKenzie. Time of game, 2 hours and 50 minutes.

*Two out when winning run was scored.

†Twohy batted for M. Shafer in twelfth inning.

Santa Clara 6, Stanford 4

We played the second game of the series with Stanford, March 13th, at the College, with a victory for us to the tune of 6 to 4. The game was close at times but the College outplayed throughout the wearers of the Cardinal.

In the first, Stanford took the initiative. Scott made first on a hit to short-stop, took second on a wild throw, stole third, and scored on Kilburn's error. Of the other men, Kilburn struck out two and the rest were easily disposed of by the infield. In Santa Clara's half Twohy hit to Cadawalder who threw him out. Arthur Shafer beat a chance to shortstop, took second without permission, third on Freine's two-bagger. Lappin hit the air three times; Broderick reached first on Owen's error; Shafer and Freine went home on the first baseman's error; Watson hit to Owen, who fumbled it, and let him sneak to first and Broderick take a tally. Meanwhile Watson appropriated second. Salberg fanned.

In the second Thiele and Cadawalder brought in two runs for Stanford, thus tying the score. Santa Clara did not retaliate until the the fifth when she collected three runs and presented them to the scorer in a bunch. Twohy led off with a drive to Cadawalder, who played with it. A. Shafer hit to left field sending Twohy to second; Shafer was caught off first; Freine hit the ball and reached first on Owen's error; while Twohy took advantage of it and raced to third. Freine stole second.

Lappin made a beautiful hit to left field just inside the foul line scoring Twohy and Freine, and then took second when no one was looking. Broderick bowed to the crowd and took three, while Lappin went in. Watson's hit to Fenton ended the fireworks.

Stanford made a gallant effort in the ninth to tie the score but in vain. The winning of the game made us victors of the second series.

STANFORD

	AB	R	BH	PO	A	E
Scott, lf	4	1	1	0	0	0
Owen, 1 b	5	0	1	15	3	3
Presley, c	5	0	3	5	3	0
Fenton, 3 b	4	1	1	1	4	0
Sampson, 2 b	4	0	1	0	4	0
Gore, r f	4	0	2	0	0	0
Wirt, c f	5	0	0	1	0	0
Witman, p	3	1	1	1	0	0
Cadwalder, ss	4	1	1	0	1	3
Totals	38	4	4	23	5	6

SANTA CLARA

	AB	R	BH	PO	A	E
Twohy, 2b	4	1	0	2	4	0
Shafer, ss	3	1	0	3	2	3
Freine, 3b	4	2	2	1	1	1
Lappin, lf	3	1	1	3	0	0
Broderick, 1b	3	1	1	7	2	0
Watson r f	4	0	0	2	1	0
Salberg, cf	4	0	1	2	0	0
M. Shafer, c	3	0	0	6	0	0
Kilburn p	4	0	0	1	2	1
Totals	29	6	5	27	12	5

RUNS AND HITS BY INNINGS

Stanford .....1 2 0 0 0 0 0 0—4
Base hits ..2 2 1 2 0 0 1 1 2—11
Santa Clara...3 0 0 0 3 0 0 0 0—6
Base hits....1 0 0 0 2 0 0 1 1—5

SUMMARY

Three Base Hits, Broderick; Two Base Hits, Freinc; Sacrifice Hits, A. Shafer; Sampson and Gore; Stolen Bases, Santa Clara 6, Stanford 1; Left on Bases, Santa Clara 6, Stanford 13; Base on Balls, off Witman 4; off Kilburn 2; Struck out by Witman 6; by Kilburn 5. Umpire, C. Doyle. Scorer, H. A. Kenzie. Time of game two hours.

Basketball

On account of the bad weather prevailing for the last month no games have been played, but the team has been practicing assiduously at every possible opportunity; with the result that now they are in a good condition to give any team a hard fight.

The basket ball grounds on the S. A. A. field have been improved and leveled so that now it is as fast a ground as any in the vicinity. Being composed of sandy soil it never becomes muddy and it dries up very rapidly. In the next issue we shall, we hope, be able to present some of the details of the coming games.

Tennis

Misfortune has been a frequent visitor at the doors of the tennis club. The last time it appeared, it assumed the shape of our good Father Minister, who, to save some valuable pipe of unknown antiquity, directed Manuel to search for it. His explorations led him into the territory of the tennis club. Manuel excavated a large part of the court in his vain search and afterwards in the turmoil of his business affairs forgot to return the court to the good condition in which he found it.

The officers of the tennis club, ably assisted by F. Cuda and H. Gallagher, set to work with firm determination to put the court in good condition, with the gratifying outcome that much of the excavated debris has been returned to its proper place and that most of tne alfalfa crop, which was becoming ripe, has been mowed down.

As things are now, it seems safe to predict that the court will be occupied by jumping players and bouncing balls a good while before the Santa Clara College tennis season starts. It has been given out officially by Harold Mc-Lane that the tournament will take place towards the latter part of April so that every one may have a chance to register and get into form.

Second Division Athletics

The western section of Santa Clara's athletic campus has had its ardor considerably dampened by the late interminable rains. The Junior team had been looking forward to trips in various directions, but the weather has postponed them. We trust, however, it is nothing worse than a postponement, and that eventually the baseball expeditions will come to pass. The team has, notwithstanding, not been entirely idle, but between showers it has played a number of practice games with nines made up from first and second teams, in which the good talent that it possesses, and the result of coach Collins' strenuous training were always in evidence. In one of these games not a single hit was registered off Johnny Jones' delivery.

A team that already rivals the Junior team has lately been organized under the energetic captaincy of Joseph Sheean. It is called "The Outlaws," and its personnel is the following: Gallager, p.; Irilarry, c.; Sheean, 1b.; Mor-

aghan, 2b; McCabe, s. s.; Watson, 3b; O'Rourke, l. f.; Hogan, c. f.; Putnam, r. f.; Coppa, sub. p.; Bowie, Basler, subs.

The coach is "Husky" Lappin, the star outfielder of the First. How effective his work is may be gathered from the fact that although a very late arrival in balldom, the team, played the seasoned and self-satisfied Juniors and held them down to a tie score. There are other games coming of course, for the rivalry is keen, when The Outlaws intend to untie the score as well as the Junior's laurels.

No account of athletics would be complete without a mention of the little Angelus team. This nine is made up of youngsters around thirteen years of age, and is under the generalship of Harry Curry. Harry has enough ginger and ambition in him to supply a regiment, and so we must not be surprised to hear that their latest victory, that over Los Gatos B. I. C., reads 39 runs to 9. These are they: Prindeville, c; Balish, p; McCord, 1b; Curry, 2b; Jeffress, ss; Wickersham, 3b: Broderick, lf; Flood, cf; Turronet, rf; O'Brien, sub. The team is under the managership of Mr. C. F. Walsh, S. J.

Fr. Foote, S. J., our Vice-President, has lately appeared in the character of a baseball magnate, and it is now manager of a team known as the "All Stars." A number of games are on the schedule, and that they will all spell victory for the All Stars cannot be doubted when it can count upon such players as Clair Wilson, R. Yorke, Castruccio, and such a captain as F. Warren.

CARLOS K. McCLATCHY, '10·

THE REDWOOD

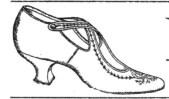

THE
REDWOOD

MAY, 1907

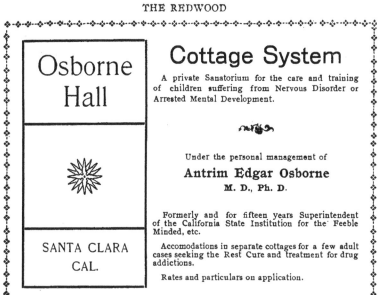

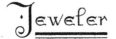

Contents.

Nace Printing Co.   Santa Clara, Cal.

Photo by Bushnell

THE HOUSE OF PHILHISTORIANS.

1.—J. C. Twohy. 2.—E. H. Wood. 3.—A. B. Diepenbrock. 4.—F. W. Dozier. 5.—J. V. Carroll. 6.—J. P. Degnan. 7.—R. J. Birmingham. 8.—R. S. Archbold. 9.—E. V. Nolan. 10.—H. A. McLane 11—C. K. McClatchy. 12.—J. R. Daly. 13.—E. P. Watson. 14.—E. S. Lowe. 15.—J. W. Maltman. 16.—Rev. P. J. Foote, S. J., Speaker. 17.—C. V. Mullen. 18.—J. M. Collins, Librarian. 19.—R. J. McClatchy. 20.—J. D. Peters. 21.—A. M. Donovan. 22.—G. J. Hall. 23.—H. R. Yoacham. 24.—H. P. Broderick, Clerk. 25.—T. F. Farrell. 26.—James C. Lappin, Treasurer. 27.—M. T. Dooling.

The Redwood.

Entered Dec. 18, 1902, at Santa Clara, Calif. as second-class matter, under Act of Congress of March 3, 1879.

VOL. VI.   SANTA CLARA, CAL., MAY 1907.   No. 8

LOST

The night is dark,
        The billows roar,
The tiny bark
That left the friendly shore,
        Returns no more.

The greedy wave
        Has caught his prey!
—A nameless grave
Beneath the glimmering spray,
        Ere break of day.

                        George J. Hall, '08.

WILLIAM WORDSWORTH--THE EXCURSION

"He found us when the age had bound
Our souls in its benumbing round;
He spoke and loosed our hearts in tears.

Our youth returned, for there was shed
Our spirits that had long been dead,
Spirits dried up and closely furled,
The freshness of an early world.

Speaking of literary criticism Goethe once said "if you would understand an author you must understand his age," and no words are more truly typical of the age in which they were written than those of Wm. Wordsworth. Europe had just undergone those cataclysms which shook her social structure to the foundations, in the throes of Revolution. France, Germany, Switzerland and even England had each suffered in their turn and were now recovering from the shock of war. There had been a decided change in the political situations throughout the world. A handful of colonies had in the Northern Continent of America formed themselves into the most powerful and progressive of states. The events which had occurred in France and which had overthrown that ancient monarchy and all the ordering of which that monarchy had been the sustaining keystone, had caused echoing convulsions throughout the Continent of Europe. New, more equal, and more humane laws, were formed, and the people became a power. Poetry, and indeed literature in general, underwent a corresponding change in the first moments of peace which had

followed upon the alarms of war and the terrors of revolution. Poetry, erstwhile the obedient interpreter of the empty moods of the upper classes, the vain nobility of a vainglorious monarchial system, had done her little turn "tricked out in court dress and rapier" and now began to

"Find tongues in trees, books in the running brooks
Sermons in stones and good in everything."

Wordsworth's course during all these events, and the influences they had on him and on his works, is not hard to trace. Briefly his history. Born at Rydal Mount in Cumberland, April 7, 1770, his parents not very well to do, he passed his early life in rather straightened circumstances, but was afforded a liberal education by his uncles who were quick to perceive signs of his genius. The education began in the grammar school at Hawkshead, he finished at Cambridge where he took his degree in the year 1791. For a time he drifted about rather aimlessly, undecided as to a career. His deeply religious nature, which is manifested in all his writings, caused him for a time to contemplate the ministry, but deeming himself unworthy, he settled upon a military life as preferable to the other alternative of law. Meanwhile he travelled, and began unconsciously to acquire in his wanderings through Europe material and color for his later works. France was no longer at the top of her golden hours when he visited that country in 1791-'92. The flames of Revolution were beginning to burn, the September massacres already filled the air with terror. Wordsworth's belief in "people's rights" and hatred of oppression needed but his military spirit to urge him to take common cause with the Girondists, and naught but the earnest dissuasions of his friends held him from this fatal step and caused him to return to England in '93. Two years later, he began the "Excursion."

The Excursion is beyond a doubt the best and most representative of the works produced in that period of the so called Metaphysical poetry. Most, indeed all, of the characters, the Wanderer, the Solitary, the Pastor, the Poet himself, are to be found in real life, in that station of life made popular by the flourishing spirit of Revolution. Wordsworth wrote, as he himself tells us, with the idea of producing a something that would live, a work which would exist on its own merits as an interpreter of life, of vibrant human emotions, and he believed that such life could nowhere be found more truly exemplified or more faithfully portrayed than in the humbler (though really higher class), the peasantry and farmers of the day. The Excursion was to have been but the middle link of three connected poems, "The Prelude," "The Excursion," and "The Solitary," making in all his contemplated masterpiece, which he was to have named "The Recluse." The Prelude dealt with the development of the Poet, his life told by himself with

minute observations upon those formative influences which go so far toward the determination of character; the Excursion follows with the Poet's observations on the different stations of life, while the Solitary would have taught the reflections following those observations. Of these, the third was never completed. The Prelude indeed was published and is the story of Wordsworth's own life, but it is with the connecting link, the most important of the three, for such it seems, that we have most to deal at present.

As a work, viewed in its entirety, it is much too complex and comprehensive to admit of any but a most cursory treatment in an article of such a nature and length as the present. Perhaps it would be wisest to pass hurriedly over the entire poem, giving a brief synopsis, then enter more into detail into some one portion deserving of more special mention.

Like Robert Boyle, who in the preface to his Occasional Reflections, said concerning spiritual thought that it mattered not "from how low a theme soever it takes its rise, being like Jacob's ladder, whereof though the foot cleaved on the earth, the top reached up to heaven," Wordsworth seems to regard no subject as too lowly for his purpose. The first book, the Wanderer, deals with the meeting of the Poet with his old friend, the Wanderer himself, the chief figure in the work that follows. He is from a lowly source, born of humble Scottish parents, raised as a shepherd, and occupying his mind with poetry while in pursuit of his lonely duties.

"Oh then, what soul was his, when on the tops
Of the high mountains, he beheld the sun
Rise up and bathe the world in light. He looked
Ocean and earth, the solid frame of earth
And ocean's liquid mass beneath him lay
In gladness and deep joy. The clouds were touched
And on their silent faces did he read
Unutterable love. Sound needed none,
Nor any voice of joy; his spirit drank
The spectacle: sensation, soul, and form
All melted unto him: they swallowed up
His animal being: in them did he live,
And by them did he die: they were his life."

Almost none but Wordsworth would have made such a man a common pedlar.

"A vagrant merchant bent beneath his load,"

but Wordsworth explains in a seeming apology

"Yet do such travelers find their own delight
And their hard service, deemed debasing now,
Gained merited respect in simpler times."

And again he likens the Wanderer in his expeditions to the minstrels of the earlier days who could open his way from "hall to hall, baronial court or royal . . . by virtue of that sacred instrument, his harp." The Wanderer is throughout the entire piece the principal actor, taking part in every "moral dialogue." The Poet and the Wanderer meet near a ruined dwelling and after listening to the story of the latter's life, the Wanderer tells of the last inhabitants. But the "ordinary sorrows of man's life," from Wordsworth's pen become singularly affecting and give a greater insight into the character the author has portrayed in the Wanderer, who relates the story.

The second and third books introduce to us and make us well acquainted with another of the leading characters, the Solitary. An early schoolmate of the Wanderer in their native village, who had undergone most of the vicissitudes of life and had retired to the mountain fastness, and was at present living in a spirit of cynical despair. The three comment upon the habits and customs of the people in the neighboring vales, the Wanderer seeking the "moral to improve the tale" and ever reproving the Solitary for his despondency. In the fourth book especially is the Solitary's despondency corrected. He is exhorted to hope and have faith. This leads to a discussion of the various sects and religions of the day, with comment on each by the Wanderer.

In the sixth, they enter another valley and approach a churchyard, where the thread of the yesterday's discourse is resumed. They meet the Pastor, a new character in this Drama of Life. The Pastor and Wanderer agree in their views, and the Pastor illustrates his remarks with an account of a few of the persons who were interred about them. The sixth and seventh books continue in the same setting and along the same theme. The characters described by the Pastor are "sketched with all the truth of Crabbe's descriptive pencil, and with all the delicacy of Goldsmith's, interspersed with many touches such as none but Wordsworth could throw in."

In the eighth we visit with them the parsonage and follow them in their discourse on the progress made of late in manufactory, and the baneful influences it exerted upon the souls of those it made its slaves. The ninth book describes their voyage over a little neighboring lake and sets down their political digressions. The sight of two innocent children at play draws from the Wanderer a discourse on the duties of a nation toward her children. The two books are replete with scenes valuable both for their poetic excellence of description, and for their arguments of hope and comfort. The poem closes in the ninth book and we leave the Solitary, not yet completely converted, but influenced by the talk of his companions. The Poet concludes with the hope that the end had in view may, at least in part, have been attained.

"What renovation had been brought; and what
Degree of healing to a wounded spirit,
Dejected, and habitually disposed
To seek, in degradation of the kind,
Excuse and solace for her own defects;
How far these erring notions were reformed;
And whether aught of tendency as good
And pure, from further intercourse ensued;
This—if delightful hope, as heretofore,
Inspire the serious song, and gentle hearts
Cherish, and lofty minds approve the past—
My future labors may not leave untold."

For separate instances worthy of more than passing notice, one has but to open the book at almost any page and the eye will find with ease a passage of surpassing beauty, each seemingly better than the last for height and depth of thought, richness of coloring, or felicity of comparison. Thus, when our poet makes the Wanderer speak of the

"One adequate support
"For the calamities of mortal life
Exists—one only: an assured belief
That the procession of our fate, howe'er
Sad or disturbed, is ordered by a Being
Of infinite benevolence and power,"

he has him sing his hymn of praise in the following few lines of almost unsurpassed excellence—

"How beautiful this dome of sky;
And the vast hills, in fluctuation fixed
At thy command how awful! Shall the soul,
Human and rational report of thee
Even less than these?—Be mute who will, who can,
Yet I will praise thee with impassioned voice:
My lips that may forget thee in the crowd,
Cannot forget thee here, where thou hast built,
For thy own glory in the wilderness!"

A reading of those lines dispels all thought of comment; they seem, like their subject, sacred, and criticism sacrilegious. But the selection grows too difficult; a passage found and seized upon is soon outshone by others far surpassing. It seems unfair to select one at the expense of many necessarily left unnoticed. The task is far too great. One reads enraptured; following the author's thought, he glories with the author in the beauty of each verse, each line, but finds his words of praise inadequate to describe the sublimity of the work.

But let us not imagine that Wordsworth is without his defects. He has been blamed time and again for his too great attention to the following out of his system, his too great faithfulness in matters of smaller detail, which though all well and good in themselves, serve oftentimes to weary and divert the reader from the lesson of the text, and cause him frequently to lay aside too readily for matter of a lighter vein a more important task. For instance, to recall a passage often quoted as an example in this regard, we refer the reader to the following description of the setting of one of his scenes, a description which, though perfectly reproducing the scene in question, is out of keeping for the reason that it draws too heavily upon the reader's application. It is—

"Upon a semicirque of turf-clad ground
The hidden nook discovered to our view
A mass of rock, resembling, as it lay
Right at the foot of a moist precipice,
A stranded ship, with keel upturned, that rests
Fearless of winds and waves. Three several stones
Stood near, of smaller size, and not unlike
To monumental pillars; and, from these
Some little space disjoined, a pair were seen,
That with united shoulders bore aloft
A fragment, like an altar, flat and smooth . . "

We are indebted to the *British Critic* for May 1815, for the following extract from a criticism on Wordsworth which we can not do better than quote in full, feeling that the word of a contemporary will have especial weight.

"But the crying sin of Mr. Wordsworth is too great refinement in the application of spiritual associations to natural objects. Agreeing with him to the full in considering this the essence of Descriptive Poetry, we yet feel and lament that he has not sufficiently distinguished between the common feelings of mankind and the wanderings of his own solitary spirit. He is too familiar with his art to see where the beginner finds difficulty. He listens to a lamb bleating, or gazes on the flight of a bird, and the visionary associations which spring up within him he takes for the ordinary stirrings of the heart, which all men who have leisure to feel at all, must feel as well as himself at the like objects. He passes abruptly from the picture to the result of the reverie it produced, and makes his writings obscure and fantastical for want of a little care in unraveling a thread of ideas so familiar to himself that he deems it easy to all mankind. . . . . If Mr. Wordsworth had reflected enough on this tendency of a life like his, he would probably have smoothed off many allusions which now come so abrupt and unexpected as to startle even his most experienced readers; and by so doing he would have come nearer the end of poetry: which is not perfected until to every man according to his measure the cup of delight and instruction be full."

However, the worst that can be said of Wordsworth is very little when set side by side with the good which his works, and particularly the Excursion, have done and will yet do. It was not for purposes of vanity and applause that poetry was given to the world, that a few men were endowed with eyes that can see deep down into the hearts and feelings of their fellow men and into the workings and providences of Nature, and with the faculty of presenting this knowledge to the world. Mill says of him:

"What made his poems a medicine for my state of mind was that they expressed not a mere outward beauty, but states of feeling and of thought colored by feeling, under the excitement of beauty. I needed to be made to feel that there was permanent happiness in tranquil contemplation. Wordsworth taught me this, not only without turning away from, but with greatly increased interest in the common feelings and common interests of human beings."

Arnold puts him above Pope, Gray, Coleridge, Goldsmith, Byron, Keats, indeed second to none but Shakespeare and Milton. "Wordsworth's name deserves to stand, and will finally stand above them all."

He himself held that every great poet should be a teacher; he wished to be considered a teacher or nothing. He wished—

"To console the afflicted; to add sunshine to daylight by making the happy' happier; to teach the young and the gracious of every age to see, to think, to feel, and therefore to become more actively and sincerely virtuous."—

A remark which can be answered in no better way than in the words of Matthew Arnold:

He found us when the age had bound
Our souls in its benumbing round;
He spoke, and loosed our hearts in tears."

ROB'T E. FITZGERALD,
Post-Grad. Course.

Oh woe is me!

I sin

So grievously,

And yet expect to win

Eternal life.

I must repent!

—I will!

Till life be spent

My purpose I'll fulfil,

Though cruel the strife.

George J. Hall. '08.

THE DAYS OF YORE

O the days of yore,
  The days of yore!
Shall I ne'er again feel
  As the shades of death steal
The spirit that made you dear friends?
  Ah, no! nevermore!
And sadly, sadly do I think,
  As I near the fated brink
Where all my sorrow ends,
  That the days of yore,
Sweet days of yore,
  Are long ago, long ago, o'er!

O ye days of yore,
  Loved friends of before!
With you did I shed my boyhood tears
  With you did I spend my boyhood years!
And I would I could hear
  E'en your echo return,
O ye days of yore!
  I would you could cheer
My hoary sojourn,
  Loved friends of before!

Ah comrades of my happy youth;
  Companions of my prime!
Why did you swiftly fly
  As in a sudden rage,
And ne'er again return
  That I my care might spurn?
Why did you die
  In my grey old age?
Why but a part of merciless time,
  O ye days of yore?

O pleasures of the heretofore
  You were fair
In the days of yore!
  And sorrows that I lightly bore
With never a thought of care,
  You, too, are friends of before!
But friends of before,
  You are friends, no, no more!

ANTHONY B. DIEPENBROCK, '08.

"THE RENUNCIATION"

A ROMANCE OF THE MISSION DAYS

I

The garden of the Mission Santa Maria Magdalena lay asleep in the noon-day sun. A torrid silence had caught the quadrangle in its spirit embrace, and the still, uncertain, enervating heat found its way into the very remotest corners. The palms, the foliage and the flowers all seemed to catch the breath of the siesta, for each of them hung drowsily and droopingly in the quiet atmosphere. The parched walks of the garden were fairly baked in the sun, and in the fountain that stood in the center of the quadrangle, not even a ripple stirred the few rose petals that had strayed upon the surface of the water. Occasionally a passing bird, or an indefatiguable bee swept across the picture; otherwise, no sign of life was visible. It was a typical summer's day in the time of the early missions.

To the left of the fountain, and not far from the heavy wooden gate stood a pergola, which was shaded from the sun by vines of passion-flower and clematis that ran riot in their entertwining embraces about the slender beams. Within the semi-coolness of this picturesque enclosure, a Franciscan Monk sat quietly sleeping on a low stone bench that leaned against the back of the pergola. By his side hung the emblem of his chosen life, a heavy wooden rosary. In his lap, lay his breviary, half open, with the forefinger of his right hand placed between the leaves. His chin rested forward on his breast, and his deep, regular breathing evidenced the fact, that upon him, too, had dropped the significance of the hour.

Just how long this peaceful scene would have remained undisturbed, is not certain, but it lacked a few minutes of the first hour after the Angelus, so presently the mission gate was opened, and a bare-footed Mexican boy, his bronzed chest showing through his soft, white shirt, opened at the neck, lazily entered the garden, dragging the gate on its hinges behind him. He stood still for a moment, and stretching out his arms, he yawned burdensomely, and then moved slowly over to the fountain. He gazed at the sun dial half hidden among the poiensettas, and later he looked up at the little tower of the church. Dipping the copper cup into the basin of the fountain he filled it to overflowing and drank long and deep of the cooling draught. This done, he walked slowly and shiftlessly on toward the church, pausing for a moment to eye the sleeping Padré in the pergola, and to make sure that the latter did not see him take the orange which lay in the dish of fruit at the good man's side. On reaching the basement of the tower, he yawningly and wearily pulled the bell-ropes, and set the bells ringing at a slow, monotonous chime. This done, he sauntered back into the garden, over past the fountain, and then out into the road.

The Padré's head rose heavily at the sound of the chimes, but he did not open his eyes. He was still in the state of coma so prevalent among the Spaniards. His mind was oblivious to his beautiful surroundings; to the rainbow of color that played among the flowers, to the orange grove and the olive orchard which for over a quarter of a century had stretched before him, just beyond the *patio*. Indeed, he might have even dropped into his sound sleep again, had not his semi-conscious attention been arrested by a full, round voice, gaily singing a snatch of an old Spanish love sung The voice was at first some distance from the garden, in the direction of the orchard, but as it drew merrily nearer, the Padré opened his eyes as if in recognition, then slowly closed them again.

"Me gustan todos, me gustan todos,
Me gustan todos in general!
Pero esa Rubia, pero esa Rubia,
Pero esa Rubia me gusta mas!"

It was Miguel Espinosa, singing with so light a heart, and the Padré knew that he was coming with good news. As the voice grew louder, Miguel swung into the orchard. He stopped to waken a sleeping magpie in its cage, and then paused for a drink at the fountain. He was a big fellow, all of six-feet-two, with the shoulders of an ox and the eyes of a dreamer. Miguel worked at the forge of Manuel Aragillá, where all of the wealthy Spaniards and Mexicans sent their horses to be shod, and their vehicles to be repaired. [He was the best mandolinist in the *pueblo*, and he could write verses that parried off all criticism. Miguel was a strange combination of laborer and poet, and what he learned at the forge he mixed with his knowledge of music and verse.

After his refreshing drink at the fountain, Miguel turned and gazed furtively around the deserted garden. His eyes wandered out through the arch at the south end, and took in the orange orchard and the olive grove whence he had come. Then he moved back to the fountain and leaned over its edge, and with his features mirrored in the clear water, he arranged his toilet, and smiled back boyishly at his own reflection. He drew in a breath of the heated air, and looked out beyond the Mission walls to where the heavens kissed the purple hill-tops, all the while his whole being trembling and vibrating with an evident emotion. He glanced at the sun and blinked in its intense light; then, he stood perplexed and thoughtful. The silence around him was majestic. Presently it was broken, ever so softly, ever so gently, broken by the low, dull sound of heavy regular breathing. Miguel's eyes shifted from left to right, his hand stole instinctively to his sombrero, which he reverently removed. Sweeping in the entire quadrangle with a glance, he tiptoed softly over to the pergola and gently drew aside the vines. The Padré José was sleeping peacefully.

Miguel smiled until his teeth shone like two bars of ivory, and drawing back, he blessed himself, and then entered the pergola from the front.

He touched the sleeping Priest on the shoulder.

"Padré, Padré," he whispered, and his soul was in his voice, "It is I, Miguel, with news; see, Padré, wake up!"

The Padré stirred, and slowly opened his eyes. He looked at Miguel, who had fallen on his knees. He smiled gently, and stretching out his hand, he rested it lightly on Miguel's soft curls.

"Ah, Miguel," he said, "it is you. *Benedicite!* I heard you singing in the orchard. What news do you bring at this hour, which usually finds you at your forge?"

Miguel's black eyes shone with a wonderful light. A rich, red glow sprang into his cheeks and his breath surged through his body with the emotion he could not suppress.

"The news! The news, Padré!" he shouted. "Oh! the Saints be praised, it is so good, it chokes me. Teresa has consented! She has told me yes! and Padré, we will be married—*manana!*"

He was shaking all over with the joy of his palpitating senses.

The Padré's face betrayed nothing. Miguel's news had made no visible im-

pression on him, but within, this man of God wondered.

It was several moments before he spoke, moments that seemed strangely still and wierdly long to Miguel.

"So, that is your news, my son," he said at length.

Miguel siezed the Padré's hand, and Spaniard-like, covered it with kisses.

"Si, Padré, si! and is it not news good to overflowing? *Manana*, Padré, *manana!* Think of it! Oh, I have waited so long for her answer. I have burned so many candles to the Virgin, and I have waited and waited, and hoped and prayed. I have worked so hard at the forge to earn some savings, and with these I have purchased the little house of Senora Cortez just off the Camino, and fitted it up gaily! And she has said yes!yes!Padré! and she will marry me—*manana!*"

The Padré smiled, but in his mind he was deeply troubled.

"Tell me," he said at length, "why do you marry Teresa tomorrow? Why not wait a week or ten days? Surely she is not prepared."

Miguel jumped to his feet.

"Oh! but she is prepared! she does not want to wait! she said, 'get it all over with quickly!' "

"And why?"

"Why? Because she loves me! Because she does not want to wait. We fixed it all to-day, Padré, we two. You are to marry us in the morning, in the church. Juanita will go with Teresa and Carlos will be with me."

The Padré knitted his brows.

"Carlos?" He repeated the name questionly after Miguel.

"Si, Padré, Carlos—Carlos Mendoza!"

Again the Padré repeated the name,— "Carlos Mendoza."

Miguel did not notice the cloud that disturbed the Padré's saintly countenance, but rambled on joyfully.

"Of course, Carlos," he said, "who else? Is not Carlos like a brother to me? Have we not been together always? We work at the same forge, we have lived always together and he plays the guitar to my mandolin! And does he not love Teresa too? Not in the way I do, of course, but as a brother loves a sister! Why, Padré there could be no wedding without Carlos!"

The Padré slowly nodded his head.

"Very well, my son," he said, "I will marry you to Teresa in the morning. Your news has surprised me, but in the end the Saints will decree all for the best. Be good to Teresa and be patient, always. She is very young, only eighteen A mere child, you see, so be good to her Miguel, my son?"

Miguel knelt before the Padré and crossed himself as the good man gave him his blessing.

"Rise, Miguel," he continued, "go into the church and light a candle to the Virgin Mother."

Miguel arose.

"I will go first to Teresa," he laughed, "and tell her the good news that you will marry us Padré. Then, I must tell Carlos also. I *will* light the candle to the Virgin Mother, Padré, I will light it—*manana*!

He picked up his sombrero and slipped a piso into the Padré's hand, and, then catching up his song, he ran happily out of the garden into the orchard, and down the road.

"Me gustan todos, me gustan todos,
Me gustan todos in general;
Pero esa Rubia, pero esa Rubia,
Pero esa Rubia me gusta mas."

The Padré listened until the song died away, then blessing himself with the cross on his beads, he slowly shook his head.

"*Manana*," he repeated. "God grant that it will come for Miguel."

And he began to say his rosary, passing out from the garden into the shade of the olive grove.

II

Carlos Mendoza was lying on a long wooden bench on the low porch which surrounded the adobe hut which he and Miguel Espinosa occupied together, and it was nearing twilight. A half-smoked cigarette hung between his lips and his eyes were barely open. One of his hands was stuffed into his sash, and in the other he held a note, scribbled on a piece of brown paper.

'Come to-night, early,' it read, 'I must see you. Teresa.'

He had been lying there for over an hour, half wondering what Teresa could want of him, and half wishing that Miguel would hurry back and prepare their supper of coffee and *frijoles*.

His latter thoughts were set at rest,

when he heard Miguel's voice down the road.

"Me gustan todos, me gustan todos,
Me gustan todos in general.
Pero esa——"

The singer stopped when he saw Carlos, and broke into a run that he might reach his friend the sooner.

"Carlos! Carlos!" he cried, as he drew near to him, "*mi amigo*, Carlos! she has consented! She has said yes, and we will be married *manana*!"

Carlos sat up lazily, as if he did not quite catch the full meaning of Miguel's words, and he looked at the latter questioningly.

"Miguel, what are you saying?" he asked. "Are you writing another verse? Who has said yes, and who is to be married?"

Miguel dropped down onto the bench beside Carlos, and placing his arm affectionately around his friend's neck, he began to talk with breathless excitement.

"*Ah! Dios!* the news is so good! Carlos, my friend, I am happy, and you, you too, will be happy when you know! To-morrow at ten we will be married, and only Pa'dré José, and Jaunita and yourself shall know of it. *Ah! Dios!* it is good to be blessed like I am! I will light two candles to the Virgin, man-ãna!"

Carlos laughed at Miguel's excitement.

"Is it too much," he questioned, "when I ask whom you are going to marry?"

Miguel now laughed even more heartily than did Carlos.

"Fool of a dog, was I," he cried, "not to have come to you directly I left the Padré. But I stopped to tell all of our friends in the village. Oh! it must be that the good news has turned my brain. Of course you shall know. It is Tereas,—Teresa, my brother, think of it! Am I not blessed? Has not good fortune smiled on me?"

All of the light went out of Carlos's face, but Miguel did not notice it. He went on at random.

"And to-night you must get your own supper, *mi amigo*, for I will go to the church and light the candles to the virgin now instead of *manana*! It is better so, not to wait. My dreams will be sweeter and the Padré would wish it so. Then will I eat supper with Teresa. And you, too, if you like! She will have better *frijoles* than we, and her coffee is stronger, and she will bake *tortillas*, nice and hot! Go to her at once, Carlos, for she will be happy when she learns that you know the good news. Go at once, *mi amigo*, and I will follow you shortly!"

Carlos did not stir. He was staring into space. Miguel noticed his friend's attitude.

"Carlos!" he cried, "are you not happy at my news; does it displease you?"

Carlos roused himself, and smiled faintly.

"Yes, I am happy," he said, "but your news has bewildered me. You took me unprepared."

Miguel laughed aloud. "Just as

Teresa took me," he went on. "I had lived and hoped on what her answer would be. I had not even dared to dream that she would tell me yes. Why, Carlos, only think of it, the Donna Teresa Martinez and my poor unworthy self. Carlos, my friend, it is like a dream come true. Often since I first met Teresa at the dance that Corpus Christi day two years ago I began to dream of her. Often, and more often I dreamed until my dreams grew into a love, such as no words could ever describe to you. I have lain awake long into the night, when you thought I was sleeping, and in visions I have seen her before me. At my forge in the day her face is always smiling at me through the flames, and at dusk her voice is singing to me in the strings of my mandolin. When I go to church I think of her as one of the Saints; when I bring flowers for the shrine her lips are on every petal. *Ah! Dios!* the Saints have blessed me with this love, and ever since it first came to me my life has been different and better. You asked me often, Carlos, why I have saved—don't you remember? And now you know! You know why I bought the Senora Cortez's cottage, and what I meant when I said, 'someday three of us would live there, we two, and one other.' I have not forgotten you in my own joy! No, *mi amigo*, for you will come and live there with Teresa and me and we will all be one happy family,—after *manana!*"

Carlos rose and walked to the edge of the porch. The air had grown dull and depressing to him and he longed to be away somewhere where he could think.

In his intense joy Miguel did not notice the effect that his speech produced in Carlos, and he continued.

"You go .at once to Teresa, Carlos, and help her to prepare the supper. I will go first to the church and light the candles, and then I will be with you both afterwards. Teresa will be happy to have you!"

Carlos turned to him. "Yes," he said, "It is better that I should go to her at once."

As he spoke, the edge of the sun dropped down behind the hills, leaving threads of red and gold behind it, and as he walked out into the soft dusk, Miguel looked after him, and he wondered if Carlos would ever be as happy as himself.

III

The home of Teresa Mendoza was in the center of the village, on a bit of slightly undulating ground. It was small and contained but two rooms, and was built of adobe. Plastered inside and out, it was whitewashed in addition. The roof was of rafters and was low and flat, and covered with tiles, thatch and clay. It was not abundantly furnished, for old Senora Mendoza and her daughter had but the scant means they earned from their carpet weaving, which in the summer time was done out of doors. In the main room they spent most of their spare time. It was clean and comfortable and contained a table, several chairs, a bench, and a bake-oven, around which was clustered a variety of cooking utensils. In one corner stood a high cupboard, filled with dishes and assortments of food. A picture or two of the commonest kind ornamented the right wall, and near the window hung an old colored print of the Blessed Virgin. Over the table on a small wooden shelf, rested a crucifix. The other chamber was used as the sleeping room.

The gathering twilight found Teresa seated beneath a great fig tree which stood a few feet in front of the house. She was knitting, it being a trifle too dark for weaving. Every now and then her hands would drop carelessly in her lap, as her fingers loosened on the yarn and the needles. Her glorious black eyes, which shone like meteors beneath her luxuriantly hair-covered brow, became like two prayers when she turned them to the sky. Her face, usually sunny and joyous, betrayed the consciousness of deep and troubled thought. Finally she ceased to knit altogether, and sat gazing thoughtfully up at a dove which pattered and cooed softly in front of the dove-cote that rested on one of the lower branches of the fig tree. As she gazed at this gentle work of God, her lips parted, and unconsciously she spoke aloud: *"Madre mia!* What shall I do?"

Old Senora Mendoza passed her at this moment and stopped before her questioningly.

"What do you murmur to yourself, my daughter?" she asked.

Teresa recovered her distracted thoughts and gathered up her knitting.

"Nothing, nothing, *mamita,*" she replied, quickly, "I was but saying a little prayer."

The old Senora grunted.

"Better be upon thy knees for such a practice. The saints love not the lazy ones."

And with this, the old lady moved on into the house.

The coming of the stars brought Teresa the answer to her note, for Carlos came to her as Miguel had asked him to. Miguel himself had gone to the church to light the candles to the Virgin Mother.

When Teresa saw Carlos coming she arose hurriedly, dropped her knitting on the bench and rushed forward to meet him.

He tried to take her in his arms, but she drew back.

"No, Carlos," she said, tremblingly, "you do not know what I have done."

He at once reassured her.

"I do know, Teresa, I do know, but I can't believe it! It isn't true, say it isn't true!"

"It is true, Carlos," replied the girl, simply.

"But Teresa, Teresa!" protested Carlos, "it cannot be! You do do not love Miguel! You cannot marry him! You do not love him!

Teresa dropped her eyes; she was trembling all over, and she did not answer.

"You do not love Miguel! Teresa, say that you do not love him!" he repeated.

Her lips quivered, and she caught nervously at the sleeve of her gown.

"No—no," she replied, "you are right. I do not love him."

Carlos took a step toward her.

"Then why," he asked impassionately, "why do you marry him?"

They had gradually moved back to the fig tree, and now Teresa sank down upon the bench, and burst into tears.

"Because, because," she sobbed, "I was afraid—afraid !"

Carlos bent over her, his knee resting on the bench.

"Afraid? Afraid of what?"

"Oh! I don't know! You would not understand!" cried the girl. "Miguel has always been so good to me, so kind, so generous and so gentle. I do love Miguel as a brother, and ever since he came into my life two years ago, it has never been different. He is so noble and has sacrificed so much for me. He has stinted himself and saved, and all for me. Oh! I know, I have watched him, and I know that it was all for me, and that some day he would ask me to marry him. To-day when he came to me, it was in my bones that he would ask me. I felt it in the touch of his hand. I saw it in the look in his eye. And when he did ask me, here in this very place, I knew that I did not love him that way, Carlos, I knew that I loved only you, but, his whole noble soul and his great beautiful heart were laid bare to me here, and my conscience whispered 'pity' into my ears and I said 'yes.' Oh! do not hate me Carlos, do not despise me! It was not

in me to tell him no; the words I wanted would not come! I told him to get it over with to-morrow; that I would go with him to the church, and to arrange it all with Padré José! Then I had planned that we should go away, away from here, where I could forget— where I could forget—you! He was so happy that his heart almost burst with the joy. Oh! I could not say 'no' to him, Carlos, when he looked at me like that! I could not say 'no' !"

Teresa buried her face in her hands, and for a moment there was a silence between them.

Finally Carlos spoke.

"And now, Teresa, what now?"

"After he had gone to see the Padré I was alone with my thoughts, and everything that I had done came back to me. I remembered how I told you that I loved you, but that you would would have to wait for my answer. I thought of how dear you and Miguel are to one another and how I was sacrificing you and my love for you! Oh! yes, Carlos, I did think of all those things, and that is why I wrote you the note this afternoon and asked you to come here, and now that you are here, and you know the truth, what must you think of me—what can you think?"

Carlos stood up erect, and moved a little from her.

"I am thinking of Miguel," he said simply.

"Of Miguel ?"

"Of Miguel. I am wondering how we can tell him."

Teresa's eyes opened wonderingly.

"Tell him? Tell him what?" she asked.

"Tell him that it can never be."

Teresa sprang to her feet with a startled cry.

"Tell him that——!"

"It can never be," interrupted Carlos, "Oh! Teresa, can't you see, can't you realize that it is all a terrible mistake? You do not love him! Then how can you make him happy, how can you make yourself happy? It would be cruel to Miguel, it would be unjust to you and to myself! Oh! believe me, I am not playing this game for myself alone! I can't see you both made miserable! I can't see you enter into such a wretched, hollow bargain. I love you, Teresa, you know that I love you, and I know that you love me. As a brother, I love Miguel, and it cuts me deep in here, in my heart, to think of what it will all mean to him, but it can never be! You are on the brink of the precipice of two human lives, upon the very edge of their happiness, and you must draw back, Teresa, you must draw back, before it is too late!"

Teresa was dazed, her heart seemed numb within her.

"What can I do, Carlos?" she asked, at length. "What *can* I do?"

"You must tell him to-night when he comes."

"It will kill him!"

"It were even better that way, than the other. Tell him quietly and gently and he will see it rightly, there is no other way. You said just now; that Miguel is good and kind and generous. He will

understand. He is coming now, see there, down the road. I will go to the Senora that you two may be alone. Tell him tenderly, and he will understand. Then tell him that you and I will go to Monterey,—*manana*."

Carlos did not give Teresa time to answer; he knew a woman's way and he slipped quietly into the house.

"Me gustan to dos, me gustan no dos,
Me gustan to dos, in general!
Pero esa Rubia, Pero esa Rubia,
Pero esa Rubia me gusta mas!"

The words of Miguel's song came to Teresa like the point of a sword. He swung through the gate, and before she could speak he had her folded in his arms.

Teresa drew back, frightened. from his embrace.

"No, Miguel, please, not that!"

He released her.

"Why? Why, Teresa, does it displease you after what has happened to-day? Ah! but I have the news that will please you though, for everything is settled with the Padré. I was with him to-day, and I caught him napping in the garden. Oh! but he was happy with the news, and he will be ready for us in the morning. Then I went quickly home, and told Carlos. Carlos was not so happy, because it means the end of our former days together. Afterwards I went to the church and lighted two candles to the Virgin Mother. Then I could not resist it to run over to the little house of Senora Cortez, and see if everything is ready. And all for you, *mi queridisima*, all for you! And not a bite have I had to eat, nor did I give anything to Carlos. He was to come here, that we might all be happy together!"

He stopped for breath, and it seemed to Teresa that his great happiness would kill her. She was almost afraid to speak, but in her heart she called to her patron Saint for strength and for courage.

"Miguel," she said falteringly, "Carlos is there, in the house."

"There?" cried the other, "then we will have him out !"

"No, no!" she advanced to him, "no, not yet. Not until I have told you."

Miguel's heart fluttered with the instinct of the Spaniard.

"Told me? Told me what?" he asked.

"Told you that it is all a mistake."

Miguel's face went death-color in a flash. He tried to move closer to her, but his feet were fixed to the ground.

"A mistake?" he whispered, "A mistake? Why, Teresa, what do you mean?"

She dug her nails into the flesh of her hands.

"I mean," she faltered, "I mean that it—that I—Oh! Miguel, can't you see, can't you understand?"

She turned fully to him, and she saw the look of despair in his face.

"*Ah, Dios!*" he cried, "speak! speak quick to me, and tell me what you mean?"

Teresa's head sank upon her breast.

"I do not love you, Miguel," she said quietly, as if the new strength and courage for which she prayed had been given her.

Miguel did not stir, he did not even flinch. He stood like a huge piece of bronze. The moon was coming up above the hills, and the stars were paling in its light. About Miguel everything was whirling, and he closed his eyes.

The whirling ceased, and he felt that the night was heavy in its profundity. As he stood there, he felt, too, a deep, painful sadness creep over him, full of strangeness and mystery, which froze his very soul, and then gradually the truth of Teresa's words, which had been slow to penetrate his strong heart, now filled it to overflowing.

She was speaking again, but he did not hear her. Inside of him, a great void was growing.

"You understand, don't you understand?" Teresa was saying. "I don't want to be cruel Miguel, don't make it too hard for me. I have always loved you for your gentleness and your kindness, but it is not the same as the love I have for Carlos; it is not the same! I could not be happy, Miguel! I could not be happy!"

She had taken Miguel's hand in hers, but he did not feel it. He had heard her say that she loved Carlos, but he did not heed it. The intensity of her words alone impressed him and they alone lingered in the depths of his heart; in this heart of Miguel which was a pure spot, difficult to manage, little understood, and where many things went on which were not revealed outside.

Carlos came quietly from the house, and as he did so, Miguel opened his eyes.

Carlos knew when he saw them there together that Teresa had told Miguel.

For a moment no one spoke. All stood like those who wait to hear a sentence passed.

At first Miguel had but half divined the truth, and it only made him trem· ble. Now that he was sure of it, it did not seem to affect him. To one whose life had been so free from suffering grief does not come suddenly. As he stood there, gazing at the other two, some· thing seemed to go wrong in his head for the moment. Was he ashamed to show his despair before them, or had his tortures numbed him?

Presently Carlos spoke.

"*Mi amigo*," he said very gently.

Mignel nodded his head.

"Has Teresa made you see," con· tinued the other, "has she made you understand?"

Miguel nodded his head again, and he loosened Teresa's hand from his.

"And it is all right?" asked Carlos, as Teresa went to him.

Miguel's eyelids quivered.

"I do not know," he said slowly. "I must have time, time to think. I under· stand, but I will go to the church, and then I will come back to you,–*manana*."

Teresa made as if to go to ·him, but he turned away, and slowly walked out into the night.

V.

When Miguel reached the church, he was surprised, even in his agitation, to find the side door unlocked. Shortly after he left Teresa and Carlos, the thought strayed to him that he might not be able to get into the church at that hour. But he had forgotten that it had been a Feast Day, and that on such an occasion the little door leading from the garden through the side of the church was al· ways left unlocked all night, as many came to pray in the hours that followed a festival in the village.

Miguel found no difficulty in letting himself in, and a sense of ·relief ·came over him when he found that the church was empty.

For a moment he stood absolutely still, and closed his eyes. Perhaps· he was trying to think, or, perhaps, he was turning over in his mind the possible ending of this first great tragedy in his life.

The church was almost in total dark· ness, the only lights being the soft re· flection of the sanctuary lamp which hung before the main altar, and Miguel's two candles lighted before the Virgin Mother. The awful stillness of the place pressed close around him, and the current of emotions within his being swayed him slowly back and forward on his feet like a pendulum, and each sway beat the time of the moments it had taken Teresa to tell him the truth. Again and again Teresa's words rang in his ears:— "I will not be happy, Miguel, I will not be happy !" And each time they echoed the same plaint upon the chords of his heart.

He reached out his hand to seek a support and it rested upon the edge of the holy-water font. In this position he remained, his eyes closed, his temples throbbing, and his pulses beating with a terrible vibration.

Then, no longer having the human power to restrain the gathered tempest within him, he threw open the flood-gate of his emotions and the agony of his soul poured out before him with all of the pain its expression could give him.

He lived over again the two years of his life since he first saw Teresa, and the wound in his heart bled freely at each touch of his memory. He counted again the days, as he had counted them before, the days that had nurtured his love. He saw Teresa as he first looked upon her that Corpus Christi day, when his desert-life blossomed like a rose. From the treasure-house of his heart, he took each look, each word of encouragement she had given him, but now, in his agony, they were dead and barren. His closed eyes burned with the fever of despair as he thought of those two years of work and ambition, when love made his life seem light and the realization of happiness was imminent. The words that he spoke to her when he asked her for her love now became as dust and ashes in his mouth. The truth of her pity for him when she gave her promise, broke upon him, cruel and naked. In his joy at her consent, he had not read

the dictates of her heart, each word of which was "Carlos !" He saw now, as he had not seen, that she had been afraid of him, and that it was terror alone that prompted her consent, and every one of these thoughts were borne to him upon the wings of her words—"I will not be happy, Miguel, I will not be happy !"

His hand relaxed on the holy-water font and he slowly opened his eyes. For a moment he stared blankly before him, then he followed with his vision, the intangible reflection of the holy light that burned before the altar. Its brightest rays caressed the Crucifix that stood above the Tabernacle, and Miguel saw the replica of the God-man upon the cross for the first time since he had entered the church. Everything else about him was darkness, save for the two candles lighted before the Virgin Mother.

As Miguel gazed up at the holy image a strange sensation stole over him, a sense of repression and of ceasing pain. The brutal words of his hopeless love became fainter in its weight, and gradually died away like an echo. A spirit of peace possessed him, and unconsciously he moved slowly toward the altar, his eyes fixed steadily upon the Crucifix. He entered the sanctuary and stood motionless at the foot of the altar. The Christ, with all of the tortures of the Redemption upon Him, looked down upon the sorrow of the man, and Miguel, as he felt the spirit of the gaze penetrating into his very soul knew that his own sorrow shrivelled into nothing. His knees weakened beneath him and he fell prostrate upon the steps of the altar.

The utter loneliness that Miguel could no longer resist now took possession of his soul, and he fell to weeping, as only strong men can weep.

Long into the night, Miguel lay there and sobbed out the depths of his sufferings; at the foot of the Cross. Each tear brought to him clearly, the only reasonable outcome of the turn of the tide, and when the tears had passed and the trembling of his sobbing body ceased, he prayed, prayed there, as the Master prayed, to give him strength to bear it all, and his prayer was answered when the supreme spirit of renunciation stole upon him. Raising himself to his feet he stretched forth his arms in supplication, and murmured in a low, hoarse voice, "Thy will be done!"

Then he slowly wended his way from the church, and as he closed the door behind him, he did not know that the draught had blown out the candles in front of the Virgin Mother.

VI.

Teresa and Carlos were sitting beneath the shade of the fig-tree when Miguel came slowly down the road. The morning was hot, but Teresa and Carlos had not noticed it. They were planning their future, for they knew what Miguel's answer would be. As the latter came before them, each felt a sense of supreme gentleness creep upon them, and they rose and went forth to meet him.

Miguel's face betrayed nothing of what he had suffered the night before. He looked a 'little sadder and perhaps a trifle tired, but beyond that, he was the same old Miguel.

Teresa extended her hand to him, and he took it without saying a word. Then he raised Carlos' hand in the palm of his own, and he placed it upon Teresa's hand. He patted their clasped hands tenderly, and then he moved away from them and walked over to the door of the cottage, and stood there rolling a cigarette.

Teresa's eyes were filled with tears, and to Carlos came the beautiful significance of friendship.

Old Senora Mendoza came out of the yard behind the house, and when she saw Miguel, she wobbled up to him.

"Ah! Senor Miguel, have you heard the news?" she asked him. "Teresa will marry Carlos, to-night in Monterey."

Miguel lighted his cigarette and did not look up when he answered.

"Yes," he said, "and they will be happy."

But, there was no bitterness in his voice.

"*Bien*," assented the old Senora as she ambled into the house to prepare for the departure.

. Teresa and Carlos approached Miguel, each still holding the other's hand.

"*Mi amigo*," said Carlos, "You will come to the wedding, to-night ?"

Miguel did not answer, he only flicked the ashes from his cigarette.

Carlos pressed Teresa's hand and she moved closer to Miguel.

For the first time she spoke to him, since her declaration of the night before "You will come, Miguel?" she asked gently.

Miguel was about to speak.

From the house came the weak, cracked voice of the old Senora Meudoza:—

Me gustan todos, me gustan todos,
Me gustan todos in general;
Pero esa Rubia, pero esa Rubia,
Pero esa Rubia me gusta mas !

She was singing Miguel's love song. Teresa placed her hand softly on Miguel's shoulder.

"If not tonight, Miguel," she said, "you *will* come, *sometime ?*"

Miguel turned toward Teresa, and he drew the cigarette from between his lips.

"Si, Senorita," he said slowly, "I will come to you both,—*manana.*"

MARTIN V. MERLE, A. M., '06.

ACERBITAS

Mad
With grief
I sought relief
In endless pleasure;
In a flood of dizzy madness
Vainly tried to drown my sadness;
Fiercely, madly strove with wine and fickle love
To soothe and solace pain.
But alas! my hope was vain;
Returning leisure
Only found me
Doubly
Sad.

D. T. M., '09.

THE VOICE OF THE SEA

Beyond the dusk, behind the sunset sky,
And far away athwart the evening sea,
What voiceless spirit calling unto me,
Forever calling, beckoning me to hie
From haunts of men, and fancy-free to lie
Encurtained mid the dreams of Poesy?
Is it the far, unknown Infinity
Beyond, behind those gates where mortals die?

Behold yon silent sea!   No sail's fresh gleam,
No flash of sea-bird poising for its prey,
Naught save the foamy fringe of spume would seem
To tell she lives.   And yet who but would say
Therein her grandeur lies!   The desolate sea
Unswept by navies, is Infinity.

N. B. P., '07.

THROUGH QUAKE AND BLAZE

I wonder if there was another family as happy in the whole city of San Francisco! I am pretty sure there wasn't. The last cent of the last installment had been paid on the house, and now it was their own. It was their own home, all theirs, and the thought of it was sweet to the heart. Independence has a charm belonging altogether to itself, and this charm was now in its first freshness.

Of course they were in duty bound to celebrate the "auspicious occasion" with a little house-warming of some kind. Mrs. Graeme wished to invite some of the neighbors to the supper, but Mr. Graeme objected that he did not want his neighbors to know too much about his financial affairs, and so it was decided to make it strictly a family feast.

There were only four of them. There was the father, a sturdy, intelligent, good-humored man, of middle age and evidently in the best of health and spirits. The mother was younger, and rather delicate, but her sweet face and kind voice betrayed none of the irritability of ill-health. And there was Mrs. Davies, the grandmother, a dear white-haired old creature, whose sole worry in life was to see that the rest of the family were well looked after and that their clothes were properly mended and arrayed in the requisite number of buttons. And last and not least there was Francis Stephen.

Francis, or Frank as mostly everybody called him, was the only child of the family. But he was a whole houseful in himself. He was not quite fourteen years of age, but so big and manly was he that he appeared older. For two years he had been attending St. Ignatius' College, a few blocks away, and there he was regarded as perhaps the brightest boy in his class. In his studies he always received very high marks, while the only flaw in his deportment was that his liveliness got at times beyond his own, if not his teacher's, control. He found it hard to keep quiet; the spirit of fun and mischief was strong within him. But he was generous, and tried hard to do his best, and if sometimes he prompted his neighbor to give an absurd answer, or even went as far as to place nitrogen iodide on some fat boy's desk or seat, we doubt if the Recording Angel went to the trouble of writing the fact down. There was no malice in it all, and moreover, repentance followed immediately, especially when he was caught and had to take his punishment like a man.

Besides leading in his class, Frank was a splendid little athlete, as his appearance, and indeed his every movement testified. It goes without saying, of course, that he was a baseball enthusiast. His favorite position was short-stop, and this he played, with remarkable skill, on the College Second Team.

Being thus an all-around good boy, it was not strange that Frank Graeme was popular with his school mates, and that he was the joy and pride of his parents. He was the light of their eyes, the core of their hearts. Yet their devotion never grew maudlin, their affection showed itself, when needed, in strictness and severity. Filial respect and obedience were thus in him a confirmed habit, and mischief-loving though he was, not a word or act of his that he could be ashamed to repeat in his parents' presence.

And so if Mr. and Mrs. Graeme felt unwonted happiness on this especial evening, you may be sure Francis Stephen was at the bottom of most of it. Yes! it was for him that they had schemed and labored, and if they wanted a spot that they could call their own, it was that they might also call it his.

It was such a cosy little home! Two stories, with three luxurious bay windows in front—two upstairs, and one below—and the exterior painted a creamy white with a slate-colored roof. No wonder that Mr. Graeme had toiled so diligently at his trade of cabinet-maker to pay off the $2500 that should make him its owner.

"Well," said he, as they sat down to the generously laden table, "I suppose April 17, 1906 must remain the red-letter day in the history of the house."

"Yes," assented his wife, with a half-sigh, "if the house is to have a history."

"Have a history! What's to prevent it? chimed in Frank. "But April 18 is the great date, Pa, for on that day we start out with a clean page. Mr. Reh was not off our hands till this afternoon so today doesn't count."

"April 18," repeated Mrs. Graeme "we may be thrown out of house and home on the 18th. 'Twixt the cup and the lip, you know."

"Heavens! what's come over the woman, anyway?" broke in Mr. Graeme, a trifle impatiently. "Why, Annie, you seem to want a death's head at the feast."

"It's her poor nerves," came the motherly voice of Mrs. Davies. "Just wait till I make her some dandelion tea —that'll fix her."

Dandelion was the old lady's panacea, and she never thought the family safe without a supply on hand.

"Jim," Mrs. Graeme deprecated, "Jim, how can you say so?"

"Now you know very well," her hus band continued banteringly," if there was a speck of cloud in the sky you'd never notice the blue."

"Pa, you're altogether too hard on mother. You know that she is just the sun of the house," said Frank as he took an extra helping of cranberry sauce.

"No, my boy, you're the son"

And Mr. Graeme laughed at his little joke with great gusto.

"Well, anyway, Mama," said he in apology, "a good laugh is about as good a luxury as you can get for nothing. My laughing is better than your sighing."

"Yes, Mama, I vote for Pa this time," interjected Frank, as he laid down the

thigh-bone of what had been a plump chicken. "What is there to worry about? Just as everything is in ship-shape, then you begin to fret. What's the use of getting up at all, if we be so afraid to fall? Pa, will you please pass some of that stuffing?"

"It's the dandelion tea that she needs to drink. That will fix up her nerves all right," declared Mrs. Davies.

"Anyway, I'm glad to hear my boy speak in rhyme, even if he does vote against me, laughed Mrs. Graeme good-naturedly. · "The college . is certainly doing you some good."

"Oh that reminds me, Pa—say, Mama, those cream puffs look awfully good to me. I bet you cooked them yourself. Thanks—Pa, of course we're all going to the entertainment at the College to-morrow night. It's to be the greatest thing out. Why, the Mayor is one of the patrons of it. The Gentlemen's Sodality are going to make it a tre-mendous success. Now you know very well you promised last week you'd—"

"Yet, but, my boy, don't you know I'm going to take out an insurance policy tomorrow. And besides, what does the Sodality want salt water in its gym. for, anyway? Isn't fresh water good enough to bathe in?"

"I should say so," sighed Mrs. Graeme. "A day may come when they would be thankful for enough water to drink, even."

"Oh Mama, what's the matter? Hon-estly your cream puffs are delicious—best thing I've ever tasted, except, of course, that cake. Gracious! you seem to read my mind. Much obliged. But anyway, how could we possibly ever want for water?"

"My dear madam," interrupted Mr. Graeme, "you're not half proud enough of our city. Don't you know we have the best water-supply in the world?"

"Of course, we have," chirruped Frank, "and in honor of the water-supply, we're all going to the show to-morrow night. Aren't we, Pa?"

Of course there was no resisting this appeal, and when two hours later, Frank made his way to his bedroom, the price of three reserved seats jingled in his pocket—three only, for Mrs. Davies insisted on staying home "to scare away burglars." The bedroom in question, though as cosy as an athletic boy could want, was lit only by a sky-light, through which from the dark blue dome of heaven, the stars were soon shining upon the deep, dreamless sleep of one of the best and happiest boys in all of mighty San Francisco.

*   *   *   *

Shortly after five o'clock on the fol-lowing morning, Frank was suddenly awakened by a violent trembling of the whole house. "Whoop," cried he, "here's an earthquake. I guess we're in for it now." And he sprang up to dress and be ready for emergencies. For a few seconds, the building shivered and danced like an animal frightened at the sight of some fearful object. Then, all at once, it gave a tremendous lurch forward, only to leap back again with equal violence. Back and forth, now to this side, now to that, the house swayed and tossed and shook, every beam and joint groaning under its torture in dreadful discord. "Good God," cried Frank, "this is frightful. Will it ever stop at all?" But just then there came a lull, and Frank breathed more freely. "Great Caesar," he ejaculated, "I thought the old thing would never get through." But lo! in the sharpest turn of a moment, the earthquake was on again, and the house was swaying and swinging, this time with a fury that was altogether terrifying. Besides the movement backward and forward, there was a twisting, torturing motion that almost knocked the boy off his feet, and brought wardrobe, shelves, bric-a-brac about his ears. He rushed to the door; it was jammed tight and would not open. "Oh my God," cried the agonized boy, "all is over; nothing can stand this." And it seemed as if nothing could. The house was behaving like a crackerbox that one smashes with an axe. Struck on one side after another, it totters to and fro; the movements become greater and greater; the connections become looser and looser, until at last they give way altogether, and with a groan and a crash down comes everything in total collapse. So it was with Frank's room—the tearing and wrenching of the creaking beams was so appalling that he but waited the movement of the final caving-in with the wild hope of dodging the falling beams and saving himself by some desperate chance. But in an instant all

grew calm and still as death! The earthquake was over!

Mr. Graeme forced in Frank's door, and found his son praying earnestly at his bedside. "Oh no! I wasn't much frightened," he protested in answer to his father's inquiry, "but I was just wild to help you and mother. She must be half dead."

But she was not, though her aged mother was almost distracted. By a common impulse they all hastened into the street, there to stand on safe ground and get time to compose their nerves. The streets were already black with people in various stages of dishabille, but, with the exception of a few women who were wringing their hands and crying softly, there was no excitement. Men seemed to be overawed by the powers of nature. A strange silence filled the atmosphere that oppressed one as with a weight. One could almost fancy that the angel of death had winged his way through the air and had stifled its vital breath. People moved about, talking softly, and surveying the damages, and many, after the first terrors were over, re-entered their homes to set things to rights.

The Graeme family proceeded to sweep out the kitchen and sitting-room, both of which were fairly covered with plaster. "So this is our own cosy house, just paid for," was the thought pictured on each one's rueful face, though none spoke it out.

"Well," laughed Mrs. Graeme, the most cheerful of the crowd, "there's many a slip, did I say? There was almost one that time."

"Yes," answered Mr. Graeme, "it nearly saved me my insurance policy."

"God be praised! any way we saved our lives, and the damage can soon be made good," added Mrs. Davies. Oh Annie, a kingdom for a cup of hot coffee!"

"Gracious!" exclaimed Frank, who had been looking through the window—"Pa, come here."

"Wheugh! it *is* a fire, sure enough, and a big one at that. Some of those storehouses or factories must have caught. But never fear, dearie," said he, seeing the pale face of his wife, "why, it's a mile away, and our fire department is the best in the world. Why; it's down at the water front—not a particle of danger!"

"Pa," whispered Frank, "let's go and see. We can fix things up here later on"

"Will you let him come, Mama?"

The mother looked at the pleading face of her boy and consented—"on condition, though, that you bring your father back before dinner."

"Oh you may be sure he won't miss dinner when you're going to cook it. He remembers last night," replied the boy with a laugh.

Perhaps the laugh was a little bit forced, for when he flung his arms around his mother and kissed her, why stood the tear in his soft, brown eye, or what presentiment was it that made his embrace so unusually long and affectionate? And why, when bidding farewell to Grandma, who had just stuffed his pockets with sandwiches for himself and his father, he begged pardon—in a whisper, of course—for all his past thoughtlessness and roughness?

"Now, we'll be back soon," said Mr. Graeme to the women," and so don't worry. Take things easy, and we'll fix things up when we return." The slender column of smoke that Frank had first seen, had now become a dense cloud.

After father and son had gone, Mrs. Graeme, feeling a great fear tugging at her heart, went to seek strength and consolation before the altar in the church of St. Ignatius. Her mother had not objected to being left alone—"You go and pray," she had said, "and I, like Martha, will look after the house." Long and earnestly the devout woman prayed not only for her own, but for the whole city as well. The church was strewn with wreckage; the gorgeous Easter decorations were piled in heaps of candelabra, candles, vases, and innumerable flowers. Beautiful statues were lying in pieces on the floor. But neither she nor the hundreds of other worshippers heeded this; the Lord of the earthquake was present before them and their souls were bent on Him alone.

After some hours soldiers arrived and ordered all out of the church. Mrs. Graeme hurried home, and on the way heard a soldier proclaim that all fires in houses were forbidden under pain of death. As she opened the door, what was her horror to find the house filled with smoke! She rushed to the kitchen, and there in a flash, took in the situation. A fire was burning in the stove, on which the coffee pot stood, and further up, flame and smoke leaped against the ceiling where the stovepipe had been disjoined. Her mother was lying motionless on the floor; the efforts of the poor woman had been directed, it was evident, not at her own safety, but at combatting the flames she had caused. Her daughter attempted to raise her inert form, but in a twinkling, a fork of fire had reached her own light clothing and set them burning. Screaming frantically and beating her dress with her hands, the unfortunate woman rushed out into the street, where friendly aid soon conquered the cruel element that was devouring her, but not before she was terribly burnt.

And the house! The flames were now bursting through crevice and window, and the awfulness of the danger came vividly home to the minds of all. A fire engine was on the scene without delay but the stream of water was so small as to be useless. The weight of despair settled on all hearts as they saw the flames devour the whole block in less than half an hour and leap across the street for more booty. The city was doomed.

It was past dinner time and Mr Graeme and his son directed their faces homewards.

"It looks pretty bad, my boy, looks pretty bad, but we're all right. It'll take a mighty big fire to jump Van Ness Avenue."

The boy said nothing. He was watching something with straining eyes.

"Look out, Frank," said the father, "the crowd will trample on you. Keep your eyes about you."

And the father's anxiety was not groundless, for although there was no panic, yet it was a rushing, jostling crowd that made its way along the streets. Nearly everybody was burdeded with his most valuable, or what was deemed his most valuable portable property. Here a man tugged away at a huge trunk, until, completely exhausted, he had to leave it to its fate. There a stout lady puffed along with a parrot in its wire cage under one arm, and a goldfish in its glass prison under the other. A long-haired man tore ahead with a violin-case in his hand and a green sack of books slung over his shoulder, while a young sport followed in his rear, tenderly bearing in his arms a dozen golf sticks. Some were carrying their children. Others carried the sick and crippled on mattrasses. Some were laden down with clothing; many had nothing to carry. Altogether it was a rough, good-natured, excited, dust and-soot-stained, wonderful crowd, but Frank's eyes were fixed on something more absorbing.

"Oh, my God! father, look at that."

He had stopped and clutched at his father's arm.

"Do you see? Hayes Valley is burning. That smoke is exactly over it."

A deadly paleness spread over Mr. Graeme's face, and a faintness benumbed his heart. He leant upon Frank for support.

"Oh my boy," he cried, "let house and home go, but where are the poor women?"

"Come along, cheer up, Pa," said Frank, shaking him kindly. "Why, there won't be one burnt; they'll all escape. Now, let us go and meet mother."

The faintness passed away, and Mr. Graeme proceeded ahead with a haste that his son could hardly equal. To all the boy's questions he had but the muttered answer: "And I left them alone, I left them alone."

When they neared the spot that had been home, they saw nothing there but brick basements and smouldering heaps of ashes. On all sides people were hurrying away from the place, carrying on their backs whatever household effects they could. But among them there was no sign of mother or grandmother. In a piteous tone, Mr. Graeme begged of a bystander to give him information of their whereabouts.

"Pa, you just wait here a moment," and Frank darted off in the direction of a woman who was staggering along under a bundle of clothes.

He was disappointed—she was only a neighbor. "Where's my mother, haven't you seen her?" he asked in a quavering voice.

"Good Heavens! don't you know, dear child?" exclaimed the woman in horror.

"What has happened? What is it—for God's sake, tell me everything."

"Now, my lad, keep up. God have mercy on us all this day! Your poor grandmother—God rest her soul—och, she wanted a sup of warm coffee, the poor old creature."

"Oh, hurry up, please, for God's sake," cried Frank wildly.

"And what did she do but start up the fire, contrary to the Government, and the pipe broke down and she was burnt. The Lord save us; I hope she had her punishment in this world," this not without a tinge of bitterness.

"But my mother," exclaimed Frank, as he shook the garrulous woman fiercely, "she was not burnt, was she?"

"No, my misfortunate lad, and at the same time yes. That is to say, she was burnt pretty bad. They carried the poor creature to the Pavilion. But I wouldn't . . ."

But Frank heard no more. Down to the Mechanic's Pavilion, the boy flew. When half way he thought of his father.

Panting and faint from the heat, the boy retraced his steps, but no father could he find. The people had taken themselves away from the fearful heat of the rapidly advancing fire.

The Pavilion had been turned into an emergency hospital where the wounded and dying had been carried by hundreds to receive whatever help physicians deprived of suitable instruments and medicines, could afford. Now even this asylum was denied them for the fire was bearing down towards it from the tall towers of St. Ignatius, which stood up against the lurid sky like twin geysers belching flame. Men and women, priests, doctors, and nuns were carrying out the patients and placing them upon whatever conveyances could be procured, automobiles, wagons, carts.

Frank ran from one vehicle to another, crying out hoarsely: "Is this Mrs. Graeme? who has seen Mrs. Graeme?"

Not finding her outside, he entered the building, and hastened, with hungry, anguished eyes, from patient to patient. At last he stopped short; a sight met his eyes that brought his heart to a standstill. There at his feet, on a heap of redwood branches—relics of a recent festivity—lay his mother.

He had recognized her by her voice as she moaned in pain. There were hardly any other means of identification. Her clothing was in tatters, her face was red and swollen, and her hair, her wavy brown hair, was burnt off almost entirely. Her hands were clenched together, suggesting excruciating suffering. Frank felt himself growing faint from horror and pity, but he forced himself bravely, and kneeling down by his mother's side said: "Mother, darling, here's your Francis Stephen; I'm going to fix you up all right."

The dying woman slowly opened her eyes and turned them upon her son. Vacant they were at first, but soon a look of recognition came into them. Long, long and wistful and searching was their gaze upon the face of her boy, while the death-film was gathering over their blue depths. A faint smile—oh far more pitiful than tears—hovered on the lips that trembled as if they fain would have spoken. Alas, they could not, and with a sigh the heart-broken mother was dead.

Frank did not cry, nor even shed a tear. The pain was too deep for tears. He kissed the dead lips passionately; he called upon her name; he took her hands in his. As he did so, his fingers touched her wedding ring, and he felt impelled to pull it off, It came off only too easily for the fingers were nearly burnt to the bone.

As he gazed at the precious memento, a soldier's rough hand seized him, and a rougher voice ordered him to drop his loot, and thank his stars he didn't shoot him at sight.

"But it's my mother's wedding ring," cried Frank. "It's all I've got of her."

"Drop it, I say, and get out," cried the hardened officer.

"But I must take her out of here. For God's sake, you surely are not going to let my mother burn, are you?"

"Get out, or we'll all be burned," ordered the soldier. And he forced the boy out at the point of a bayonet. And then it was that the tears came. A hot, blinding, bitter flood. The thought of his mother soon to be reduced to ashes was the last drop in his cup of woe. The last drop?—there was another left to fill up the measure. He sat down on a doorstep to cry out his misery.

"Get out of there, young fellow. Hurry up now." It was another soldier who spoke, roughly enough too.

Frank arose and walked on with the crowd, unheeded and unheeding. At a street crossing, the crowd stopped. Some soldiers stood before them, and ordered them to walk around the block and not cross under pain of death. Those who had already crossed were prevented by another cordon from returning. There was some murmuring at the command, and the military were on their metal.

As he turned away, Frank heard his name called, and looking around saw his father eagerly make his way toward him from the opposite side.

He was covered with perspiration and soot, and twenty years of sorrow and anxiety seemed to have passed over his head during the past two hours. The father-feeling in his haggard face was touching, almost pitiful to see.

"Go back, for God's sake," shouted the boy.

"Get back there," sternly ordered a soldier, with a gun levelled.

Whether Mr. Graeme was so overcome with joy at the sight of his heart's treasure—Frank read the accumulated love of fourteen years in the short glance he had of him—that he did not heed, or whether, as some said, he checked his step just too late, cannot be known. The bullet was sent on its fatal journey and Frank's father lay a corpse on the street.

With a piercing cry "Papa," Frank bounded forward, but was withheld by a sympathizing bystander. "Poor boy," said he, "do you want to die too?"

"Yes, yes, let me die," shrieked the lad. "Let them murder me too." But his cries were unavailing; he was forced away, almost carried, by the kind stranger. And when he returned to a more composed state of mind, and his friend—who had his own troubles to think of—had let him go, he returned to the scene to find that his father's remains had disappeared, no one could tell him whither.

*   *   *   *

Late next day, a little fellow sat on a bench in Townsend Street depot waiting for the next refugee train to pull out. His head was buried in his hands, and his whole air was so woe-begone that a young man moved over to his side and asked him whither he was bound.

"I don't know," the boy replied listlessly, "and I don't really care. They give a free passage in any direction, and I'll take the first train I can, and go as far as they take me."

"So you have no money, then?"

No—oh yes! I have. I have three dollars for the Sodality Entertainment."

S. J. C. '09.

The Redwood.

PUBLISHED MONTHLY BY THE STUDENTS OF THE SANTA CLARA COLLEGE

The object of the Redwood is to record our College Doings, to give proof of College Industry and to knit closer together the hearts of the Boys of the Present and of the Past.

EDITORIAL STAFF

EXECUTIVE BOARD

ANTHONY B. DIEPENBROCK, '08

President

FRANCIS M. HEFFERNAN, '08   MERVYN S. SHAFER, '09

ASSOCIATE EDITORS

COLLEGE NOTES	- - - -	MERVYN S. SHAFER, '09
IN THE LIBRARY	- - - -	GEORGE J. HALL, '08
EXCHANGES	- - - -	MAURICE T. DOOLING, '09
ALUMNI	- - - -	HARRY P. BRODERICK, '08
ATHLETICS	- - - -	CARLOS K. McCLATCHY, '10

BUSINESS MANAGER –

FRANCIS M. HEFFERNAN, '08

ASSISTANT BUSINESS MANAGER

JOHN W. MALTMAN, '09

Address all communications to THE REDWOOD, Santa Clara College, California

Terms of subscription, $1.50 a year; single copies, 15 cents

EDITORIAL COMMENT

It often happens that when a person clings to the customs and beliefs of the past, he is considered "behind the times," no matter what the intrinsic justice of his tenets may be.

However when the matter is duly weighed, it is no disparagement to be behind the times in some respects. It is evident that in religious questions, progress has little place. The religions most up-to-date are those ever-recurring outbursts of fanaticism and fraud and gullibility such as the country had lately the opportunity of scrutinizing in the Dowieites and the Eddyites.

In educational matters also, there is

such a thing as being too "advanced," too modern. Take, for instance, the *lecture system* so much in vogue among our universities. How much praise has been lavished upon this system! how it has been extolled to the skies! And yet when one considers the enormous deficiencies of the method, and the countless cases of "flunking" that can be laid at its door, one wonders what its merits can be, or what advantages it can claim over the tried-and-true *prelection system.*

Let us take an instance to show the logical results that nearly inevitably follow in the ordinary student—understand we speak of the *ordinary* student; exceptions are possible in extraordinary cases. A student takes a course of History, par exemple, in an institution where the Lecture system is exclusively used.

Though at first he may work assiduously at his course, in a short time, the ordinary influences prevailing, he will lose all the enthusiasm he possessed and gradually become a disinterested looker-on. He will naturally fall behind and become so negligent that he will even hardly go to class; and so on until some bright and sunny morn he will wake up to find that he has become "a gentleman of leisure."

"Why should I study? I can learn that matter in two weeks before the ex."

The end of the term comes; the gentleman of leisure begins to get anxious and he does really study. As time wears on, he labors hard, harder than ever before! But what can he do? The

examination day comes along, and the gentleman-of-leisure's situation is something like the predicament of Germanicus of old. Naturally he is mowed down by the scythe of professional lore.

Poor Flunker! You are a victim of the merciless lecture system. What can you do else than regret your life as a gentleman of leisure? Influences prevail! You are but drawn down into an abyss of circumstances! What can you do when the gravity of the lecture system is working upon you? Merely flunk.

There are thousands of cases in point in our American lecture-system universities; and but few men rise superior to their circumstances.

Let me quote a certain Yale man from our excellent contemporary, *The Yale Literary Magazine* for February, 1907:

"'It is not now as it hath been of yore.' The curriculum has become a dry, dead thing, a mere matter of note-books and lead pencils, long talks diluted with the harmless, necessary jest, fevered slumber in uncomfortable chairs. Recitations are done with now, let us sleep through the lecture. Where is the personal equation? Gone! Gone!"

This is but one of many notices we have seen that expresses such a dissatisfaction.

On the other hand let us show the prevalent forces at work in an institution where the grand, old time-tested method known as the prelection system is used, and the results of these forces.

There the young man gets an idea at the very outset. A set hour for study is laid down for him, when nothing besides study must be done; a set hour for class, with no obliging classmate able to answer roll-call for him; and a set hour for recreation, when every opportunity is given for exercise. And this order must be kept, otherwise the young gentleman finds himself in serious trouble—a whole faculty at his heels watching his every footstep, and demanding satisfaction. He finds it necessary to be prepared in his course daily, lest he be called upon for his account and found wanting, and thus fail to get the required standing. This is no small matter; for on this his monthly work is judged; and upon his monthly work the outcome of the entire year depends.

In the lecture system the whole term's standing is decided by a single examination. Can justice to the student be done by so hazardous a method?

"Some men who do thorough, conscientious term-work find it impossible, because of poor memory-power or nervousness, to do themselves justice in an examination, frequently getting into poorer grades than men who have been less faithful during the term. An examination is always more or less a lottery, and unfair as a sole standard of judgment,"

Thus writes a Princeton University man and we believe that his view is correct.

The prelection system implies, of course, much study as well as strict discipline. The very thought of these is bitterness to many, who yet are desirous of acquiring an education. But they cannot be dispensed with; they are the *sine qua non* of scholarship. If we want to succeed on the baseball diamond, on the gridiron, on the cinder-path we must go into training, we must, to use a slang phrase, put our nose to the grindstone.

This is what the prelection system forces us to do; this is where the lecture system fails.

The Retreat

In our last number, owing to lack of space—or perhaps it was the editor's natural perversity—we made no mention of the annual retreat, which always occupied the last three days of Holy Week. It was conducted this year by the Rev. John Walshe, S. J., of San Jose, who performed his difficult task very much to the satisfaction of all of us. A retreat, it goes without saying, is not meant to be a period of amusement, or "sweet-doing-nothing" or even as a mental relaxation, though that may come in incidentally. It is meant for a time of work, of serious, sober reflection and earnest amendment of life. If a little fun can be thrown in so as to make us take to the task a little more kindly, so much the better. In this respect, Fr. Walshe was excellent; he mixed the *dulce* with the *utile* in such a way as to carry us along with him with ever unabated attention. At the close of the retreat, he expressed himself highly gratified and surprised at the splendid behavior of the boys throughout the three days of silence and recollection.

Passion Play

It goes without saying that the main topic of conversation about the College is the Passion Play, now right upon us. It is a topic not confined to us, however, for throughout the whole state the keenest interest centres around it. Letters asking for additional information are coming in from north and south, and it is now very certain that a vast number of people will be unable to secure admittance to any of the six performances.

Every indication points to a most elaborate and successful production. A second gallery is being built—it is now nearly finished—at the rear of the hall, for the accommodation of the big pipe-organ and the orchestra. In addition to these, it will furnish seating room for 80 or 90 people, a very desirable circumstance, when the need for room is so pressing.

The Ryland Debate

The Annual Ryland Debate between the Philalethic Senate and the House of Philhistorians took place on Wednesday evening, April 24th. It was held in the Exhibition Hall, and as has been the case for the past three years, was open to the public.

The Honorable David M. Burnett presided, and Mr. Joseph Ryland, Prof. L. R. Smith, Hon. Wm. Veuve, and Rev. J. J. Cunningham, S. J., acted as judges.

The question in debate was: "Resolved, That the United States Senators should be elected by the direct vote of the people." The affirmative was upheld by the House in the persons of Thomas A. Farrell, Joseph M. Collins, and Ivo G. Bogan. The representatives of the Senate were James F. Twohy, Thomas W. Donlon and Robert E. Fitzgerald, who, of course, argued for the negative side of the question.

In his introductory remarks, Mr. Burnett paid a high tribute to the twin debating societies of Santa Clara College. In no college in the land, he believed, were better opportunities afforded the student of acquiring that soundness of thought and fluency of speech, and that easy "at-homeness" with his audience that marks the efficient speaker or debater. In societies of this kind a young man learns as nowhere else to think on his feet.

Mr. Farrell was the first speaker. His voice was at times rather weak, but his manner and action were forcible enough.

He dwelt at length on the character of the advocates of the proposed change in the law, and showed how the entire nation was clamorous for its adoption. He showed the wide-spread evil of graft in ths present legislative election of Senators, and argued that these evils would be removed if the election were placed in the hands of the people.

Mr. Farrell is very earnest and logical, and though his manner is as yet a little restrained, he gives every promise of developing into a very exceptional speaker.

The next in order was James Twohy. His voice was deep and manly, though towards the end rather inclined to huskiness, his articulation excellent, and his manner dignified and impressive, with, at times, perhaps a trace of stageyness, but hardly enough to detract from the general effect. His speech was a veritable jewel—orderly, logical, masterly in its reasoning, the argument was clothed in language elegant in its diction and fervid in its glowing imagery. Unfortunately he used up all the time alloted him in his first speech, and thus was unable to do any of the rebuttal work usual at the close of the debate.

His argument was divided into three parts: 1. Radical change in the constitution is an evil. 2. The proposed change has intrinsic evils peculiar to itself. 3. The advantages of the change by no means counterbalance those evils.

Joseph M. Collins followed on the affirmative. We had been wont to regard "Joe" in his baseball and athletic aspect somewhat to the exclusion of his other phases. As a public debater, we had hardly ever thought of him, and so his truly able effort on this occasion came upon us, who are not of the House, as an unmitigated surprise. He had "everything," voice, pronunciation, ease, force, and terrific earnestness. He claimed that the Senate being independent of popular suffrage was utterly regardless of popular opinion. They were in great part the result of graft and capital, and hence in them capital and the trusts found their most ready defenders. He gave a brief sketch of several of the Senators to justify his charge.

Thomas W. Donlon was the second negative. His voice was not in its usual form, not nearly so much so as when he made his stirring speeches in the political campaign of last November. His speech, however, was remarkable for its cogent reasoning. If the Senate, he claimed, were elected by the people, then invariably it would be elected on the basis of population; the lesser states would be scarcely represented—a thing directly opposed to the Federal Union. Also, the Senate would become another House of Representatives, there being between them only a distinction without a difference. Thus one of the very-foundation-stones of our system of government would be removed, the partition, namely, of the legislative power into two Chambers. The Senate is meant to be a conservative body, that will keep a restraining hand upon the less staid and grave House, which being the creation of a popular suffrage, is more liable to yield to the whims of popular feeling. But elect the Senate also by popular suffrage, and its conservative character would perish, the Senate itself would perish, and the Constitution would follow in its wake.

Ivo G. Bogan, the last affirmative, has all the qualities of a fine speaker. His delivery is excellent, the voice being strong and musical, and his manner graceful and composed. His style is clear, sufficiently florid, and at times somewhat epigrammatic, which all means that he talks in an entertaining way. Some of his invectives against the Senate, however, struck us as being unnecessarily strong. His great argument was, to use his own phrase, "that a man should choose their own Senators, if they want their interests properly safe-guarded.

The last debater to appear was Robert E. Fitzgerald. Robert is an old-timer, having begun his oratorical career in the Junior Dramatic Society when he was but a mere stripling, and thence passing to the house where for some years he was one of its most prominent members. His senior and present post-graduate year he has, of course, devoted to the Senate. This long and consistent training has borne good fruit, and his effort of April 24th, was that of a seasoned debater. His speech, particularly the lengthy and graceful introduction of it, was almost entirely extempore, and yet never a halt or stay, never a loss for a word. He applied himself to refuting the charges and arguments of the Affirmative, leaving aside his previously prepared speech, of which he brought in now and then sufficient to show that in polish of language he can hold his own. He has the genuine "swing" of the good speaker, and his energy and quickness of thought combined with his readiness of language means future forensic success for him in an exceptional degree.

The debate, all things considered, was a great success. It was noticeable how the speakers held the attention of the audience; even the irrepressible young pre-Academics forgot their restlessness. All the visitors went away favorably impressed.

The decision of the Judges will be known at the Commencement.

We must not forget to thank Prof. Buehrer for his two beautiful selections, and Messrs. Merle and Aguirre for the artistic decoration of the stage, which they transformed into a dream of palms and flowers and mosses and ferns and banners etc.

The Yard

The baseball season proper is over, but its going has brought no lull in the activity of "the yard." This activity reminds one of the proverbial college stew that we read of sometimes, in that it contains a little bit of everything. Baseball is one of these ingredients; the first nine has been submerged into the different class teams, that have sprung up from the spirit of wholesome rivalry existing between different classes of the

college. Then there are class track teams, scudding over the S. A. A. course evening after evening, and getting into condition to contest in a meet in the near future.

In the 2nd Division, great interest is excited by the rivalry of the Junior and Outlaw baseball teams. The former is the regular, orthodox, formally-selected nine, who for some time were monarchs of all they surveyed on their baseball field, and were thus led to fancy they were the whole thing in their line as far as 2nd Division went. They had the usual director of 2nd Division Athletics to oversee their movements, an efficient coach, suits made to order, and what not? All at once there springs up a team of nondescripts. Although minus all formal recognition, they assume to themselves a coach; dispossess the Juniors time and again of the diamond during practice hours by sprinting and getting there first; beat the Juniors in some practice games; beat the Juniors out of their trips by going on those trips themselves, and winning victory after victory for the alma mater. They call themselvey the Outlaws, but their outlawry is of a mild form, more nominal than real.

Another feature of yard life on the 2nd Division side is the military drill, which has been going on in full blast for over a week. The staid 1st Division rubbed its eyes in vast astonishment one bright morning when it beheld about thirty youngsters each shouldering a rifle in true military fashion, marching up and down the yard as if to the manner born, under the leadership òf General Joe Sheean, Captain Cyril Smith, and Colonel Chas. Brazell. Cowboys rounding up a thousand head of steers could hardly have made more noise or shown more energy than these valiant officers. So intense an enthusiasm and so ardent a thirst for military glory did they manage to instil into the breasts of their followers, that nothing could satisfy these but to make, on the very day of their enlisting, a forced march down to Guadalupe Creek and back again to the barracks all in the space of a little over an hour. The townspeople who knew nothing of the mushroom regiment, were greatly alarmed at the sudden invasion and discreetly retired within their garden gates. After a week, however, of this strenuous life, when the guns had worn callosites upon their shoulders, and time had worn off the novelty of the thing, their enthusiasm began to wear away too, and deserter after deserter took to his inglorious heels. Some of them were captured. One of these was the notorious John Arnold Sheehan, who was summarily court martialed and shot. Of course, only moral bullets were used, and as these had no effect whatever upon a man of his stamp, John is as alive and imperturtable as ever.

· ALVMNI ·

At the recent elections in Montana, Alexander J. McGowan, B. S., '87, formerly District Attorney of Ormsby County, Nevada, and also a member of the Nevada State Legislature, was elected to the office of Police Magistrate in Butte City.

Laurence Archer, B. S., '90, is located at Reading, Pennsylvania, engaged in the role of manufacturer. Mr. Archer is connected with the Sun Wall Paper Mfg. Company.

Henry E. Farmer, B. S. '82, holds a responsible position in the United States Customs Service in San Francisco.

In connection with his literary work in New York, James Patrick Donahue, B. S. '82, acts as New York Correspondent for the San Francisco Chronicle. In a recent letter he states that although New York has many advantages and is engaged in numberless activities, still California looks best to him, and that he will return soon.

Bradley V. Sargent, B. S. '84, M. S. '85, at one time District Attorney of the City of Monterey, is now Judge of the Superior Court at Salinas.

Located at Waipahu, Oahu, Territory of Hawaii, is Dr. Joseph McGettigan, B. S. '88. For seven years he was Government Physician, District of Haua Main, and is at present Agent of the Board of Health at Waipahu.

O. D. Stoesser, B. S. '87, is a very successful merchant in Watsonville, Cal.

At Hawthorne, Nevada, engaged also in a mercantile business is John E. Adams, B. S. '89, Com. '89.

J. L. Hudner, B. S. '76, for eight years District Attorney of San Benito County, is now entering upon his third term as City Attorney of Hollister.

From the North comes word that Eugene Breen, A. B. '98, is establishing a great reputation along lines of construction. After leaving Santa Clara Mr. Breen entered the Civil Engineering Dept. of Stanford University, from which he graduated in 1901. He is established in Seattle, Washington.

Hon. Maurice T. Dooling, Ph. D. '03, an eminent jurist of this state, was elected last week as Grand President of the order of the Native Sons of the Golden West.

We have the honor of printing the following letter from Delphine M. Delmas, A. B. '62, A. M. '63, Ph. D. '03.

New York, April 5, 1907.
Anthony B. Diepenbrock, Esq.,
THE REDWOOD,
Santa Clara, Cal.

My Dear Sir: A marked copy of the THE REDWOOD reached me a few days ago. Allow me to thank you, in the first place, for the complimentary things you are there pleased to say about myself.

As regards the remarks which you make on my classical reading, they are, in the main, true. I do keep up, as far as possible, my reading of the classics, and often find in them solace from the labors and cares of professional engagements. But whilst much of what you are kind enough to commend in my own style of these dead masters, much more is due to the loving teaching and example of him whom you name among the guides of my footsteps in Santa Clara College. Father Young was, indeed, as you say, "a most finished and elegant scholar." But he was more. He was the highest type of a gentleman —a gentleman in the broadest, most generous, and most Christian conception of the term—a gentleman such as is pictured in Cardinal Newman's matchless description. I never think of him without emotion. He was the most lovable, and in his day, among those with whom he had his being, the most beloved of men. I never saw, nor can conceive, of one who better than he

"walked
Wearing the light yoke of that Lord of love,
Who still'd the rolling wave of Galilee!"

Again thanking you, I remain
Very Sincerely Yours,
(Signed) D. M. DELMAS.

This letter was written during those busy days when the eminent lawyer was engaged on the great summing-up of the famous case which has brought his name so prominently before the country. Which goes to show that Mr. Delmas' courtesy is as exquisite as his English.

H. P. BRODERICK, '08.

·IN THE LIBRARY·

THE TRAINING ON SILAS

REV. E. J. DEVINE, S. J.

This is one of the best Catholic novels of the season. It sets forth the consolations which alleviate the hardships of a parish priest's daily routine. It shows clearly the different sorts of people he meets with in his world, and all the characters in the story are described most perfectly, particularly that of blunt, energetic, good-natured Miss Garvey.

Some passages of the book deserve special notice: The death of little Helen is pathetically told. Father Sinclair's hoaxing is very clever; the mental anguish of Silas on his bed of sickness is masterly, and Fr. Sinclair's argument with Editor Burton, in which he proves the Catholic Church to be the one true church founded by Christ, is as forcible and convincing as it is brief.

The lecture given by Prof. Flume, besides being full of the meat of sound principle, is a model of eloquence. But we would hardly expect such knowledge of the laws of the Index in these liberal days of ours, from a non-sectarian.

But still the question stands, WHO trained SILAS? Was it Miss Garvey who had a hold on his affections, or was it Fr. Sinclair who brought him to a sense of his duty to his church? We believe the honors equally divided, and think that the good result could not have been brought about without the co-operation of both. Still it does not matter much since Silas was trained and the book attained its end.

All in all we are greatly taken with this book. Whoever reads it will find himself interested, instructed, amused and improved. Would that the hint underlying the whole story were put into effect! Good Catholic free libraries! Heavens, how we need them! And it doesn't seem so hard—at least as put forth by the pen of Fr. Devine. Benziger Brothers, New York. Price $1.25.

GEORGE J. HALL, '08.

"All the world loves a laugh" some-one has wisely said, and surely that realm of buoyant youth, the college world, forms no exception to this rule. Yet we have, after a careful reading of our exchanges, come to the conclusion that humor is sadly neglected among college magazines. It seems strange indeed that, outside of those timeworn and somewhat battered repositories of musty jokes which some of our contemporaries still persist in inflicting on their inoffensive subscribers under sundry attractive labels such as 'In Lighter Vein," "Joshes," "Just a Laugh,' and the like although they contain about as much real fun as a last year's almanac, there is very little attempt at humor on the part of college writers. And when we consider that many of these attempts either descend into silliness or for some other cause fall far short of their mark we have good grounds for wonder indeed. Whether this is because there is much of the cynical in humor which only the hard knocks of after-life can develop or whether we are too busy just now laughing ourselves to furnish food for laughter in others would be hard to say. Probably the real cause lies too deeply hidden to be easily discovered, but whatever be the reason the fact remains that although we do occasionally find a hearty laugh hidden between the covers of one or another of our exchanges, they are woefully few and far apart.

"It is," however, "an ill wind that blows nobody good" and this noticeable lack of humor only serves to increase our appreciation of whatever scraps of fun we do find among our exchanges. Thus it happened that we enjoyed to the full "The Magic Hookah" in *The St. Ignatius Collegian*. This hookah is the property of the Cadiz of Ismlah and one fine day astounds that worthy by suddenly breaking out in speech. It then proceeds to sing a few songs and tell a tale or two that would do credit to any hookah. This one humorous article furnished us with so much amusement that we do not hesitate to place *The Collegian* at the head of our list.

The Williams Lit. for March contains both a poem and an essay on "Peter Pan." While we of the West have as yet had no opportunity of seeing this much praised play we are satisfied that if it possesses the quaint charm of this poem or the interest which the essay seems to indicate it has not been overrated. "A Crested Queenfisher" in the same magazine has a rather novel plot. "Quits," a sea story, presents a striking picture of heroic foolhardiness, not entirely satisfactory to the reader. True heroism should always be admired but folly, no matter how picturesque, can never be other than folly. Nevertheless there is a note of barbaric passion in this story which finds a sympathetic chord even in our civilized breast.

"The University of Oxford" in *The Mercerian* for March, the second of a series of papers on "Great Universities" now running in that magazine, is both interesting and instructive. It is written by one who knows whereof he speaks and though necessarily short it gives a comprehensive view of the quaint old customs in that historic home of learning. The value of the article is greatly enhanced by the excellent views of the University which accompany it. The other matter in this magazine is uniformly interesting if we except the josh column which flaunts itself in our face under the title "On the Campus." Why a magazine of such all around excellence retains such a department as this is a mystery to us.

One naturally expects much from the magazine of such a university as Harvard and *The Harvard Monthly* for April is no disappointment. Far otherwise; it is one of the best of our exchanges. There is so much in it worthy of praise that we hardly know where to

begin. Perhaps begin at the b article, then, is an feld: Poet," Thi who evidently l subject for it is almost tender in eminently readab accomplishes its p had finished it we with the Yiddish also good, espe Days," which in clusion reminds us lines, "The best la men gang aft'aglie and even woman in its verse, howev excels. We quote "Tusitala," that o its freshness and

We have save last. What do y found a prize st worth while but is of the month. A and a first prize i ways looked ra prize story contes ion that they w of really good w was rudely shatte call" in *The W* theme of this stor any means, but th of repression and rarely found in experienced auth served the prize a that she enjoyed one-half as much as we enjoyed the product of her pen.

TUSITALA.

Waveless sea, 'neath a cloudless sky,
  Ripples warm on the yellow shore,
And the slender palm trees, swaying high,
  Show like the columns of the mosques of yore,
Where the story-spinners of Bagdad met.
New Bagdad here, for hither sails
One whom our hearts may not forget,
  Tusitala, teller of tales!

In the dusk as the Southern Cross swings low,
  And the fire-flies flash on the opal sea,
He sits on the beach as the shadows grow,
  And the Island folk, gathered eagerly,
Brown haunch to haunch squat round about,
  While above a petulant parrot rails,
As the tired soul weaves his story out,
  Tusitala, teller of tales!

Strange flowers burst on the tropic hills,
  Gay birds whirr forth from the vine-hung caves,
And the love of life in his body thrills
  As the lithe boys leap in the seething waves.
But his heart cries out for the north again,
  For the craggy hills where the cold mist veils,
And the thin hand drives the oft wearied pen,
  Tusitala, teller of tales!

Prince of Romance, in its shades and lights,
  Yours is the magic that never fails,
In the thousand and one Samoan mights,
  Tusitala, teller of tales!

ROBERT EMMONS ROGERS,
in The Harvard Monthty.

BALLADE

The clarion calls! The horses prance,
  The long thin line into battle sways;
The mail-clad steed of the knights advance
  While the martial music plays.

The strife is on! The pennons wave,
  The knights ride into the tumult's maze—
The grim-eyed death takes his toll of the brave—
  While the martial music plays.

The victors come! The castle keep,
  Resounds with cheers in the victor's praise—
And ah! Who cares for the hearts that weep—
  While the martial music plays?

JAMES C. BARDIN,
in U. of Va. Magazine.

MAURICE T. DOOLING, JR. '09.

if it possesses the quaint charm of this poem or the interest which the essay seems to indicate it has not been overrated. "A Crested Queenfisher" in the same magazine has a rather novel plot. "Quits," a sea story, presents a striking picture of heroic foolhardiness, not entirely satisfactory to the reader. True heroism should always be admired but folly, no matter how picturesque, can never be other than folly. Nevertheless there is a note of barbaric passion in this story which finds a sympathetic chord even in our civilized breast.

"The University of Oxford" in *The Mercerian* for March, the second of a series of papers on "Great Universities" now running in that magazine, is both interesting and instructive. It is written by one who knows whereof he speaks and though necessarily short it gives a comprehensive view of the quaint old customs in that historic home of learning. The value of the article is greatly enhanced by the excellent views of the University which accompany it. The other matter in this magazine is uniformly interesting if we except the josh column which flaunts itself in our face under the title "On the Campus." Why a magazine of such all around excellence retains such a department as this is a mystery to us.

One naturally expects much from the magazine of such a university as Harvard and *The Harvard Monthly* for April is no disappointment. Far otherwise; it is one of the best of our exchanges. There is so much in it worthy of praise that we hardly know where to begin. Perhaps the best plan is to begin at the beginning. The first article, then, is an essay, "Morris Rosenfeld: Poet," This is written by one who evidently loves and admires his subject for it is sincerely sympathetic, almost tender in its treatment. It is eminently readable and what is more, accomplishes its purpose for when we had finished it we too were in sympathy with the Yiddish poet. The stories are also good, especially "Their Salad Days," which in its unexpected conclusion reminds us of Burns' well known lines, "The best laid plans of mice and men gang aft'aglie." They do indeed, and even woman is not immune. It is in its verse, however, that *The Monthly* excels. We quote one ot its best poems, "Tusitala," that our readers may enjoy its freshness and charm for themselves.

We have saved a surprise for the last. What do you think? We have found a prize story that is not only worth while but is also one of the best of the month. A prize story, mind you, and a first prize it that. We have..always looked rather sneeringly upon prize story contests, being of the opinion that they were never productive of really good work, but this opinion was rudely shattered by "Beyond Recall" in *The White and Gold*. The theme of this story is not a new one by. any means, but the writer shows sense of repression and a deftness of touch rarely found in the work of any but experienced authors. Truly she deserved the prize and we sincerely hope that she enjoyed the fruits of her labor one-half as much as we enjoyed the product of her pen.

TUSITALA.

Waveless sea, 'neath a cloudless sky,
  Ripples warm on the yellow shore,
And the slender palm trees, swaying high,
  Show like the columns of the mosques of yore,
Where the story-spinners of Bagdad met.
  New Bagdad here, for hither sails
One whom our hearts may not forget,
  Tusitala, teller of tales!

In the dusk as the Southern Cross swings low,
  And the fire-flies flash on the opal sea,
He sits on the beach as the shadows grow,
  And the Island folk, gathered eagerly,
Brown haunch to haunch squat round about,
  While above a petulant parrot rails,
As the tired soul weaves his story out,
  Tusitala, teller of tales!

Strange flowers burst on the tropic hills,
  Gay birds whirr forth from the vine-hung
    caves,
And the love of life in his body thrills
  As the lithe boys leap in the seething waves.
But his heart cries out for the north again,
  For the craggy hills where the cold mist veils,
And the thin hand drives the oft wearied pen,
  Tusitala, teller of tales!

Prince of Romance, in its shades and lights,
  Yours is the magic that never fails,
In the thousand and one Samoan mights,
  Tusitala, teller of tales!

ROBERT EMMONS ROGERS,
  in The Harvard Monthty.

BALLADE

The clarion calls! The horses prance,
  The long thin line into battle sways;
The mail-clad steed of the knights advance
  While the martial music plays.

The strife is on! The pennous wave,
  The knights ride into the tumult's maze—
The grim-eyed death takes his toll of the brave—
  While the martial music plays.

The victors come! The castle keep,
  Resounds with cheers in the victor's praise—
And ah! Who cares for the hearts that weep—
  While the martial music plays?

JAMES C. BARDIN,
  in U. of Va. Magazine.

MAURICE T. DOOLING, JR. '09.

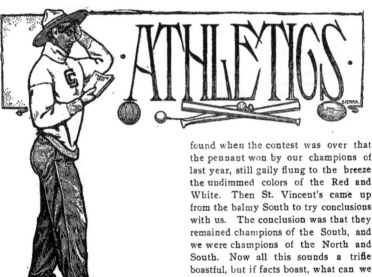

found when the contest was over that the pennant won by our champions of last year, still gaily flung to the breeze the undimmed colors of the Red and White. Then St. Vincent's came up from the balmy South to try conclusions with us. The conclusion was that they remained champions of the South, and we were champions of the North and South. Now all this sounds a trifle boastful, but if facts boast, what can we do? Facts are inexorable things.

The baseball season is over. In all modesty, we can say that with us it has been a great success. In our contests with sister colleges and universities, we lost but two games (to Stanford), and these were the first two games we played, when our boys had not as yet entirely mastered their nervousness, and were, moreover, not thoroughly drilled to machine-like perfection of team work. But when Richard was himself again, woe betide the enemy! Down they fell before us every time. We met all the strictly amateur college teams of Northern California, and we

Santa Clara College 6— Stanford 4

Santa Clara crossed bats with Stanford once more on March 27th on the College diamond, coming out of the contest with the score reading 6-4 in our favor.

The Red and Whites were in fine trim and had the best of the deal throughout, except in the sixth when the Stanfordites managed to bunch four runs. When the College came to the willow again, however, their little lead soon dwindled into the distance.

The game was free from any runs, until the last of the second, when Broderick walked to first. Taking this as his base of operations, he appropriated second, and advanced a bag on Watson's drive to Presley. Salberg obligingly made a beautiful hit to center field on which Broderick tallied. The Palo Altons had hitherto apparently been saving their efforts, for now with a whirl and rush the first four men at the bat succeeded in crossing the plate. But with this tremendous spurt, they seemed to have exhausted their strength, for nothing more was heard from them during the game.

Right back at Stanford with three runs came Santa Clara, when she stepped to the bat. Broderick led off with a· hit to left field and Salberg moved him up a peg by walking and soon after Watson sent Broderick home and Salberg to third by his two-bagger to right field. Pudgy Shafer hit to the same place scoring Salberg and putting Watson to third from whence he tallied on Kilburn's pretty hit to center field.

STANFORD

	AB	R	H	PO	A	E
Scott, cf	4	1	0	1	0	1
Owen, lf	4	1	1	2	1	0
Presley, 1b	3	0	0	6	0	0
Dailey, c	4	0	0	8	2	1
Fenton, 3b	3	0	1	0	1	1
Sampson, ss	3	0	0	2	3	0
Dudley, rf	4	0	0	2	1	0
Thiele, p	3	1	1	0	3	1
Cadwalder, 2b	2	1	0	2	1	0
Totals	32	4	3	24	12	3

SANTA CLARA

	AB	R	H	PO	A	E
Twohy, 2b	4	0	0	1	5	0
Shafer A, ss	4	0	1	0	4	1
Friene, 3b	4	0	1	1	3	0
Lappin, lf	4	0	1	1	0	0
Broderick, 1b	3	2	2	18	0	0
Watson, rf	2	1	1	2	2	0
Salberg, cf	4	2	3	0	0	0
Shafer M, c	3	1	1	4	0	0
Kilburn, p	4	0	2	0	2	1
Totals	33	6	12	27	16	2

RUNS AND HITS BY INNINGS

Stanford...........0 0 0 0 4 0 0 4
Base hits.........0 0 0 0 3 0 0 3
Santa Clara........0 1 0 0 1 3 0 1 6
Base hits........1 1 2 1 2 3 1 1 12

Two Base Hits, Shafer M., Owen and Fenton; Stolen Bases, Stanford 2, Santa Clara 3; Hit by pitched ball, Cadwalder, M. Shafer; Struck out by Thiele 6, by Kilburn 5; Base on Balls, off Thiele 4, off Kilburn 4; Umpire, Joseph M. Collins. Scorer, Sweeny. Time of game, 2 hours.

Santa Clara 4—California 2

Santa Clara College won on April 2, on the University ball-grounds, the third and deciding game of the five-game series with California by defeating the Berkeleyites by the score of 4 to 2.

On account of the many wearying games Kilburn had lately pitched, Charles Freine was substituted in his place and acquitted himself very creditably, retiring seven of his opponents without allowing them to touch the ball. The hits he allowed were well scattered, and had it not been for Ghiradelli's lucky three-bagger in the eighth, California would have been blanked.

Arthur Shafer led off with a beautiful hit, good almost for two bags, stole the next stopping place, advanced to third on a hit of Freine's and scored on the error of California's catcher.

Lappin in the fourth reached first through an error of Miller's, who misjudged his fly, stole second, and went to third an an error and scored on Broderick's heady sacrifice.

Salberg came through with a run in the eighth, reaching first by a pretty hit to Reed, advanced to second on Pudgy Shafer's sacrifice hit and tallied on Twohy's three bagger. Lappin again presented a run to the College when in the ninth he walked, stole second, and scored on Salberg's sacrifice.

California made both of her runs in the eighth. Ghiradelli drove out a three-bagger to center field and scored on Reed's single. Reed was sacrificed to second, advanced to third on an infield drive, and tallied on Wulzen's hit to right.

SANTA CLARA

	AB	R	H	PO	A	E
Twohy, 2b	4	0	2	1	0	0
Shafer A, ss	3	1	1	4	2	0
Freine, p	4	0	0	1	1	0
Lappin, 3b	2	2	0	2	1	0
Broderick, 1b	2	0	0	7	2	1
Kilburn, rf	4	0	0	2	0	0
Salberg, lf	3	1	1	3	0	0
Shafer, c	3	0	0	7	3	1
Peters, cf	3	0	0	2	1	0
Total	28	4	4	29	10	2

CALIFORNIA

	AB	R	H	PO	A	E
Reed, 2b	3	1	2	1	1	1
Causley, ss	4	0	1	2	1	1
Heister, 3b	3	0	0	2	3	0
Wulzen, 1b	4	0	1	7	1	1
Miller, rf	3	0	0	0	0	1
Schaefer, c	2	0	0	9	2	1
Sweezy, cf	4	0	0	2	0	0
Meyer, lf	4	0	0	3	0	0
Ghiradelli, p	2	1	1	1	3	1
Total	29	2	5	27	11	6

RUNS AND HITS BY INNINGS

Santa Clara......1 0 0 1 0 0 0 1 1—4
    Base hits ..2 0 0 0 0 0 2 0—4
California ....0 0 0 0 0 0 2 0—2
    Base hits ..1 0 1 0 0 0 3 0—5

SUMMARY

Three base hits, Twohy, Causley, Ghiradelli. Base on balls, off Freine 2; off Ghiradelli, 4. Struck out by Freine 8, by Ghiradelli 7. Umpire, J. G. Baumgarten. Scorer, H. McKenzie. Time of game, 1 hour, 35 minutes.

Santa Clara 1; Stanford 0

One of the best and most nerve-straining games in amateur circles for many years, was our game with Stanford on April 4th. It was played on the Stanford diamond and was witnessed by hundreds of the Stanford students, who certainly got their money's worth of baseball, even though their crack team went down to defeat.

Throughout the whole game the playing was fast and furious, and until the seventh inning it was a toss-up who should win. On both sides, the batters were hitting the dust in one, two, three, order.

Kilburn's pitching was, beyond a doubt, the principal feature of the game. That wonderful little southpaw of his held Stanford down so effectually that it secured no hits, that not a man reached second, that with the exception of two who walked, none reached first. Santa Clara's outfielders became mere figure-heads, for no flies ventured into the outfield. The bare figures of this game speak more eloquently of Kilburn's prowess than any comment of ours. Besides this, he had eleven assists, and four put outs to his credit.

In the eighth, Mervyn Shafer started the fire-works, with a clean hit to centre. Kilburn bunted, and Twohy advanced them both by another bunt. Then Art. Shafer scored his cousin by a clever sacrifice.

SANTA CLARA

	AB	R	H	PO	A	E
Twohy, 2b.............	3	0	0	1	3	0
Shafer A, ss	3	0	0	3	0	0
Friene, 3b............	4	0	0	1	2	1
Lappin, lf............	3	0	1	0	0	0
Broderick, 1b.........	4	0	1	11	0	0
Watson, rf............	3	0	0	0	0	0
Salberg, cf	3	0	0	0	0	0
Shafer M, c...........	3	1	1	7	2	0
Kilburn, p............	3	0	1	4	11	0
Total...............	29	1	4	27	14	1

STANFORD

	AB	R	H	PO	A	E
Scott, rf..............	3	0	0	4	0	0
Owen, lf..............	3	0	0	1	0	0
Presley, 1b	3	0	0	14	0	0
Fenton, 3b...........	3	0	0	2	3	1
Samson, ss	3	0	0	0	0	0
Wirt, cf..............	3	0	0	1	0	0
Daily, c..............	3	0	0	4	1	0
Goodell, p............	2	0	0	0	1	0
Cadwalder, 2b........	2	0	0	1	3	0
Total.............	25	0	0	27	8	1

RUNS AND HITS BY INNINGS

Santa Clara.........	0	0	0	0	0	0	0	1	0
Base hits	0	1	0	0	0	0	0	2	1
Stanford............	0	0	0	0	0	0	0	0	0
Base hits	0	0	0	0	0	0	0	0	0

SUMMARY

Two base hits, Lappin. Base on balls, off Kilburn, 2; off Goodell, 2. Struck out by Kilburn, 6; by Goodell, 4. Witman pitched part of game for Stanford. Umpire Scorer, H. McKenzie. Time of game, 1 hour and 45 minutes.

Santa Clara 7, St. Vincent's 4

The baseball champions of Southern California, the famous nine of St. Vincent's, met the College on April 19th on Santa Clara's diamond. The game was characterized by bad plays on both sides. If Santa Clara had played in her usual condition St. Vincent's would have been blanked.

Twohy opened the run column in the first by walking, taking second on A. Shafer's hit and third on a wild throw. Broderick drove the ball to St. Vincent's pitcher, hitting his ankle and bouncing off the diamond, and thus enabling Twohy to score.

In the third A. Shafer, Collins, and Freine accounted for three runs and in the fourth Shafer added another to the list.

In the seventh, St. Vincent's secured two runs. Wilkinson was on second base when Winnie hit to Collius, who by a misjudgment of a bad bounce, allowed the ball to go through him, scoring Wilkinson and Winnie.

In the eighth Santa Clara came back strong. Shafer added another run to his list by sousing the ball for a home run. Collins followed by walking, stealing second, and scoring on the error of Flick.

St. Vincent's made one final effort in the ninth, securing two runs but was unable to overcome the lead of Santa Clara.

The visiting team was not in good form, being very much tired out from traveling, and from almost daily games during the preceeding week. When at their best, they certainly constitute an exceptionally strong team. Our nine were in poor form also—they seemed to be unwilling to put forth their best efforts against tired-out opponents.

SANTA CLARA

	AB	R	H	PO	A	E
Twohy, 2b	4	1	0	3	2	0
Shafer A, ss	4	3	3	0	1	1
Collins, cf	3	2	0	1	1	1
Freine, 3b	5	1	2	1	2	0
Lappin, lf	3	0	0	1	0	1
Broderick, 1b	3	0	1	8	0	1
Salberg, rf	3	0	1	0	0	0
Shafer M, c	3	0	2	13	0	0
Kilburn, p	4	0	0	0	2	1
Total	32	7	9	27	9	5

ST. VINCENT'S

	AB	R	H	PO	A	E
Lamer, ss	3	1	0	1	3	1
McCann, 3b	5	1	1	1	0	0
Cuningham, cf	4	0	1	2	1	0
Snodgrass, c	4	0	2	9	0	1
Winnie, lf	4	1	1	4	0	0
Lane, p	4	0	1	0	2	0
Flick, 2b	4	0	2	1	1	3
Wilkinson, 1b	3	1	0	4	0	0
Shildwater, rf	3	0	0	0	0	0
Total	36	4	9	22	7	5

Track

The lovers of the cinder path have taken up their favorite pastime in earnest as may be seen any afternoon on the S. A. A. Sprinters, long distance men, pole-vaulters and so on down the whole line are there in abundance.

"Bum start," "lost my stride" are the expressions in the track vocabulary that take the place of baseballs, "bad bounce," "rotten decision" and so forth.

Track has been neglected in the College a good deal of late years and we are glad to see that it will not be overlooked this year. There is plenty of good material in school and with a little training there should be some good track men. The Freshmen class of the College has taken the iniative and organized a team composed of the following, some of them the best track men in the school: Donovan, McLane, Salberg, A. Shafer, Morgan, Foster, Hubbard, Hurst, Twohy, Nolan, McCabe and Degnan.

Class Games

A series of games is now being played between the Philosophy classes on one side and the amalgamated Sophomores and Freshmen on the other. The rivalry is intense, and the umpire is sure to earn his money before nine innings are over. The batteries are Kilburn and Collins for the higher classes, and Freine and Shafer for the lower.

The first game was played on May 1st, and proved more exciting than a big-leaguer. The lovers of wisdom went down before their younger rivals, the score standing 1-3 against them. A feature of the game was the rooting, Harry McKenzie leading the Philosophers and Harold McLean the Freshmen and Sophomores. The latter claim that they outrooted their opponents as well as outplayed them.

Coach Byrnes' Departure

"Jimmy" Byrnes left us for Cincinnati on the 1st of April to our keen regret. He was thoroughly liked by every one in the College; for a more unassuming, generous, jovial good fellow, it would be hard to find. He was always ready for any harmless fun that came along, and he was yet always in earnest in his work.

On the diamond he was kind but firm, ready to excuse excusable mistakes, but woe betide the negligent player! He took a special interest in each one, and showed himself most ready to help along any promising young ball-tosser in his ambition.

A successful season and a happy return to California is the wish of all his S. C. C. friends.

Second Division Athletics

(W. I. BARRY, '10.)

Things in the west side of the yard have been moving pretty fast since the bad weather blew over, a month ago. Baseball teams and leagues have increased and multiplied until now it is hard to keep track of them.

The Junior team took a trip over to Luna Park on April 18th, and there defeated the S. A. A. Juniors to the score of 6-5. The feature of the game was the squeeze play used in the ninth inning with Foster on 3rd, and Lohse at bat. The ball was punted perfectly and the winning run crossed the plate.

The "Outlaws" paid two visits to Hoitt's Academy, and came home both times with victory written all over their smiling countenances. Gallagher's curves proved an insoluble puzzle to the home team, and they couldn't do a thing with him, while the outlaws hit all over the field.

A league has lately been organized which promises to "make things hum." The teams forming it are the S. A. A. Juniors, the S. C. C. Juniors, and the Outlaws. The first encounter was between the S. C. C. Juniors and the Outlaws. As both teams were confident of victory, and as, moreover, there exists the greatest rivalry between them, players and spectators were all in a ferment from start to finish. To make a long story short, however, the score at the close read 7-2 in favor of Juniors. Foster and Gallagher pitched, and both did great work, their being but six hits off Foster and seven off Gallagher.

The next game was between the Juniors and the S. A. A. Juniors, ending in a victory for the former of 10-5. The S. A. A. Juniors showed very little team-work, and hence, in spite of good individual material, down they went. A feature of this game, as in fact of all the games, is the way in which Brown and Foster meet the ball when a hit is needed. Among the rest, Lohse is especially noted for keeping his weather eye on the ball.

The "All Stars" have played a number of games. As a rule they never give the opposing team much of a show against their own neat playing. The Angelus nine also works in the same smooth fashion. These two teams together with a third lately sprung up under the title of "Junior Outlaws" have formed themselves into a league that promises to keep the shrill echoes reverberating from breakfast to supper on holidays.

CARLOS K. McCLATCHY, '10.

And

Look

At This

Fit

"WHO SAID THAT FIT"

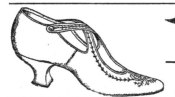

The Faculty of Santa Clara College announces the Third Production of the Famous

NAZARETH

The Passion Play at Santa Clara
under the personal direction of

MARTIN V. MERLE

At College Theater on Evenings of
May 13th, 15th, 16th and 18th and
on Afternoons of May 14th and 18th

PRICES OF SEATS, $5.00, $3.00, $2.50, $2.00, $1.50, $1.00

GENERAL ADMISSION, 50 Cents

SEATES ON SALE:

San Francisco—Kohler & Chase's
Santa Clara—Robinson's Drug Store
San Jose—University Drug Co.
Sacramento—Ing & Allee Drug Co.

Mail orders for seats will be received at the College at any time addressed to Manager Dramatic Club.

Special Rates and Excursions have been arranged for from all points. Inquire of Local Agent.

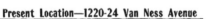

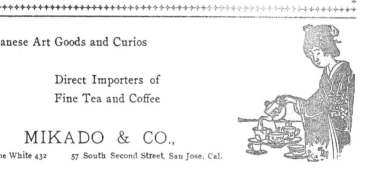

THE
REDWOOD

PHILALETHIC SOCIETY
GOLDEN JUBILEE

JUNE, 1907

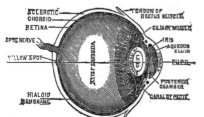

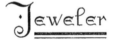

Contents.

Nace Printing Co. Santa Clara, Cal.

PHILALETHIC SENATE 1906–'07.

1.—Francis M. Heffernan, '08. Treasurer. 2.—George H. Casey '07. 3.—Floyd E. Allen, '08. 4.—Thomas J. Griffin. 5.—Cleon P. Kilburn, '08. 6.—James F Twohy, '07. Corresponding Secretary. 7.—Robert E. Fitzgerald, '06. 8.—Walter E. Schmitz, '07. Sergeant-at Arms. 9.—Joseph T Morton, S. J., President 10.—Herman F. Budde, '07. Librarian. 11.—Joseph R. Brown, '07. 12.—August M Aguirre, '07. Recording Secretary. 13.—Harry A. McKenzie, '08. 14.—J. Daniel McKay, '07. 15.—T. Weller

The Redwood.

Entered Dec. 18, 1902, at Santa Clara, Calif. as second-class matter, under Act of Congress of March 3, 1879.

| VOL. VI. | SANTA CLARA, CAL., JUNE, 1907. | No. 9 |

PHILALETHIA

Thou Philalethia!   Again
    We meet as sundered friends should meet,
Out of the warfare of the street,
Out of the soul-wring and the pain

And strangled passions of the times.
Thou drawest me to thine embrace
And I, remembering thy face,
Come to thee empty, save for rimes:

Yea, but undaunted!   For to thee
I owe this knowledge, best of all,
That nothing, nothing can befall
To thine initiate degree !

For thou and Time are not as tides
That wanton with the mobile sands
Wherein the scripture of our hands
Fronting the ocean, still abides !

                              Edwin Coolidge, '92.

FIRST PUBLIC DEBATE OF THE PHILALETHIC SENATE

Over fifty years ago, the Philalethic Senate was organized under the supervision of Father Michael L. Accolti, and decided to take part in the celebration of Washington's Birthday in 1857, by holding a public debate. The question selected by Father Accolti was "Washington Was a Greater Benefactor to Mankind than Napoleon."

Four members of the Senate, Edwin W. Johnston, F. W. Macondray, John Rae and Pierre Coombs, were chosen to carry on the debate, but who were for the affirmative, and who for the negative, I cannot now recall. Their arguments showed study, and were well delivered. At the close of the debate, the chairman—the writer of this—summed up the points presented, and gave a decision in favor of the affirmative.

The exercises, besides the debate, included vocal and instrumental music, with declamations by some of the students of the College. Among the vocal selections, Father Carreda sung "Rocked in the Cradle of the Deep" with such taste that when he had finished, the applause was great.

The celebration was largely attended, not only by the relatives of the students and the people of Santa Clara, but by many from San Jose as well. While admitting the merit of all that was done by the other performers, we, of the Senate, with that self-appreciation which sometimes characterizes college boys, thought our debate was the feature of the day.

Those who participated in the debate, except myself, have passed away. The Fathers who were then at the College, have, I think, all gone to their reward. Some of the students are now living, and one and all, look back to "the good old times," with the feeling that those were happy days.

John M. Burnett, A. M. of 1859.

A GLANCE OVER THE RECORDS OF THE PHIL-ALETHIC SENATE 1857-1907

"The weakling," says Poor Richard Jr. in his Philosophy, "lives in the memoirs of yesterday, the sluggard in the hopes of tomorrow; but there is only one day in the calendar of wisdom and that is the present."—Perhaps. But better the words of some unknown disciple in this school of thought:—"The successes of the future depend upon the actions of the present,—the present is stimulated by the glories of the past." And add to this the remembrance that our present was once the future of those bygone days in which was laid the corner-stone of our existence and the foundations of our success, and a moment of thankful retrospection becomes no less a pleasant task because a sacred duty.

And the Philalethic Senate has a past, a history of which it may well be proud. A glance at its annals and we see "spread large" upon the pages of its minutes records of intellectual feats which rival many a graver organization, and on its roster are names which have since been written across the pages of our history; names of men high in the ranks of our national industries; of leaders in the medical profession; men preeminent in the legal practice, lawyers and jurists unsurpassed and unsurpassable; men high in our educational institutions, in our army, in our government; and above all the names of those men of God which are written in letters of gold upon the Book of Life.

The Philalethic Senate, the upper House of the Literary Congress, is the outcome of the older Philalethic Debating Society which existed as such from 1857 until 1877, but the earliest record of the existence in Santa Clara College of a society devoted to debating, is found in the first few pages of the first book of minutes of the Philalethic Debating Society, which are still in existence in the archives of the Senate Library. There seems to have been a sort of informal or embryonic society, designated in the minutes as "the club," which met every Saturday afternoon under the direction of Rev. Fr. Accolti, who is mentioned as its President. No definite information could be found relative to the date of its institution, the earliest minutes being at a meeting held on Saturday, October 18, 1856. That there had been other, or at least one previous meeting is certain, as the record states that "the minutes of the last meeting were read and approved." No roll-call is given but there are the names of ten of the earliest of the college students appearing as having taken part from time to time on the various debates and it would seem the membership was limited to that number. They are T. Merry, E. W. Johnston, E. Baker, G. Reave, J. Burnett, A. Bur-

nett, T. Macondray, B. Murphy, P. Coombs, and F. Hodges. Mr. Tompkins and Mr. Ward were admitted to membership in the club in December. The first minutes are rather valuable in support of the above data and interesting as a record of the truly Californian questions they debated. The students at that time seemed to worry their souls over the problems of the State no less than their successors of today. But the minutes:

Saturday, Oct. 18, '56.

The club met pursuant to adjournment at this hall, Sat. Oct. 18, 1856. Rev. Pres. Accolti in the chair. The roll called, all the members present. Minutes of the last meeting read and approved. The following question was discussed: "Whether the pursuit of wealth is favorable or detrimental to the progress of Science. Affirmative, T. Merry and E. W. Johnston. Negative, E. Baker and G. Keane. The President, after a few remarks gave his decision in favor of the negative. The House then adopted the following question to be discussed Sat. Oct. 25, 1856,— 'Whether the immigration of the Chinese to California is beneficial or detrimental to the interests of the State.'' Affirmative, J. Burnett and G. Keane. Negative, F. Macondray and B. Murphy. Also the following question was chosen for debate Sat. Nov. 8, 1856—"Whether the gold mines are more conducive to the prosperity of California than agriculture." Affirmative, A. Burnett and P. Coombs. Negative, E. Baker and F. Hodges. The club adjourned to meet Saturday, Oct. 25, 1856.

E. W. JOHNSTON, Secretary.

Without further comment, we might state that in the next meeting the President after a few remarks gave his decision in favor of the negative.

The minutes of nine other meetings follow, containing nothing of special in-

terest. Following the ninth, which was held on January 10, 1857, there is a page missing and the next meeting recorded in the minute book was that of February 28, 1857. Somewhere between these two dates, according to the College Catalogue of that session it was on Washington's Birthday, February 22, 1857, the formal reconstruction of this club into a legally constituted organization with constitution and by-laws, occurred, and from that day we date the existence of the Philalethic Debating Society, now the Philalethic Senate.

The general end of this society, as obvious from its name, was to cultivate deliberative oratory and thereby facilitate all public speaking. Its particular province, as a further analysis of the name indicated, was to be found in the field of Ethics or Moral Law, Philalethic being defined as "Love of the Moral Law." It became known later on as the Philalethic Literary Society and was spoken of as such until the session of 1876–77, the time of its reconstruction as the upper chamber of the Literary Congress, of which we will hear more later.

The constitution and bylaws which were drawn up by the members, and to which they each affixed their signatures are indeed interesting, but too lengthy for reproduction. They are prefaced by the following preamble on the title page of the book of minutes.

"Constitution of the Philalethic Society—Preamble—

We, the undersigned, do hereby adopt and

agree to obey the following constitution and the several bylaws that may be enacted in accordance with its provisions.

Then follow the various articles of which we can only mention a few:

ARTICLE I.

This society shall be known by the name of the Philalethic Society.

ARTICLE III.

The object of this society is to accustom its members, by means of literary discussions, to speak with ease and fluency on useful and interesting subjects, avoiding everything of sectarian tendency.

ARTICLE VI.

The 22nd of February, the anniversary of the establishment of the society, shall be annually celebrated, a discourse analogous to the occasion shall be delivered by one of its members—Under the head of "Order and Decorum," we find the rule.

No member shall be allowed to read his speech or use notes but must trust to previous reflections and to his memory, and which practice would tend to form a habit which he would carry to the bar or to the Legislature.

And then a special department under the title of "Miscellaneous Rules" imposes restrictions which seem to indicate that all the excitement and turbulence with all their accompanying features which existed in California when that State was in the making, found an echo within the peaceful college walls. They remind us of the old rule which obtained in the college discipline in those days—"that the students must on their arrival at the college deposit all fire arms with the First Prefect." The rule calls up visions of booted and spurred young cavalier-students, striding into the office of the First Prefect and turning over to him their "big, black, murderous looking colts," or their "wicked little derringers" or whatever may have been the favored weapon of the times. The First Prefect thus brought about by a simple little rule, though on a somewhat smaller scale, what the Hague Tribunal has repeatedly failed to accomplish, the disarmament of nations. But to revert to our subject. One of the rules in question concerned the behaviour of the Philalethics when in their meeting hall and limited to great extent their personal liberty, besides being disturbing as regards comfort.

Rule 2nd. The use of tobacco is forbidden in the hall. No one shall assume a lolling position nor put his feet on the tables or on the sofas. No one shall enter or remain in the hall with his hat on.

The tenth rule of these same "Miscellaneous" restrictions must have interfered greatly with the principle of free speech.

No disparaging expressions as to the private character of any individual living in the State of California shall be allowed.

No reason is given why the privilege of this restriction should be limited to the citizens in this state, but it must have been inspired by the spirit of independent patriotism of those pioneer builders of California's greatness. The power and duty of enforcing these regulations were placed in the hands of the Censors, of which there were first two, and later only one, and the bylaws very aptly states that

They must bear in mind that they have been elected on account of their firmness of character and love of sound principles to fill an office so important, and they must endeavor by their conduct not to disappoint the expectations of the Society.

The constitution and by-laws were signed by the officers and members of the Society. The names are found as follows:

Michael L. Accottii, S. J., President; E. P. Baker, Vice President; Armstead L. Burnett, Treasurer; E. W. Johnston, Secretary; John Burnett, Censor; Fred W. Macondray, Junior; Pierre L. B. Coombs, James Ross, Walter S. Thorne, George Keane, Hugh Farley, B. D. Murphy, J. D. Whitney, O. M. Rowe, T. Ver Mehr and R. P. Keating.

Other names were added to these signatures from time to time as their owners became members of the club—but the ones quoted seem to be the only original signers, the charter members of our society. In September we find they have added three more names, Messrs. F. Bray, John Bray and Underwood; and in October of the same year three more are admitted, Messrs. Howard, W. F. Rowe and P. Quinens. The minutes are admirable specimens of brevity and conciseness. The meeting is called to order, roll is called, previous minutes read and approved, question debated, the President "after a few remarks" gives his decision in favor of the negative or the affirmative, as the case may be, a new question for the next meeting is proposed and the weary society adjournes. Thus the tale continues, and then two years are missing from the book. From November '57, until October '59, there is no record extant. In 1860 in the month of September some more familiar names are found. In that month there is

record of the admission into the ranks of the Philalethics, Messrs. John O'Neill, A. Durand, Stephen Smith, James J. Hughes and D. M. Delmas, during the Presidency of Rev. Florence Sullivan, S. J.

Concerning the meeting place of the Society the minutes preserve the strictest secrecy. James F. Breen, Secretary for 1860 and '61, tells us with no small degree of confidence that the "club met as usual in their hall"; the others, more discreet, simply mentioned that it "met as usual". The first tangible clue is given in the minutes of Sept. 22, 1861, when Bernard D. Murphy, who was Secretary for that year and the following, writes that "The Philalethic Debating Society convened in this Hall, commonly known as the Reading Room."

And then another gap in the minutes, this time the records of four years are missing, and they begin again with 1866. In the Roll Call for 1868, the names of Robert Kenna, John A. Waddell, Geo. O. Sedgley, Chas. F. Wilcox, Joseph McQuade, Martin Murphy, John Clapp and Clay M. Greene appear among others, Mr. Sedgley in the office of Recording Secretary. There is another roll call, also dated 1868, wherein the same names appear, and after which someone has added, probably at a later date some other little items of historical interest. After the name of Mr. Sedgley we find a note to the effect that he graduated; John Clark had "left college"; John Waddell is still "present", as is also Clay M. Greene and Martin

Murphy; Joseph McQuade had "left the Society" owing to a press of studies; Chas. F. Wilcox had graduated, while Robert E. Kenna had "joined the order of Jesuits in Santa Clara". In the same year a movement was set on foot to change the name of the Society, because, as the minutes state:

This Society had a great number of Honorary Members who were of no service to it, and who cared not for its welfare . . . . and it would be better to form a new society and have a new name, as this was the only way by which we could avoid having so many useless Honorary Members.

Happily the conservative element prevailed and the movement subsided as quietly as its rise had been stormy.

A reference has just been made to the meeting place of the Philalethics. The point is, no doubt, of interest, but very little is known of that early habitat except the statement that "they met as usual in their Hall, commonly known as the Reading Room"' and the location of the Reading Room is merely a matter of conjecture. It is possible, even probable, that they held their gatherings in the old adobe structure which was known since the later Mission Days, as the California Hotel. This building was purchased by the College in 1855 and the Catalogue of that year speaks of its "eight spacious class-rooms." It is probable that one of these was utilized as a home for the Philalethics even from the organization. At least we know that this was the room it occupied during the session of 1866-1867 and Mr. Geo. Sedgley, who was then a member, tells us that it was fully fitted up with hanging curtains, drapery, desks for the President, Secretary and Censors, and other appurtenances of a debating society, as though it had been used for such for some years past. Later, however, in 1871, it found it convenient to secure a new hall, and at that time probably moved to the large room in the second story of the old California Hotel, which was its home until the earthquake of 1906, when, though a pioneer survivor of many a heavy shock, it gave way to the greatest quake it or California ever knew. They were influenced by several reasons to make the change, one, the necessity of larger quarters, and the other the, —but we will let the *Owl* of February, 1871, tell the story:

"The Philalethic Society is very soon to have a new hall. The apartment at present occupied by that body, though handsomely fitted up and adorned with many beautiful and costly presents which cannot well be removed, and though consecrated by the memory, still green, of many of its former members whose voices, now employed on wider fields, or, perhaps, also, forever hushed, have made those old walls ring with their bursts of conviction—bearing eloquence, is too small to accommodate suitably the growing numbers of the society. There is a second objection to it. The Philalethic Society does not occupy the room exclusively, but conjointly with the Junior (Philhistorian) Society. The former meets every Wednesday, the latter every Tuesday evening. This arrangement is not altogether satisfactory. Desks and chairs suffer injury, sashes are shattered (all accidently, of course) and as the guilty party is seldom to be discovered, each society lays the blame at the door of the other and calls on the other to repair damages. To prevent the unpleasantness of such disputes, it is better that the societies should have apartments entirely separated. Then there will be peace. The new hall is a large, nicely-painted room. A handsome chair for the President is placed at the farther end, opposite the entrance, on an ample rostrum. The rostrum and floors are covered with carpets at plain design and modest color."

The article speaks for itself: evidently human nature never changes.

In the session of 1876 and 1877, Rev. Edmund J. Young, S. J., the "grand old man" of the Philalethic Society, who was then in his third term of service as President, brought about the organization of the Philalethic Society and the Philhistorian Society, which existed along with the former from 1859, into the Literary Congress of Santa Clara College, modeling it after the Congress of the United States, the Philalethic Society becoming the Philalethic Senate and the Philhistorians the House of Philhistorians, the two coordinate branches forming the Congress under the President of the College who was *ipso facto* its president. The College Catalogue of the session 1876-1867, thus gives the chief features and details of the new Congress.

LITERARY CONGRESS

Rev. A. Brunengo, S. J., President of College [ex-officio] President.

The Literary Congress consists of two coordinate branches, viz: The Philalethic Senate and the House of Philhistorians. In its form and method of procedure the Congress of the United States has been its model. By such an organization the members may not only derive all the advantages afforded by debating societies, but at the same time acquire a practical knowledge of Parliamentary Law and the manner in which Legislative bodies are conducted.

Philalethic Senate Officers: Edmund J. Young, President; O. Orena, Recording Sec. retary; V. McClatchy, Corresponding Secretary; J. L. Foster, Treasurer; H. Spencer, Librarian; E. McNally, Seargent-at-Arms.

In his paper entitled, "A Memory of an Adobe Forum," which appeared in the Sunday issue of the San Jose Mercury on August 12, 1906, Mr. Charles D. South, himself an old Senator, thus speaks of this phase: "The Literary Congress of Philalethic and Philhistorian History:"

An Original American Idea. The first American Literary Congress was instituted at Santa Clara College by Father Young. It was composed of two coordinate branches, the Philalethic Senate and the House of Philhistorians. In its form and method of procedure the Congress of the United States was taken as a model, the President of the College filling ex-officio, the place of the executive . . . .

Father Young was a native of Maine, and he bore for the Pine Tree State a truly filial love.

It was a New Englander, then, who developed in Santa Clara the ideal forum for Collegians. Only a decade ago, Yale University placed the seal of its approval on the Model Congress as exemplified at Santa Clara, and paid the Western institution the notable honor of adopting the identical idea at New Haven. New England has thus been repaid by the West for that which New England gave to the West through Edmund Young, the Jesuit,— and the plan of the mimic Congress is destined to find its way into every American college and academy.

Mr. South, in the words just quoted, paid an affectionate and well-merited tribute to that man of men, the Rev. Edmund J. Young, S. J. Born in Maine, he lived also for a long period in Washington as Professor at the University there and was a frequent visitor at the Halls of our National Legislature, where he acquired the knowledge which he combined with the spirit of indomitable energy and perseverance, inherited from a long line of Puritan ancestors, for a thoroughly perfect work, which hardly needed the warm and enthusiastic approval and encouragement of the President of the College at that time, Rev. Aloysius Brunengo, S. J.

At the time of the Golden jubilee of the College in 1901, Father Robert E. Kenna, S. J., then President of the College, received an autograph letter from Rev. Samuel H. Frisbee, S. J., President of Woodstock College, Md., and himself an old Yale alumnus. He thus speaks of the Literary Congress as formed under Father Young's fostering hands.

The last number of the Yale Alumni Weekly, for February 6th, has the following: "At a regular meeting of the Yale Union Friday evening, February 1st, it was voted to organize the Union into a Senate, modeled after the Senate of the United States . . . . Harvard has recently adopted this plan and it has

been in use thirty years in a Jesuit College in Santa Clara California.
Yours fraternally in Christ,
S. H. Frisbee,87.

There is given in another part of this issue a complete list of the Presidents who have so successfully guided this society through the various periods of its existence. Among those names, special honor is due to Rev. Father Accotti, S. J.; under whose forming hand the Society was first conceived and carefully nurtured during its early infancy; but it is to Rev. Father Edmund J. Young, S. J., that this organization, whether as the Philalethic Debating Society of early days or the present Philalethic Senate, owe in greatest part, the success of the past and the present and its sanguine hopes for the future. We have spoken of him before, we have quoted the eloquent tribute paid him by Mr. Charles D. South, and, did time and space permit, gladly would we reproduce the most eloquent panegyric pronounced by Mr. D. M. Delmas on the occasion of Santa Clara's Golden Jubilee in 1901. But we cannot forbear to point out a few of the facts of his career in connection with the Philalethic Senate, which tell better than words of praise can do what he has accomplished in their support.

It was in 1862 that he first took charge and held office for four years, the fourth President. During that period he strengthened the young society in every conceivable manner, but most of all by fusing with it the organization known as the Senior Dramatic Society, which had been in a flourishing condition for several years. Being sent to Georgetown University in '66, he remained away until the summer of 1869, but immediately resumed charge of the society on his return, and continued in this position until '72, when a press of work forced him to relinquish it. Becoming President again in 1776 he immediately began to put into reality the plans which had existed so long in his mind and which he had so carefully worked out while in Washington, the combination of the Philalethic and its contemporary, the Philhistorian Society, in the Literary Congress of Santa Clara College. The Senate immediately flourished under his careful protection and earnest assistance and the Literary Congress was firmly established forever. In 1889 he left the Senate never to return.

Such is his record, President for three different terms and for a total of twenty years, more than a third of its history. His careful guidance and indomitable energy helped it at its earliest youth; sustained it at the period of its reconstruction and made use of even its weaknesses for its greater strength. Forever, therefore, must the Senate honor and revere the memory and name of Father Edmund J. Young, their "grand old man."

In connection with the Presidents who guided the society, it is but just that we should mention the men who assisted them so well in their momentous undertakings—the officers of the Philalethic Society, but it is evidently impossible to mention all. The first election resulted in the following staff, mentioned in the early minutes:

Vice President, Edward N. Baker of San Francisco; Secretary, Edward W. Johnston of San Jose; Treasurer, Armstead L. Burnett of San Jose; Censor, John M. Burnett of San Jose.

The staff at the time of the reorganization into the Philalethic Senate may also be given. Father Young was assisted in the performance of this task by—

John W. Bellew, Clerk; George A. Young, Corresponding Secretary; Edward Pierson, Treasurer; Matthew Power, Librarian; Robert Brenham, Sergeant-at-Arms; Henry Wilcox, Assistant Librarian; John Stanton, Assistant Sergeant-at-Arms.

Another long gap and we arrive at the time of the Golden Jubilee at the college already referred to, in 1901. Fr. Ford's able assistants at that time were:

Austin Ellis, Clerk; Wm. Johnson, Corresponding Secretary; Irvin Bounds, Treasurer; Edward Cosgriff, Librarian; Thomas Ryan, Sergeant-at-Arms.

And finally we come to the time of our own Golden Jubilee, and we complete this imperfect reference with a list of the Society's official staff, bearing in mind that the President of the College is always ex-officio the Executive of the Literary Congress and therefore the highest dignitary with respect to each of its branches.

PHILALETHIC SENATE

Session 1909-1907   Second Term

Mr. Joseph T. Morton, President; Mr. James F. Twohy, Cor. Secretary; Mr. August M. Aguirre, Rec. Secretary; Mr. Francis M. Heffernan, Treasurer; Mr. Herman F. Budde, Librarian; Mr. J. Walter Schmitz, Sergeant-at-arms.

With this we must close our citations

from the official roster of the Society, and turn to a rapid survey of the other elements of its achieved and determined history. First to claim attention would of course be the subjects of the many debates; the men who took part; the remarks, if any, of the presiding officer upon the conduct of the debate in question; and his decision, which it may be recalled, has always followed Section 5, Article II of the By-Laws:

The President, or Vice President, if he presides, shall positively decide on all questions discussed in this Society, not according to the merits of the question, but according to the arguments advanced.

We have already mentioned the first few debates recorded; we are forced not to skip the forty-seven intervening years marked with their milestones of "many a forensic bout," and content ourselves with a brief review of the Public Debates between the Senate and the House of Philhistorians for the Ryland Gold Medal, awarded annually for that purpose. The first of these debates was held in the second term of the session of 1902–1903, and on the question: "Resolved that the United States of America should retain the Philippine Islands." The personnel was John M. Regan, Francis Moraghan, and Charles O'Connor for the Senate; and Thomas Leonard, Jedd McClatchy, and Harold O'Connor for the House, which won both the debate and the medal, the latter falling to Mr. Leonard. Again in the following year, 1904, they met on the question: "Resolved, that in the present war in the Far East the sympathy of the people of the United States should be with Russia

rather than Japan," and again the Representatives were victors. The Senators who defended the affirmative of the question, were John O. McElroy and James F. Johnson; the Representatives, Ralph C. Harrison and Gerald P. Beaumont, the latter winning the Ryland Medal. But in 1905 the situation was reversed and the toga-clad Senators won back their laurels from the House. The following was the question debated: "Resolved: That the opposition of the United States Senate to President Roosevelt in the matter at the Arbitration Treaties merits the approval of the country at large." The House debating-team which lost to the Senate the well fought debate, is worthy of notice; they were Representative Floyd E. Allen of Arizona, Leo J. Atteridge of Watsonville, and Robert E. Fitzgerald of Georgetown. The Senate which sustained the negative side of the resolution was represented by Senators John J. Ivancovich of San Francisco, Michael R. O'Reilly of Syracuse, N. Y., and John W. Riordan of Santa Clara, the latter team having sustained the negative side of the resolution. Senator Riordan was adjudged the winner of the medal. The earthquake of 1906 interrupted and effectually put an end to all thought of contest for that year and the two Houses next met for the Fourth Ryland Annual Medal Debate in May, 1907. The question discussed related to the method of election of the United States Senators. "Resolved: That the United States Senators should be elected by the direct vote of the people." By an odd coincidence, it seems, the Senate of Santa Clara defended its prototype the Senate of the United States in their method of election, while the House of Philhistorians, following the usual custom of that greater House, vigorously condemned it. The Senators were James F. Twohy of Spokane, Thomas W. Donlon of Oxnard, and Robert E. Fitzgerald of Georgetown; their opponents, Thomas Farrell of Sacramento, Joseph M. Collins of San Francisco, and Ivo G. Bogan of Arizona.

Since this is a historical review and in no part of the nature of a prophecy, the result of that debate on the winner of the medal cannot be given here, for in pursuance of the custom obtaining in the College, such information is reserved until the Commencement, but the Senate hopes for the best.

But we must pause, though by far the greater part of the glories of the Philalethic Senate remain untold. It would take greater space than we have room for, a longer time than we have at our disposal, to do justice to this theme. But "by their fruits you shall know them." Santa Clara has sent her sons to every country on the globe, she has her representatives in every trade and profession, and the greater part of them have carried away with them from their Alma Mater the memory of happy days spent in the "Adobe Forum." That Adobe Forum is no longer here, but the memories and associations still linger around that hallowed spot upon which the new home of the Senate has been erected, and will ever serve to influence to greater effort and emulating zeal the future members of the Philalethic Senate.

The Successes of the Future depend upon the Actions of the Present; the Present is Stimulated by the Glories of the Past.

ROBERT E. FITZGERALD, A. M., '07.

PHILALETHICA

Ode on the Golden Jubilee of the Senate Branch of the Literary Congress of
Santa Clara College

Our flag Philalethic in splendor is flashing
    To rally the kings of the forum today;
And loud through the air let your voices go crashing,
    Demosthenes, Cicero, Webster and Clay!
Ho, whiskered alumnus, explode an example
    Of spirit that flamed half-a-century back!
Ho, beardless collegians, your lung-power ample
    Must furnish the steam that the patriarchs lack.

Cheers, trumpet-din, now, and of drums the wild clatter,
    Are hailing the Senate at twoscore and ten.
Hurrah! On this birthday the welkin we'll shatter
    With shouting if never we split it again!
Each year was a nugget, a wonderful treasure;
    We've melted the fifty for purest of gold
The Senate to crown, and an exquisite pleasure
    Is ours when the diadem bright we behold!
So, wave all your laurels, you intellect-heroes,
    And thunder aloft your dynamical cheer!
To the man-making Senate what more could endear us
    Than all the rich guerdons that fell to us here?

To the realm of the Law we have furnished an army
    Puissant in Knowledge its principles yield,
With brain-bulging foreheads and voices that charm ye,
    And led by Napoleon who masters the field.
But whether Napoleon or Curran we call him,
    He stands at the head of the Barrister class.
In the temple of Fame shall the future install him
    By the old Philalethical name of Delmas!

His talents were fostered and guided and nourished
    And given their classical beauty and grace,
Right here where the genius of Learning has flourished
    Since Jesuit scholarship lighted the place.

From triumphs of mind to the conquests of battle
    An easy transition we proved it to be
When Senator Smith, 'mid the war's din and rattle,
    Made lions look tame by the Orient sea.
A chorus instead of a rythmical solo
    Were far more befitting our "General Jim,"
Whose sword rendered futile the Filippine bolo
    And captured the stars that no envy can dim.
When the President glanced o'er the list of the loyal
    For some one to govern the Philippines with,
What wonder he stopped, with a feeling right royal,
    And shouted, "Eureka! I nominate Smith!"
The million Smith votes never prompted the offer,
    Since Theodore quits at the second term's close.
That Smith's Philalethic career drew the proffer
    The Senate is privileged now to suppose.

In the southland a patriot people have builded
    A statue of bronze to the glory of one
Whose memory, hallowed and stainless, is gilded
    With rays of sublime immortality's sun.
Columbia, that laureled his brow, shall remember,
    As long as her stars gleam with Liberty's light,
Or burns in the watchfire of Freedom an ember,
    The deeds of her potent-voiced champion, White!
From his fame in the Senate, the golden lips ever
    Admonish his heirs on the scenes that he trod:
"Be honor your jewel and part with it never,
    But live for your country, your home, and your God!"

Far less to the giants of classical ages,
    Whose words set all Athens and Rome in a blaze,
Than to Young and Accolti and Shallo, the sages
    Of old love-enshrined Philalethica's days,
Owe Senators all for the breadth of their powers,
    The range of their knowledge, the eloquence rare,
That still, as of yore, in this mind-garden flowers
    Where essence of culture impregnates the air.
Nor more to the memoried past are we debtors
    Than debtors to Gleeson and Kenna who now
Foretell a Saint Claire in the Kingdom of letters
    With Varsity laurel-leaves binding her brow.
When a new tale of years makes a hundred the story
    Of Earth's Philalethical swings round the sun,
The Senate will pompously take all the glory
    For everything Kenna and Gleeson have done!

For honor and station exalted however,
    The Senators all have the qualities fit.
Like wine they all go on improving forever
    In flavor of learning and sparkle of wit.
You'll find one the bench of the Justice adorning,
    Or gracing the Governor's canopied chair;
Or clipping coupons at his bank in the morning
    Ere clipping the motor-time out in the air;
Or saving the Nation by speeches magnetic
    That flash from the stump in the torrid campaign;
Or striding away like a peripatetic
    While making an abstract philosophy plain;
Or pouring out thoughts from a brain-pan of plenty
    The age to enlighten and man to improve;
Or raising the standard of Century Twenty
    By hoisting it out of each narrow old groove.

His brow with a lofty intelligence beaming,
  The old Philalethic you'll find in the van
Of human endeavor, his bright colors streaming
  To rally the Right in the conflicts of Man!

Hurrah for the Senate! nor stint ye the cheering!
  Hurrah! and march forward new heights to attain!
Our hopes are as high as the past is endearing!
  Then speed ye the summit of glory to gain!

Thus always advancing and never retreating,
  Your banner far-flinging its folds never furled,
Spur on, till you give your full-Century greeting,
  And rouse for your Senate the cheers of the world!

                    CHARLES D. SOUTH, A. M., '01.

A PAGE FROM THE PAST

[The following humorous account of the celebration of Washington's birthday in 1862 is from the records of the Philalethic Society. We are indebted for it to the pen of the Hon. Bernard D. Murphy, who was then somewhat younger than he is at present.]

The members of the Philalethic Society had looked forward with pleasing anticipations to the dawn of this auspicious day; for upon them had developed the agreeable duty of heralding to an admiring audience the virtues and patriotism of Washington,

A week previous to the 22d, the weather had been stormy and tempestuous; and each member had entertained in his heart a secret yet intense fear with regard to its future serenity. But when the eve of the eventful day arrived, each heart glowed with satisfaction and delight, for the upward gaze detected no cloud to dim the luster of the heavens. Former doubt gave place to present certainty; the desponding tread of a week ago was now superseded by the elastic step of confidence; and each member, parchment in hand and head erect, trod the yard as if the concentrated gaze of millions were upon him.

But oh, the fallacy of human events! —the uncertainty of human felicity! when the morning dawned the sky was overcast. The lowering clouds hung thick and black in the western sky, and as they rolled eastward, mantling with gloom the azure expanse of the heavens, the rain descended with that cold, damp monotony which renders despondency more cheerless than despair.

Thus all our high-flown hopes were dissipated—all our fond anticipations crumbled into dust! And yet the gloom was but momentary. Our youthful ardor, like the frosted grass, was chilled for a while; but it burst forth again with renewed vigor. What though the rain descend in torrents? Our attractions will make people disregard the tempest. What though the day be dark and gloomy? The flashing fire of our eloquence will be more plainly visible.

Thus did the members of the Philalethic Society reason, after the first moments of dispondency; and their reasoning was as worthless as their vanity was overweening.

The hour arrived, and the audience assembled. It was a motley crew of ostlers, school-boys, hotel-keepers, clerks and itinerant preachers. In front of all, however, bloomed one solitary flower—beautiful from its very loneliness. Her presence threw a luster over the patriotic scene. And though she blushed all alone, unlike the rose of the desert, she was not "born to blush unseen."

But the exercises open. Listen! San Juan's favorite son is about to speak; and "Washington" is his theme. Attend! for Breen is skilled in "Homer's sounding line," and versed in Ciceronian eloquence. His oration is modeled after those of the ancients. His exordium is an apology for the meanness of his subject—his division, twofold, patriotism and Washington—his augmentation brilliantly metaphorical, and his peroration grandiloquently striking. A burst of applause greets. his withdrawal from the stage.

Next followed Bowie, of Georgetown memory, skilled in the mystic harmonies of music. The "Sword of Washington" was the subject and poetry the garment of his theme. Well was that poetry written, and pathetically was it delivered. Three times the speaker drew his sword; and thrice three times he gave it to the assembled Congress. He was warmed by his subject. He pointed out the gray-haired Senators; he spoke of their "pallid cheeks," their "weeping eyes;" he exemplified his ideas by gestures, and pointed to his own eyes in a manner that made. his sympathizing audience tremble for their safety.

The next performance was a debate, conducted between Messrs. R. P. Keating and B. D. Murphy. How shall I find words to speak of this admirable contest of intellect? How give an adequate idea of the reply, assertion and retort; the quick transitions, the luminous thought, and the humorous sallies? Vain were the attempt, for antiquity never listened to such a brilliant debate, nor will posterity ever desire to hear it again.

The thunders of applause which followed the debate were hushed by the applause of *Dufficy*—the same Dufficy who was born in the eminent city known as the Little Pride of the State, and vulgarly ycleped "Marysville." "The Grave of Washington," was his subject; and B. Keating the author who treated it. The theme was poetical, and "the numbered feet in easy measure came." It filled the souls of all who heard it with rapture, and reason half regretted that man's ideas ever assumed prosaic dress. But as for the speaker, his choked accents, his frightened looks, his straitened gestures and uneasy postures, almost led the audience to imagine that they actually beheld the sheeted spectre of the departed Washington.

Next followed Ball; and "Laughter" was the object of his verse. Well did he succeed. For if the audience did not laugh, at least they smiled; and if boisterous mirth did not reward his wit, neither was it chilled by choking sobs and cries.

The exercises of the day were concluded by a farce entitled, "The Correspondent," *compiled* by James Hughes of San Francisco.

The Farce consisted of two scenes.

One was the opening, the other was the closing scene.

All the incidents of the plot were connected, and might have occurred in twenty-four hours.

The number of characters was four; and the time consumed in performing the piece somewhat exceeded seven minutes.

The actors were exceedingly laughable and farcical.

It would be invidious to give the preference to any single individual;

though I cannot help mentioning with praise the names of Dufficy, Bowie, Boyle and James Hughes.

I know it would not be well to hazard an opinion on the merit of this farce, except after due deliberation. However, it may safely be said that it was, in its own way, a "little masterpiece."

But there is an orator whom I have overlooked. Not on account of the diminutiveness of his person, or the insignificance of his oration; but owing to the treachery of my memory. His name is Henning, and he hails from Missouri State. His voice was low—subdued; his accent the Missouri twang. But if his voice was low and his intonation disagreeable, the harmony of his sentences, the solidity of his thoughts, and the graceful elegance of his expressions, made us lose sight of the orator, and listen in entranced delight to the composer. Literature will yet owe some of her beauties to his pen.

"B. D. M."

LETTERS FROM OLD SENATORS

[It was our ambition to have a large number of letters from the "old boys," but owing to the short notice we were obliged to give them, we were somewhat disappointed. Of the letters, moreover, that did come, some dealt not with the Senate, but with College days in general. These we omit. The following are from Fr. Kenna, S. J., ex-Pres. of Santa Clara; Jas. H. Campbell, District Attorney, San Jose; Chas. South, Poet and Prose-writer; Rev. Jos. McQuade, S. H. Church, S. F.; James Emery, Lawyer, New York; Gerald Beaumont, City Editor San Jose Mercury, and Delphin M. Delmas.]

I

DEAR EDITOR:

You ask me to write something about the Philalethic Senate. How can I refuse you, and on the other hand how can I in a few hurried moments write anything fit for the REDWOOD? Your request carries my mind back to days that lie deep and sweet in my heart, it touches a tender cord whose response is too sacred for utterance; it brings vividly before me the Fathers and mentors of my soul, men whom I honored and obeyed, men whose very presence was a benediction and whose daily lives were an exhortation to all that is high and noble and pure. Men who wrought great things for science and religion, and whose energies were spent in laying broad and deep the foundation of this western country's welfare and progress and greatness.

It is with the deepest reverence that I write the names of those men who sacrificed all that men hold dear to make dear old Santa Clara a home of patriotism, of science, of philosophy, and of religion—Fathers Masnata, Veyret, Whyte, Sullivan, Traverso, Neri, Accolti, Brunengo, Ponte, Mengarini, Young, Caredda, and the incomparable Varsi, and others. All of them ideal educators, unselfish, and self-sacrificing even unto death, for the honor of God and the good of their fellow men!

But your request concerns more closely the Philalethic Senate whose Golden Jubilee is now at hand. The child of the princely Fr. Accolti, the Philalethic Literary and Debating Society grew to manhood ever waxing strong under the fostering and wonderful care of the great hearted Father Young during thirty years or more. It is now forty years since I had the honor of being admitted as an active member and I shall always gratefully cherish the pleasant and fruitful hours I passed at the meetings and debates whilst a student in 1867-68. This society conjointly with the Philhistorians occupied a large room in the north end of the old adobe building called in earlier times the California Hotel. This historic structure was damaged, as everyone knows, by the earthquake in 1896 and was razed to the ground. The Philalethics met on

Wednesday evenings and the Philhistorians on Mondays of the Scholastic Year. The members of the Philalethic were elected from the students of the higher classes and those of the Philhistorians from Poetry and the First Grammar class. The friendly rivalry existing between the two societies became so strong that in the seventies, the Philhistorians determined to oust the Philalethics from their position as the College Debating Society, and manouvered so skillfully that they kept the best talent, and were in fact for a time the leaders in debate. This rivalry was a source of no little unpleasantness and anxiety to the Faculty and to Father Young, but Father Young who loved both and labored so zealously for both, outwitted the Philhistorians and by a *coup-de-main*, founded the present Literary Congress. It was a thought as happy as it is American and it so captured all that it became at once a success.

The Philalethic was always a live society, its meetings were intensely interesting, and the debates lively and protracted. Everything was carried out according to strict parliamentary usage and always with a vim and snap. The elections and admission of members were almost always exciting and not infrequently gave occasion to members to display much political acumen, not to call it cunning.

Under Father Young's supervision, the Philalethic Society was a school of great ideals and its influence was for the highest and the best. He was a great teacher and possessed in an eminent degree that characteristic of all great teachers, the faculty of drawing out, bringing to the fore, the talents and powers so often so deeply hidden that the ordinary teacher does not suspect their existence, much less call them into action. He never thought to display himself but he was ever eager to bring out his boys and push them to the front. His glory was to develop his boys and to send them forth true men, honest, intelligent citizens, and good christians. The Cross and the flag were his only standards and under them he would rally all his students. He strove to send forth patriots who would sacrifice all for country and religion and whose lives would be beacon lights for all. This influence in forming character was indeed great and there are hundreds today who looking back to the hours spent with Fr. Young, will say, "Yes, I never can forget his strong, earnest words: Boys be sure you are right, and then and not till then, go ahead."

And he loved his boys. He never tired speaking of them, relating charming anecdotes about them. He more than once told us how, when Delmas was in the Philalethic Society, many of the members feared the silent student who always had a book in his hand, and who always crushed them in debate. They plotted and voted to bar him out of the debates.

The boys in their turn never tired of Father Young's company, and it was always a fine treat to stand around him and listen to him. Even now if you meet an old Philalethic you need but to mention Fr. Young's name to learn how deep and lasting is his love. An example of this we find in Mr. Delmas, whose charming eulogy of his old teacher in last April's REDWOOD does honor to both master and pupil. While I have so little time to write, I cannot close without referring to the results of the work of the Philalethic in the forming of ready and fluent speakers and also in sending forth some of the best presiding officers in the state. Fr. Young's ambition was to make his student to think accurately and speak fluently and forcibly on their feet.

Hon. Steven L. White, a great orator and one of the very best presiding officers of great assemblies, learned this latter art in the old Philalethic society. And it was a marvel to many to see White control the vast Democratic State Conventions over which he sometimes presided.

It is sweet to go back and renew in spirit the dear associations, the pleasant memories, and the strong pure friendship of our school days with their trials and triumphs, and remain once more in the hallowed company of those who taught us how to live.

Those Wednesday evenings in the old adobe room with the warm debates and the weekly reunions under Fr. Young's guidance were to me always a pleasure like that which fills the tired school boy when vacation comes. Those Wednesdays were red-letter days of the keenest

pleasure and of great profit. I trust that it is still the same with the Philalethic Senate and that there reign the same old spirit and the greatness of heart that filled the whole of 1867-68. How sweet it would be to meet the dear old boys in the same old place and in the same old way under the beaming countenance of Father Young and in the hearing of his hearty greeting and stirring words as of yore! And since it cannot be let us sometimes pass a few moments—as the much loved and honored friend of my youth, Clay Greene, so sweetly puts it—"in the tender recollections of my sweet long ago in Santa Clara College" in the classic precincts of the Philalethic hall. With the deepest affection for all who participated in that "sweet long ago"

I remain a Philalethic of 1867-68.

Very sincerely yours,

ROBERT E. KENNA, S. J.

II

DEAR MR. EDITOR:

A busy parish priest has very little time to indulge in reminiscences, even though these be of the most pleasant nature, as certainly are most, of my recollections of the old Senate days, or rather evenings. There is one incident, however, which I cannot forego telling for the reason that I figure in it myself as the — well, as the hero or victim, I don't know which. As all former members of the Philaletic Debating Society during Father Young's regime know, it was characteristic of that venerated

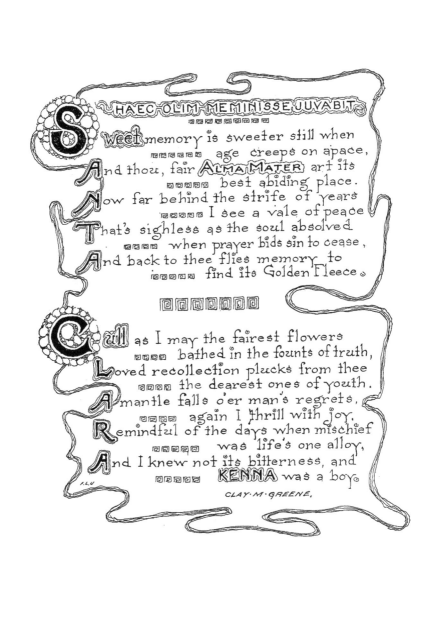

HAEC·OLIM·MEMINISSE·JUVABIT·

Sweet memory is sweeter still when
age creeps on apace,
And thou, fair **ALMA MATER** art its
best abiding place.
Now far behind the strife of years
I see a vale of peace
That's sighless as the soul absolved
when prayer bids sin to cease,
And back to thee flies memory to
find its Golden Fleece.

Cull as I may the fairest flowers
bathed in the founts of truth,
Loved recollection plucks from thee
the dearest ones of youth.
A mantle falls o'er man's regrets,
again I thrill with joy.
Remindful of the days when mischief
was life's one alloy,
And I knew not its bitterness, and
KENNA was a boy.

CLAY·M·GREENE.

professor to play upon the temperaments or the ambitions of the youthful Senators with the result that he invariably succeeded in getting what he wanted—work. It is possibly pardonable slang to say that he was always "working" us. There were among us those who were persuaded that they possessed many of the essential elements of oratory. There is no need of mentioning names, but let the reader cast his eye over the Senate of '87 and '88, which fortunately still hangs in the hall, and he can pick them out, even though he be not a contemporary. And how Father Young "worked" them! If he saw interest in a debate flag he would slyly intimate that some of the orators might raise their voices and presently the numerous elements of strength on both sides would be seen. Up would jump the orators and very often the question would be carried through two or three meetings. And so, also, with those who flirted with the Muse; he would somehow make them believe that something in their favorite line was expected from them. Father Young would go any distance and make use of any expedient to get a boy on his feet. There were those who had to be aroused and the writer recalls an incident in which he played a funny part to illustrate this trait or characteristic of Father Young. There was some question before us and the talking was in the hands of one or two. The writer must have shown unusual apathy and I guess good Father Young marked him that night for one of his "works." He rather innocently got him to his feet and got him to make a statement. Fortunately for his purpose, a member raised a point of order, which, because it happened to be most ridiculously taken, was sustained by Father Young, and what was more, he who took the point was complimented in high eulogistic terms by the president. And if ever one was tricked, fooled to the extent of making a whole circus of himself, it was the writer. For incoherent speech, frothings, inarticulate mutterings, there was nothing like it before or since in Santa Clara. He could not make noise enough or talk fast enough in denouncing the outrageous treatment. He called the President narrow-minded, unjust, mean, in fact everything. Then his pride asserted itself and despite this unfair treatment he would smother his opponent. And then happened what Father Young hoped for—the speaker begged for the floor for the entire evening. It was only when he sat down that it dawned on him that he was "worked." He thought, however, he had taken the matter too seriously and that an apology was due Father Young. He ran after him that night in the door and begged forgiveness, and Father Young could be heard chuckling until he passed into the Father's residence.

Conspicuous debaters in those days were Dante Prince, Alex ("Con") McGowan, Pedro Zabala, E. B. Martinelli, and Rev. B. J. McKinnon and J. F. Byrne.

REV. JOSEPH P. McQUAIDE, '88.

STUTTERING JIM

I knew a fellow as queer as sin
He was awkward-like and tall and thin,
Down at Santa Clara here
He joined the Senate—ah—the year—
Well say it doesn't matter now,
But he was as awkward as a cow,
    And we called him
    Stuttering Jim! ⁻

He was always willing to debate,
He haunted the Senate early and late;
And how the fellows all would screech
When stuttering Jim got up to speech!
As he floundered on in his awkward way
I can see him in fancy still today,
    As we laughed at him
    Stuttering Jim!

He said that down on the farm his "paw"
Had picked Jim out, as it were, for law.
And he said "By jings I'm goin' to try,
You fellows can go ahead and guy"
So he stumbled along in determined way,
Taking every chance in the Senate fray,
    And we laughed at him
    Poor stuttering Jim!

And then one day in the after years
In a court room—every eye dimmed with tears—
I heard a lawyer in right's defense
Pour forth in limpid eloquence,
The beauty of his noble soul,—
Back to the old Senate my spirit stole.
    And my eyes were dim
    As I listened to him,
    It was stuttering Jim.
      Harry T. Fee, B. S., '91.

III

DEAR EDITOR REDWOOD:

From 1869 to 1872 the debating societies of the college were known as the Philhistorians and the Philalethics. The division into Senate and House, which at present obtains, had not then been devised.

The dominant spirit of the Philalethics during those years was Father Young. His zeal and enthusiasm for the promotion of the art of vigorous debate were contagious, and all of the students who had any ambition to excel in oratory were stimulated to the exercise of their best efforts.

Father Young's memory was stored with recollections ot the prominent members of former days. I particularly recall an anecdote, which he used to tell to emphasize the weakness of an anti-climax, concerning a possible future rival of Daniel Webster, who in describing in a figurative manner the commencement of hostilities by a great commander said "There was no longer room for hesitation, and he drew his sword. Yes sir, *he drew it right out.*"

Father Young was an optimist. He saw the best in everyone, and by his warm and unstinted praise succeeded in promoting the natural talents of the debaters to a high degree of cultivation.

Among those who were readiest in the arts of the forum at that time was Robert Forbes. Forbes was among the most practical and shrewd of young men, and yet in decided contrast with his actual character he cultivated the appearance and affectations of an exquisite. He was the "Beau Brummel" of the college—the most dapper and finical of youths. But all these outward manifestations were but a thin crust concealing excellent, sane and sterling qualities. He was well equipped for debate by the clearness and alertness of his mind. He seized at once upon the weak point of an argument and showed great dexterity in dissecting and destroying it. He was an excellent example of the extempore speaker. He never concerned himself with the verbiage of an address but the lucidity of his mind was always revealed by an apt and fitting style of expression. He had a natural vein of humor and a rare faculty of making both his opponent and his opponent's argument seem ridiculous.

The strangest thing about it all was that he never excited enmity by his sarcasm, or contempt by his effeminacy of dress, but on the contrary he had the good will and esteem of everyone.

The one of all others to whom the mind naturally turns as a participant in the Philalethic debates was Stephen M. White. His case is the most notable one, of which I am aware, of a gradual and remarkable evolution in powers of oratory. For a considerable time after he became a member of the society his efforts attracted no attention. At a later time it was observed that he displayed a faculty of expressing himself agreeably on matters as to which it was obvious he had no opportunity for preparation. This readiness in debate became more and more noticeable until it might be said that he had become famous in this regard among his college associates.

There was never any evidence, even when time permitted it, that he gave particular attention to rhetorical display. Opportunity was utilized only in arming himself with substantial arguments to fortify his position.

The remembrance of these days recalls to mind an occasion heralded throughout the nation when the most eloquent statesmen of the Republic exhibited their powers of oratory in the United States Senate. The subject was the Philippine war and the leading journals of the country with common accord bestowed the palm of pre-eminence on the junior Senator from California—Hon. Stephen M. White.

Another member of the Philalethics at the time of which we write was John T. Malone, afterwards assistant district attorney of the County of Santa Clara, an actor of eminence, and at the time of his decease, the librarian of the Player's Club of New York City.

While an attorney of the bar of Santa Clara county, many of his efforts on public occasions were set forth at length in the public press and justly received the warmest praise for their oratorical excellence.

While at Santa Clara College, however, he was most diffident of his powers. He was one of the most inconspicuous members of the Philalethics during nearly all of the time of his connection with the society. His member-

ship seemed to result rather from the fact that all his associates were there rather than from any strong ambition to cultivate the art of debate. Still it was observable when he participated in any discussion, though in a comparatively slight degree, that he possessed the strong and sound judgment which afterward distinguished his efforts at the bar and upon the rostrum. But the fine, and, it may be said, even beautiful diction which afterward characterized his more important addresses was wholly wanting in his college days, and it was remarked at that time that it was astonishing that one who was so alive to the nice distinctions of language and could present the words of others so admirably upon the stage, was satisfied with mediocre expression in the college debating society. With him as with many others the process was one of evolution, and the foundation of his later successes was laid in the upper chamber of the old adobe building which was the battleground of the intellectual knights of the college.

During my stay at the college I was a participant in most of the important debates in the Philalethic hall. I had no aptness in extemporaneous speaking, and was always embarrassed and fearful in addressing a gathering of fellow students. I was forced to disguise this as far as possible by laborious preparation. My frequent practice as a member of the dramatic society of the college never served to give me immunity from a sort of stage-fright in debate, and the good words generously given to me by

HON. STEPHEN M. WHITE, S. B., '71

GOVERNOR-GENERAL JAMES F. SMITH, A. M., '78

Two of the Philalethic Senate's Most Honored Sons.

Father Young and others were earned, so far as they were earned at all, by hard work.

The excellent practice had not then been established of giving public debates, and in that regard the present custom of the Senate is a great advance over former methods. It is pleasing to see that these methods are bearing a rich harvest, for notwithstanding the fact that a very considerable number of the old time members of the Philalethics have since won distinction in the world, it seems to me certain that the general grade of merit in the society, judging from recent exhibitions, was never so high as at present.

JAMES H. CAMPBELL, A. B. '71,
Ph. D., '03

IV

DEAR EDITOR REDWOOD:

Had Edmund Young, the Jesuit rhetorician, done nothing more than found the first American collegiate debating Congress, his fame would still be complete, his title to immortality still secure.

The idea of replacing the ordinarily dull, monotonous, old-fashioned debating society with a mind-stimulating, ambition-spurring practical imitation of the United States Senate and House of Representatives, was conceived during his professorial career at Georgetown University, and was a product of his comprehensive familiarity with the plan, forms and customs of the American National Forum, which he visited with patriotically-interested frequency.

Santa Clara College—which, in the sphere of moral, classical and scientific education, pioneered and still leads the way on the Pacific slope—became the primal beneficiary of the learned priest's noble conception; and, in simple justice, Edmund Young must be classed among the great benefactors of the genuinely American school, college and university, public and private. His idea is today revolutionizing debating society methods in thoroughly modern institutions of learning everywhere from California to his native Maine and from the Great Lakes to the tropics.

Yale copied Santa Clara, and was the first Eastern universities to acknowledge the incomparable superiority and the progressive value of Father Young's Debating Congress; and, one by one, the colleges big and small are adopting the plan that, by virtue of its transcendant merits, will become the universal system of debate for students, who are destined to take part in the government of this free country, and who will be relied on to perpetuate the cherished principles upon which the republic stands.

Father Young was an orator of commanding powers. His personality was impressive, and with his giant intellect was combined the simplicity of a child.

He was a poet, and youth was in his soul after the snow of age had fallen. He was an American, through and through, and no son of Columbia honored more the sacred traditions of the Union or loved better the banner of the stars. Were it possible to record his deeds of kindness, a library were too small to contain the story. He taught students to think and furnished intellectual tools wherewith to shape pure thought. A master architect of moral fabrics, he taught how to lay the groundwork and rear the superstructure of character that endures and beautifies.

When in every American college and school shall flourish a debating congress modeled on the most perfect parliament in the world; when the idea borrowed by old Yale from Santa Clara shall have been adopted, as it will be, wherever the free flag floats,—then shall posterity, I trust, in justice and gratitude, accord the honor due the founder of the students' distinctively-American forum; for, if any Nineteenth Century educator was deserving of an imperishable memorial for a priceless legacy to the youth of this whole country, that educator was Edmund Young, the Jesuit.

CHAS. D. SOUTH, '78

V

DEAR EDITOR REDWOOD:

Sidney Smith declared it bad taste for any save an octogenarian to indulge in youthful memories. But our old friend Ike Marvel originated a fashion of adolescent reminiscence that seems a sufficient and adequate precedent for those of us who while still comparatively young, desire to exercise the privilege of the comparatively old. Furthermore, if the poet thought fifty years of Europe worth a cycle of Cathay, we who are reaching for the garments of the middle years may be justified in thinking an American decade worth all the European half century and securely hold that a period of more rapid development gives some claims of antiquity to modern middle age. Finally or "lastly", as Senator John Selby always put his 23rd argument on the fourth evening of his continued speech, if one had to qualify for "De Senectute" before referring to his youth, the few who in this rapid age reach the Methusalistic period would form a restricted, narrow and exasperating monopoly in reminisence, and as the tendency in this day is to regulate or prohibit monopoly, we serve a great public good by introducing the competitive recollections of the younger.

I almost hesitate to admit, though candor compells me to do so, that in my day it almost became a Senatorial custom to introduce a subtle appeal to Father Ricard's well known mathematical leanings by indulging in a form of discussion intended to predispose his judgment, namely by paralelling the discussion to a well known theory of calculus, a generous quantity of language being added or subtracted from a given subject without more than infinitesimally increasing the actual sum of thought. As I personally had no taste for mathematics, I never indulge in this crooked practice but always debated a question in the briefest possible manner —for several hours.

The Senators, to exemplify their dissipated regard for sleep; often visited the House and remained there until the wee small hours of adjournment at 9:15. In those days the House often yielded to the floor to visiting Senators, dispite the difficulty sometimes experienced in gétting it back. I recall now the impression those superior beings from the upper House made upon me when a new comer in the lower House. I remember their royal bearing, their ease and fluency of speech, the sublime dignity of their exalted position, and I could not overcome my awe of them, until one evening when Senator Sargent, being called upon to speak, had to bend his majestic figure and surreptitiously dispose :of an excess joint of "plug cut".

In his rhetorical days, the Senator divided and subdivided his subject into literary kindling wood and "scarce he opened his mouth but out there flew a trope! He worked all the topics into a single speech and combined all the possibilities of the oration on the crown and "pro Milone" in one phillipic.

But it was in the Senator's philosophical days that he struck his stride and "splitting the metaphysic hair twist north and northwest side", demonstrated the absolute viciousness of city in comparison with country life, or proved by searching appeal to fundamental moral principles that woman in politics was more dangerous to the elementary principles of republican liberty than microbes in water to infant health. During his last year he usually tackled and inclusively settled those economic and political problems that divided his countrymen and gave

final judgment on those moral issues that puzzled the philosophic mind of his day. Those things done, he seized his degree and went forth into the world the conscious captain of a cargo of knowledge for which Solomon could have exchanged his precious wisdom only by an offer of something to boot.

But the youthful egotism of the Senator was providentially balanced by the broadest and most solid training. He had a bridal portion that only his own pious and loving alma mater could give. He had lived intimately with holy men. He had thought and discussed great things with men mentally and morally great. He had, as it were, the preacher's precept reduced to daily practice. He carried in his soul an intimacy certainty that grew sweeter and more wonderful with each day's increasing knowledge of the world, with men who had given their lives for him even as the Master had given His. These are the recollections that are part forever of the finer fibers of his being, for whatever the separation of space and time, we may as we will seize the outstretched hands of a Young and a Shallo, and with them tread a memoried pathway leading to those old walls within which a living Kenna and Neri link the great past to a glorious future.

·   JAMES EMERY, '06

VI

DEAR MR. EDITOR:

I was in the Senate for only a short time and hence my recollections of it are rather lean and scanty. However, the night of my introduction to the Society will ever remain a big pleasant memory to me.

The scene comes back to me like some pleasing dream, a vision out of the night. 'Tis the ghost of the Sergeant-at-Arms, Peter Kell, that bids me enter. Dimly I hear him call my name, and as I step uncertainly across the threshold, there is perfunctory applause, the same that has greeted three other "representatives" who have preceeded me.

Ah, yes, it is the Rev. Father Kavanagh, who smiles a reassuring welcome to me from the presidential chair, and I move forward, trying to avoid strutting and yet maintain the dignity of a fledgling senator, whose wings are sprouting benegth his new-donned toga. The Sergeant-at-Arms moves solemnly ahead under the benign gaze of Recording Secretary, John J. Ivancovich, and Corresponding Secretary, Martin V. Merle. I pursue my stumbling, toga-impeded course, but withal glorious and triumphant course, between the seated rows of pompous and lordly Senators; I inwardly quaking and hurriedly reviewing my carefully prepared impromptu speech,—they glorying in their few short months' senority.

I hasten to the platform, where I sign my name on the roster, directly under that of John Riordan. I turn and gaze out upon the sea of inquiring faces. I bow—I stutter—there is a deafening applause; I stammer—there are wild cheers. I skip to the 99th chapter of my initiatory address and deliver it amidst sympathetic grins.

In perspiration I seek my seat, flounce into it with relief. The President raps for order, the applause subsides. Gradually the over-worked gavel restores calm—I soothe my injured feelings and seek to banish grieved recollections of a good speech gone wrong. "Recess over, gentlemen," says Fr. Kavanagh and Senator Jedd McClatchy, first affirmative, launches into a fiery discourse on the tariff. I am a Senator at last—

GERALD BEAUMONT, '06.

[It is with exceeding regret that we go to press without Mr. Delmas' letter. There was a misunderstanding: entirely without our knowledge, the gifted Philalethian was given just one day more wherein to favor us with a contribution than the printers could possibly wait. But we shall make up for this by giving his Commencement speech in full in our next issue. ED.]

SOME NOTED PRESIDENTS OF THE PHILALETHIC SENATE.

1.—Rev. Michael Accolti, S. J. 2.—Rev. Florence Sullivan, S. J. 3.—Rev. Edmund Young, S. J.
4.—Mr. Daniel Ford, S. J. 5.—Prof. Henry Dance, A. M.
6.—Rev. Michael Shallo, S. J.

PRESIDENTS OF THE PHILALETHIC SOCIETY 1857-1907

Rev. Michael Accolti, S. J. ....August 1857—June 1859

Rev. Florence J. Sullivan, S. J. ... " 1860 " 1861

Rev. William Moylan, S. J. .... " 1861 " 1862

Rev. Edmund J. Young, S. J...... " 1862 " 1866

Mr. Daniel Ford, S. J. .... " 1866 " 1868

Rev. Joseph M. Neri, S. J. ....
....For some months, pending the return of Fr. Young

Rev. Edmund J. Young, S. J....August 1868—June 1872

Prof. Henry Dance, A. M .... " 1872 " 1876

Rev. Edmund J. Young, S. J. .... " 1876 " 1889

Rev. Dominic Giacobbi, S. J. ... " 1889 " 1890

Rev. Jerome Ricard, S. J... .... " 1890 " 1892

Rev. Michael Shallo, S. J. .. .. " 1892 " 1897

Rev. John J. Cunningham, S. J... " 1897 " 1899

Rev. John J. Ford, S. J. .. .. " 1899 " 1902

Mr. Dionysius Kavanagh, S. J... " 1902 " 1904

Rev. Joseph P. Lydon, S. J. .... " 1904 " 1905

Mr. Joseph T. Morton, S. J. ...... " 1905 " 1907

HIC JACET MEMORIA DULCIS

(In loving memory of the Philalethic Senate Building of Santa Clara College, destroyed April 19, 1906.

What, gone, destroyed and turned again to dust,
Revered and venerable pioneer ·
That once seemed mailed against the storms of Time ?
Art thou then buried in Oblivion's rust,
From whence again but only wraiths appear,
Whose baleful shades affright one's dreams sublime?

Was Fate so kindless that a single blow,
Dealt pitilessly by a tremor's freak,
Could crush forever what had lived an age ?
Why, in its halls a scant six years ago,
I bared my head and heard Alumnus speak,
Orisons thrill, and tongues of Friendship flow.

Recalled we then what knew those crumbled walls,
Ere yet the honor-men of now were born,
And those who taught them still were acolytes.
By Memory led, there answered to our calls
The shades of Friendship's dead;—here to adorn
Thought-pictures of the youthtime's days and nights.

They passed before us cheered by song and tongue;
The armory, the silent dormitory,
The halls where boy and youth first knew debate;
The class in rhetoric of honored Young;
Traverso's learning spent on Classic glory,—
And are all these cloaked by the pall of Fate ?

Nay I defy thee, Fate, and call on Fame,
Whose sons in yon adobe Senate Hall
Vaunted their bantling eloquence. I hear
Out from the Past each honored voice and name,
Above its dust, haste at Alumni's call
To voice the memories true hearts revere.

A Partial View of Santa Clara College in 1855. The Building in the Foreground is the California Hotel, for Forty-nine Years the Home of the Philalethic Society. Erected 1818; Destroyed April 18, 1906.

Out from the graves they come in spirit form;
Out of the Halls of Justice. Voice and pen
That have swayed multitudes, are here tonight,
O fallen Senate, to contemn the storm
That laid thee low. All of them valiant men,
By Memory steeled to speak for Friendship's might.

With hearts attuned to Alma Mater's lore,
Strong manhood's voice, pitched in melodic praise,
Rings out the glories of thy honored past ;
Denying what has gone may come no more,
Nor live the splendors of the misty days
When horoscopes within thy halls were cast.

Burnett is here, Coffey, Delmas, Malone,
Barrett and White, the living and the dead,
Stand side by side, supreme in eloquence;
And sainted Varsi on the Chairman's throne
Smiled blessings on them as the moments sped.
Leaving no throb that sprang from penitence.

And I, O Senate, must be not of thee !
My voice is drowned deep in the sea of space;
And though its hush may make me listless seem,
My spirit, prayers, and flowers of Memory,
Shall there atone for a forgotten face
That's but the shadow of a school-day dream.

Thou'rt gone, destroyed and turned again to dust,
But what thou wert once cannot fade away,
For 'twixt us two are ties Fate cannot sever.
Fond recollection holds thee deep in trust,—
Senates may rise and crumble.in a day,
But Fame, Religion, Truth live on forever.

CLAY M. GREENE, '69.

IDLE NOTES

In the *Owl*, the magazine of the Santa Clara students during the years 1869-'75, there was a department for all kinds of miscellanies, called Idle Notes. Here and there throughout these Notes, mention is made of the Philalethic Literary Society. Sometimes it is the election of officers for the ensuing term; sometimes it is an appreciation of an address to the Society by some noted orator; or it is a brief account of some more than usually interesting debate. We will collate a few of these remarks of our wise old predecessor, or rather ancestor—for the *Owl* sowed the literary seed from which the REDWOOD afterwards sprang—in the hope that, interesting in themselves, they will prove yet more so when viewed through the enchantment-lending distance of the years.

The first Idle Note we find to the purpose is as follows:

The Philalethic and Philhistorian Societies, having each on their shelves a photographic album to preserve the features of their members, honorary and active, will be very thankful to their honorary members whose addresses are unknown for their pictures.—May, 1870.

Here it may be remarked that those albums proved a delusion and a snare. The photos have dropped out or have been hopelessly mixed, so that often it is impossible to tell which is which. The medleys that now adorn the walls sprang from the brain of O. D. Stoesser, B. S. '87.

In the number of June, 1870. is given the account of the Philalethic annual banquet. As there were a large number of toasts, and each toast is accorded lengthy notice, it is hardly convenient to quote it in full, and it cannot well be condensed, so with one short excerpt, we shall dismiss it.

In the evening of Thursday, the 17th of last month, came off the banquet of the Philalethic Society. Through the activity of the gentlemen of the Committee, and the generous assistance of the College authorities, "a feast of nectared sweets, where no crude surfeit reigns," bade defiance to the shadow of a complaint or after-suggestion. Fowls of the air, and fish of the sea, and everything intermediate and successive, and the drop or two which they say the stomach needs, for digestion's sake, were faultless. Accustomed for a whole year to "feasts of reason," the banqueters could appreciate more solid viands very well.—June, 1870.

The second night of the Commencement exercises, May, 1870, was under the auspices of the Philalethic Society,

The evening of Wednesday, the second day, was occupied by the Philalethic Society. This society was organized some thirteen. years since with Rev. M. Accolti, president. At the annual meeting of last year, Mr. D. M. Delmas, a talented lawyer of San Jose, and a graduate of Santa Clara, was elected to deliver the address before the society at its third annual celebration, and Mr. W. H. Rhodes, of San Francisco, the poem. The absence of Mr. Rhodes in the East, preventing his presence, Mr. James V. Coleman had kindly consented to fill his position. Wednesday afternoon at half-past six the annual meeting was called, at which, besides the active portion of the association, were present a number of honorary members. The business of the meeting was to elect honorary members, and an orator and a poet for the celebration of '71. A list comprising several distinguished men, were voted the honorary certificate and two others were chosen, to whom the society will extend its invitation to deliver the poem and address. The body then adjourned to the stage of the theater, Rev. M. Accolti now of San Francisco, there presiding.

The Rev. Father announced the subject of "Daniel Webster." Mr. M. J. C. Murphy filled twenty minutes in honor of oratory and the masterly spirit departed,

"Whose resistless eloquence', Wielded at will that fierce democratic."

The excellent periods, and fit delivery of the speaker, lent a second charm to that which the very subject carried.

To Mr. Murphy succeeded Mr. John T. Malone, who sketched the struggles and triumphs of John Philpot Curran. The words of the orator, warm with real sentiment, seemed to penetrate the feelings of his auditors. He began with the childhood of Curran, when, a handsome and noble boy, he imbibed from his mother the principles which carried him through life, and the legendary lore of his country, that afterwards served him more than his classical studies. We present no analysis of the speeches of Mr. Murphy and Mr. Malone, or of the poem and address, as the society is about to publish them.

Mr. J. V. Coleman, a graduate of Georgetown College, D. C., class of '69, then delivered the poem, "Charity". His vein, though when he dwelt with his true subject, mild as the subject herself, deviated into sarcasm when he handled her pretenders. The production was greatly admired and applauded, more especially as the brief time of its composition was known. From the outset, the purity of delivery and the sweetness of voice of Mr. Coleman enlisted the sympathy of all. The warmest thanks are due from the Society to this gentleman, who, with no little inconvenience on his own part, so kindly and ably occupied the position of the absent elected poet.

The annual address, uttered by D. M. Delmas, Esq., closed the evening and the nineteenth exercises of the College. Although a young man, Mr. Delmas ranks in the front of his profession in the State. The address evinced deep thought and careful preparation, clothed in a pleasing form of expression. After some words of congratulation to the society on the object which they professedly follow, he formally announced his subject, in these words: "While we realize, then, the importance of eloquence in a country like this, it may not be amiss to pause at times, cast a glance upon the means which may lead to its attainment, and measure the extent of the obligations which it imposes. To such an inquiry, the present hour seems propitious; and I know not how to better improve it than by choosing as the subject of my address, "The Studies and duties of the orator." With this subject he occupied the remainder of the hour, as interestingly to those grown gray in the service of oratory as to its neophytes.—Sept. 1870.

The celebration referred to in the following letters was in connection with the inauguration of the College Hall. It was postponed from June to August.

Santa Clara College, April 28, 1870.

DEAR SIR:

At the last Grand Annual Meeting of the Philalethic Literary Society, you were unanimously elected orator for 1870. Our next celebration will be held some time about the middle of June. We earnestly desire that you will deliver the address.

If I may be allowed to offer a suggestion, it is, that your oration shall not occupy less than an hour in its delivery.

I shall do myself the pleasure of corresponding with you again prior to our celebration. Hoping to hear from you at your earliest convenience, I remain your obedient humble servant,

M. J. C. MURPHY.

D. M. Delmas, San Jose, Aug. 1870.

San Jose, Cal., March 2, 1870.

DEAR SIR:

Your note of the 28th ult. reached me today. The same invitation which you have so politely extended to me I had already received from the Rev. Father Young. In answer I have already apprised him that I would be happy to accept. It only remains for me to repeat here my acceptance. Allow me to avail myself of this opportunity to beg of you to assure your Society of my best wishes, and communicate to them my sincere thanks for the unmerited honor which they have conferred upon me.

Yours, very sincerely,

D. M. DELMAS.

M. J. C Murphy, Cor. Sec. P. L. S.

Mr. Daniel Ford, S. J., a member of the Maryland Province of the Jesuit Society, who came to California on account of failing health, had charge of the Senate 1867-'68. He was a wonderfully energetic and versatile man, and highly accomplished in elocution, music, painting, poetry and literature in general. But beyond all he was a holy, religious man, and the *Owl* says of him:

We who knew him and who consider the moments spent in his society some of the happiest of our lives, can never forget him—never forget that seraphic intellect that so easily beat down the worldly arguments of men—that glory-nurtured mind that evoked from the fairy realms of poesy shapes of beauty that will ever live in our memory—that "noble manhood fused with female grace" that constituted him our beau-ideal of a perfect gentleman—that fiery eloquence that exalted while it persuaded and consoled while it reproved—that genial smile that spoke plainly of the charity that beareth all things. Farewell, thou poet-priest, we may not look upon thee again.

"Yet in these ears till hearing dies,
One set slow bell well seem to toll
The passing of the sweetest soul
That ever looked from human eyes."

As our first article this month will inform the reader, we have had, since our last issue, to lament the decease of one long and honorably connected with this institution, and universally regarded as one of its brightest ornaments. A slow consumption from which he had suffered for many years past, carried him off at length on the morning of the 24th ult. In the very prime of his manhood he was struck down,—a manhood full of brilliant promise for his friends; but the fiat had gone forth and the idol of many fond hopes is forever crushed, the tired spirit has been summoned to the bosom of its Maker, and we must resignedly bow before the Sovereign will, saying meekly "Thy will be done." The Philalethic Literary Society, of which Mr. Ford had at one time been President, sorrowfully accompanied his remains to their final resting place. He was buried according to the solemn rites of the Catholic Church.

A committee of three, appointed by the Philalethic Society to express publicly the deep grief of that body, drafted the following Resolutions, which were afterward adopted by the society.

Whereas: We are called upon to lament the untimely death of our Ex-President, Mr. Daniel Ford, S. J., who on the 24th ult was called to the enjoyment of a better life;

Resolved, That we deeply mourn the loss of so accomplished a scholar, so refined a gentleman, so sterling a Christian;

Resolved, That we will ever fondly cherish the memory of one endeared to us by so many kindly recollections;

Resolved, That as a token of sorrow our members wear mourning for thirty days;

Resolved, That we tender our earnest sympathy to the friends and relatives of the deceased in this their hour of bitter affliction;

Resolved, That copies of these resolutions be printed in the *San Jose Mercury*, the *Santa Clara Index*, and the *Owl*, and that a copy be sent to the family of the deceased.

Signed   M. J. C. MURPHY }
              JAS. H. CAMPBELL } Committee
              J. T. MALONE   }
                                    Nov. 1870.

In the next three passages, we watch the evolution of the Philalethic Hall, so well known to ensuing generations of Santa Clarans as the "Senate". It is evident that the twin debating clubs felt somewhat bitter over their 'local habitations.' But alas! Philhistorian and Philalethic, saw, not many months ago, their storied home razed to the ground.

The Philalethic Society will shortly enjoy a roomy, elegantly-fitted debating hall; the Philhistorian Society remaining in ownership of the chamber formerly occupied by both.—Oct. 1870.

The Philalethic Literary Society (seniors) is very soon to have a new hall. The apartment at present occupied by that body, though handsomely fitted up, and adorned with many beautiful and costly presents which cannot well be removed, and though consecrated by the memory, still green, of many of its former members whose voices, now employed on wider fields, or, perhaps, alas! forever hushed, have made those old walls ring with their bursts of conviction-bearing eloquence, is too small to accommodate suitably the growing members of the society. There is a second objection to it. The Philalethic Society does not occupy the room exclusively, but conjointly with the junior (Philhistorian) society. The former meets every Wednesday, the latter every Tuesday evening. This arrangement is not altogether satisfactory. Desks and chairs suffer injury; sashes are shattered (all accidently, of course) and as the guilty party is seldom to be discovered, each society lays the blame at the door of the other, and calls on the other to repair damages. To prevent the unpleasantness of such disputes, it is better that the societies should have apartments entirely separated. Then there will be peace. The new hall is a large, nicely painted room. A handsome chair for the President is placed at the farther end, opposite the entrance, on an ample rostrum.

The rostrum and floor are covered with carpets of plain design and modest colors. Two chandeliers, with four large burners each, will afford abundant light. The inauguration exercises are fixed for the 25th of January. A description of the affair will be found in our next *Owl*.—Feb. 1871.

As announced in the last *Owl*, the inaugural exercises of the new hall of the Philalethic Literary Society came off on the 25th of January—too late for an account in the last number. As the affair created quite a little stir in the college, our readers will pardon us if our description is somewhat detailed.

At seven in the evening the hall was pretty well filled with the members of the Philalethic Society, and their invited guests. Besides the Philalethic Society there were present members of three other college associations—the Philhistorian Literary Society, the Parthenian Dialectic Society, and the Dramatic Society. The Faculty, and a few specially invited gentlemen, completed the audience.

The assembly was called to order by Mr. J. C. Johnson, Chairman of the Committee of Arrangments, who acted as master of ceremonies; and the same gentleman immediately nominated Rev. A. Varsi as presiding officer for the evening. This nomination being unanimously ratified by those present, the reverend gentleman proceeded to occupy the Chair. In a few words he thanked the house for the courtesy shown him; expressed his continued friendly feeling toward the Philalethic Society; spoke of the eagerness with which he had marked its progress, and of the expectations he entertained from its influence in the college; and in conclusion, exhorted every member to pursue with unflagging zeal the object for which he had joined the society, i. e., the development of oratorical talent, and by this simple means to secure the success of the society. After the applause which followed these remarks had somewhat subsided, Mr. Charles F. Wilcox came forward and delivered the inaugural address. A brief outline of the history of the society was given, in the course of which the speaker had occasion to relate many amusing incidents connected with the memory of its earlier members. The position and efficiency of the society in the college was next touched upon; and after urging his Philhistorian brethren to "bury the hatchet" that had so long disturbed the peace of the two societies, and enter the lists as honored rivals, not as inferiors, the gentleman amid a hearty applause, resumed his seat. A well prepared oration on "History," by Mr. John T. Malone, followed. "Make Hay while the Sun Shines." came next on the program. It was an able oration by Mr. Peter Byrne. Mr. James V. Coleman was expected to deliver a poem on the occasion, but being unable through illness to fulfill the appointment, his place was filled by Prof. D. Dance, who read a laughable poem, entitled "The Fate of an English Coelebs," which appears in this number. Sensible extempore addrssses were made by members of the society, as well as by some of their guests, to a late hour in the evening, when the house adjourned. The intervals between the addresses were filled up with excellent music. "Music, and her sister, Song," a duet, was given in first rate style, Mr. J. F. McQaude taking the tenor, and during a subsequent rest "Vi Ravviso" was sung by a gentleman present to a thundering encore —March 1871.

The following four notices concern the Grand Annals of '71 and '72. The account of the banquet in the first appeals to every literary taste.

The annual banquet and re-union of the members of the Philalethic Literary Society, took place on Wednesday, May 11th. The viands that crowded the tables reflected credit on our commissary committee, and the manner in which they were served did honor to our cook. When the appetites of the gourmands began, from severe and long continued exertion, to fail, toasts became in order, and the usual toasts, the President of the College, the President of the Philalethic Society, the Philhistorian Society, and "the Invited Guests," were successfully and briefly responded to. The

presence of the founder of the Society, Rev. M. Accolti, gave occasion for an additional toast, replied to shortly by the reverend gentleman himself who thanked the members for the compliment paid him, gave them some good advice, and having excused himself for the fewness of his remarks by the infirmity of his health, expressed the wish that he might have the opportunity of speaking to them more at length later on.

The proceedings were varied by a *vegetable* toast (beats),to which Mr. James V. Coleman respoded in the following strains: (too lengthy for insertion.—ED.)

After satisfying the inner man, the company adjourned to a neighboring apartment, where some hours were spent pleasantly in dancing, singing and speech-making. At a late hour they adjourned.--June, 1871.

The Fourth Grand Annual of the Philalethic Literary Society was held on Monday, June 5th, before a very large audience. The members of the Society, both active and honorary to the number of fifty were seated upon the stage and presented a fine appearance. In the center was a chair of the presiding officer, Jas. H. Campbell, while on his right was seated the orator and on the left the poet of the evening. After some fine music by the College band, Mr. Chas. F. Wilcox was introduced to the assembly and delivered an oration on "Democracy." It was a well considered, masterly effort and was well received. The orator of the evening, Hon, Thomas P. Ryan of San Francisco, was next presented in an address to the Society on "The Duties of Educated Men in a Republic." Although Mr. Ryan gave abundant evidence of his power as an extemporaneous speaker, he labored under many embarrassments and clearly did not himself justice. The audience next listened to an eloquent panegyric on Gen. Robt. E. Lee by Mr. Peter Byrne, after which Prof. Dance of Queen's College, Oxford, as poet of the occasion, was introduced. The gifted Prof. read a beautiful poem entitled, "The Planet-born." The exercises of the evening closed with an oration on "Political, public

SPEAKERS OF "SENATE NIGHT," JUNE 25, 1907.

1.—Hon John M. Burnett, Chairman.   2.—Hon Delphine M. Delmas.   3.—Rev. Joseph McQuaide.   4.—Hon. John E. McElroy.
5.—Mr. Charles D. South.

life," by Mr. John T. Malone, which was, perhaps, the best liked of those given by the active members of the society.—Sept., 1871.

The Philalethic Literary Society will hold their Grand Annual on the evening of May 1st. It will be a select affair, and promises to pass off most satisfactorily. Many invitations have been extended to the most respected and influential citizens of our state; and the Philalethic members have resolved to make their Grand Annual one of the events of the season.—May, 1872.

On Wednesday evening, May 1st, the Philalethic Literary Society of the College, held its Fifth Grand Annual Meeting. The stage of the College Hall was tastefully decorated, and its neat and consistent appearance was much admired. The Society had sent a large number of printed invitations to many of the friends of the College, to be present at their literary festival; and it was with much satisfaction that we beheld upon the stage some of the most erudite and influential gentlemen of San Francisco, San Jose and environs. The invited guests flowed in rapidly, and seemed eager to taste of the intellectual treat about to be offered to them. Mr. Johnson was the first speaker, and held forth at some length on "Ingratitude." Mr. A. Campbell gave us a speech on "Henry Clay." Mr. J. Poujade conjured up once more the spirit of "Patrick Henry", and Mr. J. T. Malone followed with a narration entitled, "Irish Eloquence." We will not criticise, we will not show the merits or faults of each speech. It is true that they all contained points of merit, Mr. Malone's especially; but we must also say honestly that some of them were chargeable with a number of defects. The entertainment closed with a most elaborate address by Judge David Belden, of San Jose. It was a true oratorical effort, full of good sound sense and seasonable advice, and shone with all the beauties of a powerful mind.—June, 1872.

We have rejected many Notes as not being of sufficient interest, being mostly catalogues of officers of the Society. We had also to omit the numerous speeches and poems that were evoked by the Annals. Our next Note is dated June, 1873, and for the two years after this, strange to say, we hear hardly any more of the Philalethics. We are sorry that not a more pleasing ending is furnished us in the last sentences of the following, which are certainly more candid than complimentary.

The Sixth Grand Annual Meeting of the Philalethic Literary Society of this College took place on the evening of May 7th. The audience was rather small, and as, through some accident, the sun-burners could not be lighted, the hall presented quite a desolate appearance. After the "Caliph of Bagdad" had been finely rendered by the Brass Band, Mr. D. O. Furlong was introduced, and delivered an oration on the "Ravages of Time." The gentleman spoke well and his composition evinced care and attention. "Les Clochettes," polka, was played after he had finished' and then the Hon. J. W. Dwinelee delivered the address of the evening, taking for his subject, "The Duty of Citizens to Make Politics a Study." The Hon. gentleman's oration was replete with sound sense and good reasoning, and could not but be listened to with pleasure by all. His remarks were greeted from time to time with an enthusiastic round of applause. After some beautiful "Selections from Martha" had been given by the band the poem of the evening delivered by the Hon. W. H. Rhodes, who began by informing the house that it was a translation from the Chinook tongue, the real author being no less a personage than Shacknasty Jim, the Modoc hero. It consisted of a defiance supposed to be hurled by Captain Jack at the "pale faces". It was well written and delivered with much spirit. Music "Woodland March" followed. Mr. A. L. Veuve delivered an oration on the subject. "Bloody Mary." The speech was well written, but the gentleman's voice, ordinarily a strong one, failed him so completely—especially toward the end— that it became quite painful to listen to him. Music, "Then You'll Remember Me," came next, and was rendered very sweetly.

The last thing on the program was a poem entitled, "The ghost by the river," delivered by Mr. J. Poujade. From the known poetic talent of this gentleman it may be assumed that the composition was meritorious, though we were quite unable to follow the speaker, his voice being so weak that, at the farther end of the hall, hardly a word was audible. Altogether the entertainment was not as good as we had expected to see it.—June, 1873.

Commencement-Jubilee

PROGRAMME, JUNE 25, 1907

Overture.. .... .E. Boettger........................ ....Orchestra

Introductory................. ....Hon. John M. Burnett, A.M., '59, Chairman

"Past, Present, Future," ....Hon. John E, McElroy, A. B., '91

"Philalethica,"................. ....Verses written for the occasion by
Charles D. South, A. M., '01,
Delivered by James F. Twohy

Echoes of '97-'00................. ....The Cecilian Trio,
Charles A. Fitzgerald, A. B., '01, Piano
Edward I. Leake, A. B., '00, cornet
William J. Kieferdorf, A. B., '00, violin

"Venerated Names of the Dead,"................... ....
Rev. Joseph P. McQuade, A. B., '88

"Humble Beginnings," a Reminiscence................. ....
Hon. Delphine M. Delmas, A. M., '63

Hosanna!......... ....J. Granier........................... .Orchestra
The Distribution of Extraordinary Prizes and the
Conferring of Academic Degrees.

Valedictory................. ....August M. Aguirre

Address................. ....His Grace, Most Rev. Patrick W.Riordan, D. D.

Finale................. .... C. Bohm,................ ....Orchestra

FROM SHORE TO SHORE 1857-1907

Life's fickle sea for years with sullen roar,
  Has hurled my frail life-bark from foam to foam;
Now, gazing back, I see you leave the shore,
  Just putting out when I am drifting home.

I saw you leave those honored Senate halls,
  That once resounded to my boyish tread,
Whose image bright will grace my memory's walls,
  In love-thoughts wreathed, till memory be dead.

Think you the dreary booming of the Vast,
  The great world's busy cries, now sad, now gay,
Could drown the recollections of the Past,
  Or quench the thoughts of one sweet yesterday?

Two beacon fires like stars have shed their light
  Above the ruthless wrath of tide and wind;
The light of hope ahead gleamed through the night,
  That and old Memory's light from shores behind.

And now, touching the Portals of the World
  -Which lies beyond, we yield, oh youth, to thee
The Senate flag for fifty years unfurled,
  Still stainless, on this golden Jubilee.

                              James F. Twohy, A. B., '07.

The Redwood.

PUBLISHED MONTHLY BY THE STUDENTS OF THE SANTA-CLARA COLLEGE

The object of the Redwood is to record our College Doings, to give proof of College Industry and to knit closer together the hearts of the Boys of the Present and of the Past.

EDITORIAL STAFF

EXECUTIVE BOARD

ANTHONY B. DIEPENBROCK, '08

President

FRANCIS M. HEFFERNAN, '08   MERVYN S. SHAFER, '09

ASSOCIATE EDITORS

COLLEGE NOTES	- - - -	MERVYN S. SHAFER, '09
IN THE LIBRARY	- - - -	GEORGE J. HALL, '08
EXCHANGES	- - - -	MAURICE T. DOOLING, '09
ALUMNI	- - - - -	HARRY P. BRODERICK, '08
ATHLETICS	- - - -	CARLOS K. McCLATCHY, '10

BUSINESS MANAGER

FRANCIS M. HEFFERNAN, '08

ASSISTANT BUSINESS MANAGER

JOHN W. MALTMAN, '09

Address all communications to THE REDWOOD, Santa Clara College, California

Terms of subscription, $1.50 a year; single copies, 15 cents

EDITORIAL COMMENT

Five decades of years! Not such a long chapter in the annals of history, not such a long stretch in the century-paved course of the world! But fifty years is a long era in the history of a country so young as this, which though quickly developed and like a giant rejoicing to run its way, bears yet upon its features the immaturity of youth. Fifty years is a venerable age for any organization in California, and more especially so for a literary society, seeing that its birth must date back to those untutored days when the pick and the shovel were more in repute than the pen, and the lust of gold had quenched the thirst for learning.

The Philalethic Society, accordingly, may claim all the honors of patriarchal age. It is the patriarch of all the literary and debating societies now scattered over the state. It was strong and flourishing before they were born. It will survive the majority of them, ·for it has in it the elements of stability, a constitution almost unique in collegedom inspired by the same wisdom that has dictated the great charter of our country's freedom.

The REDWOOD staff gladly, then, dedicates this number of their magazine to the Golden Jubilarian. We retire as much as possible out of sight, and let its own toga-clad sons speak in our pages. Our only regret is that not more of them have spoken. We should have liked to listen to Governor-General James F. Smith from the Phillipines, and his subject officials Roman Lacson, L. L. D., and Thomas Nihill; to Matthew Walsh and Jose Pierson from Mexico City, and James Donohue from New York; to Richard de la Guardia from Panama and John V. Paul from Toronto; to Thomas Morrison from Hong Kong, and James Morrissey, S. J. from Holland. These and many others could a tale unfold of their old Senate-days to amuse and instruct us, but time was short and the distance was long. Many near at home could not find the necessary leisure to supplement their good-will; while a few alleged the modest plea that years had rusted their pen.

But what contributions we did receive are splendid—only that they make us wish for more. Father Kenna's letter will be read with interest by every Santa Claran. That it was written by snatches stolen from his many pressing duties makes us appreciate it all the more. We asked Mr. Greene for a poem, he at once set to work and produced the two gems found in the foregoing pages. Mr. South's letter and rattling poem form an addition to the obligations he has already put the REDWOOD under this year. Mr. Delmas put aside his weighty business matters from his mind to devote himself for a time to us. To these as well as all our remaining contributors we offer our thanks.

To the Philalethic Senate we say: *Esto perpetua;* to the reader, as we quit the editorial office, we bid Farewell.

The Passion Play of Santa Clara

The month of May, 1907, will be a life-long inspiring memory to many within and without the walls of Santa Clara College. During its course the far-famed "Nazareth," or The Passion Play of Santa Clara, as it is now generally known, was produced nine times, and if popular enthusiasm combined with the approval of refined and scholarly critics mean anything, each time with extraordinary success. It was a labor of love for all connected with it, from Clay M. Greene, its author, who wrote it for "sweet friendship's sake," and Martin V. Merle who came expressly from the East to stage it the second time, and Prof. John Waddell, who with a skill and a devotion engendered of over thirty years' superintendency of the green-room, "Made-up" the principal actors, down to the decemvirate of stage-hands who devoted all their free-time for days and weeks to the hundred and one mechanical jobs

that are involved in so elaborate a production. In fact, generosity was the key to the entire success of the play, and if every one of the one hundred and seventy students concerned had not put forth his most whole-hearted effort, Nazareth could never have made the impression it did.

Each one of the performances, with the exception of two extra ones which were rather unexpected by the public, was witnessed by an audience that thronged the large theatre to the doors. It was almost fortunate for us that the critical situation in—San Francisco diminished our city visitors, for, as it was, the congestion was on the verge of discomfort. Pilgrims, for such many considered themselves, came from all over the state, and at least one came from far-away Idaho. There was a Santa Clara Valley night, a Y. M. I. night, an Alumni night, a San Francisco night, and one of the matinees was for the Convent schools of the State.

Concerning the play itself, we must be necessarily brief. Anyone desirous of a more complete idea of it, may easily procure one of the very artistic souvenirs issued for the occasion.

As the asbestos drop softly rises, disclosing to view the red curtain beneath, with its gilded emblems of the Passion, a hush falls upon the people. There is an intake of the breath and a relieved sigh that is eloquent of the pent-up state of their feelings. The music plays softly, the lights are out, and the red curtain swings apart revealing to us a mountain dimly outlined against the twinkling sky. Gradually the moon emerges from behind a cloud, and in the increasing radiance we discover a plain with shepherds sleeping, and the village of Bethlehem nest led "there beneath the stars" at the foot of the hill. The shepherds awake and rehearse the story of the Messiah, some doubt its truth, but a shining angel appears to confirm it. Then the Wise Men, accompanied by Herod's emmissaries, come on the scene, and after some wrangling, set out with the half-trusting shepherds to the sacred cave.

The scenery in this act was a delight. Nothing could be more perfect than the soft moonlight sleeping on the hill and plain, and the stars sparkling in the almost cloudless sky. There was a soothing peace about it that seemed doubly sweet in view of the woeful scenes to follow.

There is not much scope for fine acting in this first chapter, as the nine divisions of the play are called. The most difficult part is that of the angel, and Masters Frank Warren and Lewis B. Ford, who took this role on alternate performances, deserve much praise for their pleasing manner and clear elocution. Ivo Bogan did well as Zoribel, the chief shepherd. For the rest of the play, Ivo was leader of the mob.

The next chapter opens in Herod's court. The emissaries return with the marvellous story of the Nativity and the Royal Child's escape. Whereupon Herod in a rage, and heedless of the cries of the people, orders every male child of two years and under to be put to the sword. At this stage begins an underplot in the play, the rupture between Jechonias, the wealthy publican and trusted friend of Herod with his son Athias, who believes in the newborn king. Athias makes no secret of his sympathies, much to his father's anger and terror, and after clamoring on bended knees for martyrdom at the hands of his once best friend, Herod's son Archelaus, he, at last, with the inconsistency of an over-zealous neophyte, suddenly becomes an exponent of muscular Christianity, and wounds Archelaus in a duel.

The scenic effects of this chapter were brilliant. The stage furniture was very handsome, the throne hangings being of rich green velvet, and the vases, rugs, tables, etc., costly and elegant. They were kindly donated for the occasion by Mrs. William Dougherty of San Jose. In the full glare of the light, the unusual richness of the costumes also became apparent. The cortege of the king was quite imposing, and the demure little pages walked to their places and into the hearts of the audience simultaneously.

Here also many of the best actors in the cast came into evidence. James Bacigalupi as Jechonias has won his spurs long ago. His part is that of a father, in his prime at first, but after the first epoch aged and feeble, who is anxious for his heterodox son, and yet groping for light to guide himself. The role admitted of no striking display of passion, but 'throughout it all, every movement, the tone of the voice, the shrug of the shoulder, bespoke the consummate artist. James Twohy as Athias had a fine field for his rare dramatic powers. Pleading, pathos, enthusiasm, indignation, all had their turn and received justice. His manner was graceful and his interpretation intelligent, but his voice unfortunately was at times quite hoarse. Of Gerald Beaumont's work we shall speak under the sixth chapter. Michael Griffith as King Herod won golden opinions from all for the naturalness of his impersonation. His powerful voice and rugged bearing lent themselves readily to the violent display of royal passion, while his manner had in it much of the dignity, if not divinity, that "doth hedge a king." Floyd Allen and Joseph Farry as the King's emissaries were excellent. They seemed to feel their parts thoroughly, and their manly, deliberate manner, and strong rich voices always gave pleasure.

The third chapter opens after an interval of thirty years. The "new-born King" is now the teacher of Israel, and

is about to make His entry into Jerusalem on Palm Sunday. The procession passes beneath the porticoes of Caiphas' council-chamber, from which the priests flee to the temple that it at least may not be defiled. Jechonias, however, views the spectacle, is much impressed and almost converted, and is reconciled to his son, now called Matthew. The priests return and hold council. Judas is lured into their presence and tempted to sell his Master; he is on the verge of yielding when the sight of the half concealed Matthew puts him to flight.

The acting of William McKagney as Caiphas deserves much praise. The stiff-necked perversity and malevolent hypocrisy of the latter Jewish Priesthood was portrayed very tangibly. Pride, cruelty, and cunning hung round him like a mist. Here, too, our first glimpse of Judas. The best tribute that can be paid to John Ivancovich is the conduct of the audience just before his appearance. A whisper runs through the house: Ah, Judas is coming,—and each one stirs nervously and braces into a more alert attitude. And the coming always brings a thrill with it. The sharp expressive countenance, the stealthy nervous movement, the rasping voice, are all in our ideal Judas. So far, however, he is necessarily suppressed, but later on he "lets himself out." The work of Edmund Lowe, the second High-Priest, deserve special mention for its excellence.

The entry of Christ into Jerusalem was not well managed. Four years ago it was one of the salient features of the

1. JAMES A. BACIGALUPI, A. B., '03
   as Jechonias;

3. WILLIAM J. McKAGNEY, '07

2. GERALD P. BEAUMONT, '06
   as Archelaus

4. JAMES F. TWOHY, '07

Photos by Bushnell

play; throughout this production it was nerveless and meaningless. One cause of it was that for some unaccountable reason the palm branches that indicate the triumphant procession passed across our view about three times as fast as the light that marks the Savior's presence. We were thus forced to disassociate one from the other. Another drawback was that the chorus of the children seemed to baffle location; they never came into the immediate neighborhood of the audience; but managed to cross the stage in some tantalizingly vague way that made one doubt whether they were in the procession at all. Their Hosannas were *"vox et praetereo nihil."*

The fourth chapter is laid in the Garden of Olives, overlooking the Holy City. It opens at sunset, and the masses of cloud piled up on the western horizon are lit up with a crimson glory that is full of sadness and mystery. The disciples, excepting Judas and Matthew are here gathered, awaiting the word to proceed to the Last Supper Chamber. Matthew enters hastily and informs them of Judas' treachery. The latter comes on the scene and proves his innocence, and all set out for the Supper Chamber. Judas, however, lags behind at a sign from Dathian, who had been lurking near, is tempted, falls, reveals his plans to Caiphas and the High-Priests, who are also abroad on this eventful night. He receives the thirty pieces of silver and disappears, and the Priests hold a council on the spot and resolve upon the Nazarene's death.

Of all the scenes of the Passion Play, this is the most touchingly and weirdly beautiful. As the curtains open we see Peter withdrawn apart from his brethren, gazing silently and sorrowfully upon the doomed city that rears its proud temples in the distance. One can almost fancy it is the prophet Isaias, or our Lord himself, he beholds, and the lament seems to echo in the air. "If thou hadst known and that in this thy day, the things are to thy peace, but now they are hidden from thy eyes. . . . Jerusalem, Jerusalem, thou that killest the prophets and stonest those that are sent unto thee, how often would I have gathered together thy children as a hen gathers her chickens under her wings, and thou wouldst not. . . Amen I say to you, there shall not be left here a stone upon a stone that shall not be destroyed."

The acting of the apostles is very good. Four only—Matthew, Peter, Judas, and John have speaking parts, but the pantomime was done with feeling and taste. And in this respect the play shows a vast improvement over four years ago.

The next chapter continues in the same scene. The apostles have returned from the last supper, and are huddled together, discussing the danger on all sides. We catch a glimpse of Judas on his way to the city after his deed of treachery. Then Peter rushes in, tells the story of the Master's apprehension, and the apostles kneel to pray for his safety.

In this scene, August Aguirre as Peter was especially fine. With a voice broken by sobs, he narrated how Jesus was betrayed and ill-treated, after which he passed on to the story of his own downfall. So genuine and heartbreaking was his grief that all were moved, and many an eye grew moist as he spoke. In a word, Aguirre made this a leading part of the play. James Daly's impersonation of John who is the angel of consolation among the apostles, must not be overlooked. His figure and carriage accorded admirably with the general conception of the "Disciple whom Jesus loved," and his elocution was clear and beautifully modulated.

The sixth chapter brings us to the court of the erstwhile Archelaus, now Herod II. Letters come from Pilate placing Jesus under the King's jurisdiction. Jechonias and Matthew come to plead for their Master—for Jechonias now declares himself a disciple—and they have won Herod over, when Caiphas bursts in upon them, and in disgust the king dismisses the case to Pilate. Before doing so however, he summons Jesus before him, and with the apparition of a bright light in an antechamber, the scene concludes.

As Archelaus in the second chapter, Gerald Beaumont's acting was characterized by naturalness and vivacity, but it was in the difficult role of Herod II. that his powers were best exhibited. It is a very difficult part. Now he is borne down with fear and remorse for the Baptist's death, now he raves in impotent hate against the name of Jesus or of Pilate. To do this well requires a delicate sensibility of feeling, and a subtle shading in tone and expression and gesture, and Beaumont did it well.

Chapter seven is set in the court of Pilate. The people, inflamed by the merchants and priests, assemble in great wrath at the news of Herod's acquittal of Jesus. Pilate's arrival is the signal for an outburst of fanaticism and hatred. The apostles endure in silence the jeers of the populace, but Jechonias and Matthew plead with Pilate. But the priests and the mob intimidate the distracted Governor, and extort the sentence of crucifixion.

This was the only act in which Pilate appears, and accordingly Leander Murphy, who takes the part, had but a brief opportunity to prove his worth as an actor. But he proved it nevertheless. The interpretation of the vacillating judge was excellent. His personal appearance much in his favor, and the square massive jaw harmonized with one's idea of a Roman soldier. His voice, however, was not overpleasant; it was harsh and lacking in flexibility.

In chapter eight, the curtains open on the sorrow-stricken apostles gathered near a stone wall that borders the route to Calvary. The faint murmur of a far-away multitude is getting louder and louder, and at last the sorrowful procession to Golgotha is upon us. Peter would rush forward to save his Master, but John closes the gate, and the Apostles kneel down to pray in the shelter of the wall. At last the tremendous procession appears. Some cavalrymen lead the way, encouraging the soldiery and the rabble, who follow in an endless throng, brandishing their spears or sticks. Then looms up a great cross, and we try to win a glimpse of the bearer, but hardly succeed. The heavy wood sways and totters painfully, and at last falls down and disappears. This is a signal for a burst of derision and angry impatience, a fiercer quivering of the weapons, a more cruel shower of mud and stones. At length the cross rises slowly, and as with a supreme effort, and passes on in its weary march, out of our aching sight. The apostles open the gate and follow their Lord at a distance. And now the unfortunate Judas creeps from his hiding-place, gazes down the road, and filled with remorse at the sight, gives vent to his incurable grief. The merchants pass by the way, and he begs them for a night's lodging, but they will none of him. Utterly hopeless he clings to his tempter Dathian, who brutally hurls him to the ground, where he lies grovelling until the High Priests discover him. He turns on them in all the wild abandonment of rage and despair, curses them, flings the blood-money at their feet, rushes off, and, as a High Priest informs us, hangs himself.

This chapter is undoubtedly the climax of "Nazareth." The procession to Golgotha is said by dramatic critics to be one of the triumphs of modern stagecraft. The angry shouting of the mob approaching from the distance, fills us with ever-increasing terror and foreboding, and when finally the mounted soldiers, and the spears and other weapons of those on foot, burst in all their rough violence and uproar upon our view, we are over-whelmed with horror at the brutal cruelty of the mob, and with pity for the gentle victim. The sight of the tottering cross brings a great tug at the heart-strings; many are unable to look upon it, and turn away their eyes. The stones that hurtle through the air inflict a feeling of almost physical pain upon the onlooker, and when the cross falls and the savagery of the mob is at its worst, the soul is stirred to the lowest depths the drama's plummet-line can sound.

The role of Judas in this chapter is terrific, and Ivancovich enacted it in a terrific way. How he held up under the strain of ten performances, sometimes twice the same day at that, is a marvel. His action was full of a nervous intensity, begot of the disquiet and restlessness of a demon-haunted conscience, and when he yielded to despair, he did it with an utterness of abandonment that was appalling. At times, it must be confessed, there was a touch of stageyness noticeable, as in the exaggerated stage-fall; and, moreover, his voice was in certain passages so indistinct as to be quite unintelligible, though his action almost conveyed his meaning.

The play concludes in the Temple

whither the people had fled for safety in the awful eclipse that shrouded the sun at the death of Christ. The merchants jeer at their cowardice, but Dathian defends their conduct, until he is savagely interrupted by the High Priest, who laughs sardonically at the fear of the people. And this, although the fearful gloom is rendered more awesome by vivid flashes of lightening and ominous rumbling of thunder. Discord ensues, and blows are about to be struck, when Pilate rushes in begging for protection and comfort. Caphas has none to give him; Jechonias shouts "Down with Caiphas," who in turn orders his soldiers to hack the people to pieces. As the melee begins, the walls of the temple sway in an earthquake, pillars fall, the "veil of the temple" is rent, and in the fitful lightning we see on calvary's crimson hill three gaunt crosses standing against the murky sky. Caiphas and his troop have disappeared, the Apostles dominate in the Temple, and our last view of the Passion Play is St. Peter standing in the midst of the kneeling multitude, his hand stretched in benediction over the rerepentent Pilate while a light from heaven streams down upon his head, who has been commissioned to diffuse the light of truth over a sin-darkened world.

All that electricity could contribute was lavished upon the last act without stint, and the combined effects of lightening, thunder and earthquake were spectacular. The ear-racking fall of the two massive pillars in the front of the great Veil was impressive in the extreme, though the climax of the chapter was not reached until our glimpse of the crucified Savior on Calvary. The acting, however, was not of extra merit. Caiphas did not tower up into that sublimity of wickedness and passion, and that madness of daring, that the occasion called for. The mob, also, was wooden. The thunder and lightning stirred no fear whatever in their souls; on the contrary they seemed quite used to it. Their mode of getting off the stage, moreover, was done too neatly; there was not enough confusion and noise about it. It was made too apparent that the earthquake was foreseen. However, this did not much detract from the general good work of the mob, which in the estimation of many competent critics, whom we have heard speak of it, was simply astonishing. The procession to Calvary, for instance, could hardly have been done with more perfect realism.

Of the music of the Passion Play we shall not say much for time and space forbid. It received universal applause. Prof. Buehrer was in charge, and he brought together the works of the great masters in such a way as to make them an echo of, and an interpretation to, the play. He had preludes taken from the best masses and oratorios for each chapter, besides the dramatic music from organ or orchestra between and during the acts. It was a grand sacred concert in itself.

Photo by Bushnell

1. JOHN J. IVANCOVICH, A.B., '05, as Judas.

2. FLOYD E. ALLEN, '08, as Ammon
   AMES R. DALY, '09

3. HARRY A. McKENZIE, '08
   FRANCIS M. HEFFERNAN, '08
   H CASRY '07

per and magazine criti-
th" have been extremely
ich so indeed as to have
ed our modesty. One
the boys were the best
r players he had ever
n, that while they lacked
experience, "the play is
the most remarkable pro-
as been seen on the coast
teur players." Of Judas'
ls us that he had "never
scene as well done by
while he thinks the "mob
with consummate skill."
verse criticism did we
in the pages of a Berkeley
s written with all the an-
rity of a school-boy.

encomiums the most
probably that of Charles
da.d. "Wonderful!" said
een profoundly impressed.
)berammergau and it does
parison with this play. It
impressive."

ing the subject, we would
le tribute to some of those
10 devoted their time and
i the cause of "Nazareth."
e we need not speak; the
iy and whatever praise is
ren him. The cast, how-
:cially grateful for his tele-
ression of good wishes.
d yeoman service in the
play, and the gratitude
ge was brought tangibly
when, on the matinee of
was called before the foot-

lights and there presented by Mr. Fox,
S. J., with an elegant gold watch in
recognition of his generous loyalty to
Alma Mater as evinced by the gratuitous
and devoted work of three months. Mr.
Fox, S. J., the Director of the Senior
Dramatic Club, was also kept very busy
with the innumerable financial and
other problems connected with such an
undertaking. Perhaps the most thank-
less task of all was that of Professor
Waddell. The Professor took charge
of this property room over thirty years
ago when he himself trod the student
boards a very close rival of the famous
John T. Malone. Ever since that time
he has given his best to it, and if it is
well furnished today, to him is largely
the credit. In "making up" the actors,
he is unsurpassed, and so generously
does he give his services that he has
actually never seen the Passion Play.
Another splendid worker is August
Aguirre, the Stage Manager. "Augie"
does the work of half-a-dozen men. He
is carpenter, painter, electrician. He
is full of devices of all sorts and many
of the most ingenious contrivances in
the stage settings were due to him.
And with him we class the stage-hands.
Those good-hearted fellows gave all
their free time for months to the labor
of getting eight heavy sets of scenery
under their most perfect and expeditious
control.

Knights of Columbus at Santa Clara

Memorial Day, 1907, will go down

the years as an event in Santa Clara's history. Never before had the institution entertained so many guests within these walls justly famed for true old Mission hospitality. The State Council of the Knights of Columbus had been invited to attend the presentation of "Nazareth," and they came along with their friends over three thousand strong.

The first feature of the day's program was the mass celebrated on a rustic altar under the shade of the trees on the boys' campus. The altar was a beautiful specimen of good taste and skill in rough woodwork. It stood on an elevated platform handsomely palisaded with cypress and palm branches. The celebrant was Rev. Fr. Giacobbi, S. J.; and the preacher of the day, Right Rev. Dr. Conaty. His sermon on The Nation's Dead was a magnificent effort.

After the sermon was concluded, the crowd filed out to dinner in the S. A. A. grounds, where 16 tables each 120 feet long, "manned" by 250 waiters, were ready to receive them.

"It can safely be said"—we quote the Mercury—"that 7000 meals (including dinner and supper) were given on the Sodality grounds yesterday. And the meals were not monastic by any means. Course followed course, and delicacy followed delicacy, until the amazed feasters wondered what was to come next. They were utterly taken by surprise. People have learned to mistrust those large picnic dinners, and some of yesterday's pilgrims had been joking beforehand about providing themselves with sandwiches in case of emergencies, but these knew not Santa Clara."

Grand Knight Buehrer of San Jose, had the engineering of the enterprise on his shoulders, and when we say that not a single unpleasant incident marred the day, and that everyone left feeling as if he had been singled out for special kind treatment, we mete him out a praise that he deserves. It may be of interest to learn that a ton and a half of chicken was disposed of, and 2000 loaves of bread. No San Francisco caterer had the hardihood to take the monster picnic in hand, and Mr. Bell of San Jose took it only when he was assured that the whole town was behind him.

The Knights to the number of 2500 attended the matinee of Nazareth at 2 p. m., the remainder awaiting the night performance. Benediction of the Blessed Sacrament was given at 7 p. m., Right Rev. Monsignor Silva of Lisbon officiating.

College Picnic

During the entire year we anxiously looked forward to the Manresa Picnic. It seemed so long coming, but alas! how quickly it was over when it did come.

Tuesday, June 4th, was the day, Rising 5 o'clock, mass 5:25, breakfast at 6, all aboard our special train 7, "toot-toot" from the engine 7:03, and we're off for Manresa by the sea. Fun? no end to it. Each of the 300 students has donned his picnic attire, the engine and coaches have been decked and festooned in the "red and white," the College brass band is there in full force.

At San Jose our special stops to sere- nade the depot and to take on "reinforcements." These latter consisted of 300 cooked chickens, 400 loaves of bread, tons of ham and Saratoga chips, five bunches of bananas, two barrels of pop-corn, a hundred pounds of peanuts, etc., etc. The freight clerks must have judged that we were taking a year's provisions for the founding of a foreign colony—but no, Fr. Gallagher was only providing for two out-door meals for the College students. Experience had put him wise as to the appetite a boy has after a sea bath.

Through the courtesy of our conductor, engineer and "brakies", all of whom suddenly grew young in the general mirth, we made short stops at several of the "big" towns en route. At Morgan Hill, Gilroy, Pajaro and Watsonville the youngsters piled off and aroused the natives with their College yell, while the band struck up its most festive tunes.

At about 10 o'clock the first glimpse of the ocean was caught and a few minutes later we were at Manresa by the sea. Many of the boys took short cuts down the crags to the beach and were diving through the breakers a few minutes after the train had come to a standstill.

A more ideal spot for a picnic can hardly be imagined. Situated on the ocean side about midway between Santa Cruz and Del Monte, Manresa possesses the combined charms of both these famous sea-side resorts. People who have traveled up and down the Pacific Coast declare that no place offers better surf-bathing.

Most of the boys spent their morning on the beach, swimming, fishing, digging clams, gathering sea-shells and curios. Others, however, having enjoyed a dip, started off to reconnoitre the surrounding hills. One of them returned with a fine mess of fresh trout caught in one of the neighboring streams.

At 1:30 P. M. at the summons of their pastors, the hungry lambs gathered for the "feed." Wonderful how the College boys like chicken feed ! I shall not attempt to do justice to the dinner, for ample justice was dealt out to it long ago by 300 ravenous appetites. At 5:30 again, after participating in the same sports during the afternoon, we returned to the rustic tables, with the same or still more !clamorous appetites. At 6:10 the train left for home bringing its passengers to the College at 9 P. M.

Twenty of the boys had a double-header of a picnic. These were the stage hands of the Passion Play, who were given a token of the Faculty's appreciation of their generous work in being invited to stay over at Manresa for a second day. They enjoyed this immensely. For the novelty of it, they slept down on the beach, wrapped up in blankets and comforters and stretched out on pine branches. A large bonfire dispelled the cold. It was very comfortable, especially as they had been fortified by a late collation of roasted clams, toast, wild raspberries and hot chocolate. It was very romantic, too, the lullaby of the mighty Pacific soothing them to slumber as they lay on the bosom of Mother Earth.

Elocution Contest

On Wednesday evening, June 12th, was held the annual Elocution Contest. An audience that filled the main floor of the spacious College auditorium listened with unabated attention to the thirteen young speakers. To quote from a local newspaper: "The boys were well-trained, had self-command, and splendid address. Since each piece was chosen on account of its intrinsic worth as well as for the opportunity it gave the individual speakers, a program of unusual merit was presented." The contestants were Andrew J. Donovan, George J. Mayerle, Marcel P. Lohse, Francis D. Warren, John J. Hartman, James B. Oswald, Albert C. Quevedo, Bernard A. Budde, Anthony J. Ivancovich, Edmund S. Lowe, James R. Daly, Maurice T. Dooling, Ivo G. Bogan.

Rev. John J. Cunningham, S. J., Rev. John J. Lally, Hon. James H. Campbell, Henry E. Wilcox, Esq., James A. Bacigalupi, Esq , and Mr. Charles D. South, acted as judges, but the decision will not be divulged until the Commencement exercises.

A Modern Stradivari

No man is a prophet in his own country. Probably few Santa Clara students are aware that working in our midst day after day is a genuine scion of the great violin-maker that established Cremona in its fame. Prof. A. W. Kaufmann has been making violins for many years, and though he is ex-tremely modest about it, his success has attracted the attention of the leading experts of the country. The following extract is from a letter from the famous Lyon & Healy music house in Chicago.

"Office of Lyon & Healy, Chicago, Ill., July 1906. To whom it may concern—Mr. A. W. Kaufmann: I have examined your violins carefully and was so surprised, even baffled, that it took me some time to find words to express my opinion. I have repaired a great many Cremona violins, and also the celebrated Hawley collection, and it seems to me impossible for any one to have accomplished what you have done, having had no other teaching than your own judgment. Your violins are perfect in tone, as in construction, and of such workmanship as to surpass most of the modern makers, including even some cremona makers. Your purfeling is superior to any I have yet seen, your scrolls and model as good as the cremonas. You are already an artist in the art of violin making, and, considering the conditions surrounding you, you have done what no one has accomplished before you, and have already made for yourself a name which makes you pre-eminent.

Yours with admiration,
JOHANN HORNSTEINER,
Violin expert of cremona violins.

Degrees

The following degrees will be conferred at the Commencement exercises: A. B. (in course), August M. Aguirre, San Francisco; Leo J. Atteridge, Watsonville; Jos. R. Brown, Napa; Herman F. Budde, San Jose; George H. Casey, Sacramento; Thomas W. Donlon, Oxnard; George J. Fisher, Coyote; J. Daniel McKay, Saticoy; J. Walter Schmitz, Madera; James F. Twohy, Spokane; Fredrick Sigwart, Placerville.

Of these the following graduated "cum laude" (with praise): Herman F. Budde, Thomas W. Donlon, George J. Fisher, J. Daniel McKay, James F. Twohy.

A. M.—Herman F. Budde, San Jose; E. Fitzgerald, Georgetown, Cal.; Jose Gaston, Philippines.

HONORARY DEGREES

A. M.—Alexander T. Leonard, M. D., San Francisco; George A. Stanley, Esq., San Francisco; Edward White, Esq., Watsonville.

Mus. D., Prof Godfrey C. Buehrer, San Jose.

Lit. D., George W. James, San Francisco.

Ph. D., James V. Coleman, Esq., San Francisco; Prof. Henry A. Dance, London; Hon. Frank J. Murasky, San Francisco; Hon. Myles P. O'Connor, San Jose; Joseph Scott, Esq., Los Angeles.

His old friends—and all who know him are his friends—were delighted to see, after an absence of two years, the genial face of John M. Regan of Boise City. "Johnnie" graduated in 1905, and though one of the youngest of our graduates, was one of the most distinguished in all-around accomplishments. He is at present engaged as assistant manager of his father's extensive properties in Boise, but from the intimate knowledge which he displays of the live political questions of the day, and his interest therein, we could easily foresee that he is very apt to gravitate, ere many years, towards our halls of Congress. However no matter what his career may be, we, his fellow students, have absolute confidence that it will be one of g$_r$ea$_t$ success, for "the child is father to the man."

Some time ago the Alumni editor, being straightened for iteresting news, wrote for the same to Robert N. Wil-liams of San Diego, who attended Santa Clara College as far back as '62. Mr. Williams wrote a letter declining the task as quite beyond him, but in the very act of refusing our request, he partially, at least, granted it. He says:

"While I cannot grant your request and write for the paper, I will tell you personally, that I have never missed a chance to visit the College when opportunity offered, and that the fondest recollections are renewed by a visit. In fact I always feel better after a visit. There is to me an atmosphere of holiness about the place arising from the revered memory of so many holy padres that I have known in the happy days of old. I should like to go for a night and borrow a bed and sleep in the big boys' dormitory.

In a recent visit to the College, I saw only one Father of the other days—Father Neri. But alas! he could not see me. Beyond the loss of sight, he seems little changed. The same kindly face and smile are still there."

The above was not intended for the REDWOOD, but we hardly think we are abusing confidence in publishing it.

When we sat down to our desk and prepared for the last time to read and criticise the familiar heap of magazines before us, we found ourselves in a particularly well disposed and benevolent frame of mind towards them and all the world, and so we resolved only to search out and mention such articles as we could freely praise and not to write a single word of adverse criticism. For this course we are indebted to several circumstances. The first and undoubtedly the strongest reason, is the fact that we must with this issue relinquish, at least for a time, a duty which we have found both pleasant and profitable. We must say farewell to the host of magazines which we have come to regard as old and trusted friends and it would seem almost a profanation of their friendship to treat them harshly now. Perhaps in other numbers we have been too ready to pick out and dwell upon their faults. If so, we hope this time to make atonement by praising their merits. Then too, we are on the very verge of vacation and who could be harsh with the call of the simple—or is it the strenuous—life ringing in his ears? Besides, there has been enough

vitriol dripping lately from the pens of—but there! We have almost forgotten our good resolution already.

We have been particularly fortunate in our search for praiseworthy articles in stumbling at once and almost by accident upon "A Serious Decision" in the May *Haverfordian*. This is a whimsical little sketch of a fancied and fanciful incident in the life of Bobbie Burns which we began to read half-heartedly enough, but so skillfully has the boyishly careless, care-free and wholly lovable character of the poet been drawn that we were fascinated by it before we had reached the third paragraph. It may be a trite wish but it is none the less sincere, that we would like to have every one of our readers have an opportunity to enjoy the extreme simplicity and naturalness of this story for himself.

"The Deserted Mine" in *The Touchstone* for May has a boldly conceived and well executed plot which gains not a little interest from the total unexpectedness of its conclusion. "Uncle His' Wisdom" is full of that pleasant rarity in college journalism, genuine humor. In fact we were pleased to notice that this number is in every way superior to the last few which preceded it.

The next contribution to our list of good articles—and it is no mean, one—is "The Soft Spot" in *The Fleur de Lis*. This is a little story, hardly more than a sketch but it contains such a subtle and well drawn comparison between the ruling passions of a staid old lawyer and his buoyant office boy that we were at once attracted by it.

In the *William and Mary Lit.* we found a romantic story of more than usual merit, "In the Reign of Terror." This, as its title indicates, deals with the French reign of terror and the author has used his dramatic material in a very effective manner. We do not think we are exaggerating when we call this story a genuine "thriller."

The work of J. C. Droste, editor of *The St. Jerome Schoolman* is especially worthy of notice. As a rule, where a single man contributes four or five articles to every issue of his magazine, his work is hardly more than mediocre but although Mr. Droste contributes almost half of the articles in *The School-man*, his work remains of a uniformly high order.

"Shakespeare's Quietus" in the *Nassau Lit.* is a clever essay on the recent attacks of Bernard Shaw, Tolstoy and Ernest Crosby on the immortal bard.

So we might multiply the number of praiseworthy articles indefinitely, but we have been warned to be brief owing to lack of space and so we will conclude by wishing our exchanges one and all a pleasant vacation.

M. T. DOOLING, JR.

·IN THE LIBRARY·

EARLY HISTORY OF THE CATHO-
LIC CHURCH IN PRINCE EDWARD
ISLAND

BY REV. J. C. MCMILLAN, D. D.

This book consists of over three hundred large octavo pages, and deals with
Catholicity in Prince Edward Island
since its first settlement to the death of
Bishop McEachern in the year 1835.
The style easy, lucid, and elegant, rising at times, particularly in the descriptions of the sufferings of the early mis-
sionaries, to great force and vividness.
The author is evidently master of his
subject, and he has marshalled an astonishing array of facts into a connected,
harmonious, and very interesting story.
The work will, we have no doubt, be
for many years hence an authority on
the subject it treats of. This is Dr.
McMillan's first book, and we would say
to him: *Perge quo coepisti.*—Evenement
Co., Quebec.

THE MYSTERY OF CLEVERLY

BY GEORGE BARTON

This is a very good story for boys. It
starts out with a fight, in which the
little hero is victorious against great
odds, and it ends up with a glorious
banquet, whereof the crisp brown
turkey, not to mention the other good
things, is enough to make an American
boy smack his lips. The story is full of
incident, and moreover gives a good
idea of the way in which things are
done in the big newspaper offices.—
Benziger Bros.—85 cents.

WHEN LOVE IS STRONG

This novel is from the pen of the
very talented young writer, Grace
Keon. It teaches a beautiful lesson of
the power of love when reinforced by a
living faith. The plot is ingenious, and
the mystery that hangs over its first
workings, rivets the attention of the

reader. Some of the passages, notably that of Carew's Confession and the frustration of his suicide, are very dramatic. —Benziger Bros.—$1.25.

IN GOD'S GOOD TIME

BY H. M. ROSS

The plot of this story is more than usually bold, though at times the execution is a trifle weak. It seems very improbable that Roderic Lestrange, the First, bright, precocious child as he was when he was kidnapped at the age of four, should have no lasting recollection of his mother and his home. And Roderic Lestrange the Second, while he is a most noble and lofty character, almost as ideal as one could wish, is not a natural creation. His father is a smooth, polished villian, and his mother, a frivolous woman of the world. And yet the boy grows up noble and generous, and so unworldly that in his opening manhood he desires to devote himself to works of charity. He strikes the reader as "too good to be true." On the whole, however, the book is a splendid story, that makes one feel the better for having read it.—Benziger Bros.—$1.25.

ROUND THE WORLD. Vols. II and III

These attractive looking books, which are issued by Benziger Bros. at 85 cts, each, form a series of interesting and very instructive articles on a great variety of subjects, from "In the Heart of the African Forest" to "The 'Blind'. Readers of the Post Office," and "From the Footsteps of the Apostles" to "Plowing in Many Lands." The articles, which are not too lengthy or full of confusing details, are yet sufficiently exhaustive to give a thorough idea of the matter in hand, and to have read the three volumes is to have acquired much of the education that comes from travel and observation. They are all profusely and elegantly illustrated.

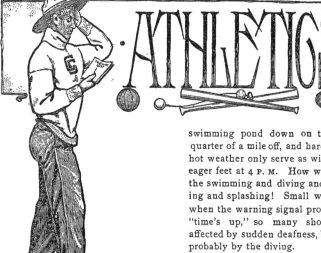

The editor has served us notice to be as brief as possible in our athletic department this month, much to our relief for there is little doing in that line at present worth talking about. The Passion Play absorbed all our surplus energies during the first three weeks of May, and the coming exams. have monopolized us ever since.

Swimming

Still we have not become paralytic, or sunk into a state of coma. We have a swimming pond down on the farm a quarter of a mile off, and hard work and hot weather only serve as wings to our eager feet at 4 P. M. How we do enjoy the swimming and diving and floundering and splashing! Small wonder that when the warning signal proclaims that "time's up," so many should be so affected by sudden deafness, brought on probably by the diving.

Old devotees of the swimming-pond will be interested to learn that the circle of poplars around the pond have been cut down and are now being diligently sawed and split into kindling wood. But let them not shed tears; those trees were a "false alarm;" to use a trope. They never warded off the cold wind which was evidently their first duty; they did ward off the warm genial sunshine, just when the shivering bathers needed it most; and they persisted in drowning their cast-off leaves in the blue wavelets of the pond, which was the most heinous crime of all. However as they are to burn for it, we shall say no more more about them, but console ourselves with the the thought that in their vacant place there will soon arise a beautiful eight-foot board fence, heavily armored with barb wire.

We are not at all joking about the barb wire. It will be intended for serious business and we hope it will do it. If not, we can call in a policeman and a brace of bulldogs. Outsiders make use of that pond who have no right to do so. The thing has been tolerated too long, and it is high time that those deadheads should be shown their place.

Baseball

Baseball has taken a back seat of late, with the exception of the indomitable Outlaw team, which has added two games to its history since Passion Play week. The energy of Manager C. Brazell is largely responsible for this.

The Outlaw record now tells the following triumphs: Hoitts, twice; Juniors 4-3; Irvington 7-4; and St. Matthews 10-2. They were defeated but once, by St. Ignatius College, bnt that was due, in part at least, to the peculiar topography of the diamond on which they played.

The little All-Stars sent a cordial invitation.to the corresponding team of St. Ignatius to come down on June 13th and get walloped. Every preparation was made for a warm reception for the visitors, and Captain Franklin Warren, Clair Wilson, Harry Curry, etc., were almost in a state of combustion for a day or two before. But alas! a shower of rain came down on the fatal morning, and though it but served to put the diamond in perfect trim, it scared away the San Franciscans. Warren & Company went to meet all the city trains, but no enemy hove in sight.

And now we close the baseball season of '07. Successful as it was, it is now a thing of the irrevocable past, but its memory will offer an exemplar and an encouragement to the teams of '08.

CARLOS K. McCLATCHY, '10·

THE REDWOOD

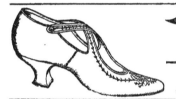

Double and Triple your Money on this Property

Must be Sold at $8,900. Cost $22,000

Big barn and out buildings; 9:20 acres; a whole or in part, beautifully situated on Bellomy street. I have another estate offered at a sacrific, at $8,000, simply grand and complete, large ground, corner lot on Jackson and Market streets (owners deceased.) I have a large list ranging from $1000 up. I have houses empty for rent now.

A. T. HELM, Real Estate City and Country **Santa Clara, Cal.**

SAN JOSE
BRICK COMPANY

MANUFACTURERS OF

Common and ✿ ✿
Ornamental Brick

Yards at Dougherty Station

SAN JOSE OFFICE:

17 North First Street   San Jose, California

Telephone Main 594

Lightning Source UK Ltd.
Milton Keynes UK
UKHW020647221118
332785UK00012B/1224/P